Teachers' Guide

LOVE AND BETRAYAL
A CATULLUS READER

BRUCE ARNOLD
Mount Holyoke College

ANDREW ARONSON
Sidwell Friends School, Washington, DC

GILBERT LAWALL
The University of Massachusetts, Amherst

with an Introduction by
SALLY MURPHY
The Windsor School, Boston, MA

A Prentice Hall Latin Reader

Prentice
Hall

Glenview, Illinois
Needham, Massachusetts
Upper Saddle River, New Jersey

Photo Credit
Cover: ©Phoenix Art Group, Inc., Richard Franklin "To Go Beyond," Courtesy of Grand Image Ltd., Seattle, WA

Acknowledgments
Grateful acknowledgment is made to the following for copyrighted material:
Acta Classica W.P. Basson. "The Riddle of Catullus 49: Some Notes on Its Interpretation." *Acta Classica* 23 (1980) 45-52. **Agon** Richard Freis. "Form and Thought in Catullus 76." *Agon* 1 (1968) 39-58. **American Journal of Philology** J.T. Davis. "Poetic Counterpoint: Catullus 72." *American Journal of Philology* 92 (1971) 196-201. E.A. Fredricksmeyer. "Observations on Catullus 5." *American Journal of Philology* 91 (1970) 431-45. David B. George. "Catullus 44: The Vulnerability of Wanting to Be Included." *American Journal of Philology* 112 (1991) 247-50. Ellen Greene. "The Catullan Ego: Fragmentation and the Erotic Self." *American Journal of Philology* 116 (1995) 77-93. Roger Hornsby. "The Craft of Catullus (*Carm.*4)." *American Journal of Philology* 84 (1963) 256-65. H.L. Levy. "Catullus, 5,7-11 and the Abecus." *American Journal of Philology* 62 (1941) 222-24. Christopher Nappa. "Place Settings: *Convivium*, Contrast, and Persona in Catullus 12 and 13." *American Journal of Philology* 119 (1998) 385-97. Delores O'Higgins. "Sappho's Splintered Tongue: Silence in Sappho 31 and Catullus 51." *American Journal of Philology* 111 (1990) 156-67. Charles Segal. "Catullus 5 and 7: A Study in Complementaries." *American Journal of Philology* 89 (1968) 284-301. **Antichthon** P.J. Conner. "Catullus 8: The Lover's Conflict." *Antichthon* 8 (1974) 93-96. **Arethusa** Gloria S. Duclos. "Catullus 11: Atque in perpetuum, Lesbia, ave atque vale." *Arethusa* 9 (1976) 79-80. Paul Allen Miller. "Sappho 31 and Catullus 51: The Dialogism of Lyric." *Arethusa* 26 (1993) 183-99. **Arion** James McCaughey. "The Mind Lays By Its Trouble: Catullus 31." *Arion* 9 (1970) 362-65. **California Studies in Classical Antiquity** Philip Levine. "Catullus c.1: A Prayerful Dedication." *California Studies in Classical Antiquity* 2 (1969) 209-16. **Cambridge University Press** Joan Booth. "All in the Mind: Sickness in Catullus 76." *The Passions in Roman Thought and Literature*, ed. Susanna Morton Braund and Christopher Gill. New York NY: Cambridge University Press, 1997, 150-68. **Clarendon Press** C.J. Fordyce. *Catullus: A Commentary*. Oxford ENG: Clarendon Press, 1961. Brooks Otis. *Virgil: A Study of Civilized Poetry*. Oxford ENG: Clarendon Press, 1963, 1st ed., 102-5. **Classical Journal** Steele Commager. "The Structure of Catullus 5." *Classical Journal* 59 (1964) 361-64. E. Courney. "Catullus' Yacht (or Was It?)." *Classical Journal* 92 (1997) 113-22. Rachael Kitzinger. "Reading Catullus 45." *Classical Journal* 87 (1992) 209-17. Marilyn B. Skinner. "Ameana, Puella Defututa." *Classical Journal* 74 (1978-79) 110-14. Elizabeth Vandiver. "Sound Patterns in Catullus 84." *Classical Journal* 85 (1990) 337-40. **Classical Philology** Sheridan Baker. "The Irony of Catullus' Septimius and Acme." *Classical Philology* 58 (1958) 110-12. H. Akbar Khan. "A Note on the Expression *solum...nosse* in Catullus." *Classical Philology* 62 (1967) 34-36. Michael C.J. Putnam. "Catullus' Journey (*Carm.*4)." *Classical Philology* 57 (1962) 10-19. E.S. Ramage. "Note on Catullus' Arrius." *Classical Philology* 54 (1959) 44-45. David O. Ross, Jr. "Style and Content in Catullus 45." *Classical Philology* 60 (1965) 256-59. Joseph Solodow. "Forms of Literary Criticism in Catullus: Polymetric vs. Epigram." *Classical Philology* 84 (1989) 312-18. **Classical Quarterly** M. Dyson. "Catullus 8 and 76." *Classical Quarterly* 23 (1973) 127-43. Ronald Mayer. "Catullus Divorce." *Classical Quarterly* 33 (1983) 297-98. M.G. Morgan. "*Nescio quid febriculosi scorti*: A Note on Catullus 6." *Classical Quarterly* 27 (1977) 338-41. J.G.F. Powell. "Two Notes on Catullus." *Classical Quarterly* 40 (1990) 199-206. W. Jeffrey Tatum. "Friendship, Politics, and Literature in Catullus: Poems 1, 65, and 66, 116." *Classical Quarterly* 47 (1997) 482-500. **Classical World** Edna S. deAngeli. "A Literary Chill: Catullus 44." *Classical World* 62 (1969) 354-56. Edward Frueh. "Sinistra Ut Ante Dextra: Reading Catullus 45." *Classical World* 84 (1990) 15-21. J.P. Holoka. "Self-Delusion in Catullus 83 and 92." *Classical World* 69 (1975) 119-20. John Rauk. "Time and History in Catullus 1." *Classical World* 90 (1997) 319-32. Carl A. Rubino. "The Erotic World of Catullus." *Classical World* 68 (1975) 289-98. **The Crowning Privilege** R. Graves, *The Crowning Privilege*, New York, 1956, 191. **Eranos** Steele Commager. "The Structure of Catullus 62." *Eranos* 81 (1983) 21-33. **Greece & Rome** Julian Ward Jones Jr. "Catullus' *Passer* as Passer." *Greece & Rome* 45 (1998) 188-94. L.A. Moritz. "*Difficile est longum subito deponere amorem*." *Greece & Rome* 15 (1968) 53-58. R.L. Rowland. "*Miser Catulle*: An Interpretation of the Eighth Poem of Catullus." *Greece & Rome* 13 (1966) 15-21. Charles Segal. "Catullan *Otiosi*: The Lover and the Poet." *Greece & Rome* 17 (1970) 25-31. **Harvard Studies in Classical Philology** Steele Commager. "Notes on Some Poems of Catullus." *Harvard Studies in Classical Philology* 70 (1965) 83-110. J.P. Elder. "Catullus 1, His Poetic Creed, and Nepos." *Harvard Studies in Classical Philology* 71 (1967) 143-49. Herbert Jennings Rose. "Some Passages of Latin Poets." *Harvard Studies in Classical Philology* 47 (1936) 1-15. **Harvard University Press** David O. Ross. "Lesbia and the Vocabulary of Political Alliance." *Style and Tradition in Catullus*. Cambridge MA: Harvard University Press, 1969, 80-95. **Helios** Ernst Fredricksmeyer. "Method and Interpretation: Catullus 11." *Helios* 20 (1993) 89-105. Paul Miller. "Catullus, C.70. A Poem and Its Hypothesis." *Helios* 15 (1988) 127-32. Marilyn B. Skinner. "*Ut Decuit Cinaediorem*: Power, Gender, and Urbanity in Catullus 10." *Helios* 16 (1989) 7-23. **Hermes** John T. Davis. "Quo desiderio: The Structure of Catullus 96." *Hermes* 99 (1971) 297-302. **Journal of Roman Studies** Eduard Fraenkel. "Vesper adest (Catullus LXII)." *Journal of Roman Studies* 45 (1955) 1-8. **Latomus** H. Akbar Khan. "Style and Meaning in Catullus' Eighth Poem." *Latomus* 27 (1968) 555-74. T.E. Kinsey. "Catullus 11." *Latomus* 24 (1965) 537-44. T.E. Kinsey. "Catullus 51." *Latomus* 33 (1974) 372-87. David Sweet. "Catullus 11. A Study of Perspective." *Latomus* 46 (1987) 510-26. D.W.T.C. Vessey. "Thoughts on Two Poems of Catullus: 13 and 30." *Latomus* 30 (1971) 45-55. **Leeds University** Lindsay Watson. "Rustic Suffenus (Catullus 22) and Literary Rusticity." *Papers of the Leeds International Latin Seminar, Sixth Volume*, eds. F. Cairns & M. Heath (1990) 13-33. **Liverpool Classical Monthly** A.J. Woodman. "Catullus 11 and 51." *Liverpool Classical Monthly* 3 (1978) 77-79. **Macmillan Publishing** Kenneth Quinn. *Catullus: The Poems*. London ENG: Macmillan, 1973 (2nd ed.). **Mnemosyne** Francis Cairns. "Catullus I." *Mnemosyne* 22 (1969) 153-58. T.D. Papanghelis. "Catullus and Callimachus on Large Women (A Reconsideration of c. 86)." *Mnemosyne* 44 (1991) 372-86. **Phoenix** T. Goud. "Who Speaks the Final Lines? Catullus 62: Structure and Ritual." *Phoenix* 49, 1995, 23-32. **Ramus** Rosemary M. Nielsen. "Catullus 9 and 31. The Simple Pleasure." *Ramus* 8 (1979) 165-73. Rosemary M. Nielsen. "Catullus 45 and Horace Odes 3.9: The Glass House." *Ramus* 6 (1977) 132-38. **Rheinisches Museum** Robert J. Baker. "Propertius' Monobiblos and Catullus 51." *Rheinisches Museum* 124 (1981) 312-24. **Transactions of the American Philological Association** Frank O. Copley. "Catullus, c.1." *Transactions of the American Philological Association* 82 (1951) 200-206. E.A. Fredricksmeyer. "On the Unity of Catullus 51." *Transactions of the American Philological Association* 96 (1965) 153-63. Donald Norman Levin. "Propertius, Catullus, and Three Kinds of Ambiguous Expression." *Transactions of the American Philological Association* 100 (1969) 221-35. W. Jeffrey Tatum. "Catullus' Criticism of Cicero in Poem 49." *Transactions of the American Philological Association* 118 (1988) 179-84. **University of Toronto Press** D.F.S. Thomson. *Catullus*. Toronto: University of Toronto Press, 1997.

Note: Every effort has been made to locate the copyright owner of material reprinted in this book. Omissions brought to our attention will be corrected in subsequent editions.

CREDITS

The authors are grateful to the following and to their students for corrections and suggestions that they made after piloting this book and its teacher's guide in 1998/1999:

Andrew Aronson
The Sidwell Friends School
Washington, District of Columbia

Karl Hayes
Elgin Academy
Elgin, Illinois

Herbert Holland
Gloversville High School
Gloversville, New York

Helene Lerner
Wayland High School
Wayland, Massachusetts

Brian McCarthy
Mt. Greylock Regional High School
Williamstown, Massachusetts

Sally Murphy
The Winsor School
Boston, Massachusetts

David Perry
Rye High School
Rye, New York

The authors are grateful to the following for numerous excellent suggestions in the final stages of preparing this material for publication:

Sean Smith
Amherst Regional High School
Amherst, Massachusetts

CONTENTS

INTRODUCTION

This introduction offers resources, suggestions, and encouragement for teachers taking on the challenge of leading their students through an extremely demanding, but highly rewarding, Advanced Placement syllabus; most of what is said here will also be of use to secondary school, college, and university teachers and professors using *Love and Betrayal* outside of an Advanced Placement course. The topics included here range from a practical teaching timetable to creative supplemental projects to innovative gearing of classroom activities toward addressing multiple intelligences. Teachers should regard this material as suggestive rather than prescriptive. The following ideas and techniques have worked successfully in classrooms where they have been implemented.

MATERIALS FROM THE EDUCATIONAL TESTING SERVICE

The Educational Testing Service (ETS) provides guides and aids to secondary teachers of the Advanced Placement syllabus through the College Board. The *Advanced Placement Course Description: Latin* is a comprehensive guide to the syllabi and format of all four AP Latin exams. The *Teacher's Guide to Advanced Placement Courses in Latin* is useful for both beginning and experienced teachers of the AP Latin exam. It contains sample syllabi from current secondary-level AP teachers and from professors who teach the same course at the college level. In addition, the book offers helpful teaching tips and an extensive list of resources. The *1994 AP Latin: Free-Response Scoring Guide with Multiple-Choice Section* is extremely helpful to both teachers and students in that it provides authentic ETS materials for use in the classroom. It includes the entire 1994 examination (with multiple choice section) along with answers and grading explanations of actual student responses. In addition, the College Board offers more practice materials including packets of ten 1994 AP Latin Exams, booklets of AP Latin free-response questions (1995, 1996, and 1997), and a five-year set of free-response questions (1993–97). These all provide convenient means of giving students more practice with real examination questions. These materials can be ordered on-line at http://cbweb2.collegeboard.org, by calling 1-800-323-7155, or by writing Advanced Placement Program, P. O. Box 6670, Princeton, NJ 08541-6670. Students and teachers should also visit the College Board's web site to access information on the AP Latin examination. It contains the syllabi, helpful suggestions for preparing for the examination, and practice multiple-choice questions (complete with answers).

Not a College Board resource, but immensely valuable to an AP Latin teacher are the previous year's free response questions with grading guides published annually in *The Classical Outlook*, a publication of the American Classical League (ACL). Students and teachers can benefit greatly from this inside glimpse into the grading process and the priorities of the graders. Non-ACL members may contact the League at Miami University, Oxford, OH 45056; telephone 513-529-7741, for subscription information.

NOTE ON THE LATIN TEXT

This edition generally follows Mynor's edition of Catullus in the *Oxford Classical Text* series, but it sometimes offers other readings, especially those found in D. F. S. Thomson's authoritative 1997 edition (see Bibliography). These other readings, including Thomson's, are usually not incorporated into the text on the right-hand pages but are given in special sections devoted to the text at the bottom of the left-hand pages. This preserves the readings of Mynors on the right-hand pages, and this is important since the AP examination questions are based on that text. Very occasionally other readings are incorporated in the texts on the right-hand pages, with Mynor's text in a note on the left-hand page. While teachers will obviously use these notes to varying degrees, it is extremely important to discuss with students the history of the transmission of Catullus' text and some of the reasons for modern editorial emendations. Examination and comparison of variant readings give students opportunities to read the passages closely and to discuss the implications of variant readings for the tone and meaning of the poems.

HOW TO USE THIS EDITION

This edition of poems from the Catullus AP syllabus is unique in the wealth of information and resources it contains for both student and teacher. Each poem is introduced by a title created by the editors and an italicized introduction summarizing the main focus of the poem. Students will find copious notes on vocabulary, grammar, poetic devices, and textual variations on the left-hand pages. The Initial Explorations which follow poems ask important questions about the grammar, translation, poetic devices, and the train of thought of each poem. The Discussion sections contain topics that invite teachers and students to explore the themes and meaning of the poems in depth. In addition, some poems are followed by literary translations, and students are invited to compare these to the original poems using criteria such as quality of writing or closeness to the original language and meaning. Teachers will find in the Teacher's Guide a literal translation of each poem and a lead-in summarizing important themes and the significance of the poem. A sample answer for each of the questions in the student's book is also given. It is important to note that these sample answers do not pretend to be definitive. Teachers and students will have other valid interpretations, and these should be encouraged in the classroom. The answers are offered simply as a guide. Finally, there is a Select Bibliography at the end of the entry for each poem. In almost all cases short, representative quotations are given from the scholarly articles or books cited in these bibliographies. The views of these scholars do not always agree with the views of the editors of this edition, and conflicting views are often given. Teachers will find these of interest in themselves, and they can also utilize them to stimulate discussion in the classroom. Many of them also provide excellent springboards for students' essays written in response to the views of this or that scholar.

It would be nearly impossible for both students and teachers to incorporate all of the material provided in this edition all of the time. Judicious decision-making as to what to focus on is a must for successful use of these books. As is remarked in the introduction to the student's book, students should be guided to efficient use of the notes and questions. At first the most important thing for them is to look for the italicized definitions of new vocabulary words. As students scan the left-hand page, they should initially ignore everything except the initial vocabulary word and the italicized definitions. Once they reach the stage of putting meaning to phrases and sentences, they should go back, examine, and use the remaining notes that will aid their comprehension. After they have completed the poem, they can then go back over the poem making full use of all the notes. Students should also use the Initial Explorations as a guide to comprehension and translation. These questions are designed to keep students "on track" as to correct meaning as they make their way through the poem. If the Initial Explorations are used as a classroom activity, the teacher might choose to focus on questions that ask about topics important for a particular day, perhaps focusing some days on a discussion of poetic devices and other days on the language or the train of thought of the poem. The same is true of the questions in the Discussion section. Teachers may choose to focus on one or two per poem, or they may have small groups of students work on different questions and report to the whole class. Teachers should also prioritize their use of material in the teacher's guide. Teachers are certainly not expected to cover every topic or point of information every day. They should use the material as a springboard, choosing what interests the class most about a poem and focusing on what they feel is important for their students to take from it. Topics and exercises of various sorts are offered for teachers and students in their editions, and teachers should make it a point to incorporate topics and exercises of each sort at some point or other in their teaching of the syllabus. It is ever important for teachers, both beginning and experienced, to try new activities and to look at poems in different ways so as not to fall into a comfortable rut. This edition makes it easy for teachers to do this since a wide range of information is provided for them and their students.

CLASSROOM PROCEDURES

There are about as many methods of teaching the AP Catullus syllabus as there are Latin teachers and Latin students. There are, however, some tried and true means that work very well and emphasize the skills and knowledge needed for a successful performance on the Advanced Placement examination. Translation of the poems has to be one of the major challenges for students. Anytime they begin to read a new author, they are faced with unfamiliar vocabulary and a unique literary style. For a relatively inexperienced Latin student, these are major hurdles to full understanding. Students will usually prepare a poem (or a section of a longer one) in preparation for the next class. They should never begin their reading without an idea of the general topic of the poem. To send them in "cold" to a poem creates anxiety and does nothing constructive to strengthen their translation skills. Teachers can, and should, use the made-up titles and italicized introductions at the beginning of each poem as a means of introducing it to students. Students can even brainstorm, with teacher guidance, as to what they think the poem will be about. They can then begin their reading with some confidence as to what the poem is going to say. When it comes to translation, students should be strongly discouraged from writing out a full translation and reading directly from it in class. They should make notes on new vocabulary, difficult constructions, and phrase groupings, but they should translate in class while looking at the Latin text itself. This Teacher's Guide contains enlarged transparency masters for each poem with the entire poem together on the page (except for poem 62), instead of being broken up into segments as often in the student's book. These may be used as masters for overhead transparencies, but they may also be photocopied and distributed to students for them to make notes on in preparation for class. Some teachers allow their students to use only these photocopied sheets and not the textbook with all of the facing vocabulary for recitation in class. In class, translation can be accomplished in many different ways. Sometimes translation will be done as a whole class with individual students translating a series of lines. Students may also work in small groups to come up with a group translation of part or all of a poem, with a reporter from each group then translating for the whole class. Alternatively, each group may turn in a written translation to be commented upon and corrected by the teacher. Students can also be asked at times to prepare a poem, and, with some teacher guidance, lead the class through a translation. In any case, each student should end up having a complete, corrected translation of every poem, from which to study for quizzes, tests, and the AP examination.

Once students understand the words and meaning of the poem, then they must begin their analysis of it as a literary, artistic work. Analysis consists of examining the ways elements such as rhetorical figures, tone, structure, meter, and so forth reflect and influence the theme and meaning of the poem. Teachers can use the questions in the Initial Explorations and Discussion sections as a means of initiating students' analysis of the poem. A working knowledge of rhetorical figures and their impact on the meaning and artistic merit of a poem is essential for any qualified AP student. Teachers should emphasize, however, that Catullus did not include rhetorical figures as a means of vexing the modern-day student, but as an integral part of his arsenal of literary expression. It may be useful to ask students whether they think that a poet consciously strives to include literary figures or whether these devices subconsciously manifest themselves in the course of the artist's expressing himself and his view of the world. Students find this an engaging topic and often make comparisons to musicians and painters as well. It is never enough for students simply to identify rhetorical figures; they must always make clear how the particular device reflects, influences, or shapes the overall theme. Identification of such devices takes practice, and students should discover them and be required to explain them every day.

In addition students must examine the tone and structure of the poems and recognize the impact of these features on overall meaning. These abstract topics can prove challenging for novice students of Latin poetry. Teachers should model this kind of analysis with students at the beginning of their study of Catullus' poetry. The questions in the student's book and the answers in the Teacher's Guide provide much helpful guidance in these areas. It is often useful to put a poem on the overhead projector and make notes of instances of key words, parallel structures, and the like. Once students are accustomed to looking at poems in this manner, they can be asked to continue to do such activities in small groups or individually.

Catullus' poetry contains engaging imagery, and this also needs to be explored carefully with students. An appreciation of the mental images created by the words of a poem is one of the great joys of reading poetry. Again, teachers should model such analysis with their students at the beginning of their study. Once they are comfortable, students can be encouraged to do such analysis on their own and in different forms. It is often beneficial, for example, for students to make visual representations of the imagery, whether by hand, with computer images, or in collages. Students can also record their reactions to certain images in writing as part of a journal-keeping assignment.

Of utmost importance in the study of poetry is its meter and interpretive reading of poems aloud. Too often students experience Latin poetry only as words on a page and are completely unaware of the oral dimension of poetry and the nuances that are created or realized only by reading the work aloud. Scansion can first be introduced as a written pattern, and students can then practice scanning poems using photocopies of the texts at the end of this Teacher's Guide. This is, of course, a skill that they will be asked to demonstrate on the actual AP exam. From the very beginning, the teacher should read poems aloud in meter, modeling proper pronunciation and rhythm. Students can then repeat and imitate the teacher. This is often most effectively accomplished in small groups as students are often hesitant to recite in a foreign language. Once the pattern is established, students should develop their ability to read with expression in correct phrase groupings with variations in tone of voice. This activity is yet another important way of testing students' comprehension of the Latin. While much reading aloud will take place in groups, each student should be expected to present at least one poem aloud by himself or herself either just to the teacher or in front of the class as a whole, depending on the anxiety level of the students. Students should be required to memorize and present at least one poem of their choice. Memorization is a skill not often practiced in upper-level classrooms, although it is an important one; students develop a real affinity for and understanding of the poem they memorize. The poem they memorize is a "gift" that they can to carry with them for years to come. In spite of initial anxiety, memorization is often one of the favorite activities that students mention in their course evaluations. Teachers who are hesitant about their abilities to read Latin poetry aloud may consult Stephen Daitz's "The Pronunciation and Reading of Classical Latin: A Practical Guide," (ISBN: 0-88432-125-8)—a set of audiocassettes with accompanying manual, which pays special attention to the meter of ancient poetry and how to teach it orally to students in five simple stages.

HOW TO WRITE SHORT CRITICAL (I.E., AP-STYLE) ESSAYS

The skill most important for any successful AP Latin student is the ability to write effective short critical essays. Students will have to do this on more than half of the AP exam. Practice, practice, and more practice is the best way for students to fine-tune their essay-writing skills. In addition to the basic skills necessary for any good essay, such as organization, clarity of thought, and appropriate use of formal written language, students must also learn other skills particular to writing an AP essay on Latin poetry. First and foremost students must learn how to cite the appropriate Latin that supports their argument effectively. Such citation is the concrete proof that the analysis is grounded completely in the Latin itself. There are several ways to cite the Latin. Students can write out the Latin and translate it or closely paraphrase it, or they can give the proper line number(s) with the Latin and a translation. A common problem is that students often cite too much Latin, believing that they must include an entire sentence or passage instead of the short phrase that is relevant. Drawing students' attention to this mistake is the best way to forestall it.

Students must also familiarize themselves with the style and format of AP questions. Often questions contain more than one topic and expect full discussion on each point. Students should become accustomed to seeing and answering questions in this format. Teachers can use some of the materials from ETS listed above in order to provide this practice. Students must also realize that AP essays are analytical; they do not ask for mere descriptions of what is taking place in the poem. Seeing as there is a time limit on the AP exam, students should be discouraged from the very beginning from including mere description or irrelevant paraphrase as a waste of time that will distract from their analysis.

There are several ways of improving students' skills at writing short critical essays. Students should begin seeing and answering authentic AP questions from the very beginning of their course. Making an outline often helps students to organize and pare down their thoughts before writing. There should be ongoing written and oral feedback from the teacher to the students, especially drawing attention to areas for improvement and places where extra work is needed. Students should have opportunities to revise some of their essays based on feedback. Critical essays should be a part of quizzes and tests, showing students that these writing skills are worthy of grades and are an extremely important way of showing their understanding. Teachers should offer anonymous models of good and bad essays and involve the class in discussions of the good and bad qualities they find in the responses. The models can come from the published answers in *The Classical Outlook* (the only "bad" models cited should come from there) and from essays from the students in the class itself. Peer-editing, a popular technique in the classrooms of our English colleagues, can also be used effectively to improve essays in the AP Latin classroom.

HOW TO LEAD AN EFFECTIVE DISCUSSION

Teachers are always striving to improve the quality of discussion, which many times depends on the personalities of the students and their willingness to speak out. There are, however, concrete steps a teacher can take to ensure that a discussion is safe, comfortable, and effective. First of all, ask the right questions. What makes a question "right"? It should be clear and understood by the students. It should invite them to think deeply about the subject. A good discussion question is one that can be answered by the students after some thought. It should be asked in a way that invites participation rather than provoking apprehension among the students. The Discussion questions in this edition are models of "right" questions.

Once the question is asked, students must be given sufficient time to think about responses before they offer them. Although silence is sometimes uncomfortable for a teacher, it is often necessary for real thought and discussion to take place. Students are also uncomfortable with silence and will speak up when they are ready. Once discussion has begun, a teacher must monitor it closely to ensure that students are exchanging ideas respectfully and that all are participating. Sometimes quiet students need extra help to become involved in the discussion. Sometimes it is effective to call on them early in a discussion before they feel all their ideas have been expressed. A teacher can also solicit an opinion if the quiet student looks ready to speak but is having trouble breaking into the conversation.

Teacher feedback that evaluates a response often hampers discussion as students become reluctant to have their ideas judged by an authority figure in front of their peers. While it is sometimes necessary to evaluate statements and offer feedback orally in order to correct or further an argument, not all discussions need to contain evaluation. A simple "thank you" is enough to make students feel their ideas are heard and appreciated.

It is important that there is not too much "teacher talk" during discussions. The teacher does not have to say something after each student speaks. In fact more productive discussion happens when students respond directly to one another without looking to the teacher for approval. Another way to lessen teacher involvement in discussion is to break the class into groups to discuss an idea or question. The teacher may or may not assign a leader for each group. The smaller numbers of a group often help quieter students feel more comfortable sharing their ideas. Teachers can move from group to group and listen in on the discussions. It is often productive to finish the discussion as a whole class after the students have had a chance to express their ideas in small groups.

The ability to articulate orally serious thoughts about a poem is a skill that will certainly benefit students in their writing of essays. Since the ability to speak effectively in front of others is becoming more valued in our modern society, it is important that teachers help students improve their discussion skills. Luckily for students in the AP classroom, Catullus' poems are chock full of interesting, provoking ideas to discuss, as is made clear on every page of the student's book.

PROJECTS AND ACTIVITIES

The AP Latin curriculum is often a rigorous challenge for teachers and students, and it is further complicated by serious time constraints. Taking time for projects and activities that differ from the regular translation/discussion/essay-writing routine is essential, however, to promoting and keeping students' interest in the material and allowing them more creative ways in which to express their understanding of Catullus' provocative poetry. Teachers can incorporate projects that help students reach a deeper understanding of the poems rather than ones that simply provide a "break" from thinking about the work at hand. The following are some project ideas that have proven effective.

Have your students graph the relationship between Catullus and Lesbia. Students set up a simple x/y graph, with the numbers of the poems under discussion on the x-axis. Students need then to come up with their own labels on the y-axis, words to summarize a tone or theme for a particular poem. While extremes such as "love" and "hate" are easy to identify, the intervening labels such as "lust" or "disillusionment" require deeper thought and understanding. Having students present their graphs to the class helps to initiate a discussion as to how different students interpret the progression of the relationship.

Students often enjoy illustrating poems or parts of poems visually, by hand, with computer images, or in a collage. This technique is especially useful in Catullus 4, for example, with its extensive personification of the ship. Students make a list of all the instances of personification in both Latin and in English and then use their lists to create a portrait of the boat as a human being. When students do artistic work, you need not give it a written grade (it is often hard to evaluate creativity with letter grades), but you may engage in an oral or written dialogue with the students as to their thought-processes and as to how effectively the artistic representations convey their thoughts.

Having students write modernizations of the poems in prose or poetic form or fashioning their own poetic translations is another activity that can deepen students' understanding of the material and help them to see the ways in which the ancient subject matter of Catullus' poems is relevant and interesting to modern readers. Students especially enjoy modernizing the friendship poems of Catullus and writing translations of the short elegiac poems at the end of the corpus. A variation on this idea is to have students write a college recommendation for Catullus using actual forms. This real-life evaluative tool offers students another way to contemplate the abstract themes of Catullus in a concrete way. Students generally give him high marks on everything (except maturity) and believe he would be a lively addition to any college community!

You may offer students the opportunity to do musical interpretations of poems. This is an especially effective way of emphasizing the lyric and oral qualities of the poetry. The class has great fun hearing the interpretations and evaluating what the composers find to be the true meaning of the poems.

The interests and strengths of your students are the best sources of ideas and inspiration for projects. Students are full of creative ideas for different ways of responding to poetry. They will also be the first to tell you that a well-conceived creative project is the best way for them to learn and retain their understanding of a poem.

NATIONAL STANDARDS FOR CLASSICAL LANGUAGE LEARNING

The national standards recently adopted for classical languages are the latest model for the highly effective and successful Latin classroom. The document containing these standards may be obtained from the American Classical League (see above). The AP Catullus classroom should incorporate and reflect these national standards. The communication standards are easily achieved in a classroom where there is careful reading and translation of poems and attention paid to making sure each student reads and hears the Latin of every poem. The cultural standards are extremely important to the study of Catullus. Without an understanding of the socio-political context of the mid-first century B.C., the long tradition of ancient lyric poetry, the place of the **poētae novī** in Latin literary circles, and a knowledge of the everyday practices of upper class Romans, students cannot fully interpret the poems or understand how they were important products of their time. The standard dealing with connections can be met in many ways. Students often see the similarities between the themes and topics of Catullus' poems and the literature they study in their English or other foreign language classes. Students especially enjoy comparing the trials and tribulations of Catullus' "life" as presented in the poems to their own experiences or to those of people they know, a way of fulfilling the connections standard. Students use the vocabulary learned and seen in the Catullan corpus and find English derivatives, and in so doing they are fulfilling the standard dealing with connections. Students can use their knowledge of Catullus' poetry in the larger community by making a presentation in another class or teaching younger Latin students one of Catullus' poems that is relevant to their present study, and in so doing they fulfill the standard concerned with communities.

TEACHING FOR MULTIPLE INTELLIGENCES

In order to make the poetry of Catullus accessible and relevant to students, teachers must continually draw upon their various strengths and interests. Howard Gardner's theory of multiple intelligences is a highly effective way of "tapping" into all kinds of students. Gardner developed his theory through his work at the Harvard School of Education. He believes that all people possess seven different kinds of intelligences: Verbal/Linguistic, Logical/Mathematical, Visual/Spatial, Bodily/Kinesthetic, Musical/Rhythmic, Interpersonal, and Intrapersonal. Although all people possess each type of intelligence, usually only one or two are strongly developed in each person. For example, a superior athlete has highly developed Bodily/Kinesthetic intelligence. Traditional classrooms have primarily included activities that focus on the development of only two of the intelligences: Verbal/Linguistic and Logical/Mathematical. Students, however, have individual strengths in all of the intelligences, a fact that is apparent to anyone who has taught a group of students. According to Gardner, teachers must be sure to include activities that employ all the intelligences. This inclusion serves different purposes. First, all students are given equal opportunity to engage in and excel at activities that are most comfortable and meaningful for them. Secondly, individuals require practice to develop all the intelligences and become more fully rounded. Finally, the use of activities that address multiple intelligences ensures a dynamic, varied learning environment. For more theoretical information, consult Howard Gardner's book, *Frames of the Mind: The Theory of Multiple Intelligences*, New York, Basic Books, 1983.

The ideas described above in Projects and Activities can all be used to engage various intelligences. The graph of the Catullus/Lesbia relationship employs Logical/Mathematical intelligence. Artistic representations of the language of the poem are a way to access Visual/Spatial intelligence. Modernizations of the poems provide another outlet for developing Verbal/Linguistic intelligence. A teacher can bring in songs dealing with similar themes to compare with a Catullus poem, using students' Musical/Rhythmic intelligence. Creating dance steps to remember the various lyric meters employs Bodily/Kinesthetic intelligence. Students can write a poem in Catullan style, each contributing one line in turn as an Interpersonal intelligence activity. Keeping a journal of personal reactions to the themes and subject matter of the poems helps students consciously use their Intrapersonal intelligence.

These suggestions are merely a starting point for developing activities addressing multiple intelligences. As was said before, students are the richest source of inspiration for activities. They benefit greatly as well, often coming to a deeper understanding of the poetry in the same amount of time as when they learn through more conventional methods. The long tradition of the AP Catullus syllabus should not discourage teachers from looking to today's students as models and inspiration for new activities and teaching techniques.

COMPARING CATULLUS' ORIGINAL POEMS WITH LATER LITERARY TRANSLATIONS

Comparing Catullus' Latin poems with translations from the Renaissance all the way to modern times is an extremely useful activity for teaching and reinforcing the skills needed for close reading of poetry. Students can easily tell which translations they like or dislike or which poems they think are "good." The first objective is to get them to explain *why* they believe a translation is good. Students should be looking at criteria such as effective use of language, use of rhetorical figures, striking imagery, complex structure, and the use of rhythm and meter. These criteria are all necessary for understanding Catullus' poems, and skill in using them is reinforced as students look at comparable English poems. Once students have answered the question of why they like or dislike a particular translation, the next step is to have them examine whether they believe the English poem is a *good translation* of Catullus' original. They can use criteria such as the translation's adherence to the tone and theme of the original, the way it translates key Catullan words such as **lepidus** or **ōtium**, and its ability to convey effectively Catullus' Latin imagery in the English language. Often students observe that the English translations, although good and interesting, have a difficult time capturing the true essence of Catullus' original. Such observations reveal a deep understanding of the structure and language of Catullus, as they show that those making them can apply their understanding in a high-level thinking activity as they judge Catullus' merits against poems in their own native language.

This exercise not only builds students' analytical skills, but concretely shows them the distinct drawbacks of relying on translations and not having the ability to read and understand literature in its original language. For some students it is the first time they realize the benefits of their ability to read in Latin. This activity also reinforces the important idea that true translation is an extremely difficult process that always involves some compromise of the essence of the original poem. Students soon come to understand that their own translations are very rudimentary. They eventually see translation as not only a skill but as an art as well.

Teachers may notice that most of the translations included in this edition are not from the twentieth century. They can consult the bibliographic resources listed at the end of this Teacher's Guide for more modern translations. *The Classical Outlook* also publishes translations and interpretations of ancient poems written by its subscribers, and these are often useful as teaching tools.

ORDER IN WHICH TO READ THE POEMS

The traditional approach to teaching the Catullus AP syllabus is to read each poem in the numerical order in which we now find them. Strong connections can be made from one poem to another, and students find the variety of themes and topics they encounter along the way enough to capture and maintain their interest. Many scholars have examined patterns in the order of the poems in the present numerical sequence, and these interpretations can be explored with students with great success. The student's book invites study of poems 1 to 11 as a structured unit.

Other teachers prefer to bring the students through the syllabus using a more thematic approach to the poems. They believe that students will find it easier to make comparisons between similar poems and that students have an easier time remembering the various topics of the numerous poems in this context. Some possible themes include love, friendship, **urbanitās**, humor, betrayal, and death.

In addition to studying Catullus thematically, some teachers incorporate the works of another AP author, either Horace, Ovid, or Cicero, into their teaching of Catullus, alternating between Catullus and the other author in the same thematic unit. Students who can effectively compare the language and style of different authors on a similar theme are usually well prepared for the challenge of discussing the authors separately on the AP examination.

For more information on various orders and sample syllabi from secondary teachers, consult the *Teacher's Guide to Advanced Placement Courses in Latin*, a publication of the College Board (ordering information can be found under the heading Materials from the Educational Testing Service above).

COVERAGE OF THE AP CATULLUS SYLLABUS

Reading the selections on the AP Catullus syllabus along with fruitful discussions, metrical readings, study of poetic devices and their impact, and putting the poems in their proper historical and social context takes the average teacher a little more than a full semester. The amount of material from the other authors is generally less than that on the Catullus syllabus, so it is reasonable to expect to spend somewhat more time on Catullus. The pacing of the class depends entirely on the skills and preparation of the students. Students at this level should be expected to read and prepare at least twenty lines per night. It is useful for a teacher to plan out a timetable for covering the poems, taking into account school holidays, time for tests and quizzes, school exam review days, and so forth. Quizzes can be given after three to six poems, depending on their length, difficulty, and thematic grouping. Tests may occur once a month, covering some or all of twelve to sixteen poems at a time through translation, multiple choice, identification, and short essay exercises.

It is a good idea to leave at least three weeks for final review before the Advanced Placement examination. Students should complete practice free-response sections and get personal feedback from the teacher. Doing sight translations and sample multiple-choice questions has proven an effective way of preparing for the AP multiple-choice section. Reviewing major thematic groupings will remind students of issues they will be expected to discuss on the examination. Finally, students should make sure to get plenty of sleep before the exam!

CONCLUSION

All best wishes for an enjoyable, productive study of Catullus' poetry with your students. It truly is a joy to share these relevant, provocative works with new groups of students each year. The enthusiasm and diligence they bring to their study of Latin literature is infectious and will continuously open your eyes to the wonder and the artistry of these poems year after year.

Translations, General Comments on Each Individual Poem, Suggested Answers to Questions in the Student's Book, Select Bibliographies

CATULLUS 1

1   To whom do I give my charming, new little papyrus roll,
2   freshly polished with dry pumice?
3   To you, Cornelius: for already you used
4   to think that my trifles were [worth] something
5   at that time when you alone of Italians dared
6   to unfold all recorded history in three volumes,
7   learned—by Jupiter!—and laborious!
8   So take for yourself whatever this [is] of a little papyrus roll
9   such as it is; which, O patroness maiden,
10   may it last/endure through the years for more than one generation/century.

or

8   So take for yourself whatever this [is] of a little papyrus roll,
9   which, such as it is, o patroness maiden,
10   may it last/endure through the years more than one generation/century.

Poem 1 records the gift of a little book of Catullus' poetry to a Cornelius, usually identified as Cornelius Nepos (but see Simpson, Select Bibliography), who had acquired some literary renown for writing a history of all time in three papyrus rolls. He had also, as it appears, expressed some warm regard for Catullus' poetry, which Catullus himself describes as **nūgae**, *trifles*. As Catullus describes the dedication copy of the papyrus roll, he also hints at the key characteristics of his poetry, which was decidedly unconventional for his own time. It is not known which of the existing poems of Catullus were contained in this little book (**libellus**), but most likely it contained at least poems 1 through 11. A sharp contrast is drawn between Catullus' light verse, his **nūgae**, and the far more pretentious historical work of Cornelius Nepos, full of learning and labor, but Catullus, after belittling the value of his own little book of trifles, prays that it may have an enduring life of its own, which it would seem to deserve for its charm, wit, and polish.

As students read other poems in which Catullus alludes to his poetic principles, preferences, likes, dislikes, and allegiances, particularly poems 22, 35, 36, 50, and 95, they should reread poem 1 as a programmatic poem in which Catullus says much about his stylistic preferences, firmly aligning himself with the Callimachean tradition of brevity, novelty, polish, and intellectual sophistication and with the neoterics of his own day and age (see Thomson, 13–22, for an excellent overview of the neoteric movement or what he calls "the reincarnation of Alexandrianism in Italy").

Poem 1 of Catullus is often compared with the first poem in Book 4 of the *Palatine Anthology*, which dedicates Meleager's *Garland* to Diocles and begins with the line "Dear muse, to whom do you bring this song with all kinds of fruits?" It is interesting to raise the question with students of whether we are to imagine Catullus as actually giving a copy of his **libellus** to Cornelius or whether the poem simply dedicates the **libellus** to him. Throughout the corpus it is important to ask to what extent and in what ways poems are presenting biographical events and to what extent and in what ways they are poetic creations that are independent of or that transcend biographical fact.

Initial Explorations

1. What qualities does Catullus ascribe to his **libellus**? (1–2)
   He calls it charming, new, little, and freshly polished with dry pumice.

2. Examine each word that Catullus uses to describe his **libellus** in the first two lines. How could each word simultaneously describe both the physical appearance of the **libellus** and also the quality of the poetry within it?
   All the terms Catullus uses can be interpreted both in a physical sense describing the smart, fresh appearance of the papyrus roll as a newly published work and in an artistic sense describing the characteristics of the poetry in the book. He calls it **lepidum**, *charming, delightful* (of the book's physical appearance) or *witty, amusing* (of the poetry inside);* **novum** describes the book as brand new but also implies the innovative poetics of its contents; **libellum** describes the book as small and may also hint at the brevity of the poems within it; **āridā modo pūmice expolītum** describes the polish of the ends of the papyrus roll but also implies the poet's attention to craftsmanship and artistry since pumice was used as a eraser when making corrections (Propertius, a poet with Callimachean allegiances, may be alluding to Catullus 1.2 when he says of his own verse, **exāctus tenuī pūmice versus eat**, 3.1.8., *may my verse go along tidied up with slender pumice stone*). All of the terms used to describe the physical appearance of the papyrus roll thus apply metaphorically to the characteristics and quality of the poetry in the book, and they reveal Catullus' allegiance to an Alexandrian or Callimachean poetic program with preference for small scale, highly polished, sophisticated verse.
      *[Wiseman (169; see Select Bibliography) suggests that a "Greek-speaking reader" might have associated the word **lepidus** as used by Catullus here with the Greek word *leptos*, "light," which was an important word in Callimachus' formulation of his poetics.]

3. Why does Catullus use the diminutive form **libellum**? (1)
   The term refers to the small size of the papyrus roll containing Catullus' poetry; it suggests the poet's modest assessment of his achievement; and it suggests that Catullus is particularly fond of the work he has produced (an endearing diminutive).

4. Identify examples of alliteration, assonance, and homoioteleuton in the first two lines. What effects are produced by these features of the verse?
   There is alliteration of *l*s, **lepidum . . . libellum**; there is assonance of *us*, **lepidum novum libellum / . . . expolītum**; and there is homoioteleuton in the last four quoted words; all of this gives the lines a musical quality. The homoioteleuton of the final **-ums** binds together all the crucial terms.

5. How is **modo** in line 2 related to **novum** in line 1? How is **expolītum** in line 2 related to **lepidum** in line 1? How do these words form a chiasmus?
   Modo and **novum** both indicate that the poetry book has just now been finished; **expolītum** and **lepidum** both indicate the papyrus roll's physically *polished* and *charming* appearance, while at the same time implying something about the craftsmanship and sophistication of the poetry inside. Chiasmus: **lepidum** A, **novum** B, **modo** B, and **expolītum** A.

6. Identify the rhetorical figure involved in the words **solēbās / meās . . . nūgās** (3–4). What is its effect?

The rhetorical figure is homoioteleuton, and it highlights the word **nūgās**. Note the effective line framing in line 4.

7. Why has Catullus chosen Cornelius Nepos as the recipient of his **libellus**? (3–4)
Because in the past Cornelius thought Catullus' **nūgae**, *trifles*, despite their modest pretensions, were *[worth] something*. Note the imperfect: Nepos *habitually regarded* Catullus' **nūgae** highly. And also note that Cornelius used to do this at a time when he himself audaciously embarked on a very different literary project.

8. How by word choice and word order has Catullus drawn an effective contrast between Cornelius' estimation of the poet's work and Catullus' own estimation of it? (3–4)
The last word **nūgās** (*trifles*) is in an emphatic position, mildly, perhaps even playfully, undercutting Cornelius' estimation of this poetry as being *[worth] something*.

9. In line 5 Catullus commends Cornelius for being a bold writer. What did Cornelius dare to produce? (5–6)
A universal history of the Greco-Roman world entitled *Chronica*. Note the emphasis on the audacity of Cornelius' literary project; this sets him and his literary work apart in a totally different order from Catullus and his **nūgae**.

10. What are the characteristics of Cornelius as a writer and of his literary production? (5–7) What stylistic devices does Catullus employ in describing Cornelius' literary achievement? What are some of the implications of Catullus' use of the two adjectives **doctīs** and **labōriōsīs** (7)?
Cornelius has alone among Italians produced a universal history in three volumes, which are the result of great learning and labor. The lines effect a somewhat grandiose tone by the long **cum** clause, the choppy arrangement of words, the heavy vocabulary, the exclamatory adjectives, and the embedded oath. The two adjectives **doctīs** and **labōriōsīs** have literary significance, implying a serious, scholarly piece of work, but also one that might be difficult and challenging to read, in contrast to Catullus' trifling and witty **nūgae**.

11. Compare line 6 with line 1, and line 7 with line 2. How do Catullus' and Cornelius' respective works of poetry and history differ? Does Catullus express unqualified admiration of Cornelius' work?
Catullus characterizes his poetry as being *charming*, *fresh*, and fitting into a small papyrus roll compared with Cornelius' more ponderous tomes of history, which cover all of recorded time in the Greco-Roman world. Also while he grants his poetry a fine polish in its craftsmanship, he characterizes Cornelius' work as being serious, scholarly stuff showing labor and learning (**doctīs . . . labōriōsīs**). The learning and labor that Cornelius has put into his writing align him with the Alexandrian school of literary practice, to which Catullus adhered as well, but the exaggeratedly grandiose terms with which Cornelius' history is described may convey some light mockery, just as in our own time a weighty scholarly work may be praised for its laborious learning but considered unreadable by most people for just that quality! Certainly there is a great disparity between Cornelius' **cartae** and Catullus' **nūgae**.

12. What attitude toward his own work does Catullus seem to reveal in his choice of the phrases **habē tibi** and **quidquid hoc libellī** and in the word **quālecumque**? (8–9) What words earlier in the poem express a similar attitude?
Catullus apparently depreciates his own poetry as being unimportant and of slight proportions in comparison with his friend's loftier work. The particular terms he uses have an offhand, disparaging, colloquial ring to them, just as did the words **libellum** and **nūgās** in lines 1 and 4.

13. To whom do you suppose the word **virgō** (9) refers?
The word refers to the muse, or collectively to the muses. No specific muse is mentioned.

14. What prayer does Catullus make to the **virgō**? (9–10)
He prays that his **libellus** may remain throughout the years for more than one generation/century; this is a modestly expressed prayer that his **libellus** may be immortal (compare the lines from Callimachus cited for comparison). By describing the muse as

patrōna, Catullus implies that both the production and the survival of his little book of poetry have been and are dependent upon the muse.

15. Explain the tension that exists between the content of the wish in the final two lines and the poet's earlier assessment of his work.

While Catullus depreciates his poetry as trivial and of slight proportions in comparison with his friend's loftier work, in the final two lines he surprisingly prays to the muse to grant lasting fame for his work, indicating that he thinks his poetry is every bit as worthy in its own distinctive way as the more conventionally dignified achievement of Nepos. Note, however, that in doing so he casts his prayer in characteristically understated terms.

16. Read the poem aloud in meter and comment on your reading. Recall the effects produced by alliteration, assonance, and homoioteleuton in lines 1–2, and comment on (a) the effect of homoioteleuton in lines 1–2, 3–4, 6–7, and 9–10, (b) the elisions in lines 5–6, and (c) the strong alliteration or consonance in lines 8–9.

Students may respond to this question in various ways, but in general they should realize how important sound is in a Catullan poem. Much of the alliteration, assonance, and rhyme either binds together key literary-critical words or enhances the tone. For example, the elisions in lines 5–6 contribute to the heavy sounding measure of the syntax, and the sound of **qu-** in lines 8–9 reinforces the depreciatory, colloquial ring of the vocabulary.

Discussion

1. What does the poem say about Catullus' **libellus** and about what Catullus valued in his poetry and thought noteworthy about it?

Catullus represents himself as giving his friend Cornelius Nepos a dedication copy of his poetry book. In physical terms, such a book would have consisted of about twenty sheets of papyrus, on average, of a width of four to nine inches, pasted together to form a continuous roll, which was then wound around a wooden, or sometimes ivory, cylinder to give the whole papyrus roll a stiff support. Rolls were normally stored vertically in a box (**capsa**). For detailed description of papyrus rolls, see Susan A. Stephens, "Book Production," *Civilization of the Ancient Mediterranean: Greece and Rome*, eds., Michael Grant and Rachel Kitzinger (New York: Charles Scribner's Sons, 1988), vol. I, pp. 421–36. See also Catullus 22.4–8.

The adjectives Catullus uses here to describe the physical qualities of the papyrus roll all have secondary, literary-critical connotations. Thus on a superficial level, the phrase **lepidum novum libellum** refers to the charming, new little book, the edges of which have been freshly polished (**modo expolītum**). But on another level, which is programmatic for Catullus' poetry, **lepidum** refers to what is witty, charming, or amusing. Catullus repeatedly uses this word throughout the corpus in contexts that characterize both the urbane style of his life and the sophisticated cleverness of his poetry. **Novum** is not just *new*, but *innovative* or *different from the ordinary*, implying the anti-traditionalist stance that is such a distinctive part of the attitude Catullus takes toward the Roman world around him and toward the conventions of poetry prevalent in that world. **Libellum** by its diminutive form signifies a small book of poetry, such as would be customary for collections of short poems, and expresses in its implied preference the familiar bias of Catullus and some of the Alexandrian poets before him against the traditional, long epic poem. The most famous of those Alexandrian poets, Callimachus, is said to have considered a big book a big evil. Finally, the idea of literary polish recalls the high ideals of refinement and sophistication that Catullus always valued in life and literature. Here the process of polishing verses is expressed not as a long and laborious task but as a quick and easy rubbing with a pumice stone, as would be appropriate for the small trifles contained in this poetry book.

Exploring the basic vocabulary of the poem in this way will help students to realize why it is important to read a finely crafted poem in its own language and in the context of its own culture. Such subtleties as are explored above cannot be communicated suitably through translation. Compare, for example, the first two lines of Andrew Lang's version in the student's book.

Also of interest, and inaccessible to the latinless student, is the way Catullus uses sound, particularly rhyme, to reinforce his meaning and his key literary terms. One may note, for example, the way final **-um** binds together all the crucial terms discussed above as a unified conception for the listener's ear in the phrase **lepidum novum libellum . . . expolītum**. Further, the rhyme in **solēbās/meās . . . nūgās** emphasizes another critical term in Catullus' poetic program, **nūgae**, *trifles*. Cornelius is thanked for having seen the value of Catullus' work, which on a superficial reading may seem trivial in its scope and treatment, but which upon close examination reveals its skillful artistry. Finally, note the words **cartīs / doctīs . . . labōriōsīs**, where once again terms that have literary significance (**doctīs** and **labōriōsīs**) are emphasized by the triple repetition of the heavy-sounding endings.

2. Is Catullus' admiration of Cornelius' *Chronica* sincere or is it tinged with sly humor?

Because Cornelius writes history, which would have been regarded by the Romans as a more serious and practical genre of literature than the slight, personal poetry Catullus prizes, some readers think that Catullus may be poking fun at his friend, no matter how compactly, learnedly, and laboriously Cornelius has composed his work. Indeed, the *Chronica* of Cornelius, a universal history of the Greco-Roman world, may receive some light mockery here in the somewhat grandiose tone of lines 5–7, where Catullus describes his friend's work. The clause is longer than usual, the arrangement of words is choppy, and the vocabulary is heavy, with its exclamatory adjectives and embedded oath. The tenor of these lines could be considered more suited to a grand subject and is very unlike what Catullus claims for his own verse. Then again, at least on the surface, Catullus depreciates his own poetry as being trivial and of slight proportions in comparison with his friend's loftier work composed in a traditionally esteemed genre of Roman literature. In the surprise coda to his poem, however, Catullus suddenly reverses himself in asking the muse to grant lasting fame for his work. Hence, in the end he reveals that, in fact, he expects his short, personal poems written in an urbane, colloquial style to be every bit as worthy in their own distinctive way as the more conventionally dignified achievement of Nepos. While the latter looks backward in chronicling the entire history of the Greco-Roman world, Catullus looks forward to a life for his poetry that will extend *more than one generation/century* into the future, thus eclipsing the achievement of his friend.

3. What is the role of the **patrōna virgō** in the final two lines?

It is customary for poets, particularly in writing epic poetry, to invoke the muse at the beginning of their work for special inspiration and divine support. Here Catullus is calling on the muse not for inspiration but as a patron of his poetry book in years to come. Calling the muse **patrōna** lends Catullus' invocation a particularly Roman air, as if the poet were assuming a special relationship to the muse as a Roman **cliēns** to his **patrōnus**. In such a relationship the former would look to the latter in difficult circumstances for legal protection and financial support. It is as if Catullus is announcing his dependence on the muse, a goddess of poetic craftsmanship and artistic quality, to help him make a case to the Roman world for the value of his literary achievement in such an unusual kind of poetry book, which does not rely on the stock heroic or historical themes of conventionally reputable poetry.

4. Consider the underlying paradox of the whole poem. Although the poet seems to downplay the significance of his poetry and to elevate the importance of Cornelius' history, the emphasis in lines 1–2 on the charm and polish of Catullus' poetry and the emphasis in line 7 on the choppy and double-edged description of Cornelius' volumes of history seem to suggest the opposite. With what final impression of the quality of the two writers' works are you left after reading the whole poem?

One may explore with students the complications in Catullus' own attitude as he presents his book of poetry to Cornelius and, by extension, to his larger contemporary and future audiences (Cornelius may be thought of at least in part as "a generic figure in this poem," as Elder, 143, suggested). Of particular importance is the seemingly self-depreciating tone that Catullus uses toward his **nūgae** and the seemingly laudatory tone that he adopts in contrast in describing Cornelius' achievement. When returning to his own work in lines 8–9, the connective **quārē**, the indefinite pronoun **quidquid**, and the indefinite adjective **quālecumque**, all beginning with **qu-**, have an off-hand, depreciatory, colloquial ring to them. Yet, in the last two lines the poet suddenly turns away from Cornelius and petitions the muse to grant that his work may attain lasting fame. The modesty that he indulges on the surface of the poem is surprisingly undercut by the request, but it is a surprise only if we have not been attuned to the programmatic clues left for us to follow in a close comparison of the way he describes his own work in lines 1–2 and that of Cornelius in lines 5–7. Catullus is making a bold claim for the importance of his own special kind of poetry, aligned as it is with the principles of the neoteric movement, but he does so in an oblique way that celebrates the artfulness of his craft.

Select Bibliography

Frank O. Copley. "Catullus, c. 1." *Transactions of the American Philological Association* 82 (1951) 200–206.

> Pressed now to say something nice about the book of the man who has so graciously praised his poems, Catullus, who was constitutionally unable to be dishonest, could come up with nothing more than a *doctus* and a *laboriosus*: "The learning that went into these books—Jupiter!—the work!" Very likely Catullus hoped that his compliment would pass muster, and that Cornelius would realize that the poet was doing his best to be appreciative; nevertheless, he is saying quite clearly that his obligation is the greater because he cannot match Cornelius' enthusiasm for his poetry with anything like an equal enthusiasm for the other's histories. (204)

J. P. Elder. "Catullus 1, His Poetic Creed, and Nepos." *Harvard Studies in Classical Philology* 71 (1967) 143–49.

> Catullus, as I read his first poem, is amiably telling Nepos that he, Catullus, is not going to do in poetry what Nepos had done in prose, i.e. that he is not going to follow the Ennian model of lengthy historical narrative. Nor the style of writing which goes along with that kind of narrative. Such must be the meaning of the puffed-up writing in lines 5–7, lines about Nepos' *Chronica*. And the meaning behind the contrasts of *omne aeuum* with *nugae*, or of *libellum* with *tribus cartis*, or of *lepidum nouum* with *doctis, Iuppiter, et laboriosis*. (146)

Francis Cairns. "Catullus I." *Mnemosyne* 22 (1969) 153–58.

> Thus Catullus, himself a neoteric poet, prefixes to his collection a dedication to Nepos giving as one of his reasons for so doing the fact that Nepos has written a neoteric historical work. . . . The virtues he attributes to Nepos are thus by implication those he is claiming for his work. (154)

Philip Levine. "Catullus c.1: A Prayerful Dedication." *California Studies in Classical Antiquity* 2 (1969) 209–16.

> This client/developing poet-patron/mentor relationship soon shifts over . . . to a deliberate comparison between Catullus *qua* aspiring poet in a new key and Nepos *qua* pioneering historian, and the erstwhile patron/mentor now emerges as a model, or perhaps better, precedent for literary innovation in a rather remarkable way through an impressive set of parallelisms that his chronological compendium offers with Catullus' own poetry. *Nouum* in v. 1 . . . alludes to Catullus' break with the poetic traditions of his Latin predecessors; the language and sonorous lilt of v. 5 (*iam tum cum ausus es unus Italorum*) effectively serve to underscore the venturesome novelty of Nepos' historical work. . . Moreover, the narrow dimensions of the poet's collection (cf. v. 1: *libellum*; v. 8: *quidquid hoc libelli*) find their analogue in the other's condensed universal history (cf. v. 6: *omne aeuum tribus . . . cartis*). And

the Callimachean quality and artistic refinement that Catullus attributes to his slender volume (cf. v. 2: *arida . . . pumice expolitum*) might well have been expressed by the very adjectives which he used to characterize the historian's publication (cf. v. 7: *doctis . . . laboriosis*). Thus almost every detail of Catullus' implicit or metaphorical description of his own poetic achievement has its explicit correlative in his account of Nepos' achievement in history. In a highly ingenious, yet typically Roman, fashion the poet justifies what he has attempted to do by relating it to an established literary precedent. (211–12)

G. P. Goold. "O Patrona Virgo." *Polis and Imperium: Studies in Honour of E. T. Salmon*, ed., J. A. S. Evans. Toronto: Hakkert, 1974: 253–64. Argues in favor of Bergk's reading **patrōnī ut ergō**, *so that, on account of its patron* (9), and gives the following version and translation of lines 8–10:

> **Quārē habē tibi quidquid hoc libellī**
> **quālecumque quidem patrōnī ut ergō**
> **plūs ūnō maneat perenne saeclō.**
> Wherefore, for better or for worse,
> Accept this little book of verse,
> That, though so slight, with patron's name
> It yet may win undying fame.

T. P. Wiseman. "The Dedication Poem." *Clio's Cosmetics: Three Studies in Greco-Roman Literature* (Leicester University Press, 1979) 167–74.

C. J. Simpson. "The Identity of Catullus's Addressee." *Revue belge de philologie et d'histoire* 70 (1992) 53–61. Suggests that the addressee is L. Cornelius Sisenna, "the most renowned historian of Catullus' day" (55) and not Cornelius Nepos.

B. J. Gibson. "Catullus 1.5–7." *Classical Quarterly* 45 (1995) 569–73. Accepts Bergk's **patrōnī ut ergō** in line 9, "so that Catullus' poem ends with the wish that Nepos assist in the survival of his [i.e., Catullus'] *libellus*" (572), but sees irony in Catullus' praise of Nepos' *Chronica*. Highly recommended.

John Rauk. "Time and History in Catullus 1." *Classical World* 90 (1997) 319–32.

Catullus' treatment of Nepos is intentionally ironic. Catullus presents Nepos as a man of great literary achievement, while at the same time implying that his admiration for Nepos is insincere. As I hope to show, however, Catullus' irony does not imply a criticism of Nepos. Rather, Catullus frames the dedication as a sort of joke; like some of his other poems, such as poem 53, it adopts a teasing attitude toward the literary activities of Catullus and his circle that is based upon the public's perception of them. Specifically, Catullus plays upon the common assumption that history, by its nature, is a higher genre than poetry. Nepos accordingly is dressed up as the imposing author of a monumental history, while Catullus, in turn, takes on the role of a lowly poet. Catullus' ironic presentation of these roles, however, shows that he and Nepos were in fact friends who were actively interested in each others' careers and whose literary values were not circumscribed by the genres they practiced. (320)

W. Jeffrey Tatum. "Friendship, Politics, and Literature in Catullus: Poems 1, 65 and 66, 116." *Classical Quarterly* 47 (1997) 482–500.

As has often been observed, the qualities attributed to Nepos' historical composition (brevity, innovation, learning, and *labor*) tend to reinforce the poet's recognition that Nepos is his ideal reader. . . . the poet's *alter ego* (485). The poet adopts "a client's posture" toward Nepos (486).

CATULLUS 2

1 **Passer**, sweetheart of my **puella**,
2 with whom she is accustomed to play, whom [she is accustomed] to hold at her bosom,
3 to whose eager attack [she is accustomed] to give her fingertip
4 and to provoke sharp bites,
5 whenever it is pleasing to the radiant object of my desire/to [her] radiant with desire for me
6 to play something or other dear [to her],
7 and [to play at] a small comfort for her heartache,

or
7 as a small comfort for her heartache,

8 I believe, so that then her heavy passionate desire may find rest;
9 if only I could sport with you as your mistress [does]
10 and relieve the sad cares of my heart.

"Poem 2 is in form and content a hymn, a prayer by Catullus to a sparrow for a special act of grace" (Bishop, see Select Bibliography, 158).

What kind of bird is Catullus referring to with the word **passer**? Instead of identifying it with the common sparrow, the *passer domesticus*, D'Arcy Thompson, *Glossary of Greek Birds*[2], 270, identified it with the *passer solitarius*, the blue thrush. Fordyce accepts that identification and quotes a passage from Samuel Butler, *Alps and Sanctuaries of Piedmont* (London, 1881), 299, describing how the bird is "easily tamed, and becomes very much attached to its master and mistress, but . . . is apt to die in confinement before very long." The *Oxford Latin Dictionary* accepts the identification with the blue thrush. Those who regard it as the common house sparrow cite the poem of Sappho where sparrows draw the chariot of Aphrodite and other passages suggesting that the sparrow was regarded as a bird of love (see Brenk, Select Bibliography). Thomson draws attention to a book by Clare Kipps, *Sold for a Farthing* (London: Frederick Muller Limited, 1953), which tells the story of how the author found a newly-hatched house sparrow on her doorstep, nurtured it, and lived with it for twelve years as an extraordinarily amiable and characterful pet, which developed a remarkable song. Either identification seems possible. We refer to the bird as **passer**, thus avoiding the need to choose one identification over the other. The issue seems to be of little importance for interpretation of poems 2 and 3.

For the obscene interpretation of the **passer** first put forward by Poliziano in the fifteenth century, see Select Bibliography. We leave the introduction of this interpretation up to the discretion of the individual teacher.

A note also on the word **puella**: we again simply use the Latin word rather than translating it as *girl* or *girlfriend*. Note also that the name Lesbia does not occur in poems 2 and 3; we believe it is better to reserve discussion of that name until poem 5 where it first appears.

Initial Explorations

1. The words **passer**, **meae**, and **puellae** in line 1 inform us of a triangle of relationships that this poem will explore. Identify the members of the triangle.
    The **passer**, Catullus , and the **puella**.
2. What does the word **dēliciae** with its range of meanings tell us about how the poet views the relationship between the **puella** and the **passer**?
    He views the **passer** as the pet of the **puella**, who has genuine affection for it and who finds delight in it such as she might find in a sweetheart.
3. Describe each of the interactions between the **puella** and the **passer** in lines 2–4.
    Within the general notion of "play," the girl clasps the **passer** at her bosom, offers him the tip of her finger to peck, and provokes him to bite her.

4. Identify the clauses of an ascending tricolon in lines 2–4.
    (1) **quīcum lūdere**; (2) **quem in sinū tenēre**; (3) **cui prīmum digitum dare appetentī / et acrīs solet incitāre morsūs**

5. In addition to its literal meaning, what suggestive meaning does the infinitive **lūdere** carry in this context? (2)
    On a literal level, the **passer** is a pet with whom the girl entertains herself in "play," but in the way the poet describes the girl's sport in the context, he puns on a connotation of **lūdere** that is appropriate to "amorous play" between humans.

6. Of the words **quem in sinū tenēre**, which one adds an erotic coloring to the scene?
    sinū

7. What is the relationship between the actions of the **puella** in line 3 and in line 4? Can something more than innocent play be seen here?
    In line 3 the **puella** offers her finger to the bird to peck in what might seem to be innocent play; in line 4 she provokes the bird to bite her sharply. This can still be seen as a kind of fast-paced give and take in fun between the two, but the provocation of sharp bites seems to indicate that something more is involved here.

8. What meaning of the verb **appetere** is most appropriate in translating the participle **appetentī** (3)? How does this word contribute an amorous overtone to the scene?
    The most appropriate meaning is *attack*, understood in the context of the bird's aggressive pecking. Like the English cognate *appetite*, however, the word can also refer to any activity motivated by instinctual desire, so that it is appropriate to amorous play between humans.

9. Why is the verb **solet** (4) important? What does it add to the description of the behavior of the **puella**?
    The verb indicates that the play engaged in by the **puella** is a regular practice of hers. The scene described here is not a special occasion but something the poet has observed a number of times.

10. Discuss the words **ācrīs . . . morsūs** (4). In what direction do these two words take the poet's description of the scene? Elsewhere Catullus uses similar language of lovers' kisses: e.g., Catullus 8.18, **Quem bāsiābis? Cui labella <u>mordēbis</u>?** *Whom will you kiss? Whose little lips will you <u>bite</u>?* and 68b.86–88, *the dove is said to snatch kisses with her <u>biting</u> beak (<u>mordentī</u> . . . <u>rōstrō</u>) more wantonly than even an especially passionate woman.* How does this affect your understanding of the scene here?
    The phrase **ācrīs . . . morsūs** colors the passage with a heightened sense of emotional intensity. The poet's description begins with the ambiguous word **lūdere**, *to play*, evoking an atmosphere of fun but also suggestive of lovemaking, and it ends with words that denote sharp pain. The poet seems to be describing the **puella** as trying to satisfy something more than a simple desire to have fun with her pet, and the comparison with Catullus 8.18 and 68b.86–88 suggests that he thinks she is engaging in vicarious lovemaking.

11. The words **dēsīderiō meō nitentī** (5) may be translated *to the radiant object of my desire* or *to [her] shining with longing for me.* Does one translation seem to be more appropriate than the other? Need one choose?
    The first translation is wholly consistent with Catullus' description of the **puella** at play; he compliments her by calling her the radiant object of his desire. The second meaning of the phrase, one suggested by Baker (see Select Bibliography) and preferred by Nisbet (see Select Bibliography) and Thomson (203), seems intended as well. It may, of course, reflect mere wishful thinking on Catullus' part.

12. Why, according to the poet, is the **puella** playing with the **passer**? (5–8) Include in your answer reference to the three line-ending words, **iocārī, dolōris,** and **ārdor.** To what extent is the **passer** described as a surrogate lover?
    The poet explains that the **puella** is engaging with her pet **passer** in some endearing play (**iocārī**) as a small comfort of her *heartache* (**dolōris**), so that her *heavy passionate desire* (**gravis . . . ārdor**) may abate. The poet speculates that play with the **passer** relieves her of her heartache and passionate desire, just as would amorous play with her beloved.

This is what Catullus was leading up to with the earlier language that was applicable to play both with the **passer** and with a human lover.

13. How does the presence of the parenthetical word **crēdō** qualify the statements in lines 7 and 8? What level of knowledge of the true intentions of the **puella** does this word suggest on the part of the poet?

The insertion of **crēdō** indicates that the poet is giving his own interpretation of the emotional purposes underlying the girl's play with the **passer**. The implication may in fact be that he is engaging in wishful thinking and projecting his own emotions onto the **puella**, imagining that her play with the **passer** must be her way of easing her emotional pain and her longing. Catullus may be saying more about himself here than about the real state of mind of the **puella**. Everything he describes up to line 6 can be seen by an observer watching the girl play with her **passer**, but in lines 7–8 the poet ventures to explain why the girl behaves as she does. He does not know for sure, but he speaks as if he has inside knowledge and imagines that she is motivated by a desire to find relief from heartache and passionate desire.

14. Is the **puella** or the **passer** the center of the poet's interest in lines 1–8?

Although the poem begins with an address to the **passer**, the **puella** is the center of the poet's interest in lines 1–8, with total focus on her in lines 5–8.

15. What is the poet's wish in line 9? in line 10?

In line 9 he wishes he could sport with the **passer** as does the **puella**, and in line 10 he wishes that he could thereby relieve the *sad cares* of his own heart (i.e., the amatory distress that he feels).

16. What is implied in the use of the imperfect subjunctive (**possem**, 9) for the poet's wish?

By using the imperfect subjunctive, the poet indicates that his wish cannot be realized. He is saying, *If only I could. But I know I can't.* He can't play with the **passer** because it is not his, but he also seems to realize that his amatory distress (**cūrae**) is too strong to be satisfied by mere play with a **passer**.

Discussion

1. What is the relationship between Catullus and the **puella**?

This is a difficult question to answer because the poem is not a narrative of a love affair as it has developed in the course of time but rather a snapshot of one scene at one moment in time with the poet as a distanced observer of the conduct of the **puella**, with no verbal communication between them. Indeed, the poem is addressed to the **passer** and not to the **puella**, and even the address to the **passer** is not made in any particular dramatic context.

The words of the poem provide only ambiguous hints as to the relationship between Catullus and the **puella**:

a. He refers to her with the words **meae puellae** (1), a phrase which implies some special relationship between the poet and the girl, but it may be a one-way relationship.

b. The words **dēsīderiō meō nitentī** (5) are ambiguous, for they may be taken to mean (1) *to the radiant object of my desire* or (2) *to [her] radiant with desire for me.*

If the phrase **dēsīderiō meō nitentī** is taken in the first of the two senses, then we must ask whether we are to suppose that the **puella** reciprocates Catullus' love and desire. Is the second interpretation of the phrase valid, or is it conscious or unconscious wishful thinking on the part of the poet?

c. The next words that tell us something about the feelings of the **puella** are the words **dolōris** (7) and **gravis . . . ārdor** (8). Here, too, however, there is uncertainty since what the poet says here is merely his interpretation, a fact that he admits with the word **crēdō** (8). Is Catullus simply projecting his own feelings onto the **puella**?

d. Finally, the words **trīstēs animī . . . cūrās** (10) tell the reader that Catullus feels the sad cares or distress of a lover, and it is clear from the words **meae puellae** and **dēsīderiō meō nitentī** and from the poem as a whole that it is the **puella** with whom he is in love and that it is because of his love for her that he feels these **trīstēs animī . . . cūrās**.

2. How satisfactory is this poem as an introduction to a cycle of poems devoted to the love affair between Catullus and the **puella**?

It is a very vivid introduction, with its focus on the **puella** and her suggestive play with her pet **passer**. It is a teasing introduction because it leaves so many questions unanswered, as we have seen above. In addition to those questions, however, there are even more basic questions that are neither asked nor answered, such as the following. Who is the **puella**? What is her name? What is her social and familial status? What kind of a relationship does Catullus expect to have with her? Something seems to be going on here outside of the traditional manners and customs that regulated the relationships between young men and young women in respectable Roman society.

It may seem that more questions are raised by the poem than are answered, but this surely makes it a splendid introduction to a cycle of love poems and entices the reader to unroll the **libellus** further to find out more about Catullus and his **puella**, since his emotional intensity and her suggestive playfulness have great potential for complex and exciting developments.

Select Bibliography

Sheridan Baker. "Catullus' *cum desiderio meo*." *Classical Philology* 53 (1958) 243–44. On ambiguity in line 5.

J. D. Bishop. "Catullus 2 and Its Hellenistic Antecedents." Classical Philology 61 (1966) 158–67. Comparison with Hellenistic epigrams on a locust and a cicada (*Palatine Anthology* 7.195 and 196).

E. N. Genovese. "Symbolism in the Passer Poems." *Maia* 26 (1974) 121–25. Sees the **passer** as "a phallic charm" (121).

Giuseppe Giangrande. "Catullus' Lyrics on the Passer." *Museum Philologum Londiniense* 1 (1975) 137–46. The *passer* as the poet's *mentula*: the obscene interpretation.

R. G. M. Nisbet. "Notes on the Text of Catullus." *Proceedings of the Cambridge Philological Society* 24 (1978) 91–115. On line 5: "*desiderio* is not dative but ablative, and the meaning is 'to her shining with longing for me'" (92).

F. E. Brenk. "*Non primus pipiabat*: Echoes of Sappho in Catullus' *passer* Poems." *Latomus* 39 (1980) 702–16. Sees in Catullus' "use of the sparrow as an amatory symbol" an allusion to Sappho's poem (number 1) in which sparrows draw the chariot of Aphrodite.

A. S. Fotiou. "Catullus' Passer Poems: Meaning and Form." *Grazer Beiträge* 9 (1980) 111–21. Develops the idea that the **passer-puella** relationship in poems 2 and 3 "can be compared with the progressive movement of Catullus' own love affair with Lesbia" (114–15), which Fotiou sees as having three stages. Discusses the erotic overtones of the language used to describe the **passer** and the **puella** in poems 2 and 3.

H. D. Jocelyn. "On Some Unnecessarily Indecent Interpretations of Catullus 2 and 3." *American Journal of Philology* 101 (1980) 421–41. Argues against the obscene interpretation of the **passer**.

Richard W. Hooper. "In Defence of Catullus' Dirty Sparrow." *Greece & Rome* 32 (1985) 162–78. Attacks Jocelyn in support of Genovese and Giangrande.

Richard F. Thomas. "Sparrows, Hares, and Doves: A Catullan Metaphor and Its Tradition." *Helios* 20 (1993) 131–142. Supports the metaphorical or obscene interpretation of the **passer**.

Julian Ward Jones Jr. "Catullus' *Passer* as *Passer*." *Greece & Rome* 45 (1998) 188–94. Toward the end of the fifteenth century, the Florentine scholar Angelo Poliziano suggested that Catullus had woven an obscene allegory into his poem, and he supported his argument by reference to the sixth epigram of Martial's eleventh book. . . . Poliziano only hinted at an indecent meaning. The Dutch scholar, Isaac Voss, in his *Observations* on Catullus published in 1684, makes the matter explicit. The Greeks, he alleges, often used the names of birds to refer to a man's penis, and similarly *passer* in poem 2 is ambiguous and at one level represents the poet's penis. By this obscene interpretation, the basic allegory of the poem would be something like this. Lesbia has great familiarity with the poet's male member. She delights in playing with it and in this way seems to satisfy her erotic impulses. The poet by means of similar play would like to take similar satisfaction for himself. He cannot because masturbation gives him no pleasure. . . . The obscene interpretation of the *passer* poems has never been generally accepted. Most scholars have seen it as an example of learned silliness and its proponents have been the butt of hearty ridicule. (188)

CATULLUS 2b

1 It is as pleasing to me as they say
2 the golden apple was to the swift girl,
3 which loosed her girdle that had been long bound.

Most scholars do not believe that Catullus 2b should be read as the conclusion of Catullus 2. Catullus 2b seems to be a mere fragment, detached from its original and now unknown context. The lone manuscript that descended to the modern era was in such poor shape that it left us with a number of such insoluble problems.

Amid discussion of whether Catullus 2b does or does not belong with Catullus 2, one should not lose sight of the important theme of female empathy or gender reversal here, as Catullus compares an experience he has had to one that Atalanta had, thus identifying himself with Atalanta.

Discussion

Could these lines make sense as an ending to Catullus 2?

This question has been as hotly debated among scholars as any other Catullan question. Brotherton's view (see below, Select Bibliography) seems reasonable, but it does not account for the switch from subjunctive (**possem**, 2.9) to indicative (**est**, 2b.1). Most other attempts to justify joining 2b to 2 rest on the obscene interpretation of the **passer** and on an obscene interpretation of 2.9–10 as referring to masturbation. Voss and Giangrande (see Select Bibliography) support their arguments with obscene interpretations of 2b as well. Thomson comments on 2b: "There can be no link with poem 2" (205).

Select Bibliography

B. Brotherton. "Catullus' Carmen II." *Classical Philology* 21 (1926) 361–63. Argues for the unity of 2 and 2b: "As the sparrow relieves Lesbia's passion, and would relieve Catullus', so the golden apple relieved the passion of Atalanta; she loved Hippomenes, and eagerly stopped her running at sight of the apple, glad of an excuse to let him win the race" (361–62).
Giuseppe Giangrande. "Catullus' Lyrics on the Passer." *Museum Philologum Londiniense* 1 (1975) 137–46. Argues for the unity of 2 and 2b by interpreting the *passer* in an obscene sense and by seeing obscene meanings in 2.9–10 and in 2b.
H. D. Jocelyn. "On Some Unnecessarily Indecent Interpretations of Catullus 2 and 3." *American Journal of Philology* 101 (1980) 421–41. Argues at great length against the obscene interpretation of the **passer**, against Voss's emendation of **possem** to **posse**, and against Voss's introduction of the idea of "self-manipulation" in 2.9–10; see 429–30.
H. Dettmer. "Catullus 2b from a Structural Perspective." *Classical World* 78 (1984) 107–10. Argues for the unity of 2 and 2b on the basis of comparison with poem 65.
Richard W. Hooper. "In Defence of Catullus' Dirty Sparrow." *Greece & Rome* 32 (1985) 162–78. Ac-

cepts Voss's emendation of **posse** for **possem** (2.9) and interprets the **passer** in an obscene sense. Hooper paraphrases: "To be able to play with myself as skillfully as Lesbia does is an idea as welcome to me as, in reality . . . , Hippomenes' golden apple was to Atalanta" (165).

CATULLUS 3

1 Mourn, O Venuses and Cupids,
2 and however many men there are who are deeply in love:
3 the **passer** of my **puella** has died/is dead,
4 the **passer**, darling of my **puella**,
5 whom she loved more than her own eyes.
6 For it/he was honey-sweet and knew its/his own
7 mistress as well as a girl knows her mother,
8 nor did it/he move from her lap,
9 but jumping about now this way now that way
10 it/he continuously peeped to its/his mistress alone;
11 it/he who now journeys on that gloomy journey
12 from which they say that no one returns.
13 But curses on you, evil darkness
14 of Orcus, you who swallow up all pretty things.
15 You have robbed me of such a pretty **passer**.
16 O misfortune! O poor little **passer**!
17 Because of your doing now the little eyes of my **puella**
18 turn red, slightly puffed from weeping.

or (Goold)
16 O misfortune, that, poor little **passer**,
17 because of your doing now the little eyes of my **puella**
18 turn red, slightly puffed from weeping.

or (Thomson)
15 You have robbed me of such a pretty **passer**
16 (O misfortune! O poor little **passer**!);
17 because of your* doing now the little eyes of my **puella**
18 turn red, slightly puffed from weeping.

   *your now refers to the **malae tenebrae / Orcī** (13–14) and not to the **passer** (16).

Poem 3 is a pendant to poem 2, both being poems in which Catullus imaginatively identifies himself with the **passer** of his **puella**. Still there are large differences between the two poems. Whereas in poem 2 Catullus makes a rather direct and moving confession of his passion and the pain it causes him, the tone and style of poem 3 are more complex and show more dramatic shifts in tone and voice. These shifts can be marked off in the symmetrical structural divisions of the poem. Lines 1–5 introduce the subject of the lament, the death of the **passer**, who is idealized as the darling of his mistress. Lines 6–10 then develop an idyllic portrait of the devoted attachment of the **passer** to the **puella**, with an implied reference to the poet's own devotion to the **puella**. Lines 11–15 abruptly shift from the romanticized view of the past to the present fate of the **passer**, described in mock-elegiac terms. The conceit of an epitaphic dirge written upon the demise of a pampered pet but delivered with all seriousness bears a distinct resemblance to a type of epigram in the *Palatine Anthology* dealing with the demise of an animal or pet (see 7.189–216 for examples) in sentimental terms. Finally, the last three lines offer a view of the tearful reaction of the **puella** to the death of the

passer, and these lines have an emotional delicacy that is very different in tone from the preceding section. Thus we move through the course of the poem from nostalgic reminiscence to mock-epic indignation and, finally, to exquisite tenderness. We can read this modulation of feeling in different ways: as a virtuoso display on the part of a lover of all the various emotions engendered by a genuinely sympathetic relationship with his beloved or, ironically, as a kind of witty exaggeration of the sufferings voluntarily undertaken by the devoted lover.

Initial Explorations

1. Whom does the poet call upon to grieve? Why does he invoke these gods and men? (1–2)
    He calls upon the *Venuses and Cupids* and upon *however many men there are who are deeply in love*. These particular gods and men are all related by their capacity to understand and appreciate the experience of love and thus can be expected to join in mourning the dead **passer** since it was the pet of the **puella** who is the object of Catullus' love.

2. Locate and analyze two ascending tricola in lines 1–2 and 4–5.
    The first tricolon, (1) **ō Venerēs**, (2) **Cupīdinēsque**, (3) **et quantum est hominum venustiōrum**, proceeds from divinities of love to men of Catullus' social ambiance who are animated by the divine qualities represented by Venuses and Cupids. The second, (1) **passer**, (2) **dēliciae meae puellae**, (3) **quem plūs illa oculīs suīs amābat**, moves from mention of the bird itself to a phrase describing the importance of the bird to Catullus' **puella** to a climactic description (note the hyperbole in the clause **quem plūs illa oculīs suīs amābat**) of how dearly the **puella** used to love the bird.

3. Lines 4–10 recall Catullus 2. Compare the relationship of the **passer** and the **puella** in these lines with lines 1–4 of Catullus 2. What are the similarities and differences?
    In both poems Catullus describes the animated, endearing relationship between the girl and her pet. In poem 2, however, he emphasizes the "play" between the two, described in terms of human lovemaking, whereas in poem 3 he emphasizes the bird's honey-sweet nature, how intimately it knew its owner, its constant presence on her lap, how it hopped about, and how it chirped continuously for its owner alone. In other words, while in poem 2 the poet focused on the play of the **puella** with the **passer**, in poem 3 he emphasizes the bird's devotion to its/his mistress.

4. With what word earlier in the poem does **mellītus** (6) correspond? How does the word **mellītus** contribute to our understanding of the relationship between the **puella** and the **passer** as expressed in this poem?
    Mellītus corresponds to **dēliciae**, meaning *delight* as well as *pet*. It emphasizes the delight the **puella** takes in her pet, which/whom she regards as *honey-sweet*, a term of endearment, which suggests that, in the eyes of the **puella**, the **passer** is like a lover.

5. The verb **nōrat** (6) may connote a knowing in carnal or sexual as well as mental terms. What limitation does line 7 place on the dual meaning of **nōrat** in this context? Why is that significant?
    Any carnal overtones of **nōrat** are immediately dispelled by the simile in line 7, which compares the bird's "knowledge" of its mistress to the way a girl "knows" her own mother, i.e., in a manner of strictly familial relationships. This is significant because it gives the bird's devotion the innocent intimacy of a girl's devotion to her mother.

6. The word **gremiō** (8) reminds the reader of **sinū** in Catullus 2.2. How has the bird's behavior at the bosom or on the lap of the **puella** changed between poems?
    In Catullus 2 the **passer** displayed aggressive behavior in pecking at the finger of its mistress, whereas in Catullus 3 it is content to frisk about on her lap.

7. Comment on the impression produced by the polysyllabic participle placed next to four choppy and elided adverbs in line 9.
    The line imitates in the polysyllabic participle and the choppy cadence of its elided sounds the bird's rhythmical hopping back and forth.

8. What do the words **ad sōlam dominam usque pīpiābat** (10) say about the relationship of the bird to the **puella**? Which meaning of the word **domina** is most appropriate? In the context of

the scene described in lines 4–10, is more than one meaning of the word applicable?

Line 10 gives us a picture of the bird's singular devotion to the **puella**. On a superficial level the word **dominam** indicates the pet's *owner*, but the singular devotion and loyalty of the **passer** to the **puella** suggests that the meaning *mistress* (i.e., the term for the female head of a household) is also appropriate here. This meaning has been anticipated by the phrase **suam . . . / ipsam** in lines 6–7, where **ipsam** is used in the technical sense of the mistress of a household in her capacity as overseer of the household slaves. The meaning *mistress* is probably most applicable in line 10, with the sparrow thinking of itself as a devoted **servus** to the **puella**.

9.   What journey must the bird now make? (11–12) How is it portrayed? What is its mythological background? Do the word **tenebricōsus** and the sentiment expressed in line 12 reinforce or undercut the gravity of the loss? Is there an element of parody here?

The bird must make the journey of the dead to the underworld, which is described as a *gloomy journey from which . . . no one returns*. The poet alludes to Orcus, who is a god of the underworld, where the souls of the dead, conceived as shades, are kept imprisoned. The scene is familiar from descriptions of the underworld in Greco-Roman mythology. The mock-elegiac quality of the language, including the word **tenebricōsum** and the sentiment expressed in line 12, underscores the seriousness of the bird's death, elevating it to a more than casual level. This parody of the general form of an epitaphic dirge recalls some epigrams in the *Palatine Anthology* (7.189–216), where the demise of a pampered pet, delivered with all seriousness, is lamented.

Note the onomatopoetic **it per iter** (11), imitating the pitter-patter of the **passer** as it hops about, and note the etymological punning on **it** and **iter**.

10.   Whom does the poet curse? (13–14) What specific reason does the poet give for uttering the curse?

He curses the *evil darkness of Orcus*, because it *swallows up all pretty things*. Note how the elisions enhance the sense here.

11.   In a surprising conclusion, what is the bird (or the shades of Orcus if Thomson's reading is accepted) blamed for? (17–18) Does the traditional text or Thomson's emendation make better sense?

The bird (or the shades of Orcus) is blamed for causing the eyes of the **puella** to *turn red, slightly puffed from weeping*. Thomson's text may be preferred by most readers, since it takes the blame off the bird and places it where it belongs, on the shades of Orcus, i.e., on death. After all, it was not the bird's fault that it died and caused the **puella** grief.

12.   What feelings does the poet express in the final line? How does he express them?

He expresses emotional sympathy with his **puella** over her grief in a tone of delicate tenderness expressed by the diminutives and the alliterative run of *l*s characterizing the emotional reaction of the **puella**. Her *little eyes* (**ocellī**) are *slightly puffed* (**turgidulī**), implying real sorrow.

13.   Where in the poem do you find shifts in sentiment and tone? Describe the sentiment and tone of each section of the poem.

Lines 1–10 develop an idyllic portrait of the bird's devoted attachment to its/his mistress. Lines 11–15 abruptly shift from the romanticized view of the past to the present fate of the **passer**, described in mock-elegiac terms. Finally, lines 16–18 offer a view of the tearful reaction of the **puella** to the death, which has a special emotional delicacy. Thus we move through the course of the poem from nostalgic reminiscence to mock-elegiac indignation and, finally, to exquisite tenderness.

14.   Read the poem aloud and in meter. Describe the effects of the various sound and metrical patterns in the poem, such as (a) the repetition of double *l*s and the resulting linkage among words, (b) the resonance of *m*s in lines 6–7, (c) the multiple elisions and onomatopoeia in lines 9–10, (d) the contrast between mono- or disyllabic words in the first half of line 11 and the polysyllabic word at the end of the line, (e) the repetitions in lines 13–15 (**malae . . . male**; **bella . . . bellum**), (f) the anaphora and exclamations in line 16, and (g) the soft liquid sounds of line 18.

(a)   The repetition of the double *l*s has a mellifluous quality, linking the honey-sweetness of the bird with the **puella**.

(b)   Perhaps also the closeness of bird to mistress, like daughter to mother, is enhanced by the alliteration of *m*s in lines 6–7.

(c)   The onomatopoeia in lines 9–10 imitates in its choppy, repetitious cadence the bird's rhythmical hopping back and forth.

(d)   The pronounced shift to the heavier word has a mock-elegiac ring.

(e–f)   The verbal repetitions, anaphora, and exclamations are part of the high style parodied in this section.

(g)   The soft liquids emphasize the two important diminutives in the last line, reflecting both the small stature of the bird and the emotional delicacy and tenderness of the scene. They also recall the same alliteration of *l*s in lines 4–6.

Discussion

1.   How is the **passer** given human qualities in the image of a lover?

Human qualities are given to the **passer** through the description of the feelings of the **puella** for it in the clause **quem plūs illa oculīs suīs amābat** (5), which is couched in terms frequently found in contexts of human friendship and love (cf. Catullus 14.1 and 104.2), through the description of the **passer** as **mellītus** (6), an adjective used as a term of human endearment (cf. Catullus 48.1 and 99.1), through the description of the **passer** as knowing its own mistress as well as a girl knows her mother (6–7), and through the description of the devoted attention of the **passer** to its/his owner/mistress alone (8–10). In all these ways the **passer** plays a very human role in the scene, thus our use of *it/he* and *its/his* in the translation and discussion.

Once seen in human terms, the **passer** assumes the personality of a lover, for the **passer** was as dear to the **puella** as her eyes (5), *honey-sweet* (6), singularly attentive to his mistress (8–9), and continuously singing to her alone (10). The statement that the **passer** *knew its/his own mistress as well as a girl knows her mother* (6–7) foreshadows Catullus' description of his love in 72.3–4: **dīlēxī tum tē . . . / . . . pater ut gnātōs dīligit et generōs** (*I cherished you then . . . / . . . as a father cherishes his sons and sons-in-law*). Now the word **dominam** in line 10 may be interpreted not only as *owner* or familial *mistress* of the household, but as amatory *mistress*, with the **passer** her singularly devoted lover. Every detail in the description of the **passer** and its/his relationship to the **puella** thus contributes to the **passer** being given human qualities in the image of a lover.

2.   How does the portrayal of the **passer** with the **puella** in Catullus 3 complement that in Catullus 2?

In poem 2 the **puella** is portrayed as playing with the **passer** in order to alleviate emotions associated in one way or another with love and desire. Focus is on the **puella**, her provocation of the **passer**, and the comfort and emotional relaxation that she appears to the poet to be experiencing through her amorous play with the **passer**. The portrayal of the **passer** and the **puella** in poem 3 focuses almost exclusively on the **passer** and its/his devotion to the **puella** as its/his **domina** (*owner*; *mistress* = female head of a household; and *mistress* = woman loved by a man but not married to him). The relationship between the **puella** and the **passer** is thus portrayed in complementary terms in the two poems, in that it is seen from the point of view of the **puella** in poem 2 and from the point of view of the **passer** in poem 3. In poem 2 the **puella** appears to be teasing the **passer** in order to alleviate her **dolor** and **ārdor** through mock amorous play, while in poem 3 the **passer** expresses its/his fondness for the **puella** through its/his devoted attention to her and its/his continuous chirping or singing to its/his one and only mistress.

The complementary images of the **puella** and the **passer** in the two poems establish a model or a paradigm of a balanced, reciprocal love relationship between a man and a woman.

It may be noted, however, that the gender roles are reversed from what was considered normal in Roman society. Thus, Khan (see Select Bibliography) remarks on poem 3, "Here . . . we meet in Catullus what we may call a reversal of sexual roles. The sparrow/Catullus personage, the male partner in the liaison, exhibits the traits of utter devotion and fidelity, which were rare and unusual in men, but highly desirable in women" (36). And, conversely, we may remark that the provocations of the **puella** in egging the **passer** on to sharp pecking are an aggressive, masculine gesture.

3. How does the death of the **passer** open the way for future developments in Catullus' love for the **puella**?

If Catullus' love for the **puella**, which he expresses in his wish at the end of poem 1 and in the image of the **passer** in poem 2, is to be allowed to develop in the form of a relationship with the **puella**, then clearly the **passer** has to go. The **puella** cannot be allowed to satisfy her longings by mere play with a bird, and Catullus' longings cannot be satisfied by sitting on the sidelines and merely watching the **puella** from a distance, as he has been doing in poems 2 and 3. The **passer** is eliminated through the brilliant poetic expedient of its death, and the stage is then cleared for Catullus to make a direct approach to the **puella**. As readers continue to roll out their papyrus rolls, they will be eagerly anticipating the next stage in Catullus' affair with the **puella**, but instead, to their disappointment, they find a poem on a totally different theme that will cause them some delay and doubtless some initial annoyance before they find the continuation of the love affair in poem 5.

Select Bibliography

H. Akbar Khan. "A Note on the Expression *solum . . . nosse* in Catullus." *Classical Philology* 62 (1967) 34–36.
    Catullus by these artistic touches attributed to the sparrow the same devotion which he felt for Lesbia. . . . (36)

CATULLUS 4

1   That **phasēlus**, which/whom you see, my friends,
2   says that it/he was the swiftest of ships,
3   and that it/he was not unable to surpass
4   the speed of any other floating timber, whether there
5   was need to fly by oars or by linen sail.
6   And it/he denies that the shore of the threatening
7   Adriatic denies this, or the Cyclades islands,
8   famous Rhodes and the choppy waters of
9   Thracian Propontis, or the savage Pontic sea,
10   where that **phasēlus** to be was formerly
11   a leafy forest; for on the Cytorian ridge it often
12   uttered a whistling sound through its speaking leaves.
13   Pontic Amastris and Mt. Cytorus bearing boxwood trees,
14   these matters have been and are fully known to you
15   says the **phasēlus**: and it says that from its
16   earliest days it stood on your summit,

17   it dipped its oars into your waters,
18   and beginning from there it carried its master
19   across so many raging seas, whether a breeze
20   summoned on the left or the right, or whether
21   Jupiter had struck each sheet at the same time
22   with a favorable wind; nor had any vows
23   to gods of the shore been made by it when it was coming
24   from the last sea all the way to this limpid lake.

or   (reading **novissimē** instead of **novissimō** in line 24)
23   to the gods of the shore been made by it when from the sea (i.e., the Black Sea) it was coming
24   after all else all the way to this limpid lake.

25   But all this was before: now it spends old age
26   in secluded rest and dedicates itself to you,
27   twin Castor and Castor's twin.

Most scholars have thought that the **phasēlus** of poem 4 was the ship on which Catullus returned in the spring of 56 B.C. (see poem 46) from his service on the governor's staff in Bithynia to his family home at Sirmio on Lake Benacus, the modern Lago di Garda or Lake Garda (see, in particular, Putnam; Select Bibliography); the map in the student's book allows the reader to trace the voyage of the **phasēlus** from Amastris to the Adriatic and then up the Po and the Mincio to Sirmio.

Some scholars regard the ship that is being addressed as a model, arguing that a real ship could not have sailed up the Po and the Mincio to Lake Garda and pointing out that sea-faring ships were not made of boxwood (taking **buxifer**, 13, as a reference to the material the ship was made of) but that model ships might be.

Thomson and Peter Glasgow (see Thomson, 213–14) hypothesize that the poem is a translation of a lost poem by Callimachus (compare Catullus' translation of Callimachus in poem 66) and that the voyage ended not at Sirmio but at Lake Mareotis in Egypt. This interpretation detaches the poem completely from Catullus' return from Bithynia and is highly speculative.

Courtney (see Select Bibliography) calls attention to an epigram of Cinna (fragment 11) in which he speaks of bringing back a copy of the Greek didactic poet Aratus as a gift for the person to whom the epigram is addressed and of bringing it back on a **Prūsiaca nāvicula**, that is, on a Bithynian ship. Cinna, as Courtney notes, "apparently came from Brescia, which is about the same distance from Lake Garda as Verona is." Courtney continues:

Cinna seems to have been in Asia Minor not just when Catullus went there as a member of the cohors of Memmius in 57–56 B.C., but also ten years or more earlier, when he brought home Parthenius. . . . Cinna himself and Catullus could be referring to the boat on which he [i.e., Cinna] returned on that earlier occasion; the poem then would have no reference whatsoever to Catullus himself. This would have one advantage. One problem has been the oddity of going to the trouble and expense of bringing the boat from the sea to Lake Garda in 56 B.C. and then virtually at once (if we may rely on the argument from silence that there is no datable reference in Catullus to anything later than 55 or 54 B.C., and infer his death soon after then) retiring it. If we put its arrival in 66 B.C. or earlier, *haec prius fuere* (25) can cover an interval of ten years or more, and we can understand that it is time for the boat to be retired. (121–22).

If the ship is that on which Cinna returned from Bithynia in 66 B.C., bringing the Greek poet and teacher Parthenius of Nicaea with him, Catullus may have had a special fondness for it. Parthenius became "the prophet of the Callimachean school" in Rome (*Oxford Classical Dictionary*, "Parthenius"). Thomson traces the influence as follows:

What Parthenius had to offer this generation of Roman youth no longer consisted in the effusions of Callimachus' followers at one or two removes, but in the works of Callimachus himself, together with those of his predecessor Philetas, and (a less worthy model for imitation, it must be admitted) of his pupil Euphorion. It was, apparently, Parthenius' influence on Catullus' friend Cinna that was decisive . . . ; and Cinna, in due course, emerged clearly as the leader of the 'neoteric,' or modern, movement in Rome. (14–15)

Regarding the **phasēlus**, then, as the ship on which Cinna returned from Bithynia in 66 B.C., bringing Parthenius and the copy of Aratus to which he refers in his epigram with him, is one more hypothesis to add to the long list of hypotheses that have been generated to explain poem 4.

Since there is no equivalent English word for the kind of ship that is being referred to with the term **phasēlus**, we have chosen to retain that term instead of giving an English equivalent such as *yacht*, that might be quite misleading. Thomson (212–13) gives the following description:

> The *phaselus* was a handy vessel, of varying size, used to convey goods, or passengers, or both, in the Mediterranean sea and on the Nile. At sea, for example, it could serve as a tender to ships which by reason of their deep draught had to stand off the shore; sometimes it was towed astern by larger ships in order to do the inshore ferrying upon arrival in port, and thus could be said to make long voyages *in statu pupillari*, as it were.

Initial Explorations

1. Who is the speaker? Whom does the speaker address? What is the speaker doing? (1)
   Nothing is said about the identity of the speaker, who is therefore presumed to be Catullus. The speaker addresses **hospitēs**, who could be *guests, visitors,* or *strangers,* and he does so as a sort of tour guide, pointing out a **phasēlus**, which they can see.

2. What claim does the speaker report that the **phasēlus** makes for itself? (2)
   The **phasēlus** is reported to claim *that it/he was the swiftest of ships.*

3. What denial does the speaker report that the **phasēlus** makes in lines 3–5? What is the tone of the denial? What is the flavor of the words attributed to the **phasēlus** here?
   The **phasēlus** denies that it/he was unable to sail faster than any other ship. The tone of the words attributed to the **phasēlus** is confident and proud and could even be called boastful. The **phasēlus** couches its/his denial in high-sounding, grandiose metaphors and diction drawn from the tradition of Latin epic poetry (e.g., **natantis, impetum, trabis,** 3, and **volāre,** 5), but it also makes metaphorical use of an endearing diminutive, **palmulīs,** *dear little palms* = oars (4; note that in poem 64, Catullus' miniature epic, he uses **palmīs,** line 7, of the oars of the Argo, but he does not use the diminutive form of the word in that epic-style poem; the **phasēlus** in poem 4 mixes high-sounding epic diction with a humble, personalized diminutive).

4. In continuing to insist on its swiftness, what tone does the **phasēlus** use in lines 6–9?
   The tone becomes one of genuine braggadocio, as the **phasēlus** lists no fewer than five places, three of them dangerous and threatening seas, that it/he claims are unable to deny its/his boast of having been the swiftest of ships, however much they might try to deny it. The heavy clash of palatals and dentals in line 6 gives that line a forceful, threatening tone. Also the heavy alliteration of *rs, ps, ts,* and final *ms* in lines 8–9 emphasizes the bombastic braggadocio of the **phasēlus**.

5. What words describe the dangers of the waters through which the **phasēlus** claims to have sailed so swiftly? (6-9)
   The words **minacis, horridam,** and **trucem**.

6. Find three words that suggest that the **phasēlus** is being personified. Find one word that suggests it is like a bird. What words suggest the personification of nature? (2–9)
   Personification of the **phasēlus**: **ait** (2), **palmulīs** (4), and **negat** (6). Like a bird: **volāre** (5). Personification of nature: **minācis Hadriāticī** (6), **horridam . . . Thrāciam / Propontida** (8–9), and **trucem . . . Ponticum sinum** (9).
   The adjectives **minācis, horridam,** and **trucem** suggest personification of these three seas, and it is essential that they as well as the **phasēlus** be personified, since what the **phasēlus** is reported to be doing here is to deny that these threatening seas and the islands mentioned in lines 7 and 8 deny that the **phasēlus** was the swiftest of ships. We hear the conflicting assertions or claims of the personified ship and the personified natural elements.
   Since the **phasēlus** is so thoroughly personified, we use both impersonal and per-

sonal pronouns in our translation and discussion.

7.   Describe a chiastic arrangement of words in lines 8–9.

Rhodum A, **nōbilem** B, **horridamque Thraciam** B, **Propontida** A. Or: **Rhodum** A, **nōbilem** B, **horridamque Thraciā** B, **Propontida** A.

8.   The speaker, quoting the denials of the **phasēlus**, leads us back to its place of origin in lines 6–9. With what words does the poet endow the **phasēlus** with human attributes and abilities when it stood as a forest on Mt. Cytorus? (10–12)

The words **comāta** (11) and **comā** (12) refer to human hair as well as to leaves on trees. The words **loquente . . . sībilum ēdidit comā** metaphorically endow the **phasēlus** in its previous form as trees on the ridge of Mt. Cytorus with the ability to speak and whistle.

Note that while in lines 2–9 the speaker is reporting the claim and the denials of the **phasēlus**, in lines 10–12 the speaker is telling the story without putting words into the mouth of the **phasēlus**.

Also note here how the *ss* in the phrase **loquente saepe sībilum ēdidit comā** suggest a fondness for sibilants even in the previous incarnation of the **phasēlus** as a shaggy forest; the letter *s* is prominent throughout this poem, particularly in its doubled form, as in the following words: **fuisse** (2) **nequīsse** (4), **fuisse** (14), **esse** (14), **cognitissima** (14), **stetisse** (16), **imbuisse** (17), **tulisse** (19), **incidisset** (21), **esse** (23), and **novissimō** (24). These words all occur in the speaker's reporting of the statements made by the **phasēlus**. The sibilant speech of the shaggy forest remains in the speech of the **phasēlus**.

9.   Whom did the speaker address in line 1? What does the speaker now address in line 13? What is the technical term for the rhetorical figure involved here?

In line 1, the **hospitēs**; in line 13, Pontic Amastris and Mt. Cytorus. The rhetorical figure is apostrophe.

10.   Once more the **phasēlus** is said to refer to an authority for its veracity. (13–15) To what does it refer now and to what did it refer for its veracity before?

To the city Amastris on the Black Sea and to Mt. Cytorus behind it. Previously it referred to the shore of the Adriatic, the Cyclades, Rhodes, the Propontis, and the Pontic (Black) Sea.

In discussing line 13 it may be mentioned that scholars have long debated the relevance of the epithet **buxifer**. Some maintain that by using this adjective Catullus is indicating that the **phasēlus** was made of box wood. This has caused problems of interpretation, since box wood, hard, close grained, and inflexible, was not used for ship building but rather for small objects such as spinning-tops, flutes, writing tablets, and combs (Griffith, see Select Bibliography, 125). Some scholars have therefore thought that it is a model boat that is being referred to in this poem. Courtney (see Select Bibliography, 119), on the other hand, has argued that Catullus' phrase **Cytōre buxifer** is simply a learned "rendition" of a phrase that Catullus read in Apollonius of Rhodes, *Argonautica* 2.942, "woodsy Cytorus"; Courtney asserts, "The idea never entered [Catullus'] head that his readers would make the mistake of inferring that the wood proverbially associated with Cytorus . . . was that used for the boat."

11.   The word **haec** (14) could refer to what comes before it or to what comes after it. Do you think it refers backward or forward? Present reasons for your answer.

Opinions will differ, but the word probably refers to the information conveyed previously in lines 10–12. The neuter plural of the pronoun is used for this kind of summarizing reference. While the pronoun may also look to what immediately follows, this way of understanding it makes less sense here, because much of the following information could not have been known to Amastris and Mt. Cytorus.

12.   What rhetorical figure is involved in the repetition of **tuō** (16, 17)?
Anaphora.

13.   Find words that continue the personification of the **phasēlus** and of nature. (14–24)

Personification is continued with the following words: **tibi . . . cognitissima** (14; as if cities and mountains "knew" things), **ait** (15), **stetisse** (16), **dīcit** (16), **palmulās** (17), perhaps **impotentia** (18; in the sense of *lacking self-control*), **vocāret aura** (20), **in pedem** (21), vōta . . . / sibi esse facta (22–23).

14. What word again calls attention to the dangers of the waters through which the **phasēlus** sailed?

> **impotentia** (18)

15. How had the **phasēlus** emphasized its versatility before? How does it do it now?

> In lines 4 and 5, the **phasēlus** claimed to have been the swiftest of ships whether propelled by oars or sail, but now (19–21) it refers to its versatility in handling the winds, whether a breeze from the left or right or a full-bodied wind from behind.

16. What is the final boast of the **phasēlus**? (22–24)

> That it never made any prayers or vows to gods of the shore when it was coming from the last sea to be reached (i.e., the Adriatic) [or *after all else*] all the way up to the clear lake. "It has not been reduced to the extremity of needing to pray for rescue to the gods with temples on the shores of the stormy Adriatic" (Courtney, see Select Bibliography, 116).

17. At what point does the speaker again stop letting the **phasēlus** speak for itself?

> At the end of line 24 the speaker again breaks off his report of the words of the **phasēlus**. He had done this before at the end of line 9, and he had then resumed reporting the speech of the **phasēlus** in line 14.

18. The words **prius** and **nunc** in line 25 complete the temporal circle of the poem, from the present (**quem vidētis**, 1) to the past (**ait fuisse**, 2) to the present (**nunc . . . senet**, 25–26). What picture does the speaker present of the **phasēlus** in its retirement?

> The **phasēlus** has passed its prime and entered into a secluded retirement in old age. Note the transferred epithet **reconditā**.

19. To whom does the **phasēlus** dedicate itself and why?

> The **phasēlus** dedicates itself/himself to Castor and Pollux, who were traditionally considered protectors of sailors and ships, thus indicating its lingering attachment to the memories of its long voyage at sea.

20. What rhetorical device used earlier in the poem is used again in the last line?

> Anaphora: **gemelle . . . gemelle**.

21. What is the effect of the meter used in this poem?

> It seems to have been chosen to imitate the rocking motion of a ship at sea and the speed of this **phasēlus**. As Courtney (see Select Bibliography) remarks, the poem is written "in pure iambics in order to match the speed of the boat" (120).

Discussion

1. Examine the structure of the poem as a whole. Define an "introduction," a "conclusion," and a "center." Then locate lines that move toward the center and lines that move away from the center.

> Introduction: line 1. Conclusion: lines 25–27. Center: lines 10–middle of 15. Movement toward the center: lines 2–9, tracing the voyage backward from its destination (the location where the speaker is pointing out the **phasēlus** to the **hospitēs**) to Amastris and Mt. Cytorus where the **phasēlus** was built and where its voyage began. Movement away from the center: second half of line 15–24, tracing the voyage forward from the launching of the **phasēlus** to its arrival at the **limpidus lacus**. The sections tracing the voyage from its destination back to its place of origin (2–9) and vice versa (second half of 15–24) consist completely of indirect statement reporting the words of the **phasēlus**.
>
> The speaker thus introduces the poem as a whole in line 1 and concludes it by describing how the **phasēlus** is old and dedicates itself to Castor and Pollux (25–27). The speaker also describes the **phasēlus** in its previous state as a leafy and garrulous forest on Mt. Cytorus (10–12). The speaker is thus knowledgeable about the present state of the **phasēlus** and about its origin. For the rest, the speaker does not tell the story of the **phasēlus** in his own words, but he lets the ship tell its own story.

2.   In what ways does the **phasēlus** betray its origin as a Greek ship?

It betrays its origin as a Greek ship by its use of Greek syntax for indirect statement in lines 2–5 and 15–21. It is not surprising that the ship, built in the Greek world, should reveal some distinctive features of the Greek language if it is going to speak or going to be reported as speaking.

3.   In what ways is the **phasēlus** similar to the legendary Argo?

Most importantly, it speaks. The Argo is the only other speaking ship from the ancient world. The name Argo means "Swift," and the **phasēlus** claims to have been the swiftest of all ships. The verb for *to swim* is used by Catullus of both the **phasēlus** (4.3) and the Argo (64.1–2: **pīnūs / dīcuntur liquidās Neptūnī nāsse per undās**). The origin of the **phasēlus** as a shaggy woods on Mt. Cytorus may allude (but see the answer to Initial Exploration question 10 above) to the origin of the Argo as pine trees on Mt. Pelion (Euripides, *Medea* 3–4, Ennius' *Medea exul*, 208–216, and Catullus 64.1: **Pēliacō quondam prōgnātae vertice pīnūs**). The Argo passed Mt Cytorus on its outward voyage (Apollonius, *Argonautica* 2.942). The Black Sea (**trucem . . . Ponticum sinum**, 9), through which the **phasēlus** sailed, was the site of the major adventures of the Argonauts on their outward voyage. Just as the **phasēlus** dedicates itself to Castor and Pollux, so the Argo at the end of its career was dedicated to Poseidon by Jason at the Isthmus of Corinth (Diodorus 4.53.2 and Apollodorus 1.9.27). Castor and Pollux were themselves participants in the voyage of the Argo. See Coleman (see Select Bibliography, 69–70) for these parallels between the **phasēlus** and the Argo. Hornsby (see Select Bibliography) comments: "That the image of the Argo, whose very name means 'swift,' lies behind the *phaselus* seems justified by the insistence Catullus makes on the ship's speed, by its ability to speak, by its carrying its master with intelligence over the *impotentia freta*, and by the fact that the ship never needed to call on the *litoralibus deis*. Furthermore, the voyage described in 6–9 is more than a little reminiscent of the famous voyage of the Argonauts" (263).

4.   The **phasēlus** is personified. What personality or traits of character does it project as the speaker reports its words?

Students should be asked to write their own character sketches of the **phasēlus** as a living person. Prominent in their sketches would be the ship's seemingly boundless energy expressed in the swiftly moving, rocking iambic meter, the ship's self-confidence, its boastfulness, its pride in having passed through such dangerous waters unscathed and without ever having to call upon the gods for help, its pride in its origins, its pride in its service to its owner, its versatility (being able to sail equally fast by oars or sail), its adaptability to the winds, its fancying itself as a modern-day Argo, its perhaps pretentious use of epic language to describe itself, and the contentment with which it dedicates itself to the gods in its quiet retirement in its old age.

5.   How do you think the speaker feels about the **phasēlus**? How do you feel about it?

The speaker of the poem for the most part simply reports the words of the **phasēlus** without any hint of his feelings toward it and apparently without twisting, distorting, or coloring the words of the **phasēlus** in any way. The speaker simply lets the **phasēlus** speak for itself, albeit indirectly. However, readers will probably feel that the speaker seems to be proud of the **phasēlus**, perhaps slightly amused at its boastfulness, its own feelings of pride, and its epic language, but basically sympathetic to it and even fond of it. Students' opinions will vary but will mostly coincide with the apparent feelings of the speaker. Students find this poem more difficult to become involved with than most other poems of Catullus.

Postscript

The following words and phrases have been identified as archaic, pre-classical, or reminiscent of the vocabulary of early Latin epic poetry: **neque . . . / nequīsse** (3–4), **impetum** (3), **trabis** (3), **volāre** (5), **negat . . . / negāre** (6–7), **horridam** (8), **buxifer** (13), and **senet** (26). More specifically, Catullus' words **natantis impetum trabis** (3) and **volāre** (5) recall a phrase in the early Roman epic poet Ennius: **lābitur ūncta carīna, <u>volat</u> super <u>impetus</u> undās**, *the ship caulked with pitch glides along, its charging force flies over the waves* (*Annals* 376). And, Catullus' words **nunc recondita / senet quiēte** (25–26) recall Ennius' description of an old, prize-winning racehorse retired to a dignified rest in its declining years: **sīcut fortis equus, spatiō quī saepe suprēmō / vīcit Olympia, <u>nunc</u> <u>seniō</u> cōnfectus <u>quiēscit</u>**, *just as the strong horse that was often victorious in the greatest racecourse at Olympia now rests worn out with old age* (*Annals* 374–75). The teacher may want to explore with students what this archaic vocabulary and these reminiscences of Ennius' epic poetry contribute to the portrayal of the **phasēlus** in Catullus 4 and its tone of voice. Taken all together, the archaic vocabulary (see Hornsby, 261; Select Bibliography) and the reminiscences of Ennius' epic poetry would give an old-fashioned flavor to the characterization and voice of the **phasēlus**. This old-fashioned epic language and the Greek flavor of the grammar of the **phasēlus** enhance its similarity to the legendary Argo.

Comparison

The following is the Latin text and an English translation of Vergil's *Catalepton* 10, a parody of Catullus 4, with which it should be compared.

1   Sabīnus ille, quem vidētis, hospitēs,
2   ait fuisse mūliō celerrimus
3   neque ūllius volantis impetum cisī
4   nequīsse praeterīre, sīve Mantuam
5   opus foret volāre sīve Brixiam.
6   Et hoc negat Tryphōnis aemulī domum
7   negāre nōbilem īnsulamve Caerulī,
8   ubi iste post Sabīnus ante Quīnctiō
9   bidente dīcit attodisse forfice
10   comāta colla, nē Cytōriō iugō
11   premente dūra volnus ēderet iuba.
12   Cremōna frīgida et lutōsa Gallia,
13   tibi haec fuisse et esse cognitissima
14   ait Sabīnus: ultimā ex orīgine
15   tuā stetisse dīcit in vorāgine,
16   tuā in palūde dēposisse sarcinās,
17   et inde tot per orbitōsa mīlia
18   iugum tulisse, laeva sive dextera
19   strigāre mūla sīve utrumque coeperat
20   <   .   .   .   .   >
21   neque ūlla vōta sēmitālibus deīs
22   sibi esse facta, praeter hoc novissimum,
23   paterna lōra proximumque pectinem.
24   Sed haec prius fuēre: nunc eburneā
25   sedetque sēde sēque dēdicat tibi,
26   gemelle Castor et gemelle Castoris.

1   Sabinus yonder, whom you see, my friends,
2   says he was once the fastest of muleteers,
3   and never was there any gig that raced along
4   whose speed he was unable to pass,
5   whether he had to race to Mantua or to Brixia.
6   And this, says he, the noble house of his rival, Trypho,
7   does not deny; nor the lodging-rooms of Caerulus,
8   where he who afterwards was Sabinus, but ere that Quinctio,
9   tells that with two-bladed shears he once clipped
10   the hairy necks, lest, under the pressure of Cytorian yoke,
11   the harsh mane might cause some soreness.
12   O cold Cremona and muddy Gaul,
13   Sabinus says that this was and is well-known to you:
14   he claims that from his earliest birthtime
15   he stood in your mire,
16   in your marsh laid by his packs,
17   and thence over so many miles of rutty roads
18   bore the yoke, whether the mule on left or on right
19   or on both sides began to flag
20   <   .   .   .   >
21   and that no vows to the gods of the by-ways
22   were made by him save this at the last—
23   his father's reins and the currycomb close by.
24   But these things are past and gone; now he sits in his ivory
25   chair and dedicates himself to you,
26   twin Castor, and to you, Castor's twin-brother.

—Translation adapted from that of H. Rushton Fairclough

Select Bibliography

Frank O. Copley. "Catullus c. 4: The World of the Poem." *Transactions of the American Philological Association* 89 (1958) 9–13. Catullus "builds his poem" on "the paradox . . . of the inanimate fabric that had life and personality" (12).

Michael C. J. Putnam. "Catullus' Journey (*Carm.* 4)." *Classical Philology* 57 (1962) 10–19.
   The boat does more than merely carry its master . . . home, it is his emotion. . . . the boat is the personification of desire. . . . the boat is . . . a reflection of the poet and his yearning for home. (14–16).

Roger Hornsby. "The Craft of Catullus (*Carm.* 4)." *American Journal of Philology* 84 (1963) 256-265.
   Develops the implicit comparison with the Argo.

H. Akbar Khan. "The Humor of Catullus, *Carm.* 4, and the Theme of Virgil, *Catalepton* 10." *American Journal of Philology* 88 (1967) 163–72.
   The humor of the poem, its chief quality, resides in the contrast between the craft's heroic and fanciful claims and the manner in which it is presented to us, as in fact of unglamorous and un-epic proportions. (172).

L. Richardson, Jr. "Catullus 4 and Catalepton 10 Again." *American Journal of Philology* 93 (1972) 215–22.
   [Catullus] describes the sound of the ship's voice. When it was still part of the forest growing on the heights of Cytorus it often gave out a whispering from its articulate foliage (11–12). . . . That this voice is the same as its present voice is conveyed by the striking emphasis on the letter *s* throughout the poem, and especially by the frequency of doubled *s* and final *-is*. (218).

K. M. Coleman. "The Persona of Catullus' Phaselus." *Greece & Rome* 28 (1981) 68–72.
   The autobiography of the personified yacht . . . yields not only a curriculum vitae but also a

vivid impression of personality. Catullus' phaselus sounds very human. (68)

John G. Griffith. "Catullus, Poem 4: A Neglected Interpretation Revived." *Phoenix* 37 (1983) 123–28.
   Revives the idea that "the *phaselus* was a model yacht, . . . a souvenir acquired in Asia and brought back by him [Catullus] to an Italian lake. . . ." (124).

E. Courtney. "Catullus' Yacht (or Was It?)." *Classical Journal* 92 (1997) 113–22. See above. Highly recommended.

CATULLUS 5

1   Let us live, my Lesbia, and let us love,
2   and let us value all the gossip of those
3   rather stern old men as worth just one cent.
4   Suns can set and rise again;
5   whenever [our] brief light has once set/once sets for us,
6   one uninterrupted night must be slept by us.
7   Give me a thousand kisses, then a hundred,
8   then a second thousand, then a second hundred,
9   then yet another thousand, then a hundred.
10 Then, when we will have reached many thousands,
11 we will confound them, so that we may not know [how many they are],

or   (with the comma after **conturbābimus** in line 11)
11   we will throw our accounts into confusion [i.e., fraudulently go bankrupt], so that we may not know them [i.e., the kisses, how many they are]

12   or some evil person may not be able to cast a spell on us,
13   once he knows there to be so great a number of kisses.

Most of the Initial Exploration and Discussion questions are based on E. A. Fredricksmeyer, "Observations on Catullus 5," *American Journal of Philology* 91 (1970) 431–45. The paragraph that follows this one and most of the answers to the questions are given in the form of quotations from Fredricksmeyer's article (these block quotations are not enclosed in quotation marks, but the source of each is acknowledged after each paragraph). One striking rhetorical feature not covered in this material is the chiasmus in lines 5–6: **brevis lūx / nox . . . perpetua**, adjective A, noun B, noun B, adjective A, with the two monosyllabic nouns in antithesis at line end and line beginning.

The poem is Catullus' exhortation and invitation to Lesbia to love as the best life. It progresses from the statement of the theme, the call to love, to two appeals designed to remove Lesbia's most likely objections and render her receptive to his quest. Then ensues the direct, passionate demand for love, and a provision to protect this love. The poem is framed thematically by *vivamus, amemus,* and *basiorum,* and by the suggestion of a threat to love and the poet's design to make it secure. This evokes the impression of a protective fence laid around the poem, the world of love, and into this world the poet calls upon Lesbia to enter, while there is time. . . . On closer examination the exhortation to love and passion can be seen to rest on rational principle, that is, to be justified both morally and intellectually, by the evaluation of love's enemies as *mali,* the *carpe diem* appeal, and the very rationality and discipline of the poem's art. By thus providing his exhortation to love with a higher rationale the poet gives it additional force and appeal. (Fredricksmeyer, 445)

Initial Explorations

1.   To whom is this poem addressed? Who is Lesbia? What does the name signify? Of what sig-

nificance is its position in the line here?

> The name "Lesbia" suggests that, whatever the woman's real identity, she inspires Catullus' poetry as well as his love, that for him she evokes and embodies the glamor and fascination of Lesbos, the traditions of poetry and love, and in particular the quality of Sappho "the Tenth of the Muses," of beauty, passion, and intelligence. The associations of the name are illustrious and imposing, of ancient date and wide-spread fame. By saying *"mea Lesbia"* the poet attracts these associations to his private sphere and introduces an atmosphere of personal intimacy and affection. The thematic hortatory words *vivamus* and *amemus* enclose "Lesbia" and thus point to her as the center of the poet's life and love. (Fredricksmeyer, 436)

2. With what two exhortations does the poet frame the first line? How does the second exhortation explain the first? How do these exhortations jar with traditional Roman values?

> The verbs mean not so much "Let us live life fully and let us love" as "Let us live in the fullest and most meaningful sense of that word, that is, let us love." Within its Roman context this appeal was no tired literary cliché. In its pungent brevity, and in the light especially of the following two lines, it shows a definite flair, a splendid audacity, for the proposition that really to live means to love, the advocacy in effect of love as a way of life, and this in express defiance of all criticism, meant to fly in the face of convention, to challenge the Roman canons of morality and rationality. The *mores et virtutes maiorum* prescribed that love for a woman as a primary concern was unworthy of a good man, to be tolerated at most as a temporary aberration of youth. The respectable life was the *vita activa* in the service of the state, or at least in the public sphere, as orator, administrator, soldier, farmer, or (big) businessman, and even one's *otium* was expected to be dignified, devoted preferably to the pursuit of moral and political philosophy. (Fredricksmeyer, 436–37)

3. How would a well-brought-up young Roman woman react to Catullus' exhortations in line 1?

> . . . the exhortation of the first verse engages the attention of the reader and was sure to evoke in Lesbia a response, a typically Roman concern for name and reputation . . . , something like "But what would people say?" (Fredricksmeyer, 437)

4. How does Catullus in lines 2–3 anticipate reservations that Lesbia might have?

> The poet anticipates Lesbia's reservations with the words:
>
> > Rumoresque senum severiorum
> > Omnes unius aestimemus assis.
>
> The *rumores* would be malicious gossip and criticism, such as *nequitia, desidia, culpa, inopia, stulti mores, insania, furor, turbo mentis, amentia, vita iners,* and perhaps worse. The poet says *senum severiorum* not merely because the expression is more vivid and personal than would be such abstracts as "society" or "people," but also because it was proverbially the *senes*, especially in patriarchal, tradition-bound Rome, who were the most censorious moralizers, intolerant of love and pleasure, inimical to all that was different and new. (Fredricksmeyer, 437–38)

5. How does Catullus encourage Lesbia to evaluate the **rūmōrēs** of the stern old men? (2–3)

> In the first line of the couplet the poet focuses on the *rumores* as such of the stern old men, and then in the second line, after a momentary pause, he takes them all up and qualifies them, *omnes*, "the whole lot of them, let us consider worth just one penny." The collocation of *omnes* and *unius* pinpoints the poet's evaluation. The hissing sibilants of the former line echo the hissing, snarling sounds of the *rumores senum severiorum*; the sibilants of the second line, in which the poet evaluates the *rumores*, emphasize his own disdain for them. He anticipates the hostility of his enemies and returns it with gusto. (Fredricksmeyer, 438)
>
> It should also be noted that **omnēs ūnius** is an oxymoron emphasizing the insignificance of the whole lot of the **rūmōrēs**.

6. What do assonance, alliteration, and word placement contribute to the effect of line 3?

> Sounds unify and consolidate the line. Note that each word ends with the letter *s*. Note the repetition of *ms* and *ēs* and the sounds of **aes-** and **ass-**. The words **omnēs** and **ūnius**

are effectively juxtaposed in opposition to one another.

7.   What is meant by the phrase **carpe diem**? How do lines 4–6 introduce this theme?

The phrase means "seize the day" and means that one should enjoy each day of one's life while one can, being fully aware of how brief life is and how swiftly time passes. Lines 4–6 introduce this theme by reminding Lesbia of how brief life is (**brevis lūx**, 5) and that death is eternal (6).

Fredricksmeyer (438) remarks, "The poet . . . anticipates a second reservation or objection from Lesbia, something like 'Not now, perhaps some other day,' and impresses upon her that there is no time to waste."

8.   Identify, analyze, and comment on the meaning of the imagery and the antitheses in lines 4–6.

The admonition is emphasized by imagery and antithesis, the great fiery orbs in the sky, the puny light of our life on earth, the black night of death underground. The image of the "suns" (nature) here connotes eternity, magnitude, power, splendor, plurality, while in contrast "the brief light" (our life) connotes ephemeralness, smallness, feebleness, and finality. The repetition of the verb *occidere* is subtly ironic and reinforces the contrast. With *soles* it is in the infinitive, without limitation by person, number, or modus, and means "to set," but applied to us it is in the finite form and means "to die." The limitlessness, expansiveness, and eternal recurrence of nature (the suns can and therefore do set and return) contrast with the limitedness, the constrictedness, and the singularity (*semel*) of our life. There is then no analogy but only a radical contrast between our life and that of nature, and the words *soles* and *lux* stand in pointedly antithetical positions. But *nox*, replacing *lux*, is placed parallel to *soles*. The images contrast the black night of death underground with the brightness and warmth of the upper world, but in their permanence death and nature are alike (and hence parallel), in contrast to our life. The brevity of life is conveyed even syntactically. "Nature" and "death" each find expression in an independent main clause, but "our life" is given in a shortened (note the post-position of *cum*) dependent clause, dependent on and anticipating its main clause, the statement of "death." Our life, as it were, is a mere brief prelude to death. The same impression is conveyed by the progressive shortening of *occidit brevis lux*, three syllables, two syllables, one syllable, the end of the line, the extinction of life. Immediately then sets in death (*nox*), and a sense of its awesome, unchanging permanence is conveyed by the heavy, melancholy rhythm of the line and its long drawn-out polysyllables *perpetuuna dormienda*. In the face of the splendorous suns who can and do set and return, our life is like a flickering, feeble light that, once extinguished, is followed by the one night of death which must be slept forever (note the contrast in *possunt* and *dormienda*, freedom and necessity). Surely, then, before this happens, and it will happen soon, *carpe diem: vivamus atque amemus.* (Fredricksmeyer, 438–39)

If one reads Catullus' poems in their numerical sequence, the death of the sparrow and the description of Orcus' actions in poem 3 may be felt to foreshadow the more ominous theme of death and the *carpe diem* message in poem 5.

9.   How does the demand for kisses (7–9) result logically from what the poet has said so far in the poem?

. . . since the poet has anticipated her [Lesbia's] most likely objections and thus rendered her receptive to his quest, there now ensues his direct, intense, and passionate demand for love. (Fredricksmeyer, 439)

10. How would you characterize Catullus' demand for kisses, and what would the stern old men think of it?

The poet demands many thousands of kisses in succession and well-nigh without a pause (*usque* and the double elision *deindusqualtera*), an impossible feat for even the most robust and ardent of lovers, a fantastic hyperbole. To the critical and unsympathetic observer, like the *senes*, this outpour would seem silly, indecorous to the point of offensiveness, and certainly completely irrational. But this is just the point. What the poet expresses is not decorum and rationality but passion, and every detail is designed to bring out this effect.

The antithesis of love and the orthodox virtues is thematic in the whole poem. First life is in effect identified with love, love then is polemically asserted against the guardians of the traditional virtues, then love is given an immediate urgency by the *carpe diem* appeal, and now love is specified as passion, unrestrained, limitless, insatiate, the radical opposite of the traditional virtues of discipline, restraint, and rationality. (Fredricksmeyer, 440)

11.   Analyze the rhetorical effects produced by sound, rhythm, and movement in lines 7–11.

To appreciate these lines fully, we must be attuned to their rhetorical effect, of sound, rhythm, and movement. After the slow and solemn cadence of line six the *basia* lines, impelled by the monosyllabic accented imperative *da*, push forward in short, staccato thrusts. These "thrusts" are produced by the alliterative anaphoras (*da*), *deinde, dein, dein, deinde, deinde, dein*. Each anaphora is given force by an ictus, asserts and reasserts itself after each short breather within and at the ends of lines seven to nine, and launches the next short unit of words. The effect is a series of forward thrusting moves which propel the numbers of kisses, love's passion, toward more and more dizzying heights in a rhythm which correspondingly increases in speed and momentum. Thus the impetus of the movement carries beyond line nine and, after being slightly inhibited by the deliberative effect of the *cum*-clause in line ten, receives sonic reinforcement from the strongly accented assertive effect of *conturbabimus* in line eleven. (Fredricksmeyer, 440)

12.   How does line 11 set up a contrast between passion and rationality?

. . . line eleven can be considered the culmination of the passion motif begun in line seven, and the listener or reader, moved along by the impetus of the movement, may well see line eleven at first as pinpointing and polarizing the thematic contrast between passion and rationality, *conturbare* vs. *scire*: "We will throw them into confusion, so that we do not know," that is, we will assert the confusion, the irrationality of passion (*conturbabimus*) over against knowledge and control (*ne sciamus*). This initial impression is sustained by the more literal meaning of the line. The demand (*da*) for more and more kisses progresses to the assertion that "when we have completed many thousands, we will throw them into confusion," perhaps by adding a profusion of additional kisses, without count, in disordered multitude, "so that we do not know (the count)," for *pauca petit qui numerare potest* [Mart., VI, 34], that is, we will make sure to set no limit to our kisses, to the magnitude and exuberance of our passion. (Fredricksmeyer, 440–41)

13.   What two threats to the love between himself and Lesbia does Catullus want to protect against? (11–13)

More than this, line eleven has a pivotal function in the poem, for when apprehended in direct conjunction with the following, last two lines, it bears yet a further significance, as part of the topos of *invidia*: "We will throw them (the count of the kisses) into confusion, so that we (ourselves) do not know (the count)," for to do so might bring us harm, as by attracting nemesis, "or (*aut*) so that no evil man can look in on us (that is, can envy and put the evil eye on us), when he knows that there are (just) so many kisses." By the pivotal function of line eleven the poem moves easily and quickly from the apex of passion to a relatively calm and rational conclusion. This turn, or development, is entirely uncontrived and natural, since the motif of love's passion and bliss, expressed by the accumulation of multitudinous kisses, evoked almost automatically for ancient man the thought of the precariousness of such a love, and with it the need to protect it. Now, this precariousness is intimated also at the beginning of the poem, in the topoi of men's malice (2–3) and the brevity of life (4–6), and thereby the motif contributes to giving the poem a frame. Against the imminence of death the lovers are defenseless, but it lends to their love a poignant urgency. Against nemesis or some similar retribution the lovers can protect themselves by insuring their own ignorance of the count of their kisses, the precise measure of their bliss (11), and against the malice and envy of men (*senes severi, malus*) they can protect themselves by totally ignoring and disdaining them (2–3) and by preventing them from putting the evil eye on them (12–13). (Fredricksmeyer, 441–42)

Discussion

1. How would you divide the poem into sections?

    The following is Fredricksmeyer's answer to this question. Thomson suggests 1–6, 7–11, 12–13.
    The poem can be divided into three major parts. Line one states the theme, the invitation to love, lines two to six offer two appeals in support of the proposition, lines seven to thirteen present the direct request for love and a provision to protect it. (Fredricksmeyer, 436)
    The device of the frame has a significant function in the poem. The words *vivamus* and *amemus* enclose and focus attention on the recipient of the poem, *mea Lesbia* (1). *Vivamus* and *amemus* (1) and *basiorum* (13) frame the poem thematically as an exhortation to love and passion. The motif of a threat to this love points up its precariousness and hence its preciousness. Most important, by suggesting, at the same time, a defense against this threat the poet creates the impression of enclosing the poem, the private world of his and Lesbia's love, with a protective ring, as it were, to secure it against the malevolence and the envy of a hostile outside world. (Fredricksmeyer, 442)

2. The **malus**, *evil person*, of line 12 is usually thought to represent the stern old men of line 2. To what extent is the following conclusion justified: "The association, or identification, of the *malus* and his envy with the *senes severi* shows them up as hypocrites, and their moral censure stands discredited"? (Fredricksmeyer, 443)

    The guardians of the *mores et virtutes maiorum* will condemn this love. A close consideration of the poem suggests that the poet undercuts and neutralizes the censure of his critics by a subtle appeal to the same principles invoked by them, but applied in a different sense. The *senes severi* will object to the poet's and Lesbia's love on moral grounds. This being so, the use of the word *malus* in line twelve is significant, for it surely refers to the *senes severi*, the guardians of the moral code. It is true, of course, that *malus* is applied from the phrase *mala lingua*, and also that a man may call someone *malus* simply because he is an enemy, but the suggestion goes further. *Invidere* (12) means not only "to cast the evil eye" but also "to envy." Therefore, the association, or identification, of the *malus* and his envy with the *senes severi* shows them up as hypocrites, and their moral censure stands discredited. The irony is obvious. The *severi* are not the *viri boni* they doubtless claim to be, and the lovers, in the light of the suggested advocacy in line one of love as a total commitment, assume a moral position, even if it is condemned by traditional prejudice. (Fredricksmeyer, 442–43)

3. In opposition to the **senēs sevērī** and the **malus**, Catullus stakes out a moral defense of the life of love in this poem. How, in lines 4–6, has he also staked out a rational defense of the life of love?

    The *severi* will also criticize this love as being irrational and foolish. We have noted that the poet revels in his passion and asserts it, by implication, over against reason and restraint. This being so, the employment of the *carpe diem* motif is significant. This carefully designed appeal to the brevity of life and the imminence of death, when all consciousness is lost, the suggestion of the insignificance of man's life and the vanity of his ambitions, lends to the poet's call for love as the most meaningful life a rational validity of its own, even if it is not accepted by the traditional code.

4. Assume that the woman addressed as **mea Lesbia** in this poem is the same as the person referred to as **mea puella** in Catullus 2 and 3. To what extent is Catullus 5 an appropriate next step in Catullus' courtship of the **puella**?

It is an excellent next step. Poems 2 and 3 show that the poet has fallen in love with the **puella**, takes a great interest in her, and has observed her closely, but there is no hint in those poems that he has approached her directly, spoken any words to her, or sent her any poems. Poem 5 is the first poem of those we have met so far in the collection that is addressed to the **puella**/Lesbia. It is, as Fredricksmeyer demonstrates, a poem of courtship or seduction, inviting Lesbia to join in a life of love with the poet, reassuring her, persuading her, and showing her how their love affair could be protected from the hostility of the outside world.

Select Bibliography

H. L. Levy. "Catullus, 5, 7–11 and the Abacus." *American Journal of Philology* 62 (1941) 222–24.

> According to my interpretation, then, Catullus thinks of himself as keeping score of Lesbia's kisses on an abacus. First a pebble in the thousands column, then one in the hundreds, then another in the thousands, and another in the hundreds, then still another in the thousands, and one in the hundreds, and then, when the thrice-told tale is done, the lovers shake the board violently (*conturbabimus*), the pebbles fly in all directions, and the score is forever obliterated. (224)

J. H. Turner. "Roman Elementary Mathematics: The Operations." *Classical Journal* 47 (1951) 63–74 and 106–8.

> There should be no need of having to show in detail that Catullus is here setting imaginary counters on thousand and hundred columns of an imaginary abacus. (74)

Roger Pack. "Catullus, *Carmen* V: Abacus or Finger-Counting?" *American Journal of Philology* 77 (1956) 47–51. "The assumption of finger-reckoning is preferable to that of the abacus" (47). Also suggests finger gestures accompanying **ūnius . . . assis** (3) and **conturbābimus** (11) and an obscene finger gesture "to avert *invidia*" in line 12 (see page 51).

Norman Pratt. "The Numerical Catullus 5." *Classical Philology* 51 (1956) 99–100.

> It is essentially the movement of the arithmetical theme which makes this little piece notable for its simple variety, cohesion, and symmetry. (100)

R. E. Grimm. "Catullus 5 Again." *The Classical Journal* 59 (1963) 15–21. The unity of the poem "is reinforced by a leitmotiv . . . drawn from the business or mercantile world. . . . " (20).

Steele Commager. "The Structure of Catullus 5." *The Classical Journal* 59 (1964) 361–64.

> The poem is built on three antitheses, all couched in numerical terms: that of life and death; that of a profusion of kisses and the single number describing them; and that of the *rumores senum severiorum* and the value to be assigned them. . . . the association of death and singleness (cf. *cum semel occidit brevis lux*) is as central to the poem as that of life and profusion: *soles occidere et redire possunt*. . . . The unknowable number of their kisses stands, then, as a defense against their love's death, just as the incalculable number of the sun's appearances is, in a sense, proof against the world's end. . . . Just as the *malus* would kill his and Lesbia's love by setting a single sum to their kisses, so Catullus will kill, or at least negate, the *rumores senum severiorum* by assigning them a single known value: *unius aestimemus assis*. (362)

Charles Segal. "Catullus 5 and 7: A Study in Complementaries." *American Journal of Philology* 89 (1968) 284–301.

> Something too of the powerful effect of Five lies in a consistent progression and juxtaposition of the large, basic terms of our existence: life and love *versus* age and death; sun and light *versus* night and darkness; infinite multiplicity *versus* number and limit; the direct involvement of passion and action *versus* distanced observation and calculation. (292)

E. A. Fredricksmeyer. "Observations on Catullus 5." *American Journal of Philology* 91 (1970) 431–45. See above. Highly recommended.

CATULLUS 6

1   Flavius, you would wish to tell Catullus
2   and you would not be able to be silent about your darling,
3   unless she should be without charm and refinement.
4   But you are in love with some feverish
5   whore: to admit this makes you ashamed.
6   For your bed, smelling strongly of wreathes and
7   Syrian perfume, silent in vain shouts out that
8   you do not lie there nights without a woman,
9   and the pillow, both here and there, equally
10 crumpled, and the shaken creaking
11 and restless motion of the trembling bed.
12 For nothing is able to keep your debauchery secret, nothing.
13 Why? You wouldn't spread out a body so worn out
14 with sex, unless you were doing something foolish.
15 Wherefore, whatever good or bad thing you have,
16 tell us. I want to summon you and your loved one
17 to heaven by my charming verse.

Catullus 6 is not included on the Advanced Placement syllabus, but it is included in this book so that the pattern of poems 1–11 may be studied in full (see page 87 of the student's book).

The poem celebrates a friend, Flavius, and his beloved whore! This is not the kind of subject matter that would be considered by traditional Roman standards as appropriate for a dignified poem, and Catullus' desire to exalt Flavius and his love to the heavens is not premised on any claim to immortality brought forward in the body of the poem regarding Flavius and his whore. Sexual infatuation and physical activity are all that distinguish their relationship.

Flavius himself sensibly insists upon concealing his affair and the name of his beloved, just as Catullus in poems 5 and 7 wishes to protect his affair from the prying **malus** and the **cūriōsī** and hides the identity of his **puella** behind a pseudonym. Ironically, Catullus here plays the role of a prying **cūriōsus**.

Initial Explorations

1. Study the diction of lines 1–5. What important words recall words used in earlier poems? What words import a new tone? What is the effect of the combination of different kinds of diction?

    The word **dēliciās** (1) recalls the term for the beloved pet in Catullus 2 and 3. The word **illepidae** (2) recalls the crucial term, **lepidus** (1.1), *charming*, describing the style and subject matter of the papyrus roll that Catullus offers to Cornelius. But here the beloved is purported *not* to be *charming* or *refined*. The words **febrīculōsī / scortī** (4–5) import a new tone, since these are the first words in any of the poems with an embarrassing reference to a lower class person crassly described. The importation of a new level of diction should alert the reader to the fact that this poem will be very different from the previous ones and may contain adult language with explicit sexual references, but the combination with the "smart" language of the earlier poems should suggest that all will be handled with grace and charm.

2. What effect is achieved by the use of **Catullō** instead of **mihi** in line 1? Note the line framing. Flavius and Catullus frame the beloved between them. By naming himself, Catullus achieves a sense of comradeship and intimacy with Flavius, as if saying *to your buddy Catullus*, thus seeking to gain Flavius' confidence.

3. What does Catullus know about Flavius' activities? What does he not know? (1–5) The poet knows that his friend has been carrying on a relationship with a woman, but he

doesn't know anything specific about her, such as her status, name, looks, or personality, because his friend isn't talking about her.

4. Based on his friend's silence about the identity of the woman he is in love with, what does Catullus assume about her? (2–5)

> He assumes that she must be *without charm and refinement* (2) and that she is probably a **febrīculōsum scortum** (4–5), of such a cheap and vulgar sort that his friend is ashamed to reveal her identity.

5. What does Catullus suggest that Flavius is ashamed to admit? (4–5) What incongruity does the juxtaposition of **scortī** and **dīligis** suggest?

> Catullus suggests that Flavius is afraid to admit that his beloved is a common whore. The words **scortī** and **dīligis** are incongruously juxtaposed since the verb is usually used not of sexual love but of affection and esteem. It is thus with some sarcasm that Catullus would say **nescio quid febrīculōsī / scortī dīligis**.

6. How is the bed personified? (7)

> It shouts.

7. What does the bed shout? (6–7)

> It shouts, i.e., it reveals, that Flavius has not been sleeping on it alone.

8. Why is the bed described as **nēquīquam tacitum**? (7)

> It is silent *in vain* since presumably in being silent it would not reveal the truth, but this bed is silent *in vain* since in spite of its silence it does reveal the truth. Flavius, of course, would have thought that since beds cannot speak the secret of his affair would be kept. Catullus is playing on a traditional theme that even inanimate objects such as beds or walls of bedrooms witness acts of sexual impropriety and may ultimately reveal them. It is in vain that Flavius would have thought the bed would keep his secret.

9. How does the bed (7–11) reveal the truth of the statement made in line 6?

> The lovers' wreaths and perfume, the bed's appearance of being used by two people (the pillow is crumpled on both sides), and its shaking and creaking and virtual walking about reveal that Flavius is spending his nights with someone.

10. Comment on word placement and sound effects in the description of the bed? (7–11)

> The close coordination of **tacitum** and **clāmat** framing **cubīle** (7) points up the irony of the situation: the bed is silent but still manages to tell its story (note the alliteration of *c*s). Note also the way **Syriō** and **olīvō** frame **fragrāns** (8), with alliteration of *ss* in the line— **sertīs . . . Syriō fragrāns**. The crumpling of the pillow equally on both sides is given verbal expression by the clever counterpoint of sounds in **pulvīnusque peraequē et hīc et ille** (9). Then enjambment adds emphasis to **attrītus**, which echoes **pulvīnus** at the beginning of the line above. Finally, the very expressive words **argutātiō inambulātiōque**, which end the sentence by renewing the personification found in **clāmat**, elide to form one single utterance that takes up the whole line and by their weight and internal rhyme give musical expression to the voice of the bed.

11. How does Catullus refer to Flavius' activity in line 12?

> As **stupra**, *debauchery* or *disgraceful conduct*.

12. What imaginary objection from Flavius is the interrogative **Cūr?** (13) meant to address?

> Catullus is replying to an imagined objection of Flavius that in spite of all the evidence Catullus has assembled so far he has no reason to think that Flavius is involved in any **stupra**, *debauchery*. "Why do you draw that conclusion?" Flavius is imagined to say. Catullus picks up the *Why?* and then adds the final, damning piece of evidence.

13. How does Catullus in line 14 evaluate Flavius' activity?

> He gives a negative evaluation of it as absurd, foolish behavior.

14. **Quārē** (15) implies that there is a logical connection between the request made in lines 15–16 and the previous part of the poem. Explain the connection.

> The poet reasons that *since* Flavius has now been proven, in a court of law as it were, to have been carrying on some kind of love affair, whether good or bad, he should tell his friend about it.

> Although Catullus infers from Flavius' appearance that he is involved in some kind

of **ineptiae**, *foolishness*, which would normally be regarded negatively, he does not set out to be judgmental but asks to be informed of whatever it is that Flavius is doing, whether it is good or bad (**bonī malīque**, 15). The implication is that whatever Flavius is doing, Catullus will be properly sympathetic.

15. In the last line and a half what does Catullus propose to do?
    He proposes to glorify Flavius and his love affair.

Discussion

1. Consider the poem as a parody of legal proceedings against Flavius. How does the mock trial develop? What language is borrowed from the courtroom? What charges are brought? Who are the witnesses? How does Flavius defend himself? What is the verdict?

   Catullus brings a charge against Flavius: *you are in love with some feverish whore* (4–5), and as evidence he cites first the bed (7–11) and then Flavius' physical exhaustion (13). Nielsen describes the mock trial in detail in her article on the poem (see Select Bibliography). She cites the verbs **dīcere** (3, 16), **tacēre** (3, 12), **fatērī** (5), and **clāmāre** (7) as creating a "rhetorical atmosphere" (107) and cites Baehrens's 1885 commentary "for analogies from the more technical vocabulary of Cicero's speeches." The words **argūtātiō** and **inambulātiō** (11) smack of the courtroom. The bed itself is the main witness, and although inanimate it shouts (**clāmat**, 7) its testimony. Flavius' debauched body (13) is the second, and clinching, piece of evidence. Flavius is to be imagined as entering an objection just prior to line 13, which is answered by the rejoinder of Catullus as prosecutor, who picks up Flavius' implied "Why do you draw that conclusion?" and cites his final damning evidence (13–14). As Nielsen remarks, Catullus "switches . . . from the role of prosecuting attorney to that of the jury in his delivery of a verdict" (105), and Flavius is judged guilty and ordered to tell whatever good or bad thing he has been up to (15–16); he is clearly convicted of being up to some sexual foolishness or other (14).

2. How do the last line and a half fit with the rest of the poem?

   The last line and a half come as a surprise. Flavius has just been convicted of excessive and repeated indulgence in sexual foolishness (**ineptiae**, 14) and debauchery (**stupra**, 12). The reader expects censure and a penalty. Instead, the poet expresses his wish to praise or glorify Flavius and his beloved to the skies (16–17). Normally such poetic praise or glorification would be a reward for virtuous conduct or for victory in some athletic or military contest. For Flavius, however, it could be seen as appropriate punishment, since it would reveal to the world what Flavius has been desperately trying to conceal. As Thomson remarks (222): "In the concluding line and a half . . . we find an unexpected twist: the friend, having been urged to share a confidence, finds that what Catullus intends is to celebrate and publish the entire affair—*te ac tuos amores*—no doubt to his (imagined) consternation."

   The ultimate irony of the final line and a half is that in composing this poem the poet has in fact already fulfilled the wish that he here expresses. *This* poem celebrates Flavius and his beloved whore. The poem is a perfect example of the sort of **nūgae**, *trifles*, that Cornelius might have thought to be [*worth*] *something* (Catullus 1.3–4), and by its inclusion in the **libellus** that Catullus prays may last **plūs ūnō . . . perenne saeclō** it immortalizes Flavius and his affair, truly summoning them to the heavens in its charming verse. Although Flavius has been convicted of involvement in a trivial, sordid, and even disgraceful affair, Catullus has turned that affair into something of perennial interest.

3. What does the poem celebrate?

   The poem celebrates Flavius, his beloved, and their affair, and in doing so it commemorates and celebrates raw physical sexual activity. The woman's qualities of charm and refinement (2), should she possess them, are irrelevant, as are any pretensions to social status on her part (4–5). The only thing of importance about her is the feverish heat of her sexuality. Flavius likewise has no concern for how others might characterize his activity, whether they would see it as **stupra** (12), as **ineptiae** (14), as **quidquid . . . bonī** (15) or as **quidquid . . . malī** (15). He is intent only on concealing his activity and enjoying it mutually with his nameless beloved. That it is a most vigorous and exhausting form of sexual activity is shown by the creaking and walking about of the bed and by Flavius' sexually enervated body. Yet it is exactly this raw physical sexual activity, nothing more and nothing less, that Catullus here celebrates and immortalizes in the verses that make up poem 6.

4.　　If Catullus arranged his poems or at least the ones toward the beginning of the corpus in the order in which we now have them, why would he have put poem 6 here?

　　　　Various reasons suggest themselves: for contrast with the three earlier love poems, which deal with Catullus' own very serious relationship to the **puella**/Lesbia; to provide light, comic relief; to bring in a glimpse of his relations with his friends or buddies; to show something of the social world within which he lived; to begin to address the issue of sophisticated or elegant behavior in his social circle; to distinguish himself further from the **senēs sevēriōrēs** of poem 5 by showing that he could take a sympathetic view of his friend's love affair, even though it is proven to be what most people would think of as a sordid and foolish affair with an unworthy partner.

　　　　Within the sequence of poems 1–11, if Catullus arranged them in the order in which we have them, poem 6 stands exactly in the middle, with five poems to either side. It celebrates raw sexuality in stark contrast to the nuanced emotional drama that plays itself out in the series of poems dealing with Catullus' **puella**/Lesbia that surround it. The richness, complexity, and seriousness of that affair are highlighted by contrast with the simple, unambiguous sexuality of Flavius and his **amōrēs**.

　　　　Poems 2, 3, 5, 6, 7, 10, and 11 all address the thematic relationship between poetry and love. Poems 4 and 6 present inanimate objects speaking. Poem 6 shares themes of speech and silence with poem 7.

　　　　It is ironic that in poems 5 and 7 Catullus is trying to protect the essence of his affair with Lesbia from prying, malevolent eyes, but in poem 6 it is Catullus himself who is the **cūriōsus**, prying into Flavius' affair and exposing it to the world.

Select Bibliography

Stephen V. Tracy. "Argutatiinambulatioque (Catullus 6.11)." *Classical Philology* 64 (1969) 234–35.
　　Effects produced by sound and rhythm.
M. G. Morgan, "*Nescio quid febriculosi scorti*: A Note on Catullus 6." *Classical Quarterly* 27 (1977) 338–41.
　　Catullus is playing on a series of Hellenistic epigrams here. In those epigrams the person of the lover is described in terms demonstrating his or her infatuation. So the lover has a sleepless look, hair disordered from a garland recently removed, panting breath, and an unsteady walk. Instead of launching into a description of Flavius along these lines, however, Catullus demonstrates his infatuation by transferring the various traits to the furnishings in his bedroom. So it is the bed which cries out; it is the bed which has recently borne the garlands; it is the pillows which are quite worn away; and it is the entire contraption which is credited—in one of Catullus' most striking hendecasyllabic lines—with an unsteady gait. This is truly a new variation on an old theme, and an elegant conceit. (340)
Rosemary Nielsen. "On the Significance of Too Much Love." *Latomus* 43 (1984) 104–10. See above. Highly recommended.

CATULLUS 7

1   You ask, Lesbia, how many of your kissings [of me]/[my] kissings of you
2   are enough and more than enough for me.
3   As great a number of Libyan sand(s)
4   [as] lie in **lāsarpīcium**-bearing Cyrene
5   between the oracle of sweltering Jove
6   and the sacred sepulcher of ancient Battus,
7   or as many stars [as], when the night is silent,
8   look down upon the stolen/secret loves of humankind:
9   for you to kiss so many kisses/to kiss you so many kisses
10 is enough and more than enough for frenzied/crazy Catullus,
11 which neither prying meddlers could count
12 nor an evil tongue bewitch.

Poem 7 is obviously a companion piece to poem 5. Both poems have a short introduction and a conclusion framing two highly elaborate poetic images of infinity. Catullus uses these images to express his love for his mistress. In poem 5 he invites her to join him in an exuberant life of love; in poem 7 he responds to her perhaps bewildered or exasperated question of how many kisses it would take to satisfy him. The specific problem Catullus addresses in the second poem is how to respond accurately to her question, that is, how to express his love for her with human language. How can he adequately describe with the limited means of words something that is so limitless? The poem also explores a second, related paradox. How can the poet, as a detached observer in an intellectual frame of mind, describe a passion that renders him personally "crazy" or "frenzied"? Hence, this poem is one of Catullus' masterpieces as an introspective examination of the paradoxes that make up his position as a poet of love in Rome.

Initial Explorations

1. What has Lesbia apparently asked Catullus? Why would she have asked such a question? (1–2)
    She has apparently asked him, "How many of my kisses are enough for you?" (But see Initial Explorations 2.) The question clearly refers to poem 5 and perhaps suggests a bewildered or exasperated response on the part of Lesbia to the profusion of kisses demanded in that poem. She apparently does not understand why so many kisses are needed, and this suggests that she does not understand the depth or the intensity of Catullus' passion. There is an imbalance in the relationship.

2. The phrase **bāsiātiōnēs / tuae** (1–2) can be translated two different ways (see note on facing page). Can you argue for translating the phrase one way or the other, or is there deliberate ambiguity here?
    If Lesbia's question here is thought of as being prompted by Catullus' demand in poem 5 that Lesbia give hundreds and thousands of kisses, then the phrase should be translated *your kissings [of me]*. Arkins (see Select Bibliography) comments: "the poem begins by assuming that the thousands of kisses demanded by Catullus elicited from Lesbia the question how many would satisfy him" (630). The phrase can, however, be translated *[my] kissings of you* (see Fordyce and Thomson). It could also be argued that since kissing involves give and take (my kisses of you and your kisses of me), Catullus could be deliberately, perhaps teasingly, ambiguous here (and also in line 9 below where the same question arises).

3. Catullus inverts his answer by placing two images of infinite number first (3–8) and then giving his statement of how many kisses would suffice (9–10). What is the first image he evokes? (3–6)
    He first evokes an image of infinity by reference to the number of sands in a specific geographical area of North Africa.

4. Generally and specifically where are the sands located? (3–6)

> The sands are located in the region around Cyrene, and more specifically between the oracle of Ammon (identified with the Roman Jupiter) in the oasis of Siwa in the Libyan desert and the sepulcher of Battus, the founder of Cyrene, which was located in the center of Cyrene. The oracle of Jove and the tomb of Battus are hundreds of miles distant from one other, so the number of grains of sand in the desert between them could easily be described as infinite.

5. The image of infinite sands (3–6) is elaborately developed. What do the connotations and associations of the following words and phrases add to the texture of the image? **lāsarpīciferīs** (4), **aestuōsī** (5), **Battī veteris** (6), and **sacrum sepulcrum** (6)

> **Lāsarpīciferīs**: lāsarpīcium or *silphium*, as the Greeks called it, was thought to have extraordinary curative powers; Paoli (*Rome: Its People, Life and Customs*, Burnt Mill, England: Longmans Green & Co. Ltd., 1963), summarizes some of these as follows: "In medicine it performed miracles. . . . to men it brought countless benefits. In convalescence, in states of exhaustion, in digestive difficulties, in circulatory and female complaints it was an incomparable tonic. . . . It even cured gout, asthma, dropsy, epilepsy, hysteria and pleurisy" (211). See Pliny, *Natural History* 22.100–106. This ornamental epithet modifying **Cyrēnīs** displays the learning (**doctrīna**) of Catullus in the Alexandrian manner (compare **būxifer** in Catullus 4.13), but it is far more important than this in the economy of the poem. Readers may remember it when in line 10 Catullus describes himself with the words **vēsānō . . . Catullō**, as *crazy* or *frenzied* and therefore in need of the remarkable curative powers of a medication such as **lāsarpīcium**. The epithet may then be seen as having a personal reference to Catullus and his deranged mental state as a lover.

> **aestuōsī**: the adjective is used of Jupiter sweltering from the physical heat at his oracle in the desert, but it also suggests the heat of his amorous passion that he felt in his numerous illicit love affairs with mortal women. It may be felt to allude to Catullus' amorous passion for Lesbia, perhaps subtly likened to Jove's illicit affairs with mortal women.

> **Battī veteris**: mention of the ancient founder of Cyrene, whom the Hellenistic Greek poet Callimachus claimed as an ancestor, is usually interpreted as an allusion to Callimachus, whom Catullus twice refers to as **Battiadēs** (65.16 and 116.2) and from whom Catullus derived so much of his poetic taste and so many of his poetic practices.

> **sacrum sepulcrum**: the grave of Battus, who is described as *ancient*, contrasts in tone with the associations of heat and passion in the image of the desert oracle of sweltering Jove. The grave of Callimachus' remote ancestor introduces a tone of intellectual detachment and distance, which is at variance with the implications of sweltering Jove and of **lāsarpīcium**-bearing Cyrene.

6. What is the second image? (7–8) How does it differ in tone and mood from the first? How is it similar? What personal reference does it contain?

> The second image of infinity is a reference to the stars of the night sky. It connotes coolness and distance (night sky) as opposed to what is hot and near (sands of the earth). Yet it also has similarities to the first image: distance is present within both images (the vast distance between the oracle of Jove and the tomb of Battus; the even vaster distance between the stars and the earthly lovers), and both images set heat and passion (Jove; the furtive lovers) against cold (the dead Battus; the distant stars of the night). The image of the stars and the lovers is usually thought to contain an allusion to Catullus' furtive affair with Lesbia, which is carried on as secretly as possible, beyond the gaze of the *stern old men* and the *evil one* mentioned in poem 5. Ideally, only the stars of the night would witness Catullus and Lesbia's **fūrtīvōs amōrēs**.

7. In line 1, Catullus refers to himself with the first person pronoun, **mihi**; in line 10 the reference shifts to **Catullō**. What is the significance of this shift from first to third person?

> By using the third person Catullus is taking a detached, objective view of himself, as if he were an observer standing apart and examining the way he behaves with Lesbia.

8. What view of himself does the speaker take in using the phrase **vēsānō . . . Catullō**?

    He takes the view that he is *crazy* or *frenzied*, that he has been driven insane by his passionate love.

9. From whom and from what does the speaker wish to protect the kisses? (11–12) What does this echo in Catullus 5?

    He wishes to protect the kisses from the calculations of prying meddlers and from the bewitching spell they may cast from their evil tongues. This echoes the spell feared from the evil eye in Catullus 5.

Discussion

1. How are Catullus 5 and 7 similar and how do they differ in basic matters of form and content?

    Each poem has a short introduction and a conclusion framing two highly elaborate sets of poetic images, which explore the concept of infinity. The sets of poetic images in poem 5 first juxtapose the limitless risings and settings of the sun to the finality of death and then demand an uncountable number of kisses, thus inviting Lesbia to join Catullus in an exuberant life of love. In poem 7 Catullus responds to the question of how many kisses it would take to satisfy him and uses two sets of poetic images, the sands of the desert and the stars in the sky, to represent infinity and to describe the limitless magnitude of his desire, which is so irrational and indescribable that he realizes that he is, in fact, **vēsānus**, *out of his right mind, frenzied, crazy.* Both poems end with warnings against the bewitchment and destruction of passion by the evil eye (poem 5) or the evil tongue (poem 7).

2. How does Catullus 7 differ from Catullus 5 in style and tone?

    There are many differences in style and tone between the two poems. Poem 5 makes use of common vocabulary and straightforward syntax; it is composed in the form of an insistent request aggressively tendered. As has often been noted, poem 7 has an Alexandrian manner with self-consciously rhetorical language, structures, and embellishments, by which the poet assumes a distanced, reflective perspective on himself and his love. Characteristic of the Alexandrian or Callimachean style are the poem's neologisms (**bāsiātiōnēs**, 1, **lāsarpīciferīs**, 4), the learned and recherché epithets (**lāsarpīciferīs . . . Cyrēnīs**, 4, **Iovis . . . aestuōsī**, 5), the blend of the extravagantly imaginative and the realistically familiar, and possible punning word play of extreme subtlety. For the latter, some commentators note that mention of the oracle of Jove may call to mind the Egyptian god Ammon, whose name may suggest punning play on the Greek word for sand, *ammos.* Moreover, the purposeful reflection of Alexandrianism in the poem is sealed by the indirect allusion to Callimachus, who is recalled in the mention of the grave of his ancestor, Battus. Poem 7 seems almost as much involved with staking out poetic territory and creating a poetic stance as it is with the on-going wooing of Lesbia and the protection of the poet's love from malicious outside influences.

3. What is the poet saying through his antithetical images of sand and stars?

    At a basic level, of course, both images offer rhetorical tropes for the idea of infinity. The intriguing point of these subtly crafted images is the way they encapsulate an ironic contradiction between the implied thoughts, "I cannot tell you how many kisses are enough" or "I cannot tell you how much I love you," and the rhetorical form that succeeds in doing just that. That contradiction is underscored by the antitheses that underlie the poetic elaboration of the images. Thus in describing the Libyan sands Catullus specifies the large territory that lies between the oracle of Jove and the tomb of Battus. The epithet applied to Jove, **aestuōsī** (5), means *sweltering* in a prosaic sense that comprehends the desert climate of the oracle, but it is commonly used in a figurative sense also to mean *lusty, passionate.* In this sense it contrasts pointedly with the epithet applied to Battus, **veteris** (6), which marks not only the remoteness of Battus in time but also the complete absence of passion in death. In addition, the landmark that bounds one side of this territory is an oracle, which speaks, while on the other side is a tomb, which is silent. Hence, the imagery incorporates a specific design of antitheses matching speech against silence and passion against death, which darkly echo the great antithesis in poem 5 between a brief but passionate life of love full of noisy **bāsia** and an eternal and silent sleep of death.

The same essential antithesis in another form is sketched in the poetic elaboration of the image likening infinity to the multitude of stars, where the silence of the cool, insensate night is juxtaposed against the passionate lovemaking of humankind. An antithesis is again recalled from poem 5: while the first set of images in that poem juxtaposes the eternal risings and settings of the sun against the brief limit of human life, the second image in poem 7 juxtaposes the eternal stars against human lovers, who are in a doubly precarious situation not only in that they are **hominēs** and not **deī** and accordingly they are subject to death but also in that their love is **fūrtīvus**. Further, the theme of furtive love recalls poem 5, for while in that poem the **senēs sevēriōrēs** and the **malus** would maliciously gossip about Catullus and Lesbia's love affair and threaten it with an envious evil eye (**invidēre**, 12), in poem 7 the stars look at (**vident**, 8) the furtive lovers with equanimity or perhaps even with approval. The celestial bodies know that the life of love makes most sense for humans, subject as they are to the harsh and absolute law of mortality, and so sympathize with the furtive lovers.

4. Why does the poet use the word **bāsiātiōnēs** instead of **bāsia**, which he used in poem 5?

Bāsiātiō is probably a neologism coined by Catullus to epitomize the relationship between love and poetry that he explores in this poem. He has affixed an abstract noun suffix **-tiō** to the verbal stem **bāsiā-**, giving the act of kissing a cerebral quality, which bespeaks a personal detachment from the emotional furor of love. Again, the contradiction between rhetorical form and content, which Catullus plays with throughout this poem, is underscored. Students might also look up **vēsānus** in their dictionaries and investigate its etymology and how it is used. Certainly it is a very strong word that connotes a complete loss of control, a kind of insanity, precisely what is contradicted by the tight rhetorical form and intellectual detachment celebrated in the body of the poem and exemplified in the distancing effect of the poet's move from the first person in line 1 to the third person in line 10.

5. How does the third-person reference in the phrase **vēsānō . . . Catullō** (10) suggest that the poet is taking a new, objective perspective on himself and his passion?

By using the third person Catullus is taking a more detached, objective view of himself, as if he were an observer standing apart from himself and examining how he feels toward Lesbia. He begins the poem by confessing the ineffable passion he feels through images of infinity, and in the end he views himself with detachment, acknowledging that there is an insane, frenzied quality to his love.

The poem is very tightly structured between question (**quot mihi bāsiātiōnēs / tuae . . . sint satis superque**, 1–2) and answer (**tam tē bāsia multa bāsiāre / . . . satis et super . . . est**, 9–10), with **satis et super** (10) echoing **satis superque** (2) and the subjunctive **sint** (2) becoming the indicative **est** (10). Then, within this frame of question and answer, **Quam magnus** (3) and **quam . . . multa** (7) correlate with **tam . . . multa** (9). By line 10 the poet realizes that the poem's central imagery has set the number of kisses that would satisfy him so high that he has clearly left himself open to the reproach, "You've got to be crazy to want all those kisses!" But he realizes also that this is exactly right. No fewer kisses will satisfy him, and if that means he's crazy, then so be it: *for you to kiss so many kisses/to kiss you so many kisses / is enough and more than enough for frenzied/crazy Catullus* (9–10).

6. What role do the **cūriōsī** play in the poem?

Just as Catullus concludes poem 5 by turning from his passionate exhortation to Lesbia to confront those who envy and would destroy his love, so also here, after confessing the magnitude of his love, he again confronts those who would bewitch and destroy his love. The poem could, of course, stand as complete without the last two lines; one reason for adding the last two lines was surely to cement the formal relationship of this poem to poem 5, reinforcing their relationship as a pair of poems to be read together, albeit with the seemingly unrelated poem 6 coming in between (contrast the immediate juxtaposition of poems 2 and 3 on the **passer**). In poem 5 the last two lines are structurally and ideologically related to the rest of the poem in that the **quis malus** who would envy and bewitch the kisses is identifiable with the **senēs sevēriōrēs** who might gossip maliciously about Lesbia if she were to respond positively to Catullus' invitation to live a life of love with him. In poem 7 the last two lines have no such connection with anything earlier in the poem. If they relate to anything other than the last two lines of poem 5, it is to the envious and malicious **senēs sevēriōrēs** of poem 5. They, gossips and rumor-mongers that they are, are here labeled **cūriōsī**, *busybodies*, to be outwitted here just as at the end of poem 5 by assuring that the number of kisses and the magnitude of love are uncountable and incomprehensible in the language of malicious gossips.

Poem 7 ends on the significant word **lingua** and the inability of the busybodies to make a proper count, because the number of kisses Catullus imagines as sufficient to satisfy his desire is beyond counting. The spiteful opponents of the poet's love are imagined as trying to make an exact count of the kisses in order to have some basis on which to cast their spell. They cannot, however, give adequate expression to such numbers, and consequently they cannot, like the poet, use language (one meaning of the word **lingua**) to any purposeful effect at all, not even a malicious one.

7. How would you, if you were Lesbia, respond to Catullus 7?

Answers to this question will obviously vary. Some may complain that the poet's feeling for Lesbia gets lost in the maze of allusive imagery. Some may feel that the poet is more interested in staking out his stance as a poet and in creating an appendage to poem 5 than he is in wooing Lesbia. Some may feel that the poet is more interested in the reaction of the **cūriōsī** to the imagined kisses than he is in Lesbia's feelings. Positive responses should include comment on the overwhelming, total commitment that Catullus appears to be making by stating that only an infinite number of kisses will satisfy him and by being willing to accept a public image of seeming frenzied and crazy for demanding so many kisses since in fact only an infinite number of kisses will satisfy him. Some students will feel that Lesbia should feel flattered that the poet is so in love with her that he is willing to appear crazy in order to be able to express his total commitment.

8. Why might Catullus have placed poem 6 in between poems 5 and 7?

He might have placed it between the two kiss poems for variety, just as he might have placed poem 4 after the two **passer** poems for the sake of variety. He might also have placed poem 6 between the two kiss poems in order to point a contrast between Flavius' carnal, sexual affair with a common whore—an affair that he tries to conceal from the public and even from his buddy Catullus—and Catullus' affair with Lesbia, which is far more serious, "spiritual," or "romantic," and which he does not conceal but rather reveals and even flaunts in the face of the **senēs sevēriōrēs**, the **malī**, and the **cūriōsī**, determined to justify it and to define it in such ways that even these most severe critics will be disarmed and unable to attack it with their malicious, envious looks and words. While there is a stark contrast, however, between poems 5 and 7 on the one hand and the carnal, sexual 6 on the other, it should be remembered that Catullus wishes to elevate Flavius and his beloved whore to the skies, that is, to eulogize them just as he eulogizes his own very different affair with Lesbia in poems 5 and 7. Perhaps the best way to conceive of the relationship between poem 6 on the one hand and poems 5 and 7 on the other and to see why Catullus might have placed poem 6 in between poems 5 and 7 is to recall the following famous lines from poem 72: **Dīlēxī tum tē nōn tantum ut vulgus amīcam / sed pater ut gnātōs dīligit et generōs**, *I cherished you then not only as anyone from the common herd [loves] a friend/prostitute, / but as a father cherishes his sons and his sons-in-law* (3–4). In these two lines of poem 72 Catullus is trying to express the two strands of his love for Lesbia, the purely carnal on the one hand and the familial on the other. Just so, in the collocation of poems 5, 6, and 7 Catullus groups together glorifications of both Flavius' casual, carnal love and of his own overwhelming romantic commitment to Lesbia. (See also the answer to Discussion question 4 for poem 6.)

Select Bibliography

A. C. Moorhouse. "Two Adjectives in Catullus, 7." *American Journal of Philology* 84 (1963) 417–18. On **lasarpīciferīs** and **aestuōsī**.

Charles Segal. "Catullus 5 and 7: A Study in Complementaries." *American Journal of Philology* 89 (1968) 284–301. On **vēsānō . . . Catullō** (10): "the poet, having passed through the distant realms of lines 3–8, sees himself at greater remove: he speaks of himself in the third rather than the first person (compare *mihi* in line 1) and recognizes his 'madness' (*uesano*)" (294).

Charles Segal. "More Alexandrianism in Catullus VII?" *Mnemosyne* 27 (1974) 139–43. Hellenistic precedents for the images of stars, night, and secret loves.

Brian Arkins. "Catullus 7." *L'Antiquité Classique* 48 (1979) 630–635.

CATULLUS 8

1 Lovesick Catullus, cease to play the fool,
2 and consider what you see to have perished as lost.
3 Once bright suns shone for you,
4 when you came again and again where your girl led,
5 she who was loved by us/me as no [other] will [ever] be loved.
6 There while those many playful experiences took place,
7 which you used to want and your **puella** was not used not to want/was not refusing,
8 truly bright suns shone for you.
9 But now at last she does not want [those things]: you too,
        [although] weak in will, stop wanting [those things],
10 and don't constantly chase after [her] who flees, and don't be wretched/lovesick,
11 but with mind set against [her] endure, tough it out.
12 Good-bye, **puella**. Now Catullus is toughing it out,
13 he will neither look for you nor woo you unwilling.
14 But you will suffer, when you will not be wooed.
15 Unfortunate [one], alas for you! What life awaits you?
16 Who now will approach you? To whom will you seem pretty?
17 Whom will you love now? Whose will you be called?
18 Whom will you kiss? Whose lips will you bite?
19 But you, Catullus, thoroughly determined tough it out.

Catullus 8 memorably expresses a theme that has great importance throughout the Catullan corpus: the divided will or self. His **puella** is no longer interested in carrying on the affair. Catullus knows rationally that this is the case, but he finds it difficult to accept reality and to withdraw from his enchantment with her. His dilemma is in fact insoluble, yet the artistry of this poem, in which he expresses it, is superb. Its structure of concentric rings, its verbal repetitions, and its patterns of sounds have often been diagrammed. Rather than providing a diagram of its structure here, we encourage teachers to have their students work out its structure for themselves, along with study of its elaborate patterns of sounds (see Discussion question 1).

Initial Explorations

1. What does the speaker's use of the vocative **Miser Catulle** (1) imply about the dramatic situation of this poem? Who is addressing whom? Why?

    The speaker, who is presumably Catullus, is addressing Catullus, i.e., is addressing himself. The poem opens as an internal monologue or dialogue. Some have seen a division here between the speaker, who represents the rational side of Catullus, and the addressee, who represents the emotional Catullus. The terms *rational Catullus* and *emotional Catullus* may be useful for purposes of discussion, but they may be too categorical for some readers of the poem. See the comments quoted from the articles of Rowland, Dyson, and Connor in the Select Bibliography.

    Students should compare the situation here with that in poem 7, line 10, where the poet refers to himself in the third person as **vēsānō . . . Catullō**, thus distancing himself from himself. Poem 8 develops as an internal monologue or dialogue with Catullus ordering himself to stop being foolish.

2. What do the words **miser** (1) and **ineptīre** (1) reveal about Catullus' view of his situation and its cause?

    The adjective **miser** indicates that Catullus recognizes that he is involved in an unhappy love affair. The infinitive **ineptīre** indicates that he attributes his unhappiness to some lack of judgment or folly on his part. His misery is due to the fact that he is being foolish.

    The word **miser** is a technical term in the vocabulary of love; love, as Allen ("Elegy and the Classical Attitude toward Love," *Yale Classical Studies* 11 [1950] 255–77) states "is regarded as a power which overrides reason, mastering the lover and reducing him either to willing servitude or helpless despair. . . . *Miser* in erotic context describes the lover whose will and reason are altogether subject to his passion" (258–59). The opposite of **miser** is **sānus**, as Allen shows with reference to Lucretius 1073–82. Booth (152; see Select Bibliography for poem 76) defines **miser** in this technical sense as *afflicted with erotic passion*—we might say *lovesick*. This meaning of **miser** should be kept in mind elsewhere in Catullus as well. Allen (260, n. 16) suggests that **nec miser vīve** (Catullus 8.10) means simply *don't be in love*.

3. Explain the point of the command expressed in line 2.

    The point is that Catullus should acknowledge the fact that what has perished should be regarded as lost forever. Since **miser** in line 1 implies unhappiness in a love affair, Catullus is apparently telling himself to regard the love affair as over. Catullus stands apart as an objective observer of the situation and clearly sees that the affair is indeed over.

4. Lines 3 and 8 serve as a frame for a nostalgic memory. What do the words **fulsēre quondam candidī tibī sōlēs** mean?

    The words mean that once upon a time Catullus' days were filled with happiness (**candidī** = *happy*; **sōlēs** = *days*).

5. What picture do we get of the relationship between Catullus and the **puella** as presented in lines 4–7?

    We get a rosy, nostalgic view of their past love affair. The **puella** used to take the lead (**dūcēbat**, 4), and Catullus, her lover, would constantly go along (**ventitābās**, 4) with her every whim. Catullus describes the **puella** as *loved by us/me as no [other] will [ever] be loved* (5); his love for the **puella** was unique. Finally, Catullus remarks that many **iocōsa**, *playful experiences* (6), took place during the course of the affair, things that Catullus *used to want* and that the **puella** *was not used not to want*.

6. What does each of the following contribute to the meaning and the tone of lines 4–7: the iterative verb, hyperbole, repetition of sounds, and litotes (**nec . . . nōlēbat**)?

The iterative verb **ventitābās** and the imperfect tenses of lines 4, 6, and 7 emphasize the duration of the happy love affair in the past. The repetition of the **-bā-/-ba-** sounds emphasizes the dominance of the imperfect tense verbs in this section. The hyperbole of line 5 stating that no woman will ever be loved as much as the **puella** was loved expresses the great devotion of Catullus to the **puella**. The consonance of *ls* ties crucial pairs of words together, such as **puella** (4) and **nūlla** (5), **illa** (6) and **multa** (6), and **volēbās** (7) and **nōlēbat** (7). The litotes, **nec puella nōlēbat** (7), *and your puella was not used not to want*, could mean simply *and your puella used to want*, but using a double negative and saying that she was not not wanting the playful things is not quite the same as saying that she was wanting them but hints that she may in fact have been indifferent (= *was not refusing*). Connor (see Select Bibliography) remarks on this phrase: "Obviously a cloud over a positive commitment to love. We get a chill perception that things were *never . . .* perfect and mutually rapturous" (95). In line 9 her indifference becomes refusal.

7. With what temporal adverb earlier in the poem does the phrase **Nunc iam** (9) correlate?

It correlates with **quondam** (3).

8. How does Catullus describe the situation as being different now? (9) How does he characterize himself, and what does he order himself to do? (9)

Now the girl no longer wants what she wanted or at least did not refuse in the past. Catullus characterizes himself as being **inpotēns** (*powerless, lacking self-control, weak in will*) but nevertheless orders himself to stop wanting the **iocōsa**, *playful experiences*, which he had with the **puella** in the past.

9. How does the pairing of **inpotēns** and **nōlī** (9) intimate Catullus' dilemma in the poem?

Catullus issues the command, **nōlī** (*stop wanting [those things]*), while ironically undercutting his command by addressing himself as **inpotēns**, thus indicating that he knows that he does not have the power or ability to do what he is ordering himself to do. This characterizes Catullus' essential dilemma in the poem, for he knows that the affair should be abandoned but knows that he does not have the willpower to abandon it.

10. How do the words **nec quae fugit sectāre** (10) reverse the memory of the relationship with the **puella** in line 4?

In line 4 it is said that Catullus used to go wherever the **puella** led, but now Catullus has to be told not to pursue the **puella** who now flees from him.

Note that Catullus uses **nec . . . nec** with imperatives here instead of the usual **nōlī** + infinitive.

11. How do the iterative verbs **ventitābās** (4) and **sectāre** (10) link and characterize Catullus' behavior before and now?

The fact that both of these verbs are iterative calls attention to the relationship between them and highlights the repeated, almost compulsive, quality of the actions. Just as Catullus constantly followed the **puella** in the past, so now he constantly chases after her.

12. Line 11 concludes Catullus' address to himself, which began in line 1. Comment on his choice of words, use of prefixes, and use of asyndeton in line 11.

The ablative of manner, **obstinātā mente** emphasizes the need for Catullus' mind to be made to stand fast *against* (**ob-**) the **puella**; **per-**, *completely*, adds emphasis to the need for endurance of what can't be changed; and the **ob-** of **obdūrā** again emphasizes the need for resolution *against* the **puella** and the affair. The asyndeton in **perfer, obdūrā** binds the two emphatic words more closely together. The line may seem like heavy-handed overkill, but it should be remembered that Catullus regards himself as **inpotēns**, *without control over himself/weak in will*, and so in need of the strong wording in this admonition that comes as the climax of the series of admonitions that began in the second half of line 9.

13. Beginning with line 12, who is now addressing whom? In what frame of mind is the speaker of this line? With what does he greet his **puella**? What will he not do? (13)

Now Catullus addresses the **puella** or at least rehearses what he plans to say to her. He plucks up his courage, greets the **puella** with a farewell, and states that he is firmly set against her (**obdūrat**). Just as he told himself in line 10 not to pursue the one who flees, so here in obedience to that voice he declares that he will neither seek out the **puella** nor woo her *unwilling* (**invītam**, 13).

On the words **nec tē requīret nec rogābit invītam** (13), Khan (see Select Bibliography) remarks: "the rasping rhotacism strives to be theatrical in its teeth-baring display of determination" (561).

It should be noted, however, that there is a possibility that Catullus' newly found resolution may waver even as he gives it expression. The adjective **invītam** at the end of the line modifying **tē** toward the beginning is predicative, and the two words could mean: *since you are unwilling, if you are unwilling,* or *as long as you are unwilling*. Only the first of these translations, *since you are unwilling*, states an unambiguous hardening against the **puella**. The latter two, *if you are unwilling* and *as long as you are unwilling*, hold open the possibility that the **puella** may change her mind and that the affair could be renewed.

14.   What is the purpose of the statement in line 14, the exclamation in line 15, and the rhetorical questions in lines 15–18? For what is the **puella** to be pitied?

Catullus is warning the **puella** of the consequences to herself of her change of heart and abandonment of the affair. Specifically, he warns her that she will be sorry, that no real life will remain for her, and that she will neither be loved nor have anyone to love.

The **puella** is to be pitied because she will be lonely and destitute when no one invites her out, no one approaches her, and no one thinks her pretty; when she will have no one to love, she will not be said to be anyone's **puella**, she will kiss no one, and she will bite no one's lips.

Note that in the first line of the poem it is Catullus who is to be pitied as *miserable* (**miser**), whereas here the tables are turned and it is the **puella** who is to be pitied (*Unfortunate [one], alas for you!* **Scelesta, vae tē!**, 15). Catullus has pulled himself out of his state of misery and confronts the **puella** as the one to be pitied.

Note also that the implied answers to the rhetorical questions are all negative, and note also that Catullus in formulating these questions assumes that he is the one and only suitor or lover of the **puella**. He assumes that she has no one else and that she will be left destitute without him. This assumption may be wrong (compare poem 11.17–20), but at this point Catullus seems blissfully ignorant of any other suitors or lovers.

15.   In warning the **puella** of the consequences of her change of heart toward him by listing the causes of grief that await her (13–18), Catullus is in fact reliving memories of his love affair with her. Do they have a beginning, middle, and end? Do they move toward a climax? What echoes of earlier poems do you find in these memories? What is happening to Catullus' professed resolve?

There is a clear progression from the initial stages of the love affair, in which Catullus looked for and courted the **puella**, to the stage at which he visited her and complimented her beauty, to the point at which she loved him and was called his, to the final stage at which she kissed him and would bite his lips. Thus the memories move from initial courting (**tē requīret**, 13) to a climactic reminiscence of lovemaking (**Cui labella mordēbis?**) The following echoes of earlier poems add verisimilitude to the reminiscences here:

8.15 **Quae tibī manet vīta?** = 5.1 **Vīvāmus**
8.17 **Quem nunc amābis?** = 5.1 **amāmus**
8.17 **Cuius esse dīcēris?** = 2.1; 3.3, 4, 17 **meae puellae**
8.18 **quem bāsiābis** = 5.7 **bāsia**, 5.13 **bāsiōrum**, 7.1 **bāsiātiōnēs**, 7.9 **bāsia . . . bāsiāre**
8.18 **Cui labella mordēbis?** = 2.4 **et acrīs solet incitāre morsūs**

In expressing these progressively more intimate reminiscences of his affair with the **puella**, Catullus' resolve weakens. He is becoming caught in his own erotic language and is falling back under the spell of the **puella**. He is losing control.

In warning and pitying the **puella**, Catullus is gloating, as it were, over how, due to his new resolve, the tables have been turned and it will now be the **puella** and not Catullus who will be miserable. Yet there may be another level here. If the **puella** only real-izes how pitiable, lonely, and destitute she will be without Catullus as her lover, perhaps she will have a change of heart. The rhetorical questions, centering on more and more in-timate reminiscences of the pleasures of the affair in the past, may revive her fondness for him. Thus, in lines 14–18, Catullus is, on one level at least, perhaps consciously, perhaps unconsciously, wooing the **puella** all over again by on the one hand warning her of her misery if she continues her isolation and on the other hand holding forth the possibility of a return to their mutually satisfying intimacies of the past. It's the old **Vīvāmus, mea Lesbia, atque amēmus** (5.1) all over again. Catullus' resolve, stated in lines 12–13 with the declaration that he would neither look for nor woo the **puella** thus vanishes in lines 14–18.

It should be remembered, however, that Catullus' resolve in line 13 was not without reservation, since the line could mean *he will neither look for you nor woo you if/as long as you are unwilling*. In other words, Catullus can be thought of as holding out the hope that the **puella** may change her mind and become willing again in the very sentence in which he states his resolve. It is with that hope in mind that he continues with lines 14–18, simulta-neously pitying, warning, and wooing the **puella**.

16.   In the last line we again hear the voice of the Catullus of the first eleven lines of the poem. Why does Catullus need to repeat at the end of the poem (19) the command that he had al-ready delivered in line 11? Compare **dēstinātus** (19) with **obstinātā mente** (11). What dif-ferent meaning does the different prefix create in line 19?

Catullus repeats the command because he sees that in lines 14–18 he lost his resolve to put an end to the affair and that he has been drawn into re-experiencing it in the hope that it might be revived (something he knows is not possible); he knows that he has lost control and that he can succeed only in making himself miserable again by recalling the happiness of the past affair. The voice of the rational Catullus must therefore reissue the command already delivered in line 11. The language used is similar; Quinn (119) sug-gests that use of the adjective **obstinātus** in line 11 "stresses the beginning of the pro-cess," while **dēstinātus** in line 19 stresses "its continuance." Catullus thus breaks in with a final exhortation, calling for a continuing process of toughing it out, in the realization that neither warning the **puella** nor wooing her will be to any avail.

17.   What effects are produced by the meter of the poem? What tone is produced by absence of enjambement?

The meter of the poem is choliambic (lit., "limping iambics"), so-called from the metrical pattern of an iambic trimeter with a spondee in the sixth foot that distorts the rhythm at the end of each line. The verse form was invented by Hipponax, who wrote satirical verses in the sixth century B.C. Catullus likewise appears to use the meter when he aims for satirical or mocking effect. Compare poems 22 and 44 among the selections in *Love and Betrayal*. The absence of enjambement reinforces the metrical emphasis on the sixth foot to give added weight to the last two syllables of each line. Notice how often in the poem Catullus has placed at the end of the line the crucial imperatives with which he ex-horts himself to make the break with his **puella**: **dūcās** (2), **nōlī** (9), **vīve** (10), **obdūrā** (11) and **obdūrā** (19). Fraenkel (see Select Bibliography) thinks that "the hard rhythm, pro-duced by the incision at the end of every single line, is in keeping with the hard tone of the whole poem" (52).

Discussion

1.   Reread the poem and note words, phrases, and sounds that are repeated. What is significant about the repeated words, phrases, and sounds? What do the repetitions add to the meaning of the poem?

The most significant repetition is of words that refer to the will and to the poet's intention to persevere in his resolve to be quit of the love affair: **volēbās . . . nōlēbat** (7), **nōn volt . . .**

nōlī (9); **obdūrā** (11), **obdūrat** (12), and **obdūrā** (19). Such clustering of words highlights the major theme of the poem, the poet's divided will. Catullus also repeats the phrase **fulsēre quondam candidī tibi sōlēs** (3) with a minor variation in line 8, emphasizing the idyllic memories of love that the poet continues to reflect on despite the present rupture in the relationship, which leaves him being **miser** (lines 1 and 10). Finally, notice how the repetition of *l* sounds enhances the leading terms of contrast in the poem, **Catulle** (1), **puella** (4), **puella** (7), **illa** (9), **puella** (12), **Catullus** (12), **nūlla** (14), **bella** (16), **labella** (18), and **Catulle** (19), but also including the key verbs **volēbās** (7), **nōlēbat** (7), **nōn volt** (9), and **nōlī** (9) and other important words like **fulsēre . . . sōlēs** (3, 8), **dolēbis** (14), and **Scelesta** (15). These *l* sounds are particularly evident in lines 12–19. The repetition of words and sounds perhaps enhances the sense of the poet's haunting memories and the predicament he finds himself in of wanting to be free from something that he still clings to emotionally.

For detailed study of sound patterns in the poem and of its structure, see the articles of Swanson and Schmiel in the Select Bibliography.

2. How does Catullus 8 fit into the story of Catullus' love affair with the **puella**/Lesbia as recorded in Catullus 2, 3, 5, and 7? Does it come as a surprise? Does it seem to fit?

The vocabulary of lines 3–8 and 13–18 of poem 8 seems to echo the bright and playful experiences recorded in Catullus 2, 3, 5, and 7. It will probably come as no surprise to most readers that the **puella** has now ceased to want the affair (**Nunc iam illa nōn volt**, 8.9), because she seemed distant in the earlier poems, paying more attention to her **passer** than to Catullus and asking how many kisses he really wanted rather than giving him the infinite number that he clearly asked for. One wonders how positive the reader of poems 2, 3, 5, and 7 is supposed to think that the **puella**/Lesbia is about the affair and whether her attitude is not best captured in the double negative **nec puella nōlēbat**, *and your* **puella** *was not used not to want [those playful experiences]* (8.7), which rather than expressing a positive *wanting* may express indifference. This seems to fit with the picture of the **puella**/Lesbia in the earlier poems. The affair was always one-sided or largely so. Her leading him on (**dūcēbat**, 8.4) implied no genuine commitment.

Select Bibliography

Eduard Fraenkel. "Two Poems of Catullus," *Journal of Roman Studies* 51 (1961) 46–53.
Roy Arthur Swanson. "The Humor of Catullus 8." *The Classical Journal* 58 (1963) 193–96.
Steele Commager. "Notes on Some Poems of Catullus." *Harvard Studies in Classical Philology* 70 (1965) 83–110.
L. A. Moritz. "*Miser Catulle*: A Postscript." *Greece and Rome* 13 (1966) 155–57. On the structure of the poem.
R. L. Rowland. "*Miser Catulle*: An Interpretation of the Eighth Poem of Catullus." *Greece and Rome* 13 (1966) 15–21. Highly recommended.
    The poem is cast in the loose form of a dialogue between two 'voices'. These have been envisaged in terms of the rational poet and the irrational lover. . . . This interpretation is attractive, . . . but the dichotomy between lover and poet is an over-simplification. . . . The basic fault of this interpretation lies in its failure to distinguish between the memories of his experience and his present attitude towards that experience. Once this distinction has been made it is possible to see the poem as depicting a dialogue between two 'voices', neither of which necessarily reflects the poet's present attitude to the experience expressed. (16)
H. Akbar Khan. "Style and Meaning in Catullus' Eighth Poem." *Latomus* 27 (1968) 555–74.
    Critics are divided in opinion as to whether Catullus had any rival in mind. Fraenkel . . . says: 'At the end, his imagination is tormented with the vision of the rival, of Lesbia embracing him.' On the other hand Fordyce . . . says 'there is no suggestion that he has a rival.' . . . no hint of a rival is given: the relationship of lover and beloved is only a two-way one, and not a triangle. (566, 568)

M. B. Skinner. "Catullus 8. The Comic *Amator* as *Eiron*." *The Classical Journal* 66 (1971) 298–309. Develops an interpretation based on "resemblances between Catullus 8 and the traditional picture of the irresolute *amator* as he appears in Roman comedy" (299). Catullus' fictional alter ego in poem 8 is a "comic *adulescens*," a "humorous character," and "Lesbia is the living embodiment of the archetypal comic *meretrix*" (305).

M. Dyson. "Catullus 8 and 76." *Classical Quarterly* 23 (1973) 127–43.

> The poem on the face of it is a sombre monologue, and one should start with the supposition that it presents an expression of unhappiness in a dilemma which one is invited to share. . . . [The poem is a] monologue in which the speaker faces his dilemma, argues himself into a decision of self-control, and finds his new strength broken at the very next onset of desire. (134)

P. J. Connor. "Catullus 8: The Lover's Conflict." *Antichthon* 8 (1974) 93–96.

> Catullus does not harshly set up two poles which rigidly focus diametrically opposed personalities. His method is much more pliable, more restrained than that. We see rather, in lively existence, two aspects of an indivisible personality. A person can experience internal conflicts without being some sort of Jekyll and Hyde. It is a perfectly human situation which, by avoiding the vulgar and easy adoption of two separate identities, Catullus has gently captured. The hints of dualism do not spread into two separate entities. It is finely caught. (93–94)

Robert Schmiel. "The Structure of Catullus 8: A History of Interpretation." *The Classical Journal* 86 (1990–91) 158–66.

Ellen Greene. "The Catullan Ego: Fragmentation and the Erotic Self." *American Journal of Philology* 116 (1995) 77–93.

> The issues of identity and allocution are especially problematical in light of the configuration of three persons in the poem: the speaker, the second-person addressee identified as "Catullus," and another "Catullus" referred to in the third person. Both the dramatic structure of the poem and the self-presentation of the speaker depend on the discontinuity of past and present, then and now. The speaker is both lamenting and renouncing an ideal past in which the speaker's love for his mistress was fulfilled. The speaker vacillates throughout the poem between conjuring up his lost happiness and attempting to renounce his passion and finally accept Lesbia's rejection of him. The poem is built on a hard structure of imperatives in which the speaker tries to reprove himself for clinging to the past and being incapable of giving up his love, despite the girl's rejection of him. (78–79)

CATULLUS 9

1   Veranius, who of all my friends is worth
2   more to me than three hundred thousand,
3   have you come home to your household gods,
4   and to your loving brothers and aged mother?
5   You have come home. O blessed news to my ears!
6   I shall see you safe and sound and listen to you
7   tell about the sights, deeds, and tribes of the Spaniards,
8   as is your habit, and I shall draw your neck to me
9   and kiss your sweet mouth and eyes.
10   Of all the men who are truly blessed,
11   who is happier or more blessed than I?

Poem 9 presents an intimate portrayal of Veranius' homecoming from Spain and his happy reception by his family and by Catullus. Veranius is one of only a handful of men in the corpus who on the basis of the poems can be unequivocally called a friend of the poet, and this poem exudes both familial affection and the warm joy of a close friendship.

Initial Explorations

1. By means again of large numbers (compare Catullus 5 and 7), what point about Veranius does the hyperbole make? (1–2)

   That he is worth more to Catullus than three hundred thousand other friends.

2. Behind the simplicity and colloquialism of the Latin in this poem are strong sentiments that celebrate the return of Catullus' close friend. How does Catullus imagine that Veranius' reunion with his home and family unfolded? (3–4)

   After arriving home, he greeted his household gods and then his loving brothers and aged mother.

3. Identify a tricolon in lines 3–4 and a chiasmus in line 4.

   The tricolon: (1) **tuōs penātēs**, (2) **frātrēsque ūnanimōs**, (3) **anumque mātrem**. The number of syllables does not increase in the third item over the second, but the items are perhaps in an ascending order of importance, with the **māterfamiliās** coming last.

   The chiasmus: **frātrēs** A, **ūnanimōs** B, **anum** B, **mātrem** A.

4. News of Veranius' arrival home precedes the anticipated reunion of Catullus with his friend. What sequence does Catullus anticipate when the two friends are reunited? How is the intimacy of their friendship revealed through the sequence? (6–9)

   Catullus mentions first that he will see that Veranius is safe and sound, second that he will hear Veranius telling of his travels, and third that he will embrace and kiss his friend. There is a progressive intimacy of sight, sound, and touch. No doubt in actuality the embrace and kiss would precede the narration of travels, but here in Catullus' telling of what will happen the most important items, the embrace and kiss are left for the climactic third place in the series of events. This is an example of the rhetorical device called hysteron proteron. The intimacy of the friendship is further revealed through the warm and graphic way Catullus describes his embracing and kissing of his friend.

5. Lines 6–9 contain three verbs; identify the members of an ascending tricolon in this sentence.

   (1) **vīsam tē incolumem**, (2) **audiamque Hibērum / nārrantem loca, facta, nātiōnēs, / ut mōs est tuus**, (3) **applicānsque collum / iūcundum ōs oculōsque suāviābor**. Again there are fewer syllables in the third member of the tricolon than in the second; it is clearly, however, the climactic member, and its verb has the most syllables.

6. As Veranius is singled out by a hyperbole at the start of the poem, who is singled out at the end by an equally strong hyperbole? (10–11)

   At the end, the poet himself, in his relationship to Veranius, is singled out by hyperbole, just as Veranius, in his relationship to Catullus, was singled out by hyperbole at the beginning.

7. Note that line 10 is almost identical with line 2 of Catullus 3. Does this repetition serve any purpose?

   The cross-reference links the two poems. Compare similar cross-references in Catullus 2.1 and 3.4 and in Catullus 5.12–13 and 7.11–12. The poem celebrating Veranius' return is thus brought into a relationship with the poem lamenting the death of Lesbia's sparrow, contrasting themes of joy and sorrow and of the poet's love for the **puella** and his close friendship and bonding with Veranius.

8. Reread the poem and note recurring sound patterns, especially of the letters *m* and *n*. What important words in the poem echo Veranius' name by beginning with the letter *v*? Where is asyndeton used effectively? What do the three elisions in line 6 highlight? Locate strongly placed front and end words in particular lines throughout the poem.

   Important words beginning with *v* and echoing Veranius' name: **vēnistīne** (3), **Vēnistī** (5), and **Vīsam** (6), all at the front of their lines.

   Asyndeton: **nārrantem loca, facta, nātiōnēs** (7).

   The elisions in line 6 highlight Catullus' excitement at seeing and hearing his friend.

Front words: **Vērānī** (1), **antistāns** (2), **vēnistīne** (3), **Vēnistī** (5), **Vīsam** (6), **nārrantem** (7), and **iūcundum** (9).

End words: **amīcīs** (1), **penātēs** (3), **mātrem** (4), **beātī** (5), **collum** (8), **suāviābor** (9), **beātiōrum** (10), and **beātiusve** (11).

At the ends of each of the final two lines emphasis is given to the poet's happiness by repetition in the words **beātiōrum** (10) and **beātiusve** (11), which echo **beātī** (5).

Discussion

1.   At what points would you divide the poem into three parts?

The poem divides naturally into three parts. In lines 1–5 Catullus announces the good news of his friend's arrival: **vēnistī** (repeated twice). In lines 6–9 he imagines his own joyful visit with his friend. In the last two lines he pronounces himself to be not only happy but even blessed, a word that can be used for describing the perfect happiness of the gods.

2.   Printed below are lines from a poem by the third century B.C. Greek poet Theocritus. Catullus may have known this poem, and he may have taken his cue for his repetition of **vēnistī** (3, 5) from the Greek words of Theocritus' poem that are translated "You have come . . . / you have come. . . . " What similarities and what differences between the two poems do you notice? What purpose might Catullus have had in mind in echoing the words from Theocritus?

Both poems express a deep emotional joy at the return of a dear friend, as is emphasized by the repeated expression, "you have come." Theocritus' poem, however, is addressed to the speaker's youthful homosexual lover who has been away only two nights and two days, perhaps deliberately playing coy in order to tease his lover, in contrast with Veranius who has been away a long time on service in Spain. The lover's joy at the return of his beloved boy in Theocritus is expressed in an elaborate string of similes, whereas Catullus' joy at the return of Veranius is expressed in terms of his seeing him safe and sound, hearing him tell of Spain, and embracing and kissing him. In Theocritus it is the lover who runs to the boy, presumably upon seeing him return, whereas in Catullus the poet simply says *I will see . . . I will hear . . . I will kiss.*

In echoing the poem of Theocritus Catullus is drawing attention to the similarities and differences between their two poems and perhaps hinting indirectly at the depth of his own love for Veranius by echoing a poem that openly celebrates homosexual love.

3.   How do the close friendship and bonding between Catullus and Veranius contrast with the relationship between the poet and his **puella** in the preceding poem?

The close bonding between the two men here contrasts strongly with the disrupted relationship between Catullus and the **puella** in the preceding poem. At the very point at which that affair seems to have come to a dead end with Catullus himself ordering himself to stop playing the fool and to realize that what has perished is lost, it is very welcome to have a poem on Veranius' return from Spain and a celebration of Catullus' close friendship with him as a new focus and anchor for his emotional life.

Select Bibliography

Rosemary M. Nielsen. "Catullus 9 and 31. The Simple Pleasure." *Ramus* 8 (1979) 165–73. Highly recommended.

In Carmen 9 . . . home is conceived of as much more than physical shelter for human life; it is a spiritual reality, one found in the bond among people enjoying the closest ties of blood and kindred. . . . Catullus describes himself as an inseparable part of Veranius' *domus*. . . .

The image of his presence in the home suggests that for Catullus friendship is the main-spring of happiness. In Carmen 9 friendship is portrayed as important as, or more important than, the physical shelter afforded by a home. Catullus has so completely integrated the two concepts that friendship seems the logical extension of the home. (169–70)

CATULLUS 10

1   My friend Varus had brought me from the Forum to go
2   and visit his love as I had nothing to do,

or
1   My friend Varus having seen me at leisure
2   had brought me from the forum to his love,

3   a dear little/young whore, as it seemed to me then at first glance,
4   not at all lacking wit and charm.
5   When we arrived here [i.e., where the woman lived], a variety of topics of
6   conversation arose among us, among which, what was [the condition]
7   now [of] Bithynia, how it was faring,
8   and by what kind of money there had been profit to me/what kind of profit I had made there.
9   I answered, that which was [= the truth], that there was nothing for the natives
10 or for the governors or for their staff

or
9   I answered, that which was [= the truth], that there was nothing either
10 for the governor himself or his staff

11 [as to] why any of them should bring home a more richly combed head of hair/
        come home better-off,
12 especially [those of us] whose governor was a
13 sexual pervert, [a fellow who] didn't care a hair for/didn't give a hoot about his staff.
14 "But nevertheless," they say, "you certainly bought what
15 is said to be native to that place,
16 men to bear a litter." To make myself out
17 in the eyes of the girl as the one [fellow] in particular [who was] rather fortunate,
18 I say, "I didn't make out so badly
19 that just because a rotten province had fallen to my lot
20 I couldn't get eight men who could stand up straight."
21 But I didn't have a one either here or there
22 who could put the broken leg
23 of an old cot on his neck.
24 At this point that [girl], as befitted the rather shamelessly opportunistic [slut], says,
25 "Please, my dear Catullus, lend those [fellows] of yours
26 to me for a little while: for I wish to be carried down
27 to the temple of Serapis." "Wait," I said to the girl,
28 "that thing that I had just now said that I had,
29 my reason escaped me/I slipped up: my good friend—
30 that's Cinna, Gaius [Cinna]—he bought [it/them] for himself.
31 But whether they're his or mine, what [is that of concern] to me/what do I care?
32 I use them just as if I had bought them for myself.

33   But you really have no wit and are annoying,
34   on account of whom it is not permitted [for anyone/for me] to be careless."

The looseness of form and straightforward narrative quality of this piece distinguish it from the other poems of the corpus. It may owe its form, at least in part, to the satires of Lucilius, who, as far as we can tell from the surviving fragments of his poetry, wrote satirical sketches that featured realistic description of everyday events and conversations. The satires of Horace, which acknowledge Lucilius as an important model, have the same kind of rambling, casual narrative structure. The Hellenistic mime may also be considered a distant relative of this kind of poem, a miniature comedy of manners.

Skinner (see Select Bibliography) summarizes the traditional interpretation of this poem as follows:

> The secret of its elusive charm resides . . . in its *urbanitas*, that aura of sophistication that elite Romans deemed essential for the fashionable man and that Catullus and his circle in turn elevated into a guiding aesthetic and moral principle. Interpreted in this way, C. 10 becomes an exercise in genial self-ridicule, for its creator presumably is recounting an embarrassing incident that had actually happened to him. In representing himself as a bungling dolt who fibs shamelessly in order to impress a pretty girl but alters his good opinion of her after she catches him out, Catullus the artist has managed to distance himself from the original experience so completely that he can report "the vicissitudes of his own fate with sublime detachment." Through the very acts of inventing a comic surrogate—the "Catullus" who narrates the piece—and of inviting us to laugh at that homonymous character, the author submits neat proof of his own impregnable poise. Paradoxically, then, C. 10 offers a parable of false *urbanitas* chastised and simultaneously manifests the ironic self-awareness that distinguishes the urbane gentleman at his civilized best. (8–9)

Skinner develops a considerably darker interpretation of the poem in her article (see Select Bibliography for a summary of her interpretation).

Initial Explorations

1. Unlike the earlier poems, Catullus 10 does not set up the situation of a dramatic dialogue in which Catullus addresses someone. There is no addressee. What form does this poem take? (1–4)

    It takes the form of a simple narrative with the poet telling a story about himself.

2. What are Catullus' first impressions of the woman that Varus takes him to visit? (3–4)

    He immediately categorizes her social status as that of a **scortum**, in contrast to Varus' more romantic reference to her as his **amōrēs**, his *love*, but his use of the endearing diminutive shows that he is favorably impressed. Furthermore, he seems pleasantly surprised at how attractive she is: **nōn sānē illepidum neque invenustum**, *not at all lacking wit and charm* (4; note the litotes), thus paying a compliment both to the **scortillum** and to Varus for his good taste in women.

3. What direction does their conversation take? (5–8)

    A variety of questions arise concerning Bithynia, from where Catullus has recently returned from service on the governor's staff. The questions move from the general to the personal, ending with the potentially embarrassing question of how much money Catullus made there.

4. Locate the members of a tricolon in lines 6–8.

    The three indirect questions form a tricolon: (1) **quid esset / iam Bīthȳnia**, (2) **quō modō sē habēret**, and (3) **quōnam mihi prōfuisset aere**. The third clause is the longest of the three.

5. How does Catullus characterize his reply to these questions? (9)

    In an aside to the reader, he states that his reply was truthful (**Respondī, id quod erat**, 9).

6. Locate three words or phrases with the colloquial flavor of everyday or street language in lines 11–13.

(1) **caput ūnctius referret**, (2) **irrumātor**, (3) **nec faceret pilī cohortem**.

7. How does Catullus characterize his service on the governor's staff in Bithynia? What complaints does he make? (9–13)

> Catullus is angry and disappointed with his service in Bithynia. No one made any money on this tour of duty. This complaint is emphasized by the triple negatives: **neque** (9), **nec . . . nec** (10). He also complains that the governor on whose staff he served was a sexual pervert who didn't give a hoot about his staff.
>
> The vehemence and acerbity of his lurid comments may be prompted by his realization that he cannot honestly boast of having made a fortune and thereby enhance his image in the eyes of Varus and the **scortillum**, who are interested especially in the topic of how much money Catullus made in Bithynia. He tries to gain control of the flow of the conversation by deflecting it to the sordid character of the governor and thereby evading the question of how much money he made there.

8. What do Varus and the **scortillum** suppose that Catullus must have acquired in Bithynia and why? (14–16)

> In spite of the fact that Catullus says that no one enriched himself during Memmius' tour of duty, Varus and his **scortillum** suppose that Catullus nevertheless must certainly have acquired litter-bearers, since they are said to be native to the place. The assumption in their minds would seem to be that any young Roman going off to Bithynia to serve on the governor's staff would be expected to return with at least a set of authentic Bithynian litter-bearers, no matter how little financial gain he made from his service.

9. Why do you suppose that Varus and the **scortillum** remark that Catullus surely acquired these? (14–16)

> They may be making the remark in complete innocence, meaning simply to carry the conversation forward by remarking that surely things weren't so bad that Catullus wasn't able to bring back what one would expect that anyone would bring back from Bithynia, namely litter-bearers, for which the place was famous. Given the vehemence, however, with which Catullus asserts that no one came back enriched from that tour of duty, it may seem more likely that Varus and the **scortillum** are mischievously attempting to see if they can make Catullus try to save face by claiming that things weren't so bad that he didn't at least bring back some litter-bearers, even though they suspect that he didn't. The polite thing for Varus and the **scortillum** to have done at this juncture in the conversation would have been to sympathize with Catullus for his misfortune and to pass on to some other topic of conversation.

10. What motivates Catullus' reply? To whom does he explain his motivation? (16–17)

> His reply is motivated by his desire to save face and make himself out in the eyes of the **puella** to be the one fellow on the governor's staff who was rather fortunate. He explains his motivation in an aside to the reader, not to the **puella** or to Varus.

11. What does Catullus say he was able to purchase? (20)

> He says that he was able to purchase eight litter-bearers (in spite of the fact that he has just said that no one made any money on the governor's staff, 11).

12. Is he telling the truth? How do we know? (21–23)

> No. In an aside to the reader, he explains that he is fibbing.

13. What does the **puella** request? (25–27) How does Catullus characterize her for making this request? (24) What reason does the **puella** give for her request? (26–27) Might she have some other reason for making it? If so, what is it?

> She requests that Catullus lend her his litter-bearers.
>
> In the phrase **Ut decuit cinaediōrem**, Catullus characterizes her as being as opportunistic as a **cinaedus**, i.e., shamelessly making the request in order to take advantage of Catullus, just as a **cinaedus** would make excessive demands in taking advantage of his lover (note the wheedling address, **Quaesō . . . mī Catulle**, somewhat overly familiar for use at first acquaintance).
>
> The **puella** explains that she would like to borrow the litter-bearers in order to be carried to the temple of Serapis. Since Serapis was a goddess of healing, the **puella** may be

implying (perhaps truthfully, perhaps not) that she is suffering from some illness that requires that she be carried to the temple rather than having to walk.

More realistically, the **puella** may be thought to be requesting to borrow the litter-bearers because she suspects that Catullus has fallen into the trap set for him by Varus and herself (14–16) and that he is fibbing. She wants to catch him up and embarrass him.

14. What does the faltering speech of lines 27–30 imply about the speaker?

It implies that he is embarrassed by being caught fibbing and that he is groping for some way to excuse himself.

15. What is unusual about the order of words in the first half of line 30? Why do you suppose the speaker does what he does here?

The inversion of **praenōmen** and **cognōmen** is unusual and may represent faltering speech as the speaker tries to concoct an explanation.

16. Is Catullus' explanation in lines 29–30 credible?

No. It reads like a lame excuse for his false claim that he did at least purchase litter-bearers. He is probably fibbing about Gaius Cinna as well—concocting a tale that cannot be verified on the spot, hoping to get away with it.

17. How does Catullus' assessment of the woman differ at the end of the poem (33–34) from what it was at the beginning (4)?

At the end he considers her to have no wit and to be annoying, whereas in the beginning he said that she appeared not at all lacking wit and charm.

18. What does Catullus imply about his behavior in referring to himself as **neglegentem** (34)?

Catullus implies that in his social circle he should be allowed to be **neglegēns**. When the **puella** calls his bluff, she is behaving inappropriately in Catullus' judgment and is called **īnsulsa male et molesta** (33). So in poem 12, dinner guests should be allowed to be **neglegentēs** (see line 3), and Asinius is criticized for taking advantage of their carelessness by stealing their napkins. So Catullus in poem 10 implies that he should have been allowed to be **neglegēns** and should have gotten away with his fib.

Discussion

1. This poem does not have an addressee, but Catullus tells a story about himself. What are the consequences of this difference in form? How does this poem differ in tone from those preceding it?

An important point that students are likely to notice is the more colloquial tone and the looser structure of the poem. Whereas Catullus' poems can often be broken up into neatly balanced sections that offer deliberate contrasts or that are tied together by elaborate devices such as ring composition, poem 10 has the form of a rambling narrative, like a story any of us might tell about our own lives with little discernible artistic shape.

A distinctive tone in this poem is created by an unusually high number of colloquial expressions and some broken syntax, all in imitation of everyday speech. The poem has a far more casual and colloquial air than those preceding it.

2. What device has the poet used to guide the reader's response to his portrayal of himself in this poem?

The poet has used the dramatic device of asides to the reader/audience. While Varus and his **puella** mischievously outmaneuver Catullus and force him to fib evasively about the litter-bearers, the poet is frank and open in his asides to the reader/audience (9, 16–17, 21–23). Through the device of these comic asides, the poet lets us see his predicament through his own eyes and allows us to take a bemused look at this Catullus who fancies himself to be so witty but comes off so poorly in this encounter with the **scortillum**.

Postscript

Catullus has been shown up, embarrassed, and discomfited by the clever and opportunistic **scortillum**, and this has forced him to revise his opinion of her. At least in Catullus' eyes the appearance that the **scortillum** projected at the beginning of being *not at all lacking wit and charm* (4) is shattered in the course of the conversation and completely reversed at the end when he sees her as having absolutely no wit (**īnsulsa male**) and being annoying (**molesta**, 33). The apparently casual and loosely structured poem is seen upon closer analysis to turn on this shattering of first appearances and reversal of the poet's judgment as he himself suffers a humiliating embarrassment by being exposed and shown up, even being victimized, by the clever, opportunistic, and aggressive **scortillum**.

It could be argued that the poem's light comedy of manners that turns on these themes foreshadows the next poem in the collection. In that poem the delicate image of the **puella**/Lesbia as she is seen in poems 2, 3, 5, and 7, which appear to provide glimpses of the early stages of Catullus' affair with her, is shattered as she is portrayed as a sexually voracious Scylla-like monster, and as Catullus now sees himself as victimized by her, his love for her destroyed like a beautiful flower cut down by a passing plow. Poem 10, both in its reversal of the poet's assessment of the **scortillum** and in its discomfiture of the poet, prefigures in its comic form the tragic reversal of the poet's evaluation of his **puella**/Lesbia and his tragic victimization by her in poem 11. Discussion of this topic should be delayed until after poem 11 is read, at which time students should review the apparently planned ordering of poems 1 through 11 in what may well have been the sequence in which these poems appeared in the **libellus** that Catullus presented to Cornelius Nepos.

Select Bibliography

W. B. Sedgwick. "Catullus X: A Rambling Commentary." *Greece and Rome* 16 (1947) 108–14. Contains much information on the poem's colloquialisms.

Rosemary M. Nielsen. "Catullus and *Sal* (Poem 10)." *L'Antiquité Classique* 56 (1987) 148–61. Studies the "interplay between the poet's self-image and its projection through the *persona*" (148).

Marilyn B. Skinner. "*Ut Decuit Cinaediorem*: Power, Gender, and Urbanity in Catullus 10." *Helios* 16 (1989) 7–23. Skinner summarizes her interpretation of poem 10 as follows:

> I do not deny that C. 10 can be appreciated as pure comedy of manners. On a deeper level, however, it also may be studied as a realistic depiction of the power dynamics operating within a society organized along hierarchical and patriarchal lines. While the surface text elicits an indulgent smile, provocative references to gross imbalances of power—between commanders and subordinates, provincial administrators and subject peoples, elites and plebeians, men and women—give rise to complex subsurface tensions. Counteracting the suave surface wit, those tensions produce disturbing insights into the uses of privilege, the association of affluence, power, and *savoir-faire*, and the employment of elegant discourse as a handy mechanism of societal control. C. 10, as I read it, deconstructs its own urbanity, first by establishing an ominous link between socioeconomic hegemony and abuse of power and then by presenting the confrontation between "Catullus" and the young woman as a paradigm of class and gender oppression, all the more insidious for taking the form of a frivolous game of wits. (10)

CATULLUS 11

1   Furius and Aurelius, comrades of Catullus,
2   whether he will enter among the Indians at the end of the world,
3   where the shore is beaten by the far resounding
4   eastern wave,

5   or among the Hyrcanians or the soft Arabs,
6   or [among] the Sagae or the arrow-bearing Parthians,
7   or [at] the sea that the seven-mouthed Nile
8   colors,

9   or whether he will cross the high Alps
10   viewing the memorials of great Caesar,
11   the Gallic Rhine, the rough sea, and
12   the distant Britons,

or

11   the Gallic Rhine and the rough and
12   distant Britons,

or

11   the Gallic Rhine rough with ice and the
12   distant Britons,

13   you who are prepared to try all these things together [with me],
14   whatever the will of the gods will bring,
15   announce to my **puella**
16   a few unpleasant words.

17   Good-bye to her/May she live and may she fare well with her adulterers,
18   embracing three hundred of them together,
19   truly loving none [of them], but repeatedly
20   busting the balls of all [of them];

21   nor let her look for my love, as in the past,
22   which has fallen/perished by her fault, just as a flower
23   at the edge of the meadow [falls], after it has been touched
24   when a plow has passed by.

Catullus 11 is one of the great poems of the corpus; it draws a poignant picture of Catullus' final separation from his **puella**, surely to be identified with his Lesbia, in language that conceals a great complexity of compositional structure and literary allusiveness. This is one of only two poems in the corpus, the other being poem 51, where Catullus uses the Sapphic meter, and in it he makes specific, unmistakable allusions to Sappho's poetry. Students will obviously want to explore this Sapphic content, but to make an initial acquaintance with the poem it will be important to ask basic questions of the poem's style and content.

Initial Explorations

1.   Analyze the grammar of lines 2–12.

a.   What two verbs are introduced by the repeated conjunction **sīve**?

b.   What two verbs are parts of subordinate clauses within clauses introduced by **sīve**?

c.   What two prepositional phrases are parallel to one another?

d.   Where has the preposition **in** been omitted where it could have been expressed?

e.   What relative adverb has been delayed?

f.   What antecedent has been placed within the relative clause dependent on it?

    a.   **penetrābit** (2), **gradiētur** (9)

    b.   **tunditur** (4), **colōrat** (7)

    c.   **in extrēmōs . . . Indōs** (2), **in Hyrcānōs Arabasque mollēs, / seu Sagās sagittiferōsve Parthōs** (5–6)

    d.   before **Sagās sagittiferōsve Parthōs** and **aequora** (8)

    e.   **ut** (3)

    f.   **aequora** (8)

2.   Examine the elements of elevated style in lines 2–12.

    a.   Identify examples of anaphora and of asyndeton.

    b.   Comment on the effectiveness of word placement in line 2. Consider in particular the placement of the verb **penetrābit**.

    c.   Identify and explain the sound effects of the words in lines 3–4.

    d.   Diagram the arrangement of nouns and adjectives in lines 5–6. Identify a chiastic noun-adjective, adjective-noun arrangement.

    e.   Describe the effect of the use of polysyllabic adjectives.

    f.   Describe the effect of adverbial and adjectival words that convey ideas of distance, size, or stature.

        a.   anaphora: **sīve** (2, 5, 7, 9); asyndeton: **Gallicum Rhēnum horribile aequor** (11).

        b.   **penetrābit** is bracketed between **extrēmōs** and **Indōs**, where its position reinforces its meaning (word-picture).

        c.   In the phrase **resonante Eōā** the interior vowels in **resonante** echo those of **Eōā**. Also the alliteration and assonance of *ts, ns, ds* and *us* in the final phrase **tunditur undā** may imitate the sound of the beating of the waves upon the shore.

        d.   **Hyrcānōs** (n.), **Arabasve** (n.), **mollēs** (adj.), **Sagās** (n.), **sagittiferōs** (adj.), **Parthōs** (n.); **Hyrcānōs** and **Sagās** stand toward the beginning of their respective lines; **Arabasve mollēs . . . sagittiferōsve Parthōs** constitute a chiasmus (ABBA).

        e.   Polysyllabic adjectives, especially those that are compound words (**sagittiferōs**, 6, **septemgeminus**, 7), belong to the elevated poetic style associated with epic. Hence, they give rhetorical weight and grandeur to the lines.

        f.   As the poet tries to express grand images of far-away places, he uses a number of modifiers that imply distance, size, or stature: **extrēmōs** (2), **longē** (4), **altās** (9), **magnī** (10), and **ultimōs** (11–12).

3.   Trace on the map the succession of places mentioned from line 2 to the end of line 12. What is the overall pattern? What word at the end rounds out the passage by echoing a word at the beginning? What do these words contribute to the tone of the passage?

    a.   At first reading, the pattern may seem somewhat random and arbitrary, but most of the places mentioned have associations with the great Greek and Roman conquerors, Alexander the Great, Crassus, and Julius Caesar. There is a general movement from the remote East to the remote North.

    b.   The word **ultimōs** (11–12) echoes **extrēmōs** (2).

    c.   These words emphasize the great distances that separated these places at the eastern and northern ends of the then-known world from Rome.

4.   The words **sagittiferōsve Parthōs** (6) allude to Crassus' expedition to Parthia, to which he set out in 55 B.C. and where he was defeated near Carrhae in 53 B.C.; lines 9–12 refer to Caesar's bridging of the Rhine in 55 B.C. and his crossing into Britain in 55 and 54 B.C. Why do you suppose Catullus included this allusion in line 6 and these references in lines 9–12?

    The grand images of far-away places evoke memories of the legendary conquests of Alexander the Great, but at the same time Catullus makes reference to the two great empire-building military campaigns of his own day, those of Crassus in the East and of Caesar in Gaul, Germany, and Britain. Allusions to Crassus' and Caesar's attempts to extend and consolidate the Roman empire give the listing of far-off places a patriotic ring. While the imagined travels to far-off places are described largely in terms of sight-seeing and adventure among romantic and unusual peoples and places, the allusions to the activities of Crassus and Caesar suggest the need for public service in the form of military and diplomatic activity on the distant borders of the empire.

5. How is the elevated style of lines 1–12 continued in lines 13–14? Include discussion of hyperbole and poetic vocabulary.

Hyperbole: it is a rather bombastic exaggeration to describe Furius and Aurelius as *prepared to try all these things . . . / whatever the will of the gods will bring* (13–14).

Poetic vocabulary: the vocabulary in these lines is heavy and elevated in the epic style, e.g., **quaecumque feret voluntās / caelitum** (13–14), the latter word being an epic circumlocution for the gods.

6. What appears to be the purpose of the imagined or projected travels? Who will decide what travels will be undertaken? What is the relationship of Furius and Aurelius to Catullus?

a. The purpose appears to be sight-seeing and adventure in distant, romantic, dangerous, and famous places.

b. The gods will decide what travels will be undertaken. The poet does not say *whatever travels I or we decide to undertake* but *whatever the will of the gods will bring* (13–14). This is perhaps equivalent to *wherever we may happen to go*. No one of the three men appears to have any specific destination or purpose in mind.

c. Furius and Aurelius are described as **comitēs Catullī**, *comrades of Catullus* (1), who are prepared to try any and all of the various travels that Catullus mentions (13–14). The adverb **simul** (14) is ambiguous, meaning either *in company/together [with me]* or *at the same time/simultaneously*. Neither meaning can be ruled out, and the latter meaning would emphasize the dedication of the two men to Catullus' projected plans for travel—they are prepared to attempt all the destinations simultaneously if that is what the will of the gods imposes. Their loyalty and their dedication to Catullus know no limits.

7. Lines 1–16 constitute one main clause of a single sentence. What is the main verb in this clause?

The main verb is **nūntiāte** (15).

8. How do lines 15–16 depart from the elevated style of lines 1–14?

The lines form a simple imperative clause, whose object, **dicta**, is modified by very common words, **pauca** and **nōn bona**.

9. What word in lines 15–16 echoes what word in lines 13–14?

The word **pauca** (15) echoes **omnia** (13). The relationship between the words, standing prominently at the beginning of their respective lines, is striking. Catullus' loyal and dedicated comrades, who are prepared to undertake *all* the aforementioned travels to far-off, exotic, and dangerous places, are in fact asked not to undertake any of these travels but merely to report a *few* unpleasant words to Catullus' **puella**.

10. Does the message in lines 17–20 come as a shock after the buildup of lines 1–16? What is shocking about it?

The message should come as a shock, since its content is vulgar and personal, compared with the idealized themes of travel, adventure, and loyalty in the previous lines.

11. How are the style, tone, and perspective of lines 17–20 different from those of lines 1–16? Is hyperbole present in lines 17–20?

The style and tone of these lines deflate the grandiose voice of the previous stanzas. The harsh word **moechīs** (17) and the pornographic description of the sexual activity of the **puella** (19–20) clash with the elevated, epic-style diction and descriptive words and phrases in the travelogue. The perspective is narrow, focusing on a single, compact scene of the woman embracing and having sex with three hundred adulterers at a time in contrast to the expansive perspective of the travelogue with its references to places scattered throughout the known world.

There is hyperbole in saying that Lesbia embraces three hundred lovers at the same time.

12. In what ways is the scene described in lines 17–20 the opposite of the travels described in lines 1–12?

Catullus is the main actor in lines 1–12, whereas the **puella** is the main actor in lines 17–20, creating an opposition of male and female. The socially-approved male bonding among Furius, Aurelius, and Catullus contrasts with the socially anathema sexual activity of the **puella** and her adulterers. The focus on lovemaking in lines 17–20 contrasts with the allusions to making war in lines 1–12. The private scene of lines 17–20 contrasts with the public world of lines 1–12. The scene described in lines 17–20 is one of moral perversion and iniquity, while the allusions to empire building on the part of Alexander the Great, Crassus, and Julius Caesar in lines 1–12 evoke concepts of socially sanctioned public activity in the service of civilization. In all these ways the scene described in lines 17–20 is the polar opposite of the travels described in lines 1–12.

13. Notice that two words are repeated in lines 17–20 from the previous stanza: **simul** (18) = **simul** (14) and **omnium** (19) = **omnia** (13). What contrast do these repetitions invite between the two groups of people and their activities, i.e., between Catullus and his male companions (**comitēs**) on the one hand and the **puella** embracing three hundred adulterers at a time on the other?

Catullus' companions are described as <u>omnia</u> haec . . . / . . . temptāre <u>simul</u> parātī (13–14), and the **puella** is described as **nūllum amāns vērē** (19). Furius and Aurelius reveal their faithful devotion to their friend by being prepared to follow him to the ends of the world, while the **puella** is exposed by her monstrous promiscuity (**quōs <u>simul</u> complexa tenet trecentōs**, 18) as faithless and unloving, merely *busting the balls* (20) of all of her lovers (<u>omnium</u>, 19).

14. What words in lines 17–20 express leave-taking? What words in lines 21–24 reiterate this message?

In lines 17–20 **vīvat valeatque** is a formula for leave-taking. The message is reiterated more indirectly in the last stanza by the poet's exhortation to the **puella** not to look for his love, which is declared to be as dead as a flower that has been cropped when a plow has passed by.

15. Examine the simile of the flower and the plow. What does the flower represent? What does the plow represent? What is the significance of the fact that the flower is at the edge of the meadow? Is there any suggestion as to whether the plowman cuts the flower accidentally or on purpose?

   a.   The flower represents the poet's love for the **puella**.

   b.   The plow represents the **puella**, who has destroyed Catullus' love for her just as a plow cuts down and destroys a flower.

   c.   The position at the edge of the meadow is a marginalized site, out of public view in a nook of the natural world, seemingly protected even from plowing.

   d.   The implication is that the flower has been cut down accidentally, since it is only grazed by a plow in passing.

16. Look at the last line in each stanza. How does each last line bring its stanza to an effective closure?

The last line of each of the first three stanzas pinpoints a significant geographical locale in the description of possible destinations for travel: first the eastern wave, secondly the Nile, and finally the uttermost Britons. The fourth stanza ends with the characterization of the message the poet wants delivered as an unpleasant one. The end of the fifth stanza characterizes the vulgar promiscuity of the **puella**, and the last stanza, the tragic demise of the poet's love (note the effective play on sounds in **flōs**, 23, and **arātrōst**, 24, when the words **arātrō** and **est** are elided).

Discussion

1. Consider this poem as part of the cycle of poems dealing with Catullus' love affair with his **puella**/Lesbia. What position does this poem occupy in the cycle? What is different from the situation in Catullus 8?

    This poem instructs Furius and Aurelius to deliver the poet's final message to his **puella**/Lesbia, bidding her farewell and describing his love for her as dead. As such, this poem could take its place as the last poem in the cycle. Students will most likely be surprised at how much seems to have happened in the affair since poem 8. That poem deals with a rift between Catullus and his **puella**, but there is no mention of other lovers in that poem, and the poet there seems to be divided equally between a desire to revive the interest of his **puella** in continuing the affair and a self-admonition to tough it out in the realization that the affair is over. There he bids farewell to his **puella** with the words **valē, puella. Iam Catullus obdūrat** (12), but his resolve dissipates in the series of questions that he addresses to his **puella**, to the point where his rational consciousness has to intervene before the questioning becomes too intimate and openly sexual and recall himself to his senses and his resolve, **At tū, Catulle, dēstinātus obdūrā** (19). There is no division of the self or wavering in poem 11; the message of farewell is firm, couched in insulting and degrading terms (<u>**cum suīs vīvat valeatque moechīs**</u>, 17), and elaborated with a visual image of the **puella** embracing and having sex with her three hundred lovers that is intended to blacken the image and reputation of the **puella** forever. Whereas in poem 8 Catullus at one level wishes to revive the affair with his **puella**, who is described simply as no longer wanting the playful things of the past (**Nunc iam illa nōn volt**, 9), in poem 11 the poet as an undivided self bids final farewell to a **puella** whom he has discovered to be a promiscuous slut and for whom he no longer has a shred of affection, love, or respect.

    While in poem 8 Catullus describes the **puella** as no longer willing and as having withdrawn herself into isolation from Catullus, in poem 11 it is the poet who withdraws his love from the **puella**: **nec meum respectet, ut ante, amōrem**, *nor let her look for my love, as in the past* (21). The fact that this withdrawal of the poet's love is final is expressed in the simile of the flower that *has fallen/perished*, after having been grazed by a plow. Catullus' love for the **puella** is now dead.

    Mayer (see Select Bibliography) points out that Catullus regarded "his love affair as a sort of marriage" and that in poem 11 "he persists in seeing the affair as a sort of marriage." "To break it off," Mayer argues, "he has adopted the Roman legal form of 'diuortium per nuntium.'" Mayer continues his argument as follows:

    > Whenever the *affectio maritalis* upon which Roman marriage was based broke down, divorce could be agreed by both partners. But a unilateral *repudium* had to be announced either *per litteras* or *per nuntium*. . . . Catullus has an eye to the proper form and appoints Furius and Aurelius to be the *nuntii* of his divorce (*nuntiate*, 15). A husband did not have to give grounds, but Catullus does so in line 17: his 'wife' has committed adultery. *Moechis* are not just lovers . . . ; the choice of word keeps to the metaphorical view of the love-affair as a sort of marriage. There was no fixed formula for divorce when the marriage was entered into *sine manu* . . . , so *uiuat ualeatque* would probably suffice for dismissal. (297)

    Mayer's observations explain much about poem 11, such as the reason why Catullus has Furius and Aurelius deliver the message, why the three hundred lovers are described as **moechī**, and why the break with the **puella** is now to be regarded as final, the affair or the "marriage" being legally terminated by the delivery of the message.

2. Gloria S. Duclos has compared the fifth stanza of Catullus 11 with Catullus 5 as follows. To what extent do you agree with her observations?

C.11 . . . is in some ways a response to . . . earlier enthusiasm. Just as Catullus now truly sees Lesbia for what she is, . . . so he also weaves into this last poem themes and verbal reminiscences from other poems to and about Lesbia. The most rapturous poem of the Catullus-Lesbia affair is c.5, which opens with the startling equation of living and loving: *vivamus atque amemus* (1). The two lovers are exhorted to live a life of loving and kissing, excluding all others. The isolation and uniqueness of Catullus and Lesbia in their love for each other are stressed in c.5. In the fifth stanza of c.11, there are ironic and bitter echoes of c.5. *Vivamus atque amemus* becomes *vivat valeatque* of 11.17. The union of the two lovers, expressed in the verbs, has been broken irrevocably and one partner now fornicates indiscriminately, to the disgust of the other. The percussive *centum, centum, centum* of 5.7,8,9 is ironically reflected in the *trecentos* of 11.18; Catullus now counts Lesbia's other lovers, not her kisses given to him. 5.1 and 11.17 show in the very word order how far apart the lovers have grown: *vivamus* and *amemus* encircle, as it were, the beloved *mea Lesbia*; living and loving should be the alpha and omega of the lovers' existence. In c.11, however, Lesbia is encircled, in the line as well as in life, by her adulterers, *cum suis . . . moechis*; she lives her life with them and thrives on her sexual excesses. The *amemus* of 5.1 is answered by the flat statement of 11.19: *nullum amans vere*, and the ecstatic exhortation of 5.1 degenerates into a true assessment of what Lesbia's "love" really is: *ilia rumpens* (11.20). It is not only Lesbia who has withdrawn from the *amemus*; Catullus' love, too, has gone, destroyed by Lesbia herself (11.21–22). Catullus had declared in c.5 that living and loving were the same thing and thus in c.11 he pictures his love dying as a flower dies; when love is gone, so is life extinguished.

(Gloria S. Duclos, "Catullus 11: Atque in perpetuum, Lesbia, ave atque vale," *Arethusa* 9, 1976, 79–80.)

Most students will probably agree with Duclos's observations. Relationships between poem 11 and other poems that Catullus may have written prior to 11 but that are included later in the corpus will be noted in our comments on those other poems, especially poem 51, which will be closely compared with poem 11. For the time being, however, we believe it is more productive to view poem 11 solely in the light of the **puella**/Lesbia poems that precede poem 11 in the present sequence of Catullus' poems.

3. The comparison of Catullus' love to a flower cut down as a plow passes by (22–24) is indebted to an image of a hyacinth in lines preserved from a wedding hymn written by the Greek poetess Sappho (seventh to sixth centuries B.C.):

like the hyacinth that shepherds trample under foot in the mountains, and the purple flower <lies crushed> on the ground. . . .

Gloria S. Duclos has written as follows on this fragment of Sappho and the image of the flower in the last stanza of Catullus' poem. Again, to what extent do you agree with her observations?

The image which dominates this stanza, the lonely flower at the meadow's edge cut down by the plough, has its origin in a fragment attributed to Sappho. Catullus had used a variant of it in another, presumably earlier, poem (62.39–47), but what is interesting about its use in c.11 is the inversion to which Catullus has subjected it. In the Sapphic fragment, the hyacinth trampled by the shepherds is presumably likened to a maiden's virginity. The passage in c.62 explicitly compares the plucked flower to a girl's maidenhood. The image, then, is traditionally used to express the finality of a girl's loss of her virginity. In c.11, the finality is still there *(cecidit,* 22) but the subject of the image has been changed, the flower has become Catullus' love for Lesbia. As he inverted the first part of the Sapphic image from feminine to masculine, so also he transforms the second element from masculine to feminine, for the passing plough of the simile must correspond to Lesbia. Not only is ploughing ordinarily a masculine activity, but the metaphoric use of ploughing to denote male sexual activity is commonplace in ancient literature.

Catullus has clearly reversed the usual terms of the image: the girl's virginity becomes Catullus' love, and the shepherds' trampling feet become Lesbia's plough. In this final renunciation of his love, the poet's tendency to think of himself in feminine rather than masculine terms is . . . apparent.

(Duclos, 86–87.)

There is more to Catullus' use of the Sapphic image. The reversal of sexual roles in Catullus' adaptation of the symbols of flower and plow is prefigured in the description of the lovemaking of the **puella** with her three hundred adulterers; she here plays the aggressive male role, embracing (**complexa**, 18) and holding (**tenet**, 18) her lovers and actively busting their balls (**īlia rumpēns**). It is exactly this aggressively male behavior, which the **puella** has assumed and which now characterizes her relations with her lovers, that has, like a plow, severed the stalk of the flower and killed Catullus' love.

Catullus has engineered another reversal as well; traditionally the crushing of the flower symbolizes the act of union in the marriage bed, but here in Catullus 11 it symbolizes the demise of Catullus' love and is described in conjunction with his message of divorce that is to be delivered by Furius and Aurelius to his adulterous **puella**. It comes at the end rather than at the beginning of the poet's union with his **puella**.

4. Divide the poem into three parts according to the tenses of the indicative verbs. In what temporal direction do the poet's thoughts move? On what note does the poem end?

To answer these questions, we again quote from Duclos's article:

The poem begins . . . as a look forward into Catullus' future travels; it regresses to the present in the pivotal forth stanza, especially in the last two lines; it dwells in the present of Lesbia's behaviour in the fifth stanza, then ends with the finality and past tenses of the last stanza. Not a logical progression, perhaps, from future to present to past, but poetically and psychologically valid, since Catullus can think about his future only because he has rid himself of his past infatuation for his mistress. (82)

The poem, bravely begun with hopeful pictures of future journeys, ends with the image of death and we realize that the Catullus of the future so grandly described in the opening stanzas is not a whole man, as it were; some part of him has died at Lesbia's hands. The sombre image with which the poem closes somehow undercuts the joyful freedom of the opening stanzas. . . . The *mea puella* to whom his words are addressed is no longer that, the words themselves are *non bona dicta*, and the final image of the poem is one of supreme negation, death. (87–88)

Postscript

Readers are usually puzzled by the apparently disproportionate length of the address to Furius and Aurelius and by the question of whether that address is ironic in light of other poems addressed to Furius and/or Aurelius (15, 16, 21, 23, 24, 26), in which the tone is abusive. To the latter it is usually answered that up to this point in the collection as we have it Furius and Aurelius have not yet made an appearance and that within this poem itself there is no suggestion of irony in the address to them. With regard to the former, it should be noted that what Catullus builds up in the lengthy address to Furius and Aurelius is a sense of their complete and absolute loyalty to Catullus; it is this that allows him to entrust to them with confidence the task of delivering the final message to his **puella**. For further views on the theme of travel with Furius and Aurelius, see the extracts quoted from Duclos's and Fredricksmeyer's articles in the Select Bibliography.

Select Bibliography

T. E. Kinsey. "Catullus 11." *Latomus* 24 (1965) 537–44.
[The] first four stanzas are meant to imply what is expressly stated in the last two; all is over between Lesbia and Catullus and he will now only address her through intermediaries. He prefers the company of his friends to hers (their faithfulness is implicitly contrasted with Lesbia's lack of it) and his mind is full of the excitement of foreign travel. For Lesbia he can spare only a short contemptuous message. (539)

G. S. Duclos. "Catullus 11: Atque in perpetuum, Lesbia, ave atque vale." *Arethusa* 9 (1976) 76–89.
See above and student's book. Very highly recommended.
Comparison of poem 11 with poem 72:
c.72 hinges on the contrast between the "past" Lesbia and the "present" Lesbia, between the

woman who once professed that Catullus was her only lover and the woman who now wantonly abandons herself to indiscriminate lust. In the halcyon days of their relationship, Lesbia had claimed that she would rather hold Catullus in her arms than Jove (*nec prae me uelle tenere Iouem*, 72.2). Whom, now, in c.11 does the "present" Lesbia hold? Not Catullus, not even Jove—but hundreds of adulterers. (80)

Comparison of poem 11 with poem 75:

Catullus' love for Lesbia . . . was ruthlessly destroyed by a human agency, as a flower is cut down by the passing plough. Lesbia herself was this agent of destruction: *illius culpa* (11.22). [Catullus] had expressed this before, in the earlier c.75: *huc est mens deducta tua mea, Lesbia, culpa* (1), but he had qualified the concept by admitting his own culpability: *atque ita se officio perdidit ipsa suo* (2). Now, however, the responsibility is totally hers. . . . Lesbia's *culpa* has been so blatant, so disgusting that it has destroyed forever Catullus' love. No longer is he poised on the horns of the dilemma of 75.3–4. . . . He can now flatly declare that his love has died because of her conduct and underline this by the finality of the image of the flower which has perished after being crushed by a passing plough. (81)

Comparison of poem 11 with poem 76:

[Catullus] is reduced to speaking of his love as a *pestis*, a *pernicies*, a *morbus* (c.76) which he prays he may shake off so that he can grow strong and whole again: *ipse valere opto et taetrum hunc deponere morbum* (76.25). Catullus can be healthy and strong only if he rids himself of his love for Lesbia. . . . By declaring that his love is dead (11.22), Catullus has attained his wish for health. . . . (80)

On the theme of travel in poem 11:

Why such an elaborate and lengthy description of his projected journeys? . . . He is free to roam over the entire world; his options, now that he is released from his emotional dependence on his mistress, are unlimited. The expansiveness of the world now opened to him is reflected in the expansiveness of his description, which ranges across the known boundaries of the Roman world, east to west, north to south. . . . The poet is free to wander wherever he wishes, and does so, figuratively, in three stanzas. (84)

A. J. Woodman. "Catullus 11 and 51." *Liverpool Classical Monthly* 3 (1978) 77–79. Argues against the view that "Catullus' address to Furius and Aurelius is ironical" (77).

Ronald Mayer. "Catullus' Divorce." *Classical Quarterly* 33 (1983) 297–98. See above.

R. T. Scott. "On Catullus 11." *Classical Philology* 78 (1983) 39–42. Similarities between Lesbia as depicted in lines 18–20 and the Homeric monster Scylla and Scylla the daughter of Nisus.

David Sweet. "Catullus 11. A Study in Perspective." *Latomus* 46 (1987) 510–26. A thorough review of the basic issues that have divided interpretation of poem 11. He presents three readings of the poem:

We have now developed two very different readings of the poem. They differ because each emphasizes a different half of the poem. If we take the poem as free of irony, we do so because we are unwilling to let the second half undercut the first. If we respond to the irony of the second half, we seem to be obliged to deny to the first half its tone of unspoiled romance. . . . I base the third reading on the primary observation that the poem, viewed from either of the two preceding perspectives, is cathartic. (518–19)

Ernest Fredricksmeyer. "Method and Interpretation: Catullus 11." *Helios* 20 (1993) 89–105. See above. Very highly recommended.

On the travels with Furius and Aurelius:

What does the message have to do with the extensive address that precedes it, or, put differently, what explains the long address to Furius and Aurelius vis-à vis the message to Lesbia that follows? . . . The flower symbolizes . . . [Catullus'] *love* for Lesbia (*amorem*, 21). This love, the poem suggests (*nec meum respectet, ut ante, amorem*, 21) and other poems confirm, has dominated Catullus' life until now, but since it is now dead, the question becomes: What will Catullus do now, what will his life be in the future? The answer is provided by . . . the first part of the poem. . . . [This] is now seen to serve the important compositional function in the poem of providing a prospectus and affirmation of Catullus' life with Furius and Aurelius in the future, to contrast with the retrospect and disavowal of his life with Lesbia in the past. . . . The new life on which Catullus now embarks contrasts with this past life in most every respect. Then he was in bondage to a worthless woman; now he will enjoy the companionship of devoted (male) friends (*comites . . . parati*, 1–14). Then, we infer, like Lesbia's present paramours held fast by her, he lived a life confined by his love in Rome; now that he is free, he will engage in travels far away from Rome and Lesbia, even to the ends of the earth. The images of the flower and the grip of Lesbia's embraces suggest that Catullus' past life was stationary and passive; his future life will bring rigorous activity, manly exertion, and hardships. . . . In short, contrasting his past life of *desidia* with his faithless, worthless woman, in his projected travels Catullus will pursue a life of adventure and action with devoted and faithful men. . . . what he declares is that his life with Lesbia is finished, and a new life with his friends is about to begin. Appropriately, he assigns to them the delivery of his repudiation of Lesbia, for they are thus given assurance of the end of his life with her, and of his commitment to a life with them in the future. (92–95)

CATULLUS 12

1   Asinius Marrucinus, it's not very pretty the way
2   you use your left hand: while others wine and dine,
3   you lift the napkins of the more careless.
4   Do you think this is witty? Fool, it escapes you;
5   it's ever so mean and ungraceful.
6   You don't believe me? Believe Pollio,
7   your brother, who is the sort who would wish
8   your thefts to be undone by means even of a talent: for he is
9   a young man chock-full of pleasantry and wit.

or
9   clearly the father [i.e., the very essence] of pleasantry and wit.

10   Wherefore either expect three hundred
11   hendecasyllables, or return the napkin to me,
12   which does not disturb me because of its value,
13   but it's a keepsake of a buddy of mine.
14   For Fabullus and Veranius sent me
15   Saetaban napkins from Spain
16   as a gift; I must love them as I love
17   my dear Veranius and Fabullus.

Poem 12 recounts a small incident of thievery. Dinner guests brought their own napkins with them when invited to dine, and Catullus claims to have lost his to the dexterous left hand of a fellow named Asinius, who had a knack for this kind of humorless antic. As so often, Catullus uses the case illustratively, not just to tell a personal story but to make a statement both about what is genuinely graceful social behavior and about the value of friendship in general and his friendship for Veranius and Fabullus in particular. Catullus turns a minor event into a poem—the appropriate witty response.

Initial Explorations

1.   What words characterize Asinius and his crime in lines 1–5?

The important words are **nōn bellē** (2), **salsum** (4), **inepte** (4), **sordida** (5) and **invenusta** (5).

2. Why does Catullus mention Pollio, Asinius' brother? (6–9)

Catullus mentions Pollio since he is Asinius' brother and therefore someone Asinius might listen to more readily than he would listen to the victim of his crime. He also mentions Pollio to embarrass Asinius and to hold up an example of a wholesomely witty person in order to put Asinius and his perversely clever acts to shame.

3. What reading in line 9 makes more sense?

Students will differ on this. The reading **differtus** + gen. is defended by Fordyce, although the word occurs elsewhere with the ablative and nowhere else with the genitive; Thomson's reading eliminates the problematical word **puer** (why would Catullus refer to Pollio as a **puer** if he is holding him up as a moral exemplar, and would a **puer** have access to a full "talent" of money with which to redeem his brother's indiscretions?), but it introduces a very bold metaphor in **pater** = *the essence* (of).

4. What threat does Catullus make in lines 10–11? What rhetorical device does he use to highlight the threat?

Catullus threatens to attack Asinius with 300 lines of hendecasyllabic poetry. The rhetorical device of hyperbole (300) highlights the threat. It may be observed that Catullus is ironically and wittily carrying out his threat in this very poem, though without the full 300 hendecasyllables.

5. The poem ends on a sentimental note. Why does Catullus really want the napkin back?

Catullus really wants the napkin back because it is a gift from his dear friends Veranius and Fabullus and was sent to him by them while on service in Spain.

6. In line 1, look closely at the two pairs of words. How do they echo each other?

Some of the sounds in **Marrūcīne** are echoed in **manū**, and some of the sounds in **Asinī** are echoed in **sinistrā**.

7. Locate other pairs of words or phrases in the poem.

Note the following doublets in balance or contrast, which have a playful, musical ring to them: **in iocō atque vīnō** (2), **salsum . . . inepte** (4), **sordida rēs et invenusta** (5), **nōn crēdis mihi? crēde Polliōnī** (6), **lepōrum . . . ac facētiārum** (8-9), **exspectā aut . . . remitte** (11), and chiastically **Fabullus et Vērānius** (15–16) . . . **Vērāniolum meum et Fabullum** (17).

Discussion

1. What key words are used in the comparison of the two brothers in lines 4–9? How do they define a conception of **urbānitās**, i.e., the sophistication and manners appropriate to a refined city-dweller?

Students will easily recognize key words in lines 4–9 that characterize the personal qualities and social talents, or lack thereof, of each brother: **salsum**, **inepte** (4), **sordida**, **invenusta** (5), **lepōrum** (8), and **facētiārum** (9). These are all words that recur repeatedly in the Catullan corpus in praise or denunciation of different persons' social sensibilities and contribute to Catullus' conception of **urbānitās**. For Catullus these words are invested with such a strongly approving or disapproving sense that they come close to constituting ethical categories. In the urbane settings Catullus is fond of describing, the man or woman who manifests a particular social gracefulness and sensitivity, for which wit is a key ingredient, is held up for our admiration, while anyone who offends against the standards of elegance and social savoir-faire is greeted with abusive ridicule.

2. The literary genre of satire is often aimed at people who act in self-interested, thoughtless, greedy, and ultimately self-destructive ways. To what extent is this poem satirical, and what strategies does the poet use in lines 1–11 to bring Asinius to his senses and to correct his ways?

Asinius thinks his pranks to be *witty*, **salsum** (4), but Catullus corrects him by saying that he is using his left hand in an ugly fashion as might any common thief. He addresses the young prankster as *unaware of what is appropriate*, a *fool*, **inepte** (4) and describes his deed as the opposite of **salsum**. Furthermore, he tries to embarrass him by bringing in his brother, Pollio, who is the kind of person who would make a considerable sacrifice to have Asinius' misdeeds *undone*. Pollio is described as someone worthy of emulation, a prince of true wit and decency in contrast to Asinius with his perverted social sensibilities. Not only is Pollio extraordinarily charming and witty (8–9), but he also does not value money above good manners. His social gracefulness is thus endowed with a particularly disinterested sense of honor. If Asinius doesn't return the napkin, Catullus threatens to attack him with 300 hendecasyllabic verses—the most potent weapon in the satirist's arsenal.

3. How does the poet's valuation of the napkin as expressed in the last section of the poem differ from that of Asinius?

Catullus makes one emphatic point in the last section: it is not the *value* (**aestimātiōne**) of the napkin that disturbs him, but the fact that it is a *keepsake* (**mnēmosynum**) of his buddies. The Latin word **aestimātiō** is usually used of the act of evaluating or estimating the worth of something, but when used in the sense that it has here of *worth* or *value*, it has a more unequivocally positive sense than the English translations can convey. Asinius sees one kind of *value* in the prize he has filched, but Catullus sees quite another. The napkin has a sentimental value. Because some were sent to him by his friends serving abroad in Spain, he loves them as he loves his friends.

4. Divide the poem into three sections. How do the themes of the poem develop from beginning to end?

The poem is best divided into the following three sections: (1) an introductory statement of the situation (1–5); (2) a comparison of Asinius to his brother Pollio (5–9); and finally, (3) a statement by the poet of the napkin's personal value, which contains an implied contrast with the attitude of the thief (10–17). It may be observed that just as the poem's rhetorical style embellishes essential contrasts, such as that between what is witty and what is foolish, between the sordid gracelessness of Asinius and the charming wit of Pollio, so also structurally the poem revolves around comparisons and contrasts, first, between Pollio and Asinius, and secondly, between Asinius and Catullus.

The poem begins with a satirical attack on Asinius for what he perversely regards as a clever or witty act—stealing a valuable napkin at a dinner party, an act repudiated as sordid and ugly by Catullus and wished undone at any price by Asinius' brother, Pollio, the epitome of true grace and wit. The first nine lines of the poem build on a contrast between perverse and true conceptions of what constitutes clever, graceful, or witty action. Asinius quite wrongly thought it a very smart prank to have filched the expensive linen napkin of his fellow dinner guest; his perverse cleverness is out of step with the true charm, grace, and wit that were the cornerstones of Catullus' conception of **urbānitās**.

In the last six lines of the poem the vocabulary of charm, grace, and wit disappears. Asinius' act is now excoriated not because it was out of step with the social ideals of the age but because it attacked and violated something more important for Catullus, namely, his emotional relationship with his dear friends Veranius and Fabullus. Asinius was doubly wrong, first in thinking that his prank was truly clever and second in placing a merely monetary value on the obviously expensive napkin. In the last lines of the poem Catullus reveals the true value of the napkin, not in monetary but in emotional terms, as a memento sent to him from his dear friends Veranius and Fabullus. The reader now realizes the true motive for Catullus' attack on Asinius earlier in the poem, and Catullus' love for his dear friends expressed at the end of the poem transcends both the earlier satirical attack on Asinius and the language of **urbānitās** in which that attack is couched. The language is now that of memory

(**mnēmosynum**, 13), friendship (**meī sodālis**, 13), gifts (**mūnerī**, 15), and love (**amem**, 16)—
Catullus' love for both the napkins and his two dear friends.

In the end the poem champions the significance of humane sensibilities and true friend-ship, such as should ideally characterize the urbane social intercourse (**urbānitās**) cultivated by the circle of friends among whom Catullus moved. The poem begins with the name *Asinius Marrucinus* and ends with *my dear Veranius and Fabullus*. These people are represen-tative examples for Catullus of two important kinds of people that make up his general por-trayal of life at Rome: first, the sordid, materialist boor, and secondly, the dear friend, whose value cannot be measured by any standard other than the pleasure his company affords.

Select Bibliography

Christopher Nappa. "Place Settings: *Convivium*, Contrast, and Persona in Catullus 12 and 13." *American Journal of Philology* 119 (1998) 385–97. Highly recommended.
In the end . . . Catullus reveals that his concern is not with the loss of the napkin, but with the role of that napkin in the maintenance of his friendship. . . . The sympotic background dis-appears, and finally Catullus emerges as one whose real concern is with proper regard for and maintenance of his personal relationships. (387)

CATULLUS 13

1 You will dine well with me, my Fabullus,
2 in a few days, if the gods favor you,
3 if you bring a fine big
4 dinner, not without a pretty girl
5 and wine and salt/wit and all kinds of laughter.
6 If, I say, you bring these things, my charming fellow,
7 you will dine well—for the little purse
8 of your Catullus is full of cobwebs.
9 But in return you will receive pure love/the essence of love
10 or if there is anything more delightful or more elegant:
11 for I will give perfume, which
12 the Venuses and Cupids bestowed on my girl,
13 which when you smell [it], you'll ask the gods,
14 Fabullus, to make you all nose.

Poem 13 is addressed in a teasing, intimate voice to one of Catullus' good friends who had served with Veranius in Spain (see 12.14–17). Readers have always responded to the humor and charm of this piece. Dinner parties are part of the stylish ambiance that Catullus is fond of describ-ing. As we saw in poem 12, such scenes can provide the poet the means not only of portraying the manners of the age but also of sketching some of his own most cherished values, for the Roman din-ner encompasses fundamental aspects of Roman mores and social practices. One should particu-larly take note, in this regard, of the status that usually accrues to the person extending the invita-tion and the reciprocal debt of obligation incurred by his guests. On the surface at least, this poem seems to stand the host-guest relationship on its head.

Initial Explorations

1. What will Fabullus do? Where? When? On what condition? (1–2)
    Fabullus will dine well. At Catullus' house. In a few days. If the gods favor him.

2.   What does Catullus imagine that Fabullus will bring? (3–5)

   Catullus imagines Fabullus as bringing the basics for the dinner: lots of good food, a girl for companionship, wine, salt/wit, and all kinds of laughter. With regard to the *salt/wit*, Nielsen (see Select Bibliography for poem 10) remarks, "*sal* is arranged in a word-order that evokes on one side its culinary aspect, by juxtaposition with wine, and on the other its spiritual character, by juxtaposition with merriment" (149). Note also that the conventionally pious condition **sī tibi dī favent** (2) gives way to a series of conditions in lines 3–5, making the opening of the poem into an apparent joke.

3.   Why can't Catullus provide the usual essentials of a good dinner? (7–8)

   Catullus can't provide the essentials because he has no money (or so at least he claims).

4.   What will Fabullus receive in return? (9–10)

   In return, Fabullus will receive *pure love.*

5.   What specifically will Catullus give Fabullus? (11–12)

   Catullus will give perfume, which the deities of love gave to his **puella**.

6.   What will this make Fabullus do? (13–14)

   It will make Fabullus wish he were all nose.

7.   Structure:

   a.   Analyze the chiastic arrangement of phrases and words in lines 1–7 by finding in lines 6 and 7 words and phrases that correspond in reverse order to the following phrases and words in lines 1–4: **Cēnābis bene** (1), **mī Fabulle** (1), **sī . . . attuleris** (3), **cēnam** (4).

      The correspondences noted here and in b and c below should be diagrammed visually by marking them on an overhead projection of the text.

      The words and phrases in lines 6–7 that correspond to those in lines 1–4 are: **Haec** (6, referring to the **cēna** and the other things that Fabullus will bring), **sī . . . attuleris** (6), **venuste noster** (6, echoing the vocative **mī Fabulle**), and **cēnābis bene** (7).

   b.   What three words positioned at the beginning of three of lines 1–7 echo one another?

      Cēnābis (1), **cēnam** (4), and **cēnābis** (7).

   c.   The arrangement of words that you have analyzed in lines 1–7 reinforces the tight logic of the statement being made in these lines, namely, that Fabullus will dine well if he brings the dinner, etc., with him. What Catullus will contribute is described in lines 9–14. Discuss the significance of the following correspondences between phrases and words in these lines and in lines 1–7: **accipiēs merōs amōrēs** (9) = **Haec . . . attuleris** (6); **unguentum dabo** (11) = **attuleris . . . / cēnam** (3–4); **puellae** (11) = **puellā** (4); **deōs** (13) = **dī** (2); and **Fabulle** (14) = **Fabulle** (1).

      accipiēs merōs amōrēs (9) = **Haec . . . attuleris** (6); **unguentum dabo** (11) = **attuleris . . . / cēnam** (3–4); these correspondences highlight the reciprocity of giving and receiving, with the perfume that Catullus will give matching the dinner, etc., that Fabullus will contribute.

      puellae (11) = **puellā** (4); this echo invites comparison between Catullus' **puella**, to whom the deities of love have given an extraordinary perfume, and the **puella** that Fabullus will bring, who is **candida** but not extraordinary in any way.

      deōs (13) = **dī** (2); **Fabulle** (14) = **Fabulle** (1); these repetitions neatly round out the poem and invite the reader to compare the end with the beginning and to reflect on the unity of the poem that consists of the contrast between the contributions to the dinner that are imagined as being made by Fabullus on the one hand (first half of the poem) and the contribution made by the poet on the other (second half of the poem).

Discussion

1.   This poem is often described as an invitation to dinner. Is it? What would a normal dinner invitation be like, and how does this poem invert and parody what one would expect in a dinner invitation? How does this inversion and parody produce a humorous and comical effect?

As students will be able to realize without much prodding, Catullus 13 works humorously because it inverts the basic sense of a dinner invitation. It may be compared with the following from Horace, *Epistles* 1.5.1–11:

> If you can recline at my table on couches made by Archias, and are not afraid of "a dinner of herbs" only, from a modest dish, I shall expect you, Torquatus, at my house at sunset. You will drink wine that was bottled in Taurus's second consulate between marshy Minturnae and Petrinum near Sinuessa. If you have aught better, bid it be sent, or submit to orders. Long has my hearth been bright, and the furniture made neat for you. Dismiss airy hopes and the struggle for wealth, and Moschus's cause. To-morrow, the festal day of Caesar's birth, gives excuse for sleeping late; without penalty shall we be free to prolong the summer night in genial converse.
>
> —trans., H. R. Fairclough

If hospitality is in the Roman understanding both a display of one's own personal largess and status as well as a token of affection for one's friends, Catullus cuts a comical figure by stating that his friend will dine well at Catullus' house only if he brings all the food and entertainment with him, reversing the normal roles. Catullus imagines the event taking place but offers virtually nothing that would under ordinary circumstances constitute a formal invitation. Everything is hypothetical (*You will dine well . . . if . . . if*), and even the date is left vague (*in a few days*). The poem is, in fact, not an invitation at all but a fantasy, a description of a hypothetical, purely fictive dinner party, at which the usual conventions are comically turned upside down with the guest bringing the dinner and the entertainment.

2. How does Catullus set up an opposition between the dinner that Fabullus will provide and the perfume that Catullus will offer? Note the verbal correspondences that you analyzed above.

The poem divides easily into three sections. Lines 1 to the middle of line 7 state and restate the basic hypothesis, with an elaborate chiastic arrangement of phrases and words that bundle these lines together as a closed unit within the poem. The second half of line 7 and line 8 offer an undoubtedly facetious explanation for why Fabullus himself must bring the dinner, etc. Then the poet's promise to provide the perfume and his description of the perfume and its effect constitute the third section of the poem, and these lines (9–14) contain words and phrases that correspond to words and phrases in the first section, making it clear that the gift of the perfume is Catullus' way of reciprocating Fabullus' bringing of the food and other party makings. Thus the first and the third sections of the poem set the putative dinner that Fabullus is solicited to bring against the perfume that Catullus will bestow on his part, and they set the eating and good humor that one might anticipate on such an occasion against the olfactory delights that Catullus offers in exchange.

3. What is the point of the inverted situation of guest and host in which the guest brings all the food, etc., and the host supplies only the perfume?

Many interpreters of the poem see this inversion only as an elaborate joke, but there is no reason Catullus cannot be serious at the same time as he is being humorous and ironic. Here for example, the opposition between the substantial dinner and the almost intangible scent holds some significance. The poet assumes that his good friend can supply a notable dinner with all the stylish accessories, while he himself pleads poverty. Catullus, therefore, is confessing that he is unable to compete with Fabullus on the level of material assets. One should keep in mind, however, that Catullus came from a well-to-do family, had several villas, and was probably of equestrian rank. The plea of poverty may simply be a way for Catullus to set up the contrast between what Fabullus will bring and what he himself will provide.
However that may be, Catullus does have something that he claims is more than suffi-

cient compensation for his acknowledged lack, namely, a special perfume that the Venuses and Cupids have given his girl. Anointing oneself with a fragrant scent was conventional behavior at a dinner party, but nevertheless it would strike the Romans as odd to put the scent on an equal basis with a substantial dinner. The scent is by its very nature insubstantial, something that one cannot eat but that lends atmosphere and grace to the proceedings. Thus the comic inequity of the situation in the first part of the poem is ultimately resolved by the assertion that such is the excellence of the poet's perfume that Fabullus, having once smelled it, will no doubt prefer to be *all nose*, that is, will prefer the immaterial delights that Catullus is able to offer even to eating. The poem contrasts, therefore, not only the two respective contributions to the party that the poet and his friend are deemed capable of providing, but also the respective abilities of the poet and his more fortunate friend in vying with each other for the superior distinction that naturally falls in Roman social interactions to the one who is able to provide more by way of hospitality. Surprisingly the ostensibly cash-poor poet is confident of coming out ahead in the exchange.

4. What precisely is the perfume that Catullus will give? Is it more or less important than what Fabullus is asked to contribute to the imagined dinner?

Since the perfume in question has been bestowed upon the poet's beloved **puella** by the divinities most responsible for creating and fostering love, we may understand it as a tangible symbol of Lesbia's charm, or as we would call it, her sex appeal. Catullus first introduces the scent in the poem rather abstractly as **merōs amōrēs** (9), in which the plural conveys a generalizing sense, *the essence of love*. Furthermore, the two critical adjectives that define the unguent, **suāve** (*delightful*) and **ēlegāns** (*elegant*), are appropriate also to describing the nature and atmosphere of love. The former is used elsewhere in the corpus (61.7; 64.87) of pleasant odors in an erotic context, while the latter has a more social and less physical connotation to it, being paired with **urbānus** in 39.8. Hence, the scent has properties that embrace both the physical and the emotional qualities of love, a totality of conception common in Catullus.

In addition, Fabullus is described as **venuste noster** (*my charming fellow*), a phrase that is difficult to translate adequately but the first word of which anticipates by its etymological root the later reference to the **Venerēs Cupīdinēsque**, who are the source of the perfume. Thus the friend of Catullus is recognized as someone who could very possibly appreciate the power of love that the poet celebrates in this poem, even to the point of acknowledging the superiority of the poet's unusual hospitality. Although Catullus ostensibly cannot provide a big dinner, he can in accordance with his own sense of what is genuinely important provide something even more delectable, which derives directly from his life as a lover. It is this understanding of the special advantages of his own life, materially deprived as he may claim it to be, that he wishes to impart to his friend.

5. Is the poem a serious description of a possible dinner with Fabullus, or does it have some quite different purpose? If so, what is it?

Lesbia's charm is the catalyst of the poem and of the poet's own realization of what is valuable in his life. With the **unguentum**, Catullus will tantalize Fabullus to the extent that Fabullus will wish he were all nose so that he could take in the fragrance completely. Thus by the end of the poem the facetious description of an imagined dinner is virtually forgotten, and the focus has shifted to the charm or sex appeal of Catullus' mistress and the extraordinary effect it has on men. The **candida puella** that Fabullus is invited to bring with him will not stand up to comparison. Like Poem 86, in which Quintia is compared with Lesbia to the former's great disadvantage, Poem 13 is a tribute to that very special essence that the deities of love have bestowed upon Catullus' beloved.

Select Bibliography

D. W. T. C. Vessey. "Thoughts on Two Poems of Catullus: 13 and 30." *Latomus* 30 (1971) 45–55.
The *unguentum* symbolizes the exceptional, indeed, divine, beauty which Lesbia possesses; a beauty with which Venus herself has endowed her. Catullus is subtly complimenting his mistress. . . . It can be seen from this that the poem is only nominally addressed to Fabullus; in reality its central purpose is to compliment Lesbia. The poet may not have money in his wallet, but he does have a beautiful and enthralling mistress. This is the point that is wittily brought out at the end of the poem; in fact it is the *raison d'être* of the whole fantasy. For fantasy it is: the imaginary dinner-party, which gives the poem its shape and unity, serves only to affirm Catullus' good fortune. (47–48)

Brian Arkins. "Poem 13 of Catullus." *Symbolae Osloenses* 54 (1979) 71-80. Very highly recommended.

James Helm. "Poetic Structure and Humor: Catullus 13." *Classical World* 74 (1980–81) 213–17. The poem contains three jokes, each with its own punch-word, first **cēnam**, second **arāneārum**, and third **nāsum**.

Miroslav Marcovich. "Catullus 13 and Philodemus 23." *Quaderni Urbinati di Cultura Classica*." 40 (1982) 131–38. Suggests that **merōs amōrēs** (9) refers to "love stories" (135) or "pure love poetry" (136). "*Lesbia's* perfume is worth more than a complete banquet" (137); "Catullus' intention with this poem" is "to create a playful compliment to Lesbia" (137).

Amy Richlin. "Systems of Food Imagery in Catullus." *Classical World* 81 (1988) 355–63 (356–58 on Catullus 13).

Christopher Nappa. "Place Settings: *Convivium*, Contrast, and Persona in Catullus 12 and 13." *American Journal of Philology* 119 (1998) 385–97. A perceptive study of poems 12 and 13 as a diptych. Highly recommended.
The joke of the invitation—come to dinner, and bring it—allows Catullus to divide the *convivium* in two: the material aspect supplied by food, wine, and entertainment, and the spiritual essence consisting of the pure, unimpeded enjoyment of pleasure—that is, the company of Fabullus and the *puella*. (391–92) Here the poet has given us two poems which make a more or less clear attempt not only at connecting his poetry to a social milieu, but also at contrasting a set of personal values with those of that milieu. The poet has, however subtly, used his *nugae* as an attempt to scrutinize his social environment and the value systems which support it. (395–96)

CATULLUS 22

1	That Suffenus of yours, Varus, whom you know so well,
2	he's a charming, sharp-witted, urbane fellow,
3	and yet at the same time he writes far too many verses.
4	I suppose thousands [of verses]—ten or more [thousands]—have been written
5	by him, and not—as ordinarily happens—written down on
6	used papyrus: [but] sheets fit for kings, brand-new papyrus rolls,
7	brand-new bosses, red tie-strings for the parchment wrapper,

or

6	used papyrus: [but] sheets of papyrus for the papyrus roll [that are] fit for kings and new,
7	brand-new bosses, red straps, parchment wrappers,

8	and all of it ruled with lead and smoothed down with pumice.
9	When you read these things, that smart and urbane

10   Suffenus seems at another moment [to be/to become] any old goat-milker
11   or ditch-digger: he's so different and changes.
12   What should we consider this to mean? The same man who just
13   a bit ago seemed a real wit, or if there is anything smarter than this,
14   is more witless than the witless countryside/more bumpkinish than a country bumpkin,
15   as soon as he has set his hand to poetry, and at the same time
16   never is/feels so happy as when he is writing a poem:
17   so delighted is he in himself and he himself admires himself so much.
18   Clearly we all make the same mistake, nor is there any one
19   whom you could not see [as a] Suffenus in some respect.
20   Each one of us has been allotted his own delusion;
21   but we don't see [the part] of the knapsack that is on our back.

Poem 22 offers an amusing portrait of a poetaster whom Catullus classifies as a "poison" in 14.19, but the poem manages through its humor to make a fairly serious point about literature and about human nature in general. As is the case with so many of Catullus' poems, we know next to nothing about the background of this piece. Varus may well be the same addressee that Catullus refers to in poem 10, but it is uncertain whether we should identify him as the famous literary critic Quintilius Varus, or Alfenus Varus the jurist and later consul suffectus in 39 B.C., or some other friend of that name. Of Suffenus nothing is known at all beyond what we can infer from the two poems of Catullus in which he appears.

Students will no doubt notice the deceptively simple, colloquial manner in which Catullus fills out his sketch of the charming, sociable fellow who has pretensions to writing grand tomes of poetry. Despite the prosaic feel to Catullus' verse, there is a shimmering elegance of wit and precise use of language here that is entirely characteristic of his style and his understanding of what a poem should be: a natural piece of description or conversation that becomes by its elusive art something more meaningful than is first apparent.

Initial Explorations

1.   In lines 1–2, how does Catullus characterize Suffenus as a person?
       With the words **venustus**, **dicāx**, and **urbānus**, Catullus characterizes Suffenus as a charming, witty, and urbane person.
2.   What picture of Suffenus as a poet does Catullus build up in lines 3–8?
       Suffenus is a poet who writes far too many verses; he does not use sheets of erased papyrus, which one would normally use for such scribblings, but he pretentiously writes his tens of thousands of verses on rolls of regal papyrus, elegantly decorated and equipped, with the papyrus neatly ruled and the ends of the papyrus rolls smoothed off with pumice stone.
3.   Does Catullus seem to approve or disapprove of Suffenus as a poet?
       The phrase **longē plūrimōs . . . versūs** (3) and the expression of an indefinitely large number of verses written by Suffenus (**mīlia aut decem aut plūra**, 4) seem to indicate disapproval, as does the suggestion that Suffenus wastes expensive writing materials instead of using second-hand papyrus, as would be usual for such scribblings.
4.   According to lines 9–11, what contradiction is noticed when one reads Suffenus' poetry?
       One sees that no matter how smart and urbane Suffenus is as a person, as a poet he is nothing better than a country bumpkin, a goat-milker or a ditch-digger. The **urbānus** proves to be **rūsticus**.
5.   How does Catullus further describe the contradictions in Suffenus? (12–15)
       As a person he is a supremely witty **scurra**, whereas as a poet he is more witless than the crude countryside.
6.   How does Suffenus feel about his activity as a poet? Are his feelings justified? (15–17)
       He is never so happy nor does he take as much pleasure in himself or admire himself so greatly as when he is writing poetry, but this is all a delusion since his poetry is so bad.

Compare poems 12 and 84, in which someone is described as doing something that he thinks is witty or sophisticated but that is just the opposite.

7. What observation on human nature does Catullus make in lines 18–21?

He observes that all people have their own delusions and that they do not see their own faults.

8. How many elisions can you find in line 4? What effect do they produce?

There are five elisions in the line; they make the line jerky and may be intended to imitate the poor versification of Suffenus' poetry.

9. Find an example of asyndeton and describe its effect on the reader.

Lines 6 and 7 list four or five items with no connectives. The rapid-fire, breathless listing of the elegances of Suffenus' papyrus rolls enhances the vividness of the description.

Discussion

1. Repetition is an effective device in poetry; the same word or phrase used two or three times can emphasize a point or feeling. How does the repetition of **īdem** (3, 14, 15) reinforce the theme of this poem?

Īdem is a small, prosaic word of everyday occurrence, but its thematic repetition enhances the clever point at the heart of the poem. As used in lines 3, 14, and 15 it introduces an inconsistency or a contradiction and is best translated *at the same time* or *on the other hand*. Suffenus is such a charming, urbane, even articulate man to all appearances, but when he attempts to write poetry he becomes *at the same time* (**īdem**, 3) the antithesis to all that can be called wit and good taste. Things are different from what they seem at first sight. Suffenus does well in the social circles in which he moves; he has the requisite urbanity and grace. Nevertheless, he understands nothing of the first principles of what makes literature charming, urbane, accomplished, and worth reading. This same point is made again in lines 12–14, with the same word **īdem** in the same position in line 14 as in line 3 and with the same meaning. Finally, in line 15 the word again introduces an inconsistency or contradiction, in that Suffenus, who has just been described as *more bumpkinish than a country bumpkin, / as soon as he has set his hand to poetry*, is described as being *at the same time* (**īdem**, 15) happy, delighted, and proud of himself, under the illusion that he is as charming and urbane as a poet as he is as a person.

2. Why are the terms **caprimulgus** and **fōssor** (10) appropriate descriptions of Suffenus when he publishes his poetry?

These agricultural terms offer a natural antithesis to the description of Suffenus in the previous line as **urbānus**. Further, milking the flock and digging ditches, mundane tasks, are appropriate metaphors for Suffenus' practice of poetic composition, because they imply a sordid and endless routine that requires no thought or intellectual skill in the least. That is just the way Suffenus approaches the poet's task when he composes *thousands [of verses]—ten or more [thousands]* (4).

The country connotes for the style-conscious neoterics a realm of illiteracy and uncultivated manners. All the Latin poets of this period of whom we have any secure knowledge had their roots in provincial towns but migrated to Rome and became attached to its cultural life and to elite circles that set the standards of literary fashion. For some of them, practicing the vocation of a poet would become synonymous with living the life of the cultured man of the city. Catullus is certainly to be included in that category.

3. What point of literary criticism does Catullus make in this poem?

This poem addresses, at least in part, important questions of literary standards in Catullus' day. While many of Catullus' poems imply literary statements of one variety or another by the very precise literary allusions that underlie them, some, like poem 22, enunciate their literary criticism in a much more straightforward manner. The Hellenistic poets, from whom Catullus and other neoterics derived fundamental elements of their literary programs, put a premium upon small scale, polished, and finely crafted verse of an original nature. Thus Callimachus, the standard-bearer of the Alexandrians, criticized strongly the imitators of Homeric epic who wrote long narrative poems on traditional heroic subjects. In corresponding fashion, Catullus criticizes with his usual vehemence those purveyors in Latin verse of long epic poems, many of which were modeled on the *Annals* of Ennius and dealt with traditional military and political exploits in Roman history (cf. his remarks on the *Annals* of Volusius in poems 36 and 95). We do not know what Suffenus wrote about, only that he wrote at great length and, as we may infer from his being compared to the witless countryside, with little attention to style and craft, qualities that could only be acquired by a sound education. The short poem was the preference of Catullus and his fellow neoterics, and even when Catullus attempted a longer piece, like his epyllion, poem 64, he made it much shorter than a full-scale epic and deliberately undercut traditional narrative structures with a variety of sophisticated poetic techniques. The neoteric epyllion was actually a rebuttal of the style and aims of traditional epic compositions.

4. Compare the external appearance and the inner contents of Suffenus' **librī** with those of Catullus' **libellus** as he describes it in his first poem.

There is an interesting correspondence between the position of Suffenus as a poet and that of Catullus. Students may recall from poem 1 how Catullus himself used a physical description of his little papyrus roll as a figurative image of the important poetic standards he had incorporated in his poetry. The poetry book of Catullus professed by its appearance an attachment to the very wit and stylistic polish that are everywhere visible in his poetry. The situation of Suffenus is the reverse. The appearance of his book promotes an image of royal magnificence and a claim to be taken seriously, but the contents belie such a profession by their lack of wit and literary merit.

Suffenus' defect may be seen as symptomatic of a larger blindness in the whole culture of the age, which as a result of its generally flawed, poorly educated literary understanding could not distinguish between surface and content, between the literarily trite, vulgar outpourings of Suffenus, grandly packaged as they were, and the deft, ironic sophistication, clothed so naturally, even casually, which defines the Catullan aesthetic. Catullus is not at all angry at Suffenus. Rather, the poetaster is pitiful, the way the general literary output of the times is pitiful in the eyes of the accomplished poet.

Compare poems 43 and 86 for the contrast between public opinion and Catullus' aesthetic.

5. What larger moral does Catullus draw from his observations on Suffenus?

The most important problem with Suffenus is that he is completely unaware of what he is doing as a poet. He not only writes wretchedly, but he is blissfully ignorant of the fact that he does so. The external accouterments of his poetry books are smart and impressive to match his own charming and urbane manners, but the content of his work is hopelessly rustic in nature, that is, uneducated in some basic ways. If he were aware of the discrepancy in himself, it would be blatant hypocrisy, but as he himself cannot see the part of the knapsack that is on his back (21), Catullus can describe the defect as a general characteristic of human nature—one that is encapsulated in a fable of Aesop. There are various versions of the story, but the general outline of the tale represents a man carrying two knapsacks, one on his front that holds his neighbor's faults and the other on his back that contains his own (see Phaedrus, *Fables* 4.10, which is quoted for comparison). Thus Catullus expands the moral of the piece to encompass the universal human folly of being blind to one's own faults.

Select Bibliography

Lindsay Watson, "Rustic Suffenus (Catullus 22) and Literary Rusticity," in *Papers of the Leeds International Latin Seminar, Sixth Volume*, eds. F. Cairns & M. Heath (Leeds University 1990) pp. 13–33.
Suffenus' poetic ineptitude can be summed up under one head—*rusticitas* (lines 10–14). This means that he belongs to that large class of persons in Catullan verse, the non-*urbani*; for to be *urbanus* was to belong to an exclusive club, the rules of entry to which were laid down solely by Catullus and his friends. (15–16) Suffenus . . . embodies three distinct but related contradictions, of which the most important is that between his *urbanitas* as a social being and his rusticity as a versifier. (17) 'Rustic' was in vogue [among the neoterics] as a critical term for artistic ineptitude, and . . . from the time of Catullus at least 'rusticity' came to signify the reverse of Callimachean artistry. (23)

CATULLUS 27

1   You, boy, who serve the old Falernian,
2   pour me cups of wine mixed with less water,
3   as the law of our mistress Postumia commands,
4   she who is more addicted to drink than the addicted grape.
5   But, water, depart from here to wherever you please,
6   you who are the ruin of wine, and go live with
7   the puritans. Here is a follower of Bacchus who drinks his wine undiluted.

Poem 27 is modeled on short sympotic epigrams that are familiar to us from Greek lyric poetry, in which the wine pourer at a banquet is directed to give the guests either a moderate or an immoderate mixture of wine and water. The closest example to our poem comes from Diphilus 58K, given as a comparative reading: "Now pour us something to drink. Stronger stuff, by Zeus, boy! For everything watery is an evil for the soul!" Generally, wine was diluted with water to reduce the alcoholic content. At a banquet someone would be appointed as the **arbiter bibendī** or **magister bibendī**, whose function it was to set limits on how much wine the attendants at the party would drink and how strong the alcoholic content of the wine was to be.

Initial Explorations

1.   Consider possible ambiguity in line 1. After the words **Minister vetulī**, do you expect the line to end with the name of a person or of a wine? Is the wine being personified here?
    After **minister**, *servant, attendant*, and the genitive **vetulī**, *good old*, the reader might well expect the name of a person in the genitive at the end of the line, and some commentators have taken **Falernī** as a proper name, i.e., as the name of the host of the drinking party. Most commentators now interpret **Falernī** as short for **vīnī Falernī**, but the arrangement of words in the line and the endearing diminutive **vetulī** may well suggest that the wine is being personified. In lines 5–7 water is personified, partly by being referred to as **lymphae**, *water-nymphs*, and partly through the two verbs **abīte** and **migrāte**.
2.   How is the juxtaposition of the words **vetulī** and **puer** particularly effective?
    Age and childhood are arrestingly set side by side.
3.   Explain the figure of speech in the phrase **inger . . . calicēs amāriōrēs**.
    The sense is not *pour in drinking cups with less water*, but the word for *cups* stands by metonymy for the contents of cups, namely *wine*, and so the phrase means *pour wine with less water into the cups*.
4.   What is unusual about the person in charge of the drinking on this occasion?

It is unusual for the person in charge of the drinking to be a woman; it would be even more unusual if she is the Postumia who was the wife of Servius Sulpicius Rufus and was rumored to be the mistress of Caesar. This identification, however, is by no means certain.

5.   What is striking about the choice, sound, and arrangement of the words in line 4? Locate an example of personification and an example of a transferred epithet.

First, the repetition, *ēbriōsō . . . ēbriōsiōris*; second, the elisions that join the whole line together into a single "word" with a result meant perhaps to imitate the effect of slurred or tipsy speech; third, the assonance of *o* sounds and the repetition of the *iō* sounds, and fourth, the personification of the grape, described as *ēbriōsus*, *addicted to drink*, a transferred epithet since it is surely those who drink wine made from grapes who are addicted to drink and not the grape itself.

6.   What rule for the drinking was laid down by Postumia? (2–4)

Apparently she laid down the rule that the wine was to be drunk mixed with water, but not with as much water as the boy serves it with. Thus, the speaker has to ask for wine mixed with less water, in keeping with Postumia's rule.

7.   How does the speaker go beyond Postumia's provisions for drinking? (5–7)

He orders the water to depart so that the wine can be drunk unmixed.

Discussion

1.   Where does the poem divide into segments, and how does line 4 fit in?

Like many Catullan poems, this one divides simply into two parts that balance each other. In the first four lines, the poet exhorts the serving boy to pour him another round of drinks, but to make them stronger, as the ruling of Postumia requires. In the last three lines, on the model of the formula of **aversiō**, *averting* (an evil by directing it onto someone or something else), Catullus dismisses the waters that reduce the alcoholic effect of wine and sends them packing off to the **sevērī**. The fourth line is given particular emphasis both by being at the center of the poem and by its striking choice and arrangement of words.

2.   Compare this poem with the lines of Diphilus quoted below. What are the similarities? How does Catullus' poem move to a climax?

In both poems the speaker asks for stronger drink, and water, which would dilute the wine, is criticized in both poems.

Catullus' poem is not only longer, it is far more complex. It involves a little drama that can be reconstructed from the words of the poem. Apparently the slave boy who has been serving the drinks at the drinking party (presumably a **commissātiō**) has not been obeying the rules laid down by Postumia, who had been chosen (presumably by the chance of the dice) to serve as the **magistra bibendī**, the person entrusted with the responsibility of determining how much wine will be consumed and in what proportion the wine will be diluted with water. Since the slave boy has not been obeying Postumia's prescriptions, the speaker has to order the boy to pour *cups of wine mixed with less water, / as the law of our mistress Postumia commands* (**calicēs amāriōrēs, / ut lēx Postumiae iubet magistrae**, 2–3). The striking fourth line, describing Postumia's extreme addiction to drink, then pivots the poem toward its climax. The speaker apparently either thinks that Postumia is now too drunk to notice his next move, or else he is sure that she, wine-lover that she is, will not disapprove of or interfere with it. In any case, in the next sentence (5–7), the speaker himself assumes the role of **magister bibendī** and orders the water to depart and to take up its abode elsewhere, with the **sevērī**, perhaps the same stern old men who gossip disapprovingly in poem 5. The climax of the poem then comes when the speaker as self-styled **magister bibendī** proclaims **Hīc merus est Thyōniānus**, a phrase that has puzzled commentators and the meaning of which is still not completely certain but which surely means that the wine at this drinking party will not be well-diluted with water as the **puer** first served it or even less-diluted (**amārius**) as the bibu lous Postumia had originally ordered but that it will be the pure and undiluted spirits of the son of Thyone. This is the climactic proclamation toward which this brief poem inexorably moves.

3. What role do the **sevērī** play in this poem? How does their role here compare with their role in Catullus 5?

In both poems the **sevērī** serve as foils to the interests of the poet. In poem 5 they would gossip disapprovingly of Catullus' and Lesbia's love, and here in poem 27 they, as water-drinkers, are the antithesis of the speaker's total allegiance to Bacchus. The **sevērī** seem to represent the values of traditional Roman society rejected by Catullus. He will not love as they do, write as they do, or drink as they do.

Select Bibliography

Michael C. J. Putnam. "On Catullus 27." *Latomus* 28 (1969) 850–57. Interprets the words **vetulī . . . Falernī** (1) as referring not to Falernian wine but to the host of the drinking party—"a privileged mortal, perhaps even a god" (852).
Francis Cairns. "Catullus 27." *Mnemosyne* 28 (1975) 24–29. Close study of the poem's language, humor, and wit.

CATULLUS 31

1   Sirmio, jewel of the peninsulas and the islands,
2   whichever Neptune of both sorts holds afloat
3   on clear lakes and on the vast sea,
4   how gladly and how joyfully I look upon you,
5   scarcely believing myself to have left behind Thynia
6   and the Bithynian plains and to see you in safety.
7   O what is more blessed than to be rid of cares,
8   when the mind lays aside its burden, and we come
9   worn out by our labors abroad to our own household god,
10   and we rest in the bed that we have longed for?
11   This is what alone makes up for such great trials.
12   Greetings, O lovely Sirmio, and rejoice in your master
13   who rejoices, and you, O Lydian waves of the lake,

or
13   who rejoices, and you bright/transparent waves of the lake,

14   laugh with whatever raucous laughter you have in store.

Poem 31 has been celebrated for its sentimental articulation of the love for home that all of us customarily experience after returning from a long trip. Though it is a short poem, its composition is very elaborate and deserves close reading and discussion. In the first three lines, Catullus addresses his villa at Sirmio to which he returns in the spring of 56 B.C. with great relief after his term of service in Bithynia. The poem should be read along with poem 46, which records Catullus' feelings as he sets out on his return trip from Bithynia. Here in poem 31 Catullus feels exceedingly blessed to be able to come home and rest, particularly after the cares and burdens he suffered abroad, serving under the governor Memmius, whom he found very distasteful (see poem 10.9–13 and poem 28, which is not in this book). The central section of poem 31 focuses the reader on the poet's sense of relief in putting away his exhausting burdens of the past and in returning at present to his **lar**, the god of his family estate that watches over and protects it from baleful influences from the outside. The basic thematic development of the poem, therefore, mirrors Catullus' own physical and psychological journey as he returns from labors undertaken in the administration of empire to the private pleasures of unburdened ease at home. As in many Catullan poems, the final section, lines 12–14, offers a restatement of the poem's beginning with some modification. He repeats his personal address to Sirmio, this time in less formal language, bidding her and the lake to rejoice with raucous laughter, even as he rejoices.

Initial Explorations

Our treatment of this poem is indebted in particular to Francis Cairns's excellent article (see Select Bibliography).

1. What is the tone of the poet's opening address to Sirmio? (1–3)
     The tone is elevated and formal, as appropriate for a eulogy. The lines have an exalted ring to them, characteristic of epic apostrophe. It is formulaic to address someone in epic as being "the best of this group or that." So for example, Ennius, *Annales* 491: **optima caelicolum Saturnia magna deārum**. Moreover, **uterque Neptunus** is a stylized expression by metonymy for "fresh water" and "ocean," as the elaboration **in liquentibus stagnīs marīque vastō** makes clear. Also contributing to the tone are the balanced pairs of words and phrases (see next question), the use of metaphor (**ocelle**), inclusion of the god's name, and the grand, universal sweep of the relative clause, which includes reference to all the islands and peninsulas in the world.
2. What words and phrases are paired in these lines? Which words are arranged in a chiasmus? Find an example of homoioteleuton.
     Paired words: **īnsulārum . . . īnsulārum** (1). Paired, chiastic phrases: **liquentibus stagnīs / marīque vastō**. Homoioteleuton: **īnsulārum . . . īnsulārum** (1).
3. What does the poet reveal in lines 4–6 about what he is doing now and what he has done in the recent past?
     He reveals that he is happily looking upon Sirmio scarcely able to believe that he has returned safely from Thynia and the Bithynian plains; in simpler terms, he reveals that having left Bithynia he is arriving at Sirmio (presumably after his vexed and unprofitable year of service on the staff of Gaius Memmius, cf. poems 10 and 46, although he says nothing about that service in this poem).
4. Locate an example of anaphora in lines 4–6. Locate three pairs of words in these lines. What effect do such figures of speech and pairing of words have on the reader?
     Anaphora: **quam . . . quam**. Pairs of words: **libenter** and **laetus** (4); **invīsō** (4) and **vidēre** (6); and **Thȳniam** (5) and **Bīthȳnōs / campōs** (5–6). Cairns says that such rhetorical features "are meant to convey the plenitude of Catullus' emotions and to give the impression of a man carried away by his feelings" (5).
5. What further factual information does the poet reveal about himself in lines 7–10?
     He reveals that he has returned home (**larem ad nostrum**, 9) and that he has arrived home exhausted from his labors abroad (8–9).
6. What emotions or feelings does the poet express in lines 7–10?
     Joy (**beātius**, 7), relief (**mēns onus repōnit**, 8), exhaustion (**fessī**, 9), and contentment (**dēsīderātōque acquiēscimus lectō**, 10).
7. Locate the members of an ascending tricolon in lines 7–10. Which of the three clauses in the tricolon is the longest? Which is climactic?
     The members of the tricolon are **mēns onus repōnit** (8); **peregrīnō / labōre fessī vēnimus larem ad nostrum** (8–9); and **dēsīderātōque acquiēscimus lectō** (10). The second clause is the longest, but the tricolon ascends to a climax with the picture of the

speaker resting on his desired bed in the third clause; the desired end of rest after exhausting labors abroad has been reached.

8. What words or phrases in lines 7–10 are set in contrast or concordance with each other?

The following are possible examples: **solūtīs . . . cūrīs** (7) and **mēns onus repōnit** (8); **peregrīnō / labōre** and **larem ad nostrum** (9); **fessī** (9) and **acquiēscimus** (10); **labōre** (9) and **lectō** (10).

9. With what word in line 7 does **labōribus** (11) correspond?

It corresponds with **cūrīs**. This echo brings this section of the poem to a close and leaves the poet free to make his final greeting of Sirmio and the lake in the final three lines.

10. Locate the members of an ascending tricolon in lines 12–14. Which clause is longest? Is it also climactic?

The members of the tricolon are: (1) **Salvē, ō venusta Sirmiō** (12); (2) **erō gaudē / gaudente** (12–13); and (3) **vōsque, ō Lȳdiae lacūs undae, / rīdēte quidquid est domī cachinnōrum** (13–14). The final clause is longest and climactic.

11. Identify the transferred epithet in the phrase **Lȳdiae lacūs undae**. Some editors eliminate the learned allusion in the description of the lake as Lydian and substitute descriptive adjectives instead (see **Text** on the opposite page). What arguments could you make for and against the substitution of descriptive adjectives?

The transferred epithet is **Lȳdiae**; normally the adjective would describe the lake and not its waves.

Those in favor of the substitution argue that the learned reference in "Lydian" = Etruscan is out of place in a poem as direct as this one. Those against the substitution argue that learned references of this sort are never out of place in Catullus, who adhered to the Alexandrian school of poetry that often incorporated learned references of this sort.

12. How do lines 12–14 echo lines 1–3? How do these sets of lines provide an effective frame for the poem? How is the tone of lines 12–14 different from that of lines 1–3? Why is it different?

In both sets of lines the poet addresses Sirmio; each set is three lines long, and these lines thus form a frame or ring enclosing the rest of the poem.

Initially Sirmio is viewed from a rather distant, geographical perspective as a little gem in the midst of all the peninsulas and islands of the world, and the highly rhetorical language reinforces this sense of distance between the poet and his subject. By the time we come to the end of the poem, however, Sirmio is addressed in much more colloquial language, seen from up close now as the poet's beloved and charming home, in whose bosom he finds rest and hearty laughter. Students should by now recognize the characteristically Catullan, conversational idiom in the syntax of **quidquid est domī** as well as in specific, colloquial vocabulary like **venusta** and **cachinnōrum**. The tone of the final lines is thus more personal and intimate than that of the opening lines. In the last lines Sirmio and the waves of the lake are personified. All of this contrasts starkly with the elevated, formal tone of the opening lines.

The tone has changed because of what has happened in the body of the poem, in which the poet has expressed his own intensely personal relationship to the long-desired place to which he has returned from his exhausting service abroad. This leads appropriately to the highly emotional address to Sirmio and the lake at the end of the poem, which just as appropriately *began* with the formal, distanced address to Sirmio.

Discussion

1. This poem is an example of a literary genre that the ancients described with the Greek word *epibaterion*, which refers to a speech or poem recited by someone who steps onto the shore of his homeland upon returning from travels abroad. The Greek poem translated below is an example, representing the words of Ulysses upon his return home after the Trojan War and his subsequent wanderings. What similarities do you find with Catullus' poem? What differences?

Similarities: address to the homeland and theme of joyful return after labors and sufferings abroad.

Differences: the Greek poem has no initial encomium of the homeland as does Catullus; Ulysses has suffered on the sea, while Catullus suffered in a foreign land; Ulysses describes his return as a coming to his native soil, whereas Catullus speaks of coming to his household god and his bed (curiously omitted by Ulysses, for whom his bed in his home was of supreme importance); Ulysses speaks of his hope of seeing his father, wife, and son, while Catullus mentions no people at all; it is love for the members of his family that brought Ulysses home, whereas Catullus seems exclusively attracted by Sirmio as a place of rest, devoid of people; Ulysses concludes by intellectually drawing a moral from his own experience, whereas Catullus concludes with an appeal to Sirmio and the lake to share in the joy that he feels upon his return home.

2. What role does personification play in Catullus' poem? How is it important?

Personification is evident in some of the language Catullus uses to describe Sirmio. Not only is Sirmio addressed personally, but it is called **ocelle** in line 2, a diminutive of endearment used as in poem 50.19 for someone held in great affection. In lines 12–13, Sirmio is addressed as if it had human feelings that enable it to take as much joy in Catullus' return as he does (**erō gaudē / gaudente**), and in line 12 Sirmio is given the epithet **venusta**, which elsewhere in Catullus is reserved for charming people or their charming manner of expressing themselves, referring as it does to the grace that only the goddess of beauty and love, Venus, can bestow. The final point of personification in the poem is also its most beautiful poetic image, the rippling waves of the lake's surface, which are enjoined to laugh with all the laughter they have (13–14), as if welcoming Catullus back.

The personification turns what could have been a quite ordinary effusion of joy on returning home into one of the most extraordinary pieces of Latin literature. One can perhaps see this best by comparing it with the epigram quoted from the *Palatine Anthology* on Ulysses' return home. In that epigram there is no personification of Ithaca but rather an insistence on the physical presence of the soil onto which Ulysses steps. What is emphasized is Ulysses' anticipation of seeing the members of his family again. It is this human contact to which Ulysses looks forward—and emphatically contact with his parents (last word in the poem). Catullus' poem is highly unusual in that it contains no mention of people, neither father (probably still alive at the date of Catullus' return) nor mother and neither male nor female friends or lovers. Catullus does not return to any people or any human being, but to Sirmio (1, 12–13), the **lar** of his household (9), his *long desired bed* (10), and the *waves of the lake* (13). It is Sirmio that he addresses with a term of endearment (**ocelle**, 2), it is Sirmio that he looks upon with gladness and joy (4), and it is Sirmio and the waves of the lake from which he expects some recognition of his return in the form of an emotional response (12–14). He greets Sirmio (**Salvē**, 12), addresses her as a charming woman (**ō venusta Sirmiō**, 12), and enjoins her to share the joy he feels upon his return (**erō gaudē / gaudente**, 12–13). The peninsula of Sirmio has been transformed into a human being with whom the poet can communicate and who can reciprocate the poet's emotion. In lines 13–14, the same thing happens with the waves of the lake. They are to laugh to their fullest as a greeting of the poet upon his return. There is intimate, reciprocal contact and communication with nature here (the peninsula and the lake), but a total exclusion of contact or communication with people—members of his household or society at large (a particularly striking absence for a person as sociable as Catullus!). It is this intimate relationship between the poet and personified nature that makes this poem of return home so extraordinary.

3. Compare Catullus 31 with Catullus 9 on Veranius' return home. What similarities and what differences do you find?

Some of the language in lines 4–9 of poem 31 is similar to expressions used by Catullus in receiving his friend Veranius upon his return from Spain in poem 9. Compare, for instance, **quam tē libenter quamque laetus invīsō . . . et vidēre tē in tūtō** (31.4–6) with **ō mihi nūntiī beātī! vīsam tē incolumem audiamque. . . .** (9.5–6). In poem 31 Catullus uses the word **beātius** (7) to express his happiness upon returning to his **lar** (9); this recalls his use of the word **beātius** in describing his joy in poem 9.11 upon receiving his friend, who has come home to his **penātēs** (9.3). These verbal similarities only serve to highlight the fundamental difference between the two poems, which is that in poem 9 Veranius returns to *people*, namely to his brothers (9.4), his aged mother (9.4), and to his dear friend Catullus (9.6–11), while in poem 31 Catullus returns to no *people*, but rather to the peninsula Sirmio and to the waves of the lake. It is with these that he establishes verbal and emotional contact and communication.

Select Bibliography

Michael C. J. Putnam. "Catullus' Journey (*Carm.* 4)." *Classical Philology* 57 (1962) 10–19. See 12–13 for poem 31.
> The implications of the word *venusta* are not now unexpected. Though such an adjective might well be applied to a geographical spot, it only takes on its full significance if applied to a woman, whose beauty manifests inner charm. (13)

James McCaughey. "The Mind Lays By Its Trouble: Catullus 31." *Arion* 9 (1970) 362–65.
> So, in a sense, the phrase "cum mens onus reponit" does not only say what the poem is "about," it describes what happens in it. As the poet sinks to rest in his retreat, so the reader, who was at first somewhat taxed, is lulled to a pleasant repose. The poem unwinds as the mind unwinds, moving from complication to simplicity. Purging itself of the slightly manic exuberance of the opening, it moves to its elegant conclusion. The last three lines return to Sirmio, but in a different way. Earlier she was more talked about than addressed: here she is almost a living woman. Earlier all the verbs described the visitor—"inviso," "videre," "venimus," etc.—now house and lake are called to life and Catullus listens to them. His gladness becomes theirs. (364–65)

Francis Cairns. "Venusta Sirmio. Catullus 31." *Quality and Pleasure in Latin Poetry* (Cambridge University Press 1974) 1–17. A detailed study of the poem's craftsmanship, learning, imagery, language, style, and originality. The questions and answers above are frequently indebted to Cairns's discussion of the poem.

Rosemary M. Nielsen. "Catullus 9 and 31. The Simple Pleasure." *Ramus* 8 (1979) 165–73. Highly recommended.
> The atmosphere in [the] final verses is one of liveliness and laughter; here is a natural environment uniquely conducive to Catullus' desire for personal renewal. It is only at Sirmio that Catullus can lay aside wariness required by a life in a more public place, and particularly that demanded by residence in a strange and distant land. It is clear why Catullus has chosen to personify his home as his closest human friend. This personification of Sirmio also clarifies the thematic similarity between poems 9 and 31: Veranius and Sirmio are the models of a special kind of human fellowship; the pleasure of another's continued presence and support is the sole requirement for happiness. (172)

CATULLUS 34

1   We are under Diana's protection,
2   girls and boys who are chaste:
3   <of Diana let us sing, boys and girls>
4   who are chaste.

5   O daughter of Latona, great
6   child of greatest Jove,
7   to whom your mother gave birth beside
8   the olive tree on Delos,

9   that you might be the mistress of mountains
10   and of green forests
11   and of secluded wooded pastures
12   and of resounding rivers:

13   you have been/are called Juno Lucina
14   by women suffering in childbirth,
15   you [have been/are called] powerful Trivia and you have been/are called
16   the Moon with borrowed light;

17   you, goddess, who measure out the
18   year's path with your monthly course,
19   fill up the farmer's country sheds
20   with good produce.

21   Be sanctified by whatever name
22   you please, and as you were accustomed
23   of old, with good aid preserve
24   Romulus' race.

Poem 34 is a jeweled hymn to Diana composed with careful craftsmanship in the manner one expects of supplications for divine intervention. Ostensibly it is composed in a form to be sung by a choir of boys and girls, but it will never be known whether it was actually sung on any particular public occasion, as was Horace's *Carmen saeculare*. See Wiseman (Select Bibliography) for a suggestion as to when it may have been composed and sung. Its meter, a system of three glyconics followed by a pherecratean, goes back to the Greek lyric poet Anacreon (sixth century B.C.) and his *Hymn to Artemis*.

The basic nucleus of an ancient hymn consists of an invocation to a god or goddess, followed by an honorific celebration of some of his or her most important divine attributes and titles, and concluding with a request for divine blessing or intervention. Catullus follows the formula here in a very traditional manner. The first stanza sets the scene; the second stanza gives the invocation; the next three expatiate upon Diana's powers and divine names; and the final stanza offers the poet's own supplication for divine intervention and aid. The whole composition reveals a deft adherence to the rather stringent restraints of meter and form. The lines are short, and yet each stanza, brief as it is, functions as a self-contained unit of thought.

Initial Explorations

1.   How does the first stanza introduce the hymn?
        The first stanza introduces the hymn by identifying the makeup of the chorus and the
        goddess to be celebrated.
2.   How do anaphora, conduplicatio, and chiasmus contribute to the tone of the first stanza?
        Anaphora (**Diānae**, 1, and **Diānam**, 3), conduplicatio (**puellae et puerī integrī**, 2, repeated in **puerī integrī / puellaeque**, 3–4), and the chiastic (ABBA) arrangement of words
        in the repeated phrases contribute to a tone of formality and solemnity in the first stanza.
3.   How is Diana invoked in the second stanza? What is implied or stated about her parentage
     and her birth?
        Diana is formally invoked with ō and her title Latonia, which contains her mother's

name (**Lātōna** = Leto); her father was Jupiter; and Diana/Latonia was born on Delos near a sacred olive tree.

4. What deities do the adjectives **maximī** (5) and **magna** (6) describe? Why is it tactful for the adjective **maximī** to come before the adjective **magna**?

The adjective **maximī** describes Jupiter, and the adjective **magna** describes Diana. This placement of the words tactfully avoids offending Jupiter, who presumably would not have appreciated having praise of his daughter come before praise of himself.

5. What activities of Diana are celebrated in the third stanza?

The third stanza celebrates Diana in her familiar role as goddess of wild nature (mountains, woods, pastures, and rivers) and, by implication, of the wild animals that live in or near those locations—and, further, of hunters who stalk the wild animals residing there.

6. What is the effect of the positioning of words in the third stanza?

The positioning of the nouns in the genitive plural at the beginning of each line and of their modifiers in the second half of each of the last three lines gives an effect of regularity and mastery (both of the goddess over her domains and of the poet over his words). Note also that there is a descent from lofty mountains to woods to wooded pasture lands to rivers (presumably flowing in the valleys between the mountains).

7. Locate the members of an ascending tricolon articulated by anaphora in lines 13–20.

The repeated pronouns (**tū**, 13, **tū**, 15, and **tū**, 17) introduce the members of the tricolon, consisting of (1) lines 13–14, (2) lines 15–16, and (3) lines 17–20.

8. Now look at the fourth stanza (13–16), and locate the members of a tricolon in this stanza. Is it an ascending tricolon?

The fourth stanza can be regarded as containing its own tricolon, consisting of (1) lines 13–14, (2) the words **tū potēns Trivia** (15), and (3) the words **nothō es / dicta lūmine Lūna** (15–16). Each member of the tricolon contains a name of the goddess (**Lūcīna . . . Iūnō**, 13–14, **Trivia**, 15, and **Lūna**, 16). It is not an ascending tricolon because the second member is the shortest and the first is the longest. The existence of this tricolon within the larger tricolon extending over stanzas four and five and articulated by the anaphora of **tū** is significant for the articulation of the thought in these two stanzas, since stanza four presents Diana in her three grand aspects and then stanza five elaborates on just one of them.

9. What three aspects or manifestations of Diana are celebrated in the fourth stanza (13–16)? To what three Greek goddesses is she equivalent in these roles? What three realms are involved here?

First, Diana is celebrated as **Iūnō Lūcīna**, goddess of childbirth (corresponding to the Greek goddess Eileithyia); second, Diana is celebrated as **Trivia**, goddess of the crossroads (corresponding to the Greek goddess Hecate); and third, Diana is celebrated as **Lūna**, goddess of the moon (corresponding to the Greek goddess Selene). The Greeks had long since amalgamated these three deities (Eileithyia, Hecate, and Selene) into the person of Artemis (the Greek equivalent of Diana). The three realms involved are the sky (Diana as **Lūna**), the surface of the earth (Diana as **Iūnō Lūcīna**, presiding over childbirth among mortals), and the underworld (Diana as **Trivia**, goddess of the underworld, the spirits of the dead, and magic and sorcery that are dependent on the powers of those spirits).

10. Which manifestation of Diana mentioned in the fourth stanza is elaborated in the fifth (17–20)? How does Diana in this manifestation benefit mankind?

Diana as goddess of the moon, mentioned last in stanza four, is developed more fully in stanza five, in which the moon measures out the months, thus allowing crops to be planted, to grow, to be harvested in due season, and to fill farmers' sheds with produce.

11. What two prayers are expressed in the sixth stanza (21–24)? What is the relationship between them?

First, the prayer that Diana may be sanctified by whatever name pleases her; second the prayer that she may preserve the Roman race. The implication is that only if human beings worship Diana properly and sanctify her with all the titles that please her will she, in return, grant their prayers for aid and preservation. It is the basic Roman **dō ut dēs** relationship of human beings to god, in which human beings give the deity something the deity wants and the deity will in turn give the human beings something that they want. Here there is an alternate prayer, as the poet prays **ut solita es . . . / sōspitēs** (23–24), in effect, **dā ut dedistī**, *give as you have given.*

12.   How is the last word, **gentem** (24), a fitting conclusion for the hymn?

The hymn is a public song, sung by specially chosen youths and maidens for the purpose of establishing a correct relationship between the human community and the deity addressed. The entire community stands to benefit from the hymn, and so it is fitting that the poem ends with a word referring to that community.

Discussion

1.   What conception of the goddess Diana is presented in the three stanzas (9–20) that celebrate her powers, and how does the poet organize his presentation of that conception of the deity?

The first of the three stanzas (9–12) celebrates Diana as mistress of wild, untamed nature, the mountains, woods, wooded pastures, and rivers, and presumably by implication the stanza celebrates Diana as mistress of the wild animals that inhabit these regions and of hunters who track them down and kill them (this is a traditional, paradoxical role for Diana as both mistress of the wild beasts and goddess of hunters who seek to kill them).

The third of the three stanzas (17–20) celebrates Diana as a goddess who measures the year into months and so makes it possible for farmers to reap bountiful harvests. The first and the third stanzas are thus complementary in celebrating the powers of Diana as a nature goddess, first in the realm of wild, untamed nature and then in the realm of agriculture.

The second stanza (13–16) celebrates the goddess in her three manifestations as goddess of childbirth, goddess of sorcery, and goddess of the moon, presiding over the three realms of earth, the underworld, and the sky.

Diana, as was her Greek counterpart Artemis, is traditionally regarded as having powers in all three realms; she is the **dīva triformis** (Horace, *Odes* 3.22.4). Accordingly, it is appropriate that Catullus has devoted three stanzas to celebration of her powers, and he has played on her triple powers by arranging the clauses in the central of the three stanzas (13–16) in a tricolon, with each colon celebrating one of her powers and one of her realms. Catullus has further played on the association of the number three with Diana by arranging the clauses of the second and third of the three stanzas devoted to her powers into an ascending tricolon articulated by anaphora of the pronoun **tū** (13, 15, 17).

The final element in a tricolon is the most important. Thus, in the tricolon contained in the central stanza (13–16), Diana's manifestation as the moon may be regarded as the most important. Her manifestation as the moon is then the subject of the entire third of the three stanzas that celebrate her powers (17–20). This stanza is in turn the third member of the ascending tricolon that is articulated by the repeated pronoun **tū** (13–20). It is also, of course, the third of the three stanzas devoted to celebrating the goddess's powers.

The three stanzas that celebrate Diana's powers are thus carefully organized around the number three, and they climax with the stanza describing Diana's role in filling rustic sheds with good produce for the farmer.

The hymn's final prayer builds on this positive portrayal of Diana's powers, as the youths and maidens pray that the goddess may preserve the race of Romulus with good aid.

2.   To what extent does Catullus present, celebrate, and appeal to Diana as a particularly Roman goddess?

The Roman Diana was identified with the Greek Artemis. Like Artemis the Roman Diana was a goddess of wild nature, the moon, and childbirth, and was thus assimilated also with Luna, the moon goddess, with Juno Lucina, who protected women's lives in childbirth, and with Trivia (the Greek Hecate), goddess of the earth, the underworld, witchcraft, and sorcery. Hence, in her important Roman cult at Aricia Diana was worshiped as a three-form goddess and invoked as **Diāna triplex**, **dīva triformis**, and **tergemina Hecatē**, common appellations of the goddess elsewhere in Roman literature.

The religious formulation of the hymn's supplication also has a distinctive Roman cast to it. The girls and boys address the goddess in the first line by assuming the position of clients: **Diānae sumus in fidē**. Furthermore, the last stanza consists of distinctively ancient Roman religious formulas and language: **sīs quōcumque tibi placet sāncta nōmine** (21–22), and **sōspitēs** (24). It is customary in Roman religion to invoke a god by several possible names and by the kind of open-ended formula found in lines 21–22 in order to avoid giving offense and to ensure the divinity's goodwill.

Select Bibliography

T. P. Wiseman. "Catullus in Context." *Catullus in His World.* Cambridge ENG: Cambridge University Press, 1985, 92–101. Speculates that the hymn may have been composed for performance at a festival of Artemis on the island of Delos in the course of Catullus' return from Bithynia in 56 B.C.

CATULLUS 35

1   I would like you, papyrus sheet, to tell
2   the tender poet, my friend Caecilius,
3   to come to Verona and leave the walls
4   of Novum Comum and Lake Larius' shore.
5   For I want him to receive certain thoughts/opinions
6   of a friend of mine and his.
7   So, if he's smart, he'll tear up the road,
8   even though a pretty girl calls him back
9   a thousand times when he tries to go, and throwing
10 both her hands around his neck asks him to stay.
11 If the report I have is true, she is now miserably
12 stuck on him with a passion she can't control.
13 For from the moment she read your "Mistress of Dindymus,"
14 [the poem you've only just] begun, from that moment
15 the fires [of passionate love] have been eating at the insides of [the girl made]
          wretched/lovesick.
16 I forgive you, girl more learned than Sappho's
17 muse: for the "Great Mother"
18 has been charmingly begun by Caecilius.

Poem 35 has long puzzled readers. It is a verse epistle to Catullus' friend Caecilius, requesting him to come to Verona so that he may receive the thoughts or opinions of an unnamed mutual friend, but in the second half of the poem the focus is on Caecilius' girlfriend, a **candida puella**, who fell in love with Caecilius when she read a poem on the **Magna Māter** that Caecilius had begun to write but had not yet finished. By the end of the poem the request that Caecilius come to Verona is forgotten, and there is no further mention of the thoughts or opinions of the mutual friend, which Catullus was so insistent that Caecilius come to Verona to receive early in the poem. The poem is also unusual in that Catullus never addresses Caecilius directly in it, trusting the sheet of papyrus on which he is writing to do the talking for him, but he does address the **puella** directly and eulogizes her as **Sapphicā puella / mūsā doctior** (16–17). The poem ends with praise for Caecilius' poem, which *has been charmingly begun* (**venustē / . . . incohāta**, 17–18).

Initial Explorations

1. How is Caecilius described in the first line? Identify the elements of a chiasmus.

    > He is described as a tender poet and as Catullus' crony. The Latin words are arranged chiastically: noun A, adjective B, adjective B, noun A.

2. Note that Catullus addresses the papyrus (2) on which he is writing and not Caecilius. How is this unusual? Why do you suppose he does this?

    > When Catullus has something to say to a person, he usually addresses that person directly in the vocative at the beginning of a poem. The address here is also unusual in that the papyrus is personified by being in the vocative case and by being directed to tell Caecilius something (as if the papyrus could speak). Explanations will vary as to why Catullus does this. It puts a certain distance between Catullus and Caecilius (it would have been far more intimate to address him directly). It involves a certain amount of humor in the personification of the papyrus. It softens the delivery of the message; instead of an imperative we have an indirect command (**veniat**, 3). Catullus may feel that all of this is appropriate in conveying his invitation to his *tender* poet/friend.
    >
    > Ovid similarly addresses a writing tablet in *Amores* 1.12.27–30; Ovid is angry at the tablet because it has returned from his mistress with an unpleasant message.

3. What does Catullus want the papyrus to tell Caecilius? (3–4)

    > That Caecilius should come to Verona.

4. Why does Catullus want Caecilius to come to Verona? (5–6)

    > Because he wants Caecilius to receive the thoughts of a mutual friend.

5. Is there any suggestion as to what the **cōgitātiōnēs** (5) might be and who the mutual **amīcus** (6) might be?

    > There are none. Some commentators speculate that the **cōgitātiōnēs** might be thoughts or opinions about the poem that Caecilius has begun (see lines 13–18), but there is no evidence that they are. Likewise, there is no evidence as to who the mutual **amīcus** might be. Some commentators believe that in the words **amīcī . . . suī meīque** (6) Catullus is referring to himself, but this seems unlikely.

6. What will Caecilius do if he is wise? (7)

    > He will come to Verona with all speed.

7. How is the person of the verbs **veniat** (3), **accipiat** (6), **sapiet** (7), and **vorābit** (7) dependent on Catullus' choice of addressing the sheet of papyrus instead of addressing Caecilius directly? How does the person of the verbs affect the tone of what is said here?

    > The verbs are all third person because in addressing the papyrus Catullus tells it to tell Caecilius to come. The third-person verbs then continue: *I want him to receive. . . .*; *if he's smart, he'll. . . .* The tone is objective, somewhat distant, and mild rather than being forceful, personal, or emotional.

8. Who may hold Caecilius back in Novum Comum? (8–10) Why do you suppose she would do this?

    > A **candida puella** may hold Caecilius back in Novum Comum. Judging from her insistence (**mīliēs**, 8) and from her action in lines 9–10, one would assume that the **candida puella** is in love with Caecilius and cannot bear to be separated from him.

9. What physical means of gaining her end does the **puella** employ? (9–10) How does the arrangement of words reflect her action?

    > She places both of her hands on Caecilius' neck in order to hold him back while she pleads with him to stay. The word **collō** is surrounded by the two words referring to both of her hands (**manūs**, 9, and **ambās**, 10), just as her hands surround his neck (word picture).

10. Is your answer to the second part of question 8 confirmed by lines 11–12?

Yes. The **puella** holds Caecilius back in Novum Comum because she is in love with him.

11. Why is it tactful for Catullus to include the words **sī mihi vēra nūntiantur** (11)?

It may be tactful because Catullus seems to be drawing conclusions from what he has heard by way of gossip or rumor rather than talking about the love of the **puella** for Caecilius on his own authority. It may also be playful: "I've heard about his girlfriend!"

12. How does the description of the love of the **puella** for Caecilius harmonize with her imagined actions described in lines 8–10?

The description of the **puella** madly in love with Caecilius (12) explains why she brazenly throws her arms around Caecilius as she pleads with him to stay.

13. When did the **puella** fall in love with Caecilius? (13–15)

When she read a poem that Caecilius had begun to compose on the **Magna Māter**.

14. How does Catullus describe the intensity of the love felt by the **puella**? (14–15) Was the **puella** wretched (**misellae**, 14) before or after she fell in love? Why is the word **misellae** placed so early in its clause?

Catullus describes the love felt by the **puella** vividly with reference to fire and to physiological imagery. It is her love that makes the **puella** wretched; it is not that she was wretched before she fell in love. One could translate: *the fires [of passionate love] have been eating at the insides of the puella [and have been making her] wretched.* The adjective **misellae** is proleptic. For **miser** as an erotic term, see Catullus 8.1 and note.

The early placement of **misellae** also allows it to be heard with **ex eō**, *from that moment wretched*, before it is construed as a genitive with **medullam** in the next line.

15. For what does Catullus pardon the **puella**? (16)

He pardons her for falling violently in love with Caecilius upon reading the poem he had begun writing.

16. Up to this point the **puella** and her actions have been described in the third person. What reasons can you think of as to why Catullus now refers to the **puella** in the second person (**tibi**, 16) and addresses her directly in the vocative (**puella** / . . . **doctior**, 16–17)?

Perhaps because he is so sympathetic with her plight or because he admires her good taste so much that he cannot resist addressing her directly.

17. Why does Catullus pardon the **puella**? (16–18)

He pardons her because Caecilius' poem titled **Magna Māter** has been begun *charmingly* (**venustē**). That is, the poem that Caecilius has begun writing is so charming that Catullus cannot blame the **puella** for having fallen desperately in love with Caecilius when she read what he had written. The context thus draws out a secondary meaning of **venustē**—*in a manner that inspires erotic passion.*

18. What word is repeated in the last line from the first section of the poem? What is the effect of this repetition?

Caeciliō. The repetition recalls the opening of the poem and thereby brings it to a satisfying conclusion.

Discussion

1. Outline the poem's structural symmetry.

The structure of the poem is symmetrical. In the first six lines, Catullus makes his request that Caecilius come to Verona to hear **quāsdam cōgitātiōnēs** (5). In the next six lines, the poet states his reasons for being concerned about his friend's ability to come: Catullus conjectures that a pretty girl who has fallen madly in love with him may retain him in Novum Comum and not let him come to visit Catullus. In the final six lines, Catullus describes the girl's consuming passion and addresses her directly with sympathy for her plight.

2. What message is conveyed in the last six lines of the poem?

The last six lines of the poem appear to contain its main message. They first describe how intensely the **puella** has been in love with Caecilius since reading the beginnings of his poem. Then Catullus addresses the girl, praises her poetic taste as being superior even to that of Sappho, and pardons her for having fallen in love with Caecilius—an entirely understandable event since Caecilius' poem has been begun *charmingly* (**venustē**, 17). (One may compare the effect that Catullus' poetic encounter with Calvus has on him in poem 50.) For a poem that is **incohāta**, i.e., that has only just been begun, to have had such a profound effect on a girl described as more discriminating than Sappho (**Sapphicā . . . / mūsā doctior**, 16–17) is a truly remarkable tribute to the poetic genius of Caecilius and the quality and impact of his poetry. Solodow (see Select Bibliography) remarks: "the girl's ardor measures Caecilius' poetic distinction: the more passionate she, the greater poet he—and she is very passionate" (315). There may be a touch of ironic humor in describing the **puella** as more learned than Sappho, and there may be humor and wry irony in describing the passionate love of the **puella** for Caecilius and attributing it solely to her having read the "first draft" as it were of Caecilius' poem. But the last line and a half conclude the poem with a focus squarely on Caecilius and the remarkable quality of the poem he has begun. Just as poem 13 concludes with a tribute to the charm of Catullus' **puella**, so this poem ends with a tribute to the **venustās** of Caecilius' poem. Everything else in the poem builds up to this extraordinary compliment.

Solodow remarks that the poem itself with its praise for Caecilius' poetry expresses the **cōgitātiōnēs** that Catullus wanted Caecilius to come to Verona to receive (314). Compare poem 12, which itself expresses the criticism of Asinius that is threatened in the 300 hendecasyllables. This may or may not be the case, and the reference to the mutual friend (6) is still puzzling. Solodow is surely on the right track, however, in seeing the poem as "praise for Caecilius' poetry, praise conveyed in a way that is indirect and looks casual but is, on the contrary, deliberate and effective" (314). Catullus is surely not criticizing Caecilius' poem for being unfinished or imperfect—an interpretation found in much of the scholarly comment on this poem and voiced even by Thomson ("Caecilius ought to welcome the criticisms which C. was in a position to pass on to him," 293). The last line and a half of the poem will simply not allow such an interpretation. Papanghelis (see Select Bibliography for poem 86) rightly comments: "According to F. O. Copley . . . *incohata* in 35, 18 means that Caecilius' poem is stylistically unfinished and Catullus invites his friend to Verona in order to suggest improvements. But the expression *venuste . . . incohata* tells against this notion" (376, n. 13).

Select Bibliography

The following articles by Copley, Fisher, Khan, and Fredricksmeyer allow one to follow the history of interpretation of Catullus 35 and of attempts among English-speaking scholars to reconstruct the situation that may have lain behind the poem; Solodow's interpretation, which is in substantial agreement with the interpretation above, seems best to account for the poem itself.

Frank Copley. "Catullus, 35." *American Journal of Philology* 74 (1953) 149–60.

J. M. Fisher. "Catullus 35." *Classical Philology* 66 (1971) 1–5.

H. Akbar Khan. "Catullus 35—and the Things Poetry Can Do to You!" *Hermes* 102 (1974) 475–90.

E. A. Fredricksmeyer. "Catullus to Caecilius on Good Poetry (C. 35)." *American Journal of Philology* 106 (1985) 213–21.

Joseph B. Solodow, "Forms of Literary Criticism in Catullus: Polymetric vs. Epigram." *Classical Philology* 84 (1989) 312–19. See above.

Jonathan Foster. "Poetry and Friendship: Catullus 35." *Liverpool Classical Monthly* 19 (1994) 114–21.

CATULLUS 36

1   *Annals* of Volusius, papyrus expelled as excrement,
2   fulfill a vow on behalf of my girl.
3   For she vowed to holy Venus and Cupid
4   that if I would be reinstated in her favor and
5   would cease hurling my fierce invectives,
6   she would hand over to the slow-footed god
7   the choicest/very worst works of the worst poet
8   to be burned with the wood of a cursed tree.
9   And the worst girl saw that she was making
10   this vow to the gods playfully and wittily.
11   Now then, you who were born from the blue sea,
12   who [live in] holy Idalium and open Urii,
13   also in Ancon and reedy Cnidus,
14   and who live in Amathus and Golgi,
15   and in Durrachium, the inn of the Adriatic,
16   receive the votive offering and regard the vow as fulfilled,
17   if it is not without wit and charm.
18   But no matter how that is, you go into the fire,
19   full of country bumpkinese,
20   *Annals* of Volusius, papyrus expelled as excrement.

A **puella** (presumably Lesbia) has vowed that if Catullus would be reinstated in her favor and ceased hurling fierce invectives, she would sacrifice *the choicest/very worst works of the worst poet*. The invectives referred to may well be what is contained in poem 37, a particularly scathing indictment of a **puella** (again presumably Lesbia) for flagrant promiscuity. Her vow to sacrifice what she regards as worthless trash can scarcely be taken seriously (in fact, it is said that she made the vow **iocōsē lepidē**, *playfully and wittily*, 10). Catullus takes the initiative and fulfills the vow for her by consigning the *Annals* of Volusius to the flames. Nothing further is said about Catullus being reinstated in the favors of the **puella** or about his fierce invectives. No reconciliation is in sight. The poem seems to be making an elaborate joke based on some private incident involving the **puella** and Catullus, and it ends with focus on the *Annals* of Volusius rather than the **puella**. It has generated much controversy and many conflicting interpretations. What is offered here simply tries to build on what the poem itself says. In any case, it offers a number of interesting points of comparison with Catullus 35.

Here is a translation of Catullus 37, perhaps the poem referred to as *fierce invectives* (**trucēs . . . iambōs**) in 36.5:

1   You friends who hang out at that tavern of ill-repute,
2   the one nine doors down from the Capped Brothers,
3   do you think that you alone have cocks,
4   that you alone may screw all the girls
5   and think the rest of us are goats?
6   Or because the whole stupid lot of you sit there in a line,
7   a hundred or two hundred of you, do you think
8   I wouldn't dare to let you have it—in the mouth—even as you sit?
9   Go ahead and think so: for I'll draw penises
10   for you all over the front of the tavern.
11   For my girl, who fled from my embrace,
12   she who was loved as no other woman will ever be loved,
13   for whom I waged mighty wars,
14   she has taken a regular place there. She's the one all you
15   rich and noble men love, and what's really shameful,

16   all you small-time, back street adulterers;
17   you above all those long-haired fellows,
18   son of bunny-bountiful Celtiberia,
19   I mean you, Egnatius, who have risen far by your bushy beard
20   and teeth brushed clean with Spanish urine.

Initial Explorations

1.   What is Catullus addressing in the opening lines and what command does he give? (1–2) On whose behalf is his command to be carried out? Who is the **puella**?

      He is addressing the *Annals* of Volusius, and he orders them to fulfill a vow. The vow is to be fulfilled on behalf of Catullus' **puella** (presumably Lesbia).

           With the address to the *Annals* of Volusius here, compare the address to the papyrus in poem 35.2.

2.   Analyze the first line as a chiasmus. What role do alliteration and assonance play in the effectiveness of the line?

      The line forms a chiasmus with a noun followed by a modifier and then a modifier followed by its noun. The alliteration and assonance in the phrase **cacāta carta** effectively link and highlight the two words.

4.   What can we infer about recent events in the relationship of Catullus and his **puella** from lines 4 and 5?

      We can infer that there has been some kind of rift between them, with Catullus separated or withdrawn from his **puella**, and that Catullus has been hurling fierce invectives, presumably directed against his **puella** and attacking her for whatever it was that caused the rift between them. From poem 37, which Thomson argues is the fierce invectives referred to here, it can be assumed that it was sordid promiscuity with other men on the part of his **puella** that caused Catullus to separate or withdraw from her.

5.   What exactly did the **puella** promise, and on what conditions? (3–8)

      She promised that she would burn the choicest/very worst works of the worst poet if Catullus were reinstated in her favor and if he stopped hurling fierce invectives.

6.   What might the **puella** have had in mind when she spoke of **ēlēctissima pessimī poētae / scrīpta**? (6–7)

      Commentators usually take the phrase to refer playfully to the poetry of Catullus. She would be referring to him in the words **pessimī poētae** (6), just as he refers to her with the words **pessima . . . puella** (9). Thus O'Higgins (see Select Bibliography for poem 51): "[Poem 36] includes a drama between Catullus and his beloved, who has been injured by his angry iambics. She wants to burn the poems, but Catullus deliberately misinterprets and consigns Volusius to the flames instead" (160–61).

7.   Locate elements of humor and wit in the vow as it is quoted in lines 3–8.

      a.   There is an element of humor in that the **puella** addresses her prayer to Cupid as well as to the more august *holy Venus* (3).

      b.   The phrase **ēlēctissima pessimī poētae / scrīpta** (6–7) is itself a kind of witty oxymoron, as if one could even speak of *the* <u>*choicest*</u> *works of the* <u>*worst*</u> *poet* (Thomson takes the phrase to mean *the very worst. . . .*). In any case, the word **ēlēctissima** is a clever word for the **puella** to use in her vow because one normally promised the *best* of something as an offering to a deity.

      c.   Referring to Vulcan with the phrase **tardipedī deō** is a witty circumlocution, echoing the high style of epic epithets without naming the god explicitly, and it may wittily refer to the "limping" iambics that she vows to consign to the flames (poem 37).

      d.   Finally, there is humorous parody of the language of true religious rituals in the phrase **īnfēlīcibus ūstulanda lignīs** (8).

8.   How does a phrase in line 9 answer a phrase in the vow of the **puella**?

      The reference to the **puella** as **pessima . . . puella** (9) answers her phrase **pessimī poētae** (6). If poem 37 is the poem referred to in the phrase **trucēs . . . iambōs** (5), it would be her debauched promiscuity that has earned her the label **pessima puella**.

9. What do lines 9–10 tell us about the attitude of the **puella** toward the vow she made?

The lines tell us that she saw herself as making the vow **iocōsē lepidē**, *playfully and wittily* (10), i.e., as a clever joke. Part of the cleverness of the vow is the language in which it is expressed (see above), but there is more to it than that (see the suggested answer to the next question).

10. What is bizarre about the vow made by the **puella**? How can it be said truly to have been made **iocōsē lepidē**?

Normally when one would make a vow one would promise to do, give, or sacrifice something of value to both the human being making the vow and to the deity to whom the promise is made. Here, however, the **puella** promises to sacrifice something she herself describes as of no value, **ēlēctissima pessimī poētae / scrīpta** (6–7). The *choicest/very worst works of the worst poet* are surely nothing that she places any value on, nor does the phrase imply that she thinks that the deities of love, Venus and Cupid, would put any more value on them than she does. Promising to sacrifice what she regards as trash is bizarre indeed and turns her whole vow into a farce. She is not taking the gods seriously, and she is standing her vow on its head. She is saying that if Catullus is reinstated in her favor and ceases his fierce invectives, she will sacrifice what she regards as worthless trash. If she seriously wanted Catullus reinstated in her favor and really wanted him to cease his fierce invectives, she would vow to sacrifice something of great value to her in order to gain these ends. Her vow is instead nothing but a joke, and both she and Catullus realized this, as the poet acknowledges when he says that she saw herself making the vow *playfully and wittily*, **iocōsē lepidē** (10).

11. What does the word **Nunc** (11) signal with regard to the structure of the poem?

It signals a major shift. While lines 3–5 indirectly quote and then comment on the facetious vow, lines 11–17 are direct address expressing Catullus' invocation of Venus and his prayer to her.

12. What is the tone of the poet's invocation of Venus? (11–15) How does it display the poet's learning? Is it entirely serious, or does it contain some humor? Is it a respectful eulogy of Venus' power?

In incorporating traditional elements of hymns in recounting the birth of the deity and listing the places where the deity is worshiped, the invocation is serious and solemn. It displays the poet's learning by mentioning no less than seven sites where the goddess is worshiped. It contains, however, some elements that may be felt to detract from a potential tone of high seriousness. The first phrase, **ō caeruleō creāta pontō**, sets a lofty tone with the interjection **ō**, the traditional ornamental epithet, and the evocation of the goddess by referring to her birth without actually naming her. The next two lines (12–13) become problematic in naming two famous Greek sites traditionally associated with Aphrodite but by sandwiching two Italian sites in between, one of which can no longer even be identified with certainty and has no known connection with Aphrodite or Venus. The chiastic order (Greek **Īdalium** followed by Italian **Ūriōs**; then Italian **Ancōna** followed by Greek **Cnidum**) emphasizes the playful intermingling of Greek and Italian sites. In the final citation (**Dyrrachium Hadriae tabernam**, 15) the humor comes to the fore, especially for readers who remember the description of the city's inhabitants in Plautus, in the implication that the city is the brothel of the Adriatic, playfully highlighting the goddess's most mundane role among mortals. Whether regarded as solemn, mock-solemn, or humorous, however, Catullus' invocation of the deity constitutes a respectful eulogy of her universal power.

13. What does the poet request of Venus (16) after his invocation of her?

He requests that she receive the votive offering and thereby regard the vow made by the **puella** as discharged or fulfilled. The **puella** in making her vow did not specify particular writings of a particular poet, although she and Catullus may have understood the reference to be to Catullus' poetry. Catullus on his own initiative has now brought the *Annals* of Volusius. In lines 1–2 he ordered them to fulfill the vow on behalf of the **puella**; he now requests that Venus receive them as the votive offering (**acceptum face**) and regard the vow made by the **puella** as fulfilled (**face redditum**).

14. Explain how the descriptive phrases in line 17 apply to the two different things that are referred to with the word **vōtum** in line 16.

   The original vow was said to have been made **iocōsē lepidē** (10), and so it can be described as **nōn illepidum neque invenustum** here (note the litotes); Catullus' proffering of the *Annals* of Volusius as the votive offering can also be described as witty and charming, as he turns the tables on the **puella** and cleverly gets the jump on her in fulfilling her own vow.

15. What does the use of the qualifying word **intereā** (18) imply?

   The poet has ordered Venus to receive the *Annals* as the votive offering and to regard the vow as fulfilled (16), *if it is not without wit and charm* (17), but whether Venus will regard it as *not without wit and charm* and whether she will receive the votive offering and regard the vow as fulfilled are questions that only Venus can answer. However that may be (**intereā**, 18), Catullus takes the initiative without waiting for a sign from the deity and consigns the *Annals* to the flames.

16. How does line 18 echo line 2?

   Line 18 echoes line 2 by again ordering the *Annals* of Volusius to discharge or fulfill the vow, but now more specifically by ordering them to go into the fire.

17. How does line 20 echo line 1?

   It echoes it by repeating it and thus bringing the poem full circle back to where it began, but with the reader now having far greater knowledge of the situation.

18. What is accomplished by Catullus' violating the symmetry of the opening and closing lines of the poem by adding line 19?

   The line expands on the description of the *Annals* of Volusius. So far we have been told only that they are **cacāta carta** (1). Now they are described as the diametric opposite of the urbanity and wit that Catullus valued and embodied both in his poetry and in his life. As such they are totally worthless, and Catullus shows why they deserve being addressed with the scatological phrase **cacāta carta**, *papyrus expelled as excrement.*

Discussion

1. What does the poem imply about the present and future relationship between Catullus and the **puella**?

   Very little. What will happen when Catullus will have fulfilled the vow made by the **puella**? Does his fulfillment of it mean that he is reinstating himself in her favor and promising to cease his invectives? Will she allow him to be reinstated in her favor? Will he actually cease his fierce invectives? Nothing is said about any of these matters in the poem. There is no hint of a reconciliation or in fact of any communication between Catullus and Lesbia subsequent to her making of the vow. What stands out above all in the poem is the incredible vulgarity of the opening and closing lines describing the poet's own private fulfillment of the vow. The poem concerns Volusius and his *Annals* as much as or more than it concerns the **puella**, and, remarkably, the poet rises above it all with his own charming and witty prayer to Venus (11–17), a veritable paradigm of neoteric verse.

2. Compare Catullus 36 with Catullus 35. What are some of the similarities and differences?

   Similarities:
   The poems deal with evaluation of poetry and with love affairs.
   Both poems are addressed to papyrus: **papȳre** (35.2) and **cacāta carta** (36.1).

Differences:

Poem 35:
Caecilius' *Magna Mater*: good poetry
Unnamed **puella**
Beginning of a love affair
Puella praised, described as **Sapphicā puella** / **mūsā doctior** (16–17).
Puella reacts to her reading of Caecilius' *Magna Mater* by falling desperately in love with him.

Highest praise for both Caecilius' *Magna Mater* and the **puella**.

Poem 36:
Volusius' *Annals*: bad poetry
Catullus' **puella**, presumably Lesbia
Estrangement of lovers
Catullus' **puella** described as **pessima . . . puella** (9)
The **puella** reacts to her reading of Catullus' fierce invectives (perhaps those preserved in poem 37) by formulating her vow.
Condemnation of Volusius' *Annals* and unresolved relationship between Catullus and the **puella** (presumably Lesbia).

The major similarity between the two poems is the intermingling of themes of love and poetry. The extravagant love of the **puella** for Caecilius in poem 35 contrasts with the estrangement between Catullus and the **puella** in poem 36, and Catullus' high praise of Caecilius in poem 35 contrasts with his scatological denigration of Volusius' poetry in poem 36. In both poems it may be that the themes of literary evaluation are more important than the love themes. Certainly the first and last lines of poem 36 are its most memorable.

Select Bibliography

H. Comfort. "An Interpretation of Catullus XXXVI." *Classical Philology* 24 (1929) 176–82. Summarizes earlier scholars' explanations of the circumstances that gave rise to poem 36 and offers one of his own that admittedly contains "much speculation" based on "few facts" (180).

Joseph Solodow. "Forms of Literary Criticism in Catullus: Polymetric Vs. Epigram." *Classical Philology* 84 (1989) 312–19. Compares poems 35 and 36 as pieces of literary criticism.

CATULLUS 43

1 Greetings, girl with a nose that's not very small
2 and a foot that isn't pretty and eyes that aren't dark
3 and fingers that aren't long and a mouth that's not dry
4 and a tongue that's certainly none too elegant.
5 You who are the paid mistress of the bankrupt from Formiae,
6 does the province describe you as pretty?
7 Is our Lesbia compared with you?
8 O foolish and tasteless age!

Poem 43 is a piece of invective aimed at the mistress of the bankrupt from Formiae. The dissipated spendthrift is generally agreed to be Mamurra, Caesar's chief engineer (**praefectus fabrum**) in the Gallic campaigns and a particular object of hatred for Catullus from one end of the corpus to the other (see poems 29, 41, 43, 57, 94, 105, 114, and 115). He is an important figure in the poetry of Catullus, because he appears to represent what Catullus was most enraged by in the society of his day. The poet accuses him of being the worst kind of upstart, a man of unworthy origins—hence the reference to the small and insignificant town of Formiae in the present poem—who used his connection with Caesar to amass a tremendous, yet undeserved, fortune, which he then squandered—hence he is a bankrupt—in the most scandalous fashion on luxurious living and innumerable women. His **amīca**, who is called Ameana in poem 41, is to Catullus' way of thinking one revealing specimen of his debauched taste and character.

Compare poems 22 and 86 for the contrast between public opinion and Catullus' values.

Initial Explorations

1. Specifically, what does Catullus find distasteful about the girl? (1–4)

    She has a large nose, ugly feet, the wrong color of eyes, short fingers, and a drooling mouth, and she lacks elegance in her speech.

2. Identify examples of litotes in lines 1–4, and explain why the device is effective.

    With a nose that's not very small = with a big nose; with *a foot that isn't pretty* = with an ugly foot; with *eyes that aren't dark* = with eyes of an unfashionable color; with *fingers that aren't long* = with short fingers; with *a mouth that's not dry* = with a drooling mouth; with *a tongue that's certainly none too elegant* = with a very inelegant tongue. The device is devastating because instead of simply describing ugly characteristics it emphatically denies the presence of attractive ones.

3. What other rhetorical device heightens the impact of lines 1–4? How is line 3 related to line 2 in positioning of words? What word in line 4 corresponds to **minimō** in line 1? How is line 4 an appropriate climax in the series?

    Anaphora (repeated **nec**) heightens the impact by hammering on each item in the series. The words in line 3 are positioned exactly parallel to those in line 2, except for the phrase **ōre siccō**, in which the order of the noun and the adjective is the reverse of that in the other phrases, so that the last word, **siccō**, echoes the first adjective, **bellō** (2). The word **nimis**, *too much*, corresponds to **minimō**, *very small*, in line 1. The effect of all of this very careful rhetorical and stylistic arrangement of words is to highlight the poet's masterful control of his language and thought as he relentlessly attacks the girl's appearance and character.

4. What does line 5 add to the disparaging attack on the girl?

    It attacks both her moral character and her good judgment by describing her as the paid mistress of a notorious bankrupted spendthrift, presumably Mamurra.

5. What is the tone of the last three lines? What two rhetorical devices add to the effect?

    The tone is one of righteous indignation. The tone is emphasized by anaphora (**tē**, 6, **Tē**, 7), rhetorical questions (6, 7), and by the interjection **Ō** introducing the final rhetorical exclamation.

6. What generalization does Catullus make in the last line? What has led him to this conclusion?

    Catullus concludes that the age in which he lives is *foolish* and *tasteless*, since the woman described in the poem is thought of as pretty and is even compared with his Lesbia.

7. How might this poem give us a glimpse of what the poet found most attractive about Lesbia?

    The poet's horror at the thought of this woman's being compared with his Lesbia suggests that Lesbia possesses all the good characteristics that are denied to the woman in the poem, so that it would be implied that Lesbia has a very small nose, beautiful feet, eyes fashionable in color, long fingers, a dry mouth, and a very elegant tongue. It would also be implied that she is sufficiently virtuous not to be a paid mistress of anyone and that she would have enough sense not to associate with people like the bankrupt of Formiae.

Discussion

1. Summarize how Catullus in such a brief span draws a devastating portrait of the **puella** and her lover.

    The first five lines offer the girl a greeting, which begins in a friendly manner with **Salvē**, as if he were addressing an acquaintance in an amicable tone of voice. But the vocative of address, **puella**, is extended in grotesque fashion by layer upon layer of qualifying descriptions that build up in a crescendo of controlled but bitter invective. The word **nec** is repeated five times with devastating denials of individual attributes of beauty in the girl. She is the antithesis of all that is commonly considered **bella** in a woman. The catalogue of blemishes marks her physical repulsiveness point by point but ends with climactic emphasis by denying her any elegance of tongue or wit. Her personality is as coarse and as crude as her looks. And what seals her fate as a *femme manquée* is, finally, her association with the monstrous spendthrift Mamurra. Only he could lavish his fortune on someone so obviously unsuitable.

2.   Why does the poet mention Lesbia in such an unpleasant context?

The poem is a piece of rancorous invective, but still the poet cleverly manages to work in an indirect compliment to Lesbia, his own beloved. In the logic of the poem's argument, we are drawn to associate her with all the positive qualities denied to Ameana. The idealized portrait of womanhood negated by her repulsiveness turns out to have a source after all. This source is not merely a catalogue of stereotypes but the very image of Lesbia herself, a model of beauty and of social wit and gracefulness, to which Catullus refers all his judgments in taste. The province of Cisalpine Gaul where Caesar had his winter quarters may shockingly think of Ameana as a beauty, but this only proves how foolish and tasteless are the times. The gross standards of taste and decorum of the age are an outrage to the humane and sensitive poet. His own ideal, however, his beloved Lesbia, measures their deficiency in every respect.

Select Bibliography

H. D. Rankin. "Catullus and the Beauty of Lesbia (Poems 43, 86 and 51)." *Latomus* 35 (1976) 3–11.
      Of Catullus' possible reasons for omitting to describe Lesbia's appearance in his poems, the most obvious suggestion that springs to mind is that of poem 86: he was interested in her as a complete person rather than an embodiment of handsome features. (3)
Marilyn B. Skinner. "Ameana, Puella Defututa." *The Classical Journal* 74 (1978–79) 110–14.
      To this arrestingly ugly *amica* Catullus then opposes her complete antithesis, the perfect *bella puella*. In the province Ameana does have her admirers; in the province she is actually being compared to his own splendid Lesbia. There is no need to debate which province, or to wonder how the author's flesh-and-blood mistress came to be renowned in some remote corner of the Roman empire. In poem 43 Lesbia's function is primarily symbolic: she evokes Catullus' own criteria of grace and elegance and incarnates that set of poetic, social and aesthetic values which forms his ideal of *urbanitas*. Correspondingly, "the province" stands for a metaphorical region beyond the pale of sophisticated society, the spiritual domain of the *inurbani*. In that cultural wasteland Ameana's presumption has been rewarded; there she is proclaimed as a formidable rival to the pattern of all feminine beauty. *O saeclum insapiens et infacetum*: an age which takes her claims seriously, and cannot perceive their absurdity, must be thick-skulled indeed. (113–14)
W. C. McDermott. "Catullus, Clodia and Ameana." *Maia* 36 (1984) 3–11. On poems 41 and 43; conjecturally reconstructs Catullus' relationships with Ameana.

CATULLUS 44

1   O estate of mine, whether Sabine or Tiburtine
2   (for those to whom it is not pleasing to hurt Catullus
3   call you Tiburtine, while those to whom it is pleasing
4   argue on any stake that you are Sabine),

5   but whether you are Sabine or more truly Tiburtine,
6   I gladly spent time in your villa located close to
7   the city, and I drove a nasty cough out of my chest,
8   which my stomach, as I surely deserved,
9   while I was seeking sumptuous dinners, gave me.
10   For wishing to be a "Sestian guest,"
11   I read his speech against Antius, a candidate [for office],
12   which is full of poison and pestilence.
13   Thereupon a chilly cold and constant cough
14   shook me continually, until I fled to your bosom,
15   and healed myself by rest and stinging nettles.
16   So now restored I extend to you greatest
17   thanks for not punishing my error.
18   Nor do I offer any prayer, if in the future I take up
19   Sestius' abominable writings, to prevent their frigidity
20   from bringing a cold and cough, not to me, but to Sestius himself,
21   who only invites me to dinner when I read his nasty book.

The poem is usually regarded as simply an excuse for the pun on **frīgus** or an attack on Sestius' literary style, but there is more to the poem than that. It is important to recognize the poem as a parody of an address to a deity and to see its critique of society as directed on the one hand against Sestius and all that he represents and on the other hand against the poet himself for falling prey to the attractions of Sestius' morally bankrupt social world. Catullus' country estate effects a double cure, both of Catullus' cold and of his hunger for status in Sestius' world, and he accordingly addresses it as if were a savior god and prays that Sestius may be hoist on his own petard.

Initial Explorations

1.   In what two ways do people refer to Catullus' country estate? (1–5)
       They refer to it as either Sabine or Tiburtine.
2.   Why do some people refer to it in one way and some the other way? (2–4)
       Some people do not want to hurt Catullus and so accept it as being Tiburtine (i.e., in more prestigious territory), thus supporting Catullus' pretensions to economic status; other people want to hurt Catullus and so insist that it is Sabine (i.e., in less prestigious territory), thus lowering Catullus' apparent economic profile.
3.   What word in line 5 indicates how Catullus would like people to refer to his country estate?
       The word **vērius** implies that he regards his estate as Tiburtine.
4.   How does line 5 echo line 1?
       The words **seu . . . sīve** in line 5 echo **seu . . . seu** in line 1, and the vocatives **Sabīne** and **Tiburs** are repeated in 5 from 1, thus rounding out the first segment of the poem.
5.   Why was Catullus glad to be at his country estate? (6–7)
       He was glad because he got rid of a bad cough there.
6.   How does Catullus describe himself in line 8? What figure of speech does he use?
       He describes himself as *not undeserving* (litotes, = *deserving*). He means that he deserved the bad cough.
7.   Judging from line 9, why does Catullus describe himself as **nōn inmerentī** in line 8?
       Catullus seems to imply that he deserved the cough because he was hungering after sumptuous dinners. Since he caught the cough under these circumstances, he has only himself to blame, for the argument apparently runs that he would not have caught the cough if he had not been hungering after sumptuous dinners.
8.   What does the phrase **Sestiānus . . . convīva** (10) imply about the status of being invited to dinner by Sestius?
       The phrase is far more formal than **convīva Sestiī** would have been and even somewhat pompous. It confers a formal status on being a dinner guest of Sestius and seems to imply

that being such means that one has arrived in high society.

9. When did Catullus read Sestius' oration against Antius? Why do you suppose he would have read it? (10–12)

He read it while he was wishing to be a guest at Sestius' table. Catullus, after being invited to dinner at Sestius', could have thought that he should read the oration in order to be prepared for possible discussion of it at table. It is also possible that the reader at this point in the poem is to think of Sestius as inviting Catullus to come to dinner and suggesting or even requiring that Catullus read his oration ahead of time so as to be prepared to comment on it (favorably, of course!) at dinner.

10. How does Catullus describe the oration? (12)

He describes it as full of poison and plague.

11. What happened to Catullus when he read the oration? (13–14)

He caught a *chilly cold* and a *constant cough*.

12. How does the description of the oration in line 12 prepare for or explain what happened to Catullus as described in lines 13–14?

The implication seems to be that he caught the cold and the cough from the poison and plague of Sestius' oration.

13. How did Catullus treat his illness? (14–15)

He treated his illness by fleeing to his country estate and treating himself with rest and medicinal vegetables. The implication is that he did not attend dinner at Sestius'.

14. For what two things is Catullus grateful? (16–17)

He is grateful for being restored to health (**refectus**, 16), and he is grateful that his country estate did not punish him for his **peccātum**, *error, fault*.

15. What was Catullus' **peccātum** (17)? What word earlier in the poem is recalled by Catullus' blaming himself for a **peccātum** here?

It would seem that his **peccātum**, *error/fault*, was to have hungered after invitations to sumptuous dinners in the first place, and secondly his error was thinking that he had to read Sestius' oration prior to Sestius' dinner in order to be able to please or flatter his host at dinner. Catullus' blaming himself here recalls his phrase **nōn inmerentī** in line 8. There he realized that he was guilty and deserved the cough; here he is grateful that his country estate did not punish him for the error of his ways but instead restored him to health. (In the process, Catullus has presumably learned his lesson and will no longer hunger after invitations to great men's dinners and will not even dream of preparing to flatter them at their dinner parties.)

16. The prayer as stated in lines 18–20 begins with a double negative, literally, *And I offer <u>no</u> prayer <u>to prevent</u>*. . . . Rephrase and translate it as a positive prayer, introduced by *I pray that.* . . .

Translation: *I pray that now, if I take up Sestius' abominable writings, a chill/their frigidity (of rhetorical style) may bring not to me but to Sestius himself a cold and a cough.*

17. Explain how the poet puns on the two different meanings of the word **frīgus** (20).

The word **frīgus** can refer either to chilly temperature, as in winter, or to frigidity of rhetorical style/flatness in a speech. With the first sense of the word, Catullus prays that a chill in the temperature might cause Sestius to catch cold; with the second sense, he prays that the frigidity of the style of Sestius' abominable writings should cause Sestius to catch cold, just as it caused Catullus to catch cold previously (8–12).

18. What words earlier in the poem are recalled by the following words: **nefāria** (18), **gravēdinem et tussim** (19), **frīgus** (20).

The word **nefāria** recalls **plēnam venēnī et pestilentiae** (12); the phrase **gravēdinem et tussim** recalls **gravēdō frīgida et frequēns tussis** (13); and **frīgus** recalls **frīgida** (13). Catullus thus prays that Sestius pay for the suffering he brought upon Catullus by suffering the same himself.

19. Why does Catullus think that Sestius deserves to catch a cold? (21)

Line 21 implies that Catullus thinks that Sestius deserves the fate that Catullus prays will afflict him because he has the bad taste and the effrontery to invite people to dinner only when they have read his nasty book (expecting that in exchange for the dinner they will flatter him by praising his book, thus demeaning themselves by turning themselves into hypocrites since anyone reading the book would recognize that it is trash). Line 21 as interpreted here helps answer question 9 above, for the line makes it clear that the reader is to think of Sestius as having suggested or required that Catullus read the book before coming to dinner (perhaps Sestius is to be thought of as having sent a copy of the book with the invitation).

Discussion

1. Consider the poem as a kind of address to a deity.   Locate the following:
    a.   Invocation
            Lines 1–5, Catullus' address to his country estate
    b.   Narrative of service rendered by the deity
            Lines 6–15
    c.   Expression of thanks by the speaker
            Lines 16–17
    d.   Prayer
            Lines 18–21

2.   In calling upon their deities, the Romans tried to be as inclusive as possible in listing the deities' names, epithets, or places of worship (see, for example, Catullus 34.9–22 and 36.12–15). How does Catullus work this inclusiveness of epithet into his invocation of his country estate? (1–5)

         Catullus' invocation of his country estate as **seu Sabīne seu Tiburs** (1), reinforced by the repetition in line 5 (**seu Sabīne sīve . . . Tīburs**), may be interpreted as a parody of invocations of deities. This along with the opening interjection **ō**, which often introduces invocations of deities (see Catullus 36.11), suggests that Catullus is invoking his country estate as a deity.

3.   The Romans tended to preserve archaic words and forms in their religious language. Locate the archaic words and forms in this poem.

         They are: **autumant** (2), **-que et** (15), **grātēs** (16), and **recepsō** (19).

4.   What phrase and words in lines 17–18 add to the religious tone of the poem?

         nōn es ulta (17), **peccātum** (17), **dēprecor** (18)

5.   In one common form of ancient prayer, the suppliant prays that a god may turn some evil back upon its perpetrator, e.g., "If someone wrongs me, turn the wrong back upon him." How does Catullus' prayer in lines 18–21 fit this pattern?

         He prays that Sestius' poisonous **frīgus** of rhetorical style be turned against Sestius instead of against Catullus and give Sestius, not Catullus, a cold.

6.   How is Sestius described and evaluated as a social figure in this poem?

         He is a person who gives sumptuous dinners, to which people are eager to be invited for the lavish food served; a guest will also earn the prestige of being known as a **Sestiānus conviva**. But Sestius exacts a price in that he invites guests only if they have read his nasty book, presumably in the expectation that they will praise it and flatter Sestius as the great orator/writer that he imagines himself to be. At the end of the poem Catullus prays that Sestius suffer an appropriate punishment by himself suffering the chill that he inflicts on his guests. In the last line Sestius is condemned for only inviting Catullus when the latter has read Sestius' nasty book. The pompous Sestius lacks manners, insults the intelligence of his guests, and tries to turn them into hypocrites.

7. How comfortably does Catullus fit into the social world evoked by this poem?

From the very beginning we see that Catullus has difficulties in his social world. He has his friends and enemies, his supporters and detractors, those who flatter him by describing his country estate as Tiburtine and those who try to cut him down by describing it as Sabine. Catullus then portrays himself as a kind of comic parasite figure, hungering after sumptuous dinners and even being willing to read the poisonous and pestilential speech of the great man in his eagerness to earn the status of being a **Sestiānus convīva**. But he finds that he can not stomach it, and his **venter** (8) gives him a **malam . . . tussim** (7). He is not blind to his fault, however, but realizes that he deserved what he got (**nōn inmerentī**, 8), and he thanks his country estate for healing him rather than punishing him for his **peccātum** (17). He seems to have emerged from the refuge of his country estate both cured of his cold and wiser in his outlook on his social world, for instead of hungering after sumptuous dinners of the rich and powerful he prays that the latter in the person of Sestius may receive poetic justice for their effrontery and he sees how morally bankrupt they are who only invite guests to dinner who have read their nasty books. Thus Catullus, brought to physical and mental health at his salubrious country estate, extricates himself from the social world epitomized by Sestius, satirizes it in this meditative prayer addressed to his country estate, and directs the sickness of that morally bankrupt social world back upon itself. Perhaps he will also have learned not to care whether people call his country estate Sabine or Tiburtine but will appreciate it in the future for what it is in its own right—a salubrious retreat—and not worry about it as a status symbol.

Select Bibliography

C. P. Jones. "Parody in Catullus 44." *Hermes* 96 (1968) 379–83. A close study of the language and the sequence of thought in the poem.
Edna S. deAngeli. "A Literary Chill: Catullus 44." *Classical World* 62 (1969) 354–56.
What Catullus has done here can be understood best as a witty parody on the cold legalistic prose of Publius Sestius as displayed in his oration against a certain Antius. (355). The poem with all its oddities bids fair to be a parody of the infelicitous Sestian style. (355). The awkward and stilted language, the inappropriateness and incongruity of tone contribute to the poem's message. (356)
David B. George. "Catullus 44: The Vulnerability of Wanting to be Included." *American Journal of Philology* 112 (1991) 247–50.
Catullus is angry because Sestius would not invite him on his own account—simply because he was a nice guy. He would only invite him because the poet would read and presumably flatter Sestius' work. But more importantly when one reflects on the first five lines, the point is that the poet was willing to suffer this indignity. He, as he says, deserved to get sick (*non inmerenti quam mihi meus venter, . . . dedit*, 7–8). Catullus was willing to do whatever it took to be considered Tiburtine rather than Sabine. In doing so he made himself vulnerable to those who would exclude him. He is hurt by those who would reject his real estate claims; he is made sick by his attempts to be invited to dinner. Thus he is as much the butt of his joke as Sestius. The rich well-connected aristocratic orator showed his bad taste in his style, Catullus in his desperate desire to be included in Sestius' company. (250)

CATULLUS 45

1   Septimius, holding his beloved Acme
2   on his lap, said, "My Acme,
3   if I don't love you desperately and am not prepared
4   to love you on and on unceasingly for all my years,
5   as desperately as the most desperate lover can,
6   may I alone in Libya or scorched India
7   meet face-to-face a green-eyed lion."
8   When he said this, Amor sneezed his approval
9   as before on the left [so] on the right.
10   But Acme, gently bending back her head
11 and kissing with those rosy lips of hers
12 the drunken eyes of her sweet boy,
13 said, "Dear Septimius, my life,
14 so may we continuously serve this one master,
15 as surely as a much greater and fiercer
16 fire burns in my tender marrow."
17 When she said this, Amor sneezed his approval
18 as before on the left [so] on the right.
19   Now having set out after this good omen,
20 they love and are loved with mutual hearts.
21 Wretched little Septimius prefers Acme
22 alone to all Syrias and Britains:
23 faithful Acme finds her
24 pleasure and lovemaking/pleasurable lovemaking with Septimius alone.
25 Who has seen any persons more blessed,
26 who has seen a more auspicious Venus/more auspicious lovemaking?

Poem 45 may be called a love idyll, but it is impossible to classify it by genre or by precedents in classical literature.

All but a few of the short poems in the Catullan corpus are presented as if they derive from the poet's own personal experience, treating people whom he knew with some degree of verisimilitude. That does not mean there is no fictional element or exaggeration in them, but they present themselves as pieces drawn from the poet's own life. Acme and Septimius, however, are perfectly drawn stock characters in the literature of love. She is a Greek freedwoman; he is a Roman soldier. (Because Acme has a Greek name and is free to be courted by a Roman soldier, she is assumed to be a Greek freedwoman.) His love is expressed in the most manly terms, as undying devotion and a supreme sacrifice to the service of love; her love is described in stereotypically feminine terms as heartfelt faithfulness and ardent passion. There is thus an utterly conventional quality to their oaths and a peculiarly symmetrical harmony to their relationship that places them more securely in an artificial and literary world than in the urbane tussling that characterizes the social ambiance of Catullus and his friends.

Initial Explorations

1. Describe the scene as presented in lines 1–2.
    Septimius is holding Acme on his lap and speaking to her.
2. How do the first two words and the people to whom they refer contrast with one another?
    There are several contrasts: Greek vs. Latin words; Greek vs. Roman people; feminine vs. masculine nouns; female vs. male people; freed person vs. free-born person; accusative vs. nominative case; direct object vs. subject. In other words, opposites in gender, social status, and grammar.

3.   How does the arrangement of subject and object in the first line visually undercut the sense of the line?

> Although Septimius holds Acme, she surrounds him in word placement. Compare this with poem 35.9–10, **manūsque collō / ambās iniciēns**, with the words describing the girl's hands placed to either side of the word for neck.

4.   What letter do the words **Acmēn Septimius . . . amōrēs** have in common?

> If one thinks of long and short vowels as being different letters, then the letter *m* is the only letter the words have in common. Judging from her speech in lines 13–16, this is Acme's favorite letter, and here it joins her to the name of her lover.

5.   Septimius describes his love for Acme in a conditional sentence with its protasis introduced by **nisi**, *unless* (3). What does Septimius say about himself in the protasis? (3–5)

> He says that he loves Acme *desperately* (3) and that he is prepared to love her *on and on unceasingly for all [his] years* (3–4) and *as desperately as the most desperate lover can* (5).

6.   What does Septimius wish or pray for in the apodosis (6–7) of his conditional sentence?

> He prays that, if he does not love Acme as he declares that he does (3–5), he may come, alone, face to face with a green-eyed lion in Libya or parched India.

7.   How do Septimius' words characterize his declaration of his love? (2–7)

> His words convey a strong declaration with a rhetorical flourish in the three clauses in the protasis and a vivid, fanciful wish or prayer in the apodosis. The adverbs **perditē**, **porrō**, **assiduē**, and **plūrimum** add force to his words and emphasize his desperation, his eternal loyalty, and the intensity of his love. His declaration that he is prepared (**parātus**) to love through all his years (**omnēs . . . annōs**) as much as anyone who is able especially *to perish in love/to be madly in love* (**perīre**) suggests the language of a soldier declaring his loyalty unto death. He declares his love with the intensity and commitment of a noble Roman soldier willing to suffer the ultimate fate (death in the maws of a wild lion) if he is untrue to his cause.

8.   Study the alliteration of *ps*, *ss*, and *qs* in lines 3–5. How does sound reinforce sense?

> The alliteration of *ps* hammers at the most important words in Septimius' speech: **perditē . . . porrō / . . . parātus . . . / . . . pote plūrimum perīre** (the letter also links to Septimius' name in line 1). The *ss* highlight his declaration of eternal loyalty: **omnēs sum assiduē parātus annōs**. The *qs* add weight to the first half of line 5, **quantum quī**.

9.   For the Greeks "right" was regarded as lucky and "left" as unlucky; the reverse was true in early times for the Romans, but later they tended to adopt the Greek way of thinking. Remember that Acme is Greek and Septimius Roman and that Acme is sitting in Septimius' lap and facing him. How would you interpret Amor's intentions here? (8–9)

> Amor seems to be wanting to make sure that his favorable omen of sneezing will be clear to both the Greek woman and the Roman man, no matter which direction each of them is facing (see Rose, Select Bibliography).

10.   What is Acme's physical response to Septimius' declaration of his love? (10–12)

> She responds by tilting her head and kissing Septimius' eyes.

11.   How does Acme's declaration of her love for Septimius (13–16) differ from his for her (2–7)? Include in your answer a description of how Acme's wish or prayer expressed with the optative subjunctive differs from that of Septimius.

> It is shorter, but she says that her love is greater. Acme addresses Septimius with a diminutive (**Septimille**, 13), while Septimius addressed her simply as **Acmē** (2); she also expands his **Mea . . . Acmē** to **mea vīta Septimille** (13). She does not speak in the first person singular as did Septimius. She expresses her wish or prayer (14) in the first person *plural*, thus including Septimius and herself, in contrast to Septimius' expression of his wish or prayer in the first person *singular* (6–7). She speaks of serving a master (Eros), while Septimius spoke in terms of actions prompted by free choice. In addressing Septimius, Acme uses the metaphor of life, **mea vīta** (13), while Septimius couched his declaration in terms of death (**perīre**, 5, and lines 6–7). Septimius spoke of far-off, exotic lands (**Libyā Indiāque tostā**, 6), while Acme expresses her love in terms of her physical, inner being (**mollibus . . . in medullīs**, 16). While the heat that Septimius mentioned was only

in the far-off lands of Libya and India (6), Acme speaks of a fire burning inside of her (16). While Septimius spoke of the duration and intensity of his love (4–5), Acme claims that a much greater and fiercer fire burns in her inner self (15–16). While Septimius used the words **amō** and **tē** that set Acme and himself apart, Acme never uses these words but instead uses the inclusive **serviāmus** (14).

12.   Study the alliteration of *ms*, *ls*, and *ss* in lines 13–16. How does sound reinforce sense? How many *ps* did Septimius use in his speech? How many *ms* does Acme use? How are these letters related to the names Septimius and Acme?

The liquid *ms* and *ls* are appropriate to Acme's softer language about her inner feelings, in contrast to Septimius' plosive *ps*, and Acme's favored letters link the name of her lover with her inner feelings when the diminutive that she uses to address him, **Septimille** (13) is echoed in the words referring to the inner seat of her burning passion, **mollibus . . . medullīs** (16). Her *ss* link the name of her lover **Septimille** (13) first with her desire for continuous servitude to Eros (**usque serviāmus**, 14) and then with the fire that burns inside her: **ignis mollibus . . . medullīs** (16). Septimius used 6 *ps*; Acme (in fewer lines) uses 9 *ms*. The two lovers take their favorite letters from their names: Septimius with his *ps* and Acme with her *ms*.

13.   What words in Acme's speech repeat or recall words in Septimius'?

mea (13) = **Mea** (2); **usque** (14) = **porrō** (3) and **assiduē** (4); **ignis** (16) = **tostā** (6).

14.   In what ways does the language of line 19 suggest an army marching out to battle?

The participle **profectī** suggests setting out on a journey or setting out for battle, and before setting out for a journey or for battle the Romans would take the auspices. Septimius and Acme have, as it were, taken the auspices by testing Amor's responses to their declarations of love, and they then set out on the journey of love, instead of setting out for warfare. There is a play here on the common ancient conceit of lovemaking as a form of warfare and of the lover as a soldier. As the two lovers set out here, Acme is clearly ready to surrender to Septimius.

15.   In what two ways does line 20 emphasize the reciprocity of Acme and Septimius' love?

First with the phrase **mutuīs animīs**, *with hearts mutually loving*, and then with the active and passive forms of the verb in the words **amant amantur**. Any suggestion of conqueror and conquered implied in the military allusions in line 19 is here negated in the insistence on reciprocity, as both Acme and Septimius love and are loved, i.e., conquer and are conquered.

16.   Compare the arrangement of words in line 21 with that in line 1.

The arrangement of words is very similar with the grammatical object (**Ūnam . . . Acmēn**) still surrounding the subject (**Septimius misellus**). **Septimius** is still the second word, but **Acmēn** has now become the last instead of the first word. Note that the placement of the words **Ūnam** and **Acmēn** in line 21 could be reversed without violating the meter, thus preserving the initial placement of **Acmēn** as in line 1. Catullus, however, places **Ūnam** first in line 21, because he is looking toward anaphora with **ūnō** in line 23, which underscores the striking parallel between the two lovers explored in the matching pairs of lines 21–22 and 23–24.

It should also be noted that the order of adjectives and nouns in the surrounding phrase (**Ūnam . . . Acmēn**) and the embedded phrase (**Septimius misellus**) is chiastic: adjective, noun; noun, adjective.

17.   What is said about Septimius in lines 21–22?

It is said that, wretched with desire (**misellus**, 21), Septimius prefers Acme, i.e., Acme's love, to Syrias and Britains, i.e., to military service on the borders of the empire, which could bring great honors and wealth to ambitious young Romans.

18.   What is said about Acme in lines 23–24?

It is said that Acme, faithful (**fidēlis**, 23), takes her pleasures and engages in lovemaking with Septimius alone.

19.   Identify the corresponding words in lines 21 and 23 and in lines 22 and 24.

Lines 21 and 23: **ūnam** = **ūnō**; **Septimius** = **Septimiō**; **misellus** = **fidēlis**; **Acmēn** = **Acmē**.

Lines 22 and 24: **Syriās Britanniāsque = dēliciās libīdinēsque**. Note that **Syriās** and **Britanniās** are feminine nouns, as if the poet was saying that Septimius preferred Acme to all other women, and note that making these nouns plural creates close correspondence to the plurals **dēliciās libīdinēsque** in line 24.

Note that lines 21–24, in which the poet comments on the two characters, recall elements from each of their speeches above: **misellus** (21) recalls the diminutive **Septimille** (13); Septimius' Syrias and Britains (22) recall his mention of Libya and India earlier (6); the adjective **fidēlis** (23) recalls Acme's prayer that the two lovers continually serve one master, Eros (14); and the words applied to Acme, **facit dēliciās libīdinēsque** (24), recall her description of her inner emotional experience in line 16, **ignis mollibus ārdet in medullīs**.

20. Identify the corresponding words in lines 25 and 26.
    Quis = quis; **hominēs = Venerem**; and **beātiōrēs = auspicātiōrem**.
21. What is the expected answer to the rhetorical questions in lines 25 and 26?
    The question is phrased in such a way as to anticipate the answer "No one." These people are the happiest of mortals; their sexual union is the most auspicious. See Discussion question 3, however, for irony in the poem.

Discussion

1. Divide the poem into its three major sections, and divide the third section into subsections.

    The poem shows a complete symmetry of form. Septimius speaks in the first stanza of nine lines, which concludes with a two-line refrain. Acme then speaks in a second stanza of nine lines, which concludes in the same manner as the first. The final stanza is of eight lines (2 + 2 + 2 + 2), in which the four lines in the middle offer a complementary image of the devotion of each lover.

2. Septimius and Acme have been described as "spokesmen, as it were, of their sexes." Discuss the way they are portrayed in the poem and evaluate the applicability of this statement.

    This aspect of the poem is addressed in the following extracts from scholarly articles, the first by Nielsen and the second by Freuh (see Select Bibliography).

    Nielsen:
    The details in their speeches show how adroitly Catullus makes them the spokesmen, as it were, of their sexes. . . . Septimius is no less faithful than Acme because he speaks of foreign lands. The romanticism of his vow to her is perfectly suited to a male-oriented view of the world and to his prerogative of facing physical hardship on her behalf. In turn, Acme reflects in every line of the second stanza (10–18) those qualities that make her the ideal woman in any man's eyes. She physically stirs his passion by her tender kisses, lavishes on him words of endearment (13), and manifests her subservience to her emotion as she invites him to make love. When she speaks of a keener flame in her marrow (15–16), there is no boast intended. These words fill a psychological need in her lover; they are the signal of voluntary surrender. (135)

    Edward Freuh:
    Septimius concentrates not on everyday life but on the wider world of romantic adventure and the sphere of public action. His discourse opens out in space to embrace geographical extremes. He conjures up the antithesis of a life of shared passion: solitude and death at the nearly indistinguishable ends of the earth:
        solus in Libya Indiaque tosta
        caesio veniam obvius leoni.
    The specific lands which he mentions evoke physical hardship, heat and thirst, vast

expanses of space, and a life spent in military campaigns.

To the public world and language of Septimius, Acme opposes her own private domain. She internalizes what he has made external. He was grandiose and paradoxically confounded love and death: *perdite . . . amo . . . amare . . . perire . . . veniam obvius;* she associates love and life: *mea vita, usque serviamus.* Her endearing diminutive, *Septimille,* and particularized demonstrative, *huic uni,* contrast with his expansive evocations. His eternal future is her intensely felt now. His universe of adventure and burning foreign lands has become her world of the body and the fires of a deeply felt physical love:

ignis mollibus ardet in medullis.

The body of the lover replaces the exotic geography of amorous rhetoric.

Acme preserves grammatical complexities as the closely worded "sic. . . ut" construction of her speech shows. Unlike Septimius, she presents her remarks as a statement of fact. To Septimius' use of antithetical imagery, she opposes her own more personal comparison. Acme focuses exclusively on the here and now of everyday life. Septimius' language evoked military service in distant lands and the motif of *militium amoris.* Acme's words—note particularly *serviamus*—evoke the daily servitude of love and the motif of *servitium amoris.* The imagery of love's fire recalls sun-scorched Libya and India but on a smaller, wholly personalized scale. Septimius talked of grand emotions; in one line he used the verb *amo* twice. Acme never uses the word *amare;* she speaks only of her personal feelings. Septimius used the first person of verbs—*amo, sum, veniam*—and the second person pronoun—*te.* Acme uses only a neutral third person verb—*ardet,* to refer to the fire of love—and a first person plural—*serviamus.* Grammar and language in Septimius' speech separate the lovers; in Acme's speech grammar and language bind them together. (18–19)

3. Some readers have thought that the picture of an ideal love affair presented in the poem is too good to be true and have seen ironic double meanings undercutting its idyllic surface. What elements of irony, if any, do you detect in the poem?

This is a question that has bedeviled countless readers of the poem. First, some have seen studied ambiguity in the manner in which Amor sneezes his approval on the left and the right, apparently pronouncing the omen of Septimius and Acme's love to be propitious according to both Roman and Greek religious systems, since ancient Romans believed the left to be lucky, while Greeks contrariwise favored the right. His sneezes might be understood as propitious or unpropitious depending on the viewpoint from which one chooses to interpret them.

Furthermore, there is certainly an unmistakable degree of artifice and exaggeration in the rhetoric of the lovers' sentiments, in the perfect symmetry of their parts, and in the conventional quality of their romantic poses. Many readers have thought such exaggerated perfection to be on the face of the matter incredible. In the Catullan corpus, where betrayal of love (e.g., poems 70 and 72) or non-reciprocated love (e.g., poem 87) are common themes, such description of love as we find here seems difficult to take at face value. Some readers, noting that poem 45 seems to have been written about the same time as poem 11 because of the references to the Parthians, Syria, and Britain in the two poems and because of the similarity of the words **omnēs . . . parātus** (45.4) and **omnia . . . / . . . parātī** (11.13–14), have felt that Catullus could not possibly have written a straightforward portrayal of amatory bliss at a time when he was sending **nōn bona dicta** to Lesbia and accusing her of having destroyed his love through her gross infidelities.

Teachers and students will have to make their own decisions on this point of interpretation (see Select Bibliography for quotations of some scholars' views).

4. What lines show Septimius' adherence to the saying "Make love, not war"? To what extent did Catullus share this preference?

Lines 21–22. The poem has been read as a highly expressive image of the perfect life of love and leisure that is opposed constantly by Catullus to the life of business and duty that would carry one off to the provinces, the Syrias and Britains (22), where the great martial enterprises of the day were being carried out. This reading is consistent with one of the most commonly found themes of the polymetrics: the depiction of everyday people and affairs as being important in their own right, even in comparison with traditionally dignified subjects, such as the martial enterprises forsaken by Septimius.

Select Bibliography

John Barker Stearns. "On the Ambiguity of Catullus XLV.8–9 (= 17–18)." *Classical Philology* 24 (1929) 48–59.

Herbert Jennings Rose. "Some Passages of Latin Poets." *Harvard Studies in Classical Philology* 47 (1936) 1–15. On lines 8–9 and 17–18:

> The question where the commas should go is, I submit, one which Catullus would laugh at, for the point of the lines is that they cannot be misread. The words *hoc ut dixit* are unambiguous; since they immediately follow a speech of one of the lovers, the subject cannot be *Amor*. For the rest, whether one recites *Amor, sinistra ut ante, dextra sternuit approbationem* or *Amor sinistra, ut ante dextra, sternuit approbationem*, the couplet is true and appropriate to the situation both times. The pair are sitting, as many thousands of pairs have done before and since, with the lass on the lad's knees, or perhaps she is lying in his arms (*tenens in gremio*, 2, could mean either). Acme, in any case, is facing Septimius, for to kiss his eyes she has but to tilt her chin (*leuiter caput reflectens*; to speak pedantically to the pedants, the movement must be in the vertical, not the horizontal plane, for on the latter supposition she must turn her head clean around, which is anything but moving it *leuiter*). Also, a gaze swimming with rapture (*ebrios ocellos*) is not very likely to be directed at the back of her head, however well her hair may have been arranged. So what is left to her is right to him. Thus, whichever side Love stands on, his sneeze comes from left and right also. Moreover, he is a Roman, she a Greek, in name and culture if not race. Therefore, her lucky side is right, his is left, by the usual rule of ancient divination, Greek and Italo-Etruscan respectively. So, by an arrangement of the omens quite good enough for any people as happy as they are, anything that happened must be construable as somehow favourable for one or the other, and therefore for both. (1–2)

Howard Comfort. "Analysis of Technique in Catullus XLV (Septimius and Acme). *Transactions and Proceedings of the American Philological Association* 69 (1938) xxxiii. "In addition to the larger triple division of the poem, Catullus has echoed, balanced, and contrasted words, phrases, sentiments, and alliteration with unique skill" (xxxiii)—many examples are cited in this brief but useful note.

Sheridan Baker. "The Irony of Catullus' Septimius and Acme." *Classical Philology* 53 (1958) 110–12. Catullus sees the green pastures of this idyll, I think, as nothing more than a very young Roman's after-dinner couch. Charm, honor, ideal, and all the rest of it, seem, at least to one reader, undone by a honed and skeptical irony, ending in a quaintly unanswerable question mark. (112)

David O. Ross, Jr. "Style and Content in Catullus 45." *Classical Philology* 60 (1965) 256–59. The poem is ironic: "While the words say one thing, form subtly implies the opposite" (257). Ross sees poems 11 and 45 as "genuine companion pieces," so that "Carm. 45 represents, all at once, both Catullus' desire to be free of Lesbia and his longing for a perfect love that he thought for awhile might have been, yet which could not be. Catullus' deepest emotions are often expressed in the most abstract and impersonal settings, and 45 is a poem of this nature" (258).

H. Akbar Khan. "Catullus 45: What Sort of Irony?" *Latomus* 27 (1968) 3–12. He did not use these characters to let his feelings about his own love affair filter through to the reader. . . . Catullus' treatment of the love theme reflects his affiliation to the apolitical and hedonistic principles of the *homo otiosus*, as against the active and conformist Roman attitudes of the noble *uir fortis et strenuus*. (3–4)

David Singleton. "Form and Irony in Catullus XLV." *Greece and Rome* 18 (1971) 180–87.

Rosemary M. Nielsen. "Catullus 45 and Horace Odes 3.9: The Glass House." *Ramus* 6 (1977) 132–38. See above.

Edward Frueh. "Sinistra Ut Ante Dextra: Reading Catullus 45." *Classical World* 84 (1990) 15–21. See above.

> There is no answer to or single explanation of Catullus 45; the poem is simultaneously a charming idyll of perfect love, an ironic questioning of that or of any love, and a sophisticated exploration of the creation of meaning and desire out of the myriad ambiguities of words and signs. (20–21)

Rachel Kitzinger. "Reading Catullus 45." *Classical Journal* 87 (1992) 209–17.

> The poet presents us with four different "voices": the narrator, Amor, Septimius, and Acme; and in addition the poem ends with two questions addressed to the reader which ask him to look back into the poem and use these voices to make a judgement on the two issues central to the poem: the state of the lovers and the attitude of Venus towards them. Since each voice offers a different perspective, the questions force the reader to confront a problem of reading and reconciling signs—whether those signs be lovers' vows, Amor's sneezes, or the narrator's poetic statement—and they deliberately open up the possibility of multiple responses as integral to the meaning of the poem. (210) In fact, I would argue that Catullus has made his language as difficult to interpret as possible, so that no honest reader can confidently answer the question with which the poem ends. (214–15)

Rick M. Newton. "Acme and Septimius Recounted: Catullus 45." *Syllecta classica* 7 (1996) 99–105.

CATULLUS 46

1   Now spring brings back warm days free of chill,
2   now the fury of the sky at the equinox begins
3   to quiet down before the pleasant breezes of the west wind.
4   Let the Phrygian plains, Catullus, be left behind
5   and the fertile field of sweltering Nicaea:
6   let us fly away to the famous cities of Asia.
7   Now my thoughts excited in anticipation are eager to roam,
8   now my feet happy with enthusiasm begin to grow lively.
9   O sweet bands of comrades, farewell;
10 whom, having journeyed far from home,
11 different paths by different routes bring back.

Poem 46 should be read along with poem 31 on Catullus' arrival at Sirmio on his return home from Bithynia and with poem 10, with its scathing remarks on the governor Memmius (see also poem 28, which is not included in this book). Poem 4 is also often read along with 46 and 31 on the assumption that the **phasēlus** describes Catullus' voyage home from his service in Bithynia.

Poem 46 is often cited as a model Catullan poem in the lyric manner, because in its brief scope the poet manages to express that particular emotional excitement we all feel upon departing on a journey home. Thus the poem serves for some as an essential example of Catullus' general program of not treating ideas, but emotional states of mind, and of speaking everywhere in a unique voice.

Initial Explorations

1.   What do the first three lines of the poem celebrate and what feelings do they evoke? What

does Catullus urge in lines 4–6? What does he state in lines 7–8? Whom does he address and with what feelings in the last three lines?

    The first three lines celebrate the coming of spring, and they evoke feelings of relief at the passing of bad weather and joy at the coming of the pleasant breezes of springtime.

    In lines 4–6 Catullus urges that the Phrygian fields and the sweltering plain of Nicaea be left behind and that he fly off to the famous cities of the province of Asia. In lines 7–8 he states that his mind and feet are eager for travel. In the last three lines he nostalgically addresses the groups of his companions who set out for Bithynia together but will return by different routes.

2.   Repetition of words, letters, and sounds is significant in this poem. Why is the word **iam** repeated four times?

    It is repeated four times to emphasize the new arrival of spring (1–2) and the new frame of mind that this has produced in Catullus (7–8).

3.   Words that have the letter *v* in them are central to the poem. Locate these words and describe the pattern that you see in their use. What sounds link words in lines 4, 5, and 9?

    The words are: **vēr** (1), **volēmus** (6), **avet vagārī** (7), **vigēscunt** (8), **valēte** (9, and **dīversae variē viae** (11). At least one word with this letter in it occurs as a key word in each of the sections of the poem identified in question 1 above. The words with these letters thus help emphasize the theme of each section of the poem. The final section (9–11) contains the most words with this letter of any section (five occurrences).

    The sounds of the underlined letters link words in lines 4, 5, and 9:

    Line 4: **Catulle, campī**.

    Line 5: **Nicaeaeque . . . aestuōsae**.

    Line 9: **comitum . . . coetūs**.

4.   Compare and contrast line 1 with line 7 and lines 2–3 with line 8. How does the arrival of spring influence and mirror the poet's state of mind?

    The idea of spring bringing back *warm days free of chill* (1) is echoed in the description in line 7 of the minds of Catullus and his friends, aflutter with anticipation of travel.

    Lines 2–3 describing how the stormy season calms down with the delightful west winds are echoed in line 8 in the description of feet coming alive, happy with enthusiasm for travel. The inceptive verb **vigēscunt** (8) echoes the inceptive verb **silēscit** (3).

5.   Find a chiasmus in lines 7–8. What is its effect?

    The chiasmus—**mēns** (7) A, **praetrepidāns** (7) B, **laetī studiō** (8) B, **pedēs** (8) A—sets **mēns** and **pedēs** in sharp contrast while inviting the reader to see similarities between the two modifiers, **praetrepidāns** (7) and **laetī studiō** (8).

6.   Does the tone of the last three lines differ from that of the rest of the poem? If so, how?

    Yes; it differs in being bitter-sweet, with Catullus' nostalgic farewell to his sweet bands of comrades. His happy memories of how they all set out together in the past contrast with the necessarily sad separation of the groups of friends for their return journeys. But their journeys carry them back home, and on that happy note, expressed in the verb **reportant**, the poem ends.

Discussion

1.   Divide the poem into groups of lines as follows:
    a. 1–3
    b. 4–6
    c. 7–8
    d. 9–11
How do lines 7–8 relate to lines 1–3?

    This question invites deeper probing of the contrasts identified in Initial Explorations question 4.

Spring in lines 1–3 is compared with the mind, heart, and thoughts of Catullus and his friends (7–8), and the calming of the stormy weather of late winter in lines 2–3 is set against the joyful enthusiasm for traveling that takes hold of the feet in line 8.

In this way the poem induces us to read the depiction of spring, an external phenomenon, in relation to an inner emotional state. Just as the cold and storms of late winter give way to pleasant breezes for traveling, so too the inner personality becomes excited in anticipation of being off, and the enthusiasm for movement seizes the whole body.

How do lines 9–11 relate to lines 4–6?

In lines 4–6 certain geographical areas are about to be left behind and others approached; in lines 9–11 the focus is on friends who are about to be left behind and the groups of companions that journeyed together in the past but are now about to set out on separate return journeys. Geography in lines 4–6 is set against concerns for human companions in lines 9–11.

Note that the structure of the poem can be reduced to two parts, each beginning with the anaphora of **iam**. The first six lines announce the onset of the season for travel in the full tide of warm spring weather. The last five lines depict the emotional state of Catullus and his companions as they take leave of each other in departing on their journeys home.

2. Study the poet's use of the following words in the poem: **ēgelidōs** (1), **volēmus** (6), **praetrepidāns** (7), and **vigēscunt** (8). How is each word especially appropriate and expressive in its context?

This vocabulary is very precise and apt for Catullus' purposes. The warm days are described as **ēgelidōs**, which has just the right touch for indicating the departure of chill and thus signals the return of life and vitality. The verb **volēmus** vividly expresses both the departure on a journey, which is the natural climax to the poet's thought here, and the intensity of the moment, conveyed by the connotations of speed that the word carries. The descriptive adjective **praetrepidāns** conveys very precisely the mounting excitement that hits one in anticipation of setting off: it is the moment when "spring fever" catches hold of us, just before the bad weather has actually receded in full. The verb **vigēscunt** is also vividly expressive of spring's vitality emotionally taking hold of the body; the simpler form of the verb, **vigēre**, is regularly used of the flourishing of forces of growth in nature, such as is characteristic of springtime. Hence, many of the poet's choices of diction in this poem are supremely apt, and students may want to discuss other words that seem particularly appropriate.

Select Bibliography

Michael C. J. Putnam. "Catullus' Journey (*Carm.* 4)." *Classical Philology* 57 (1962) 10–19. See 11–12 for poem 46. Comparing poems 46 and 31:
> The emotion first experienced in Bithynia is similar to that which he experiences upon arrival at Sirmio, the only difference being that 46 portrays the birth of yearning, contemporaneous with the coming of spring, while 31 denotes its fulfillment. . . . These two poems . . . run on two levels which are so interconnected as hardly to be separable. On the one hand there is the actual description of the journey's beginning and end, but this is also equivalent to the emotion of desire, the journey's cause, which is aroused in 46 and attained in 31. (12)

CATULLUS 49

1   Most eloquent of the descendants of Romulus,
2   as many as are and as have been, Marcus Tullius,
3   and as many as will be in the years to come,
4   to you Catullus offers the greatest thanks,
5   Catullus, the worst poet of all,
6   as much the worst poet of all
7   as you are the best advocate of all.

Tatum's comments (see Select Bibliography) on this poem are as valid today as they were when he wrote them in 1988:

> Catullus 49 has long attracted the interest of scholars, and its seven hendecasyllabic lines have inspired a bibliography out of all proportion to the literary merits of the poem. The reason for this curiosity is clear enough: Catullus addresses Cicero and, as one recent critic observes, "it is the sole communication between these great men which has been preserved or even attested to us." A glimpse—or rather the hope for a glimpse at the relationship between two of the first century's leading literary men is an undeniable enticement; that the piece is fascinating, however, is the only point regarding this poem on which classicists are agreed. Otherwise the history of its scholarship is a record of disagreements. The poem's tone, whether it is sincere or ironic, is contested, and very various occasions for the poet's grateful gesture toward the orator have been postulated. All in all, Catullus 49 remains a puzzle. (179)

Laughton and Basson (see Select Bibliography) and the standard commentaries summarize some of the many theories critics have postulated concerning this poem. Most critics interpret the poem as ironic, although there is little agreement as to what elements of it are ironical. Batstone (see Select Bibliography) sees the poem as a calculated riddle of identities.

Initial Explorations

1.   What is the effect of the anaphora in lines 2–3?
       It hammers home the point that Cicero is the most eloquent of any and all Romans, ever.
2.   What is the effect of the particular way Cicero is addressed in line 2?
       It is emphatically formal in tone.
3.   Locate five superlative adjectives in the poem.
       Disertissime (1), **maximās** (4), **pessimus** (5), **pessimus** (6), **optimus** (7).
4.   Locate examples of parallel word order.
       . . . pessimus omnium poēta (5)
       tantō pessimus omnium poēta (6)
       quantō . . . optimus omnium patrōnus (7)
5.   Locate examples of alliteration.
       quot . . . quot . . . / quot (2–3), **pessimus . . . poēta, / . . . pessimus . . . poēta / optimus . . . patrōnus** (5–7), **omnium . . . / omnium . . . / . . . optimus omnium** (5–7).
6.   Locate examples of homoioteleuton.
       aliīs . . . annīs (3), **grātiās . . . maximās** (4), **pessimus . . . / pessimus . . . / optimus . . . patrōnus** (5–7), **omnium . . . / omnium . . . / omnium** (5–7).
7.   What is the structure of the poem?
       The poem is symmetrically structured around line 4, which expresses the central statement of the poem's theme—the thanks that Catullus renders to Cicero. The first three lines are direct address to Cicero; the last three lines describe Catullus as he measures himself against Cicero.

Discussion

1. What indication, if any, does Catullus give for why he is thanking Cicero with this poem?

    Catullus does not explicitly state why he is thanking Cicero. The only word that could be interpreted as a hint is the word **patrōnus** (7), which could suggest that Cicero has protected or supported or defended Catullus in some formal capacity. But the word need not point in that direction; the word could be used here simply as a general description of Cicero in contrast to Catullus' description of himself in lines 5–6 as a **poēta**. Some readers hear a disparaging description of Cicero in the words **omnium patrōnus**, translating *patron of everyone/anyone.*

    Poem 49 is a conundrum in that Catullus has deliberately withheld an explanation of his reason for thanking Cicero; the wide variety of conjectural explanations offered by scholars demonstrates just how effectively Catullus has kept the explanation a secret. One may compare poem 73, in which Catullus expresses not thanks but a grievance, but in which he withholds an explanation of the cause of his grievance as well as the name of the party that has aggrieved him. Likewise, in poem 77, Rufus' perfidy is described in only the most general terms, and readers are left to speculate as to what Rufus actually did to provoke Catullus' responding with this poem. In all three poems Catullus is interested in expressing his emotional response to others' treatment of him rather than in describing the circumstances that led to his emotional states. The precise poetic craftsmanship with which the emotional states are described takes precedence over revelation of autobiographical facts. The situation in poem 49 is further complicated for those who read it as ironic.

2. On the surface, this is a very flattering poem of thanks to Cicero. Some readers have felt that it is ironic. What is there in the poem that could lead one to suspect irony on the part of Catullus?

    There are a number of elements in the poem that have led some readers to think of irony. Consider, for example, (1) the high-sounding and exaggerated tone (hyperbole) of the many superlatives; (2) the grandiose expression **Rōmulī nepōtum**, *descendants of Romulus*, line 1; (3) the use or parody in line 2 of a solemnly official style of address, such as was used in the Senate and on formal occasions, namely **Mārce Tullī**; (4) the heavy use of alliteration and homoioteleuton in lines 5–7; (5) the fact that the poet would not normally be expected to take seriously his description of himself as **pessimus omnium poēta** in line 5, repeated in line 6 (compare the phrase **pessimī poētae** in 36.6), and so his description of Cicero as **optimus omnium patrōnus** in line 7 is not to be taken seriously either. Basson (see Select Bibliography) suggests that Catullus may be using the word **disertus (Disertissime**, 1) in the sense of *glib, smooth-tongued*, indicating "that Catullus had no intention of praising Cicero as an orator in this poem" (48). Also note the playful verbal echo of <u>Mārce Tullī</u> (2) in the poet's own self-reference, <u>-mās</u> **Catullus** (4), to which Wormell (see Select Bibliography) calls attention (60). Readers will make up their own minds as to whether they regard the poem as straightforward or ironic.

Select Bibliography

D. E. W. Wormell. "Catullus 49." *Phoenix* 17 (1963) 59–60. See above.

D. F. S. Thomson. "Catullus and Cicero: Poetry and the Criticism of Poetry. *Classical World* 60 (1967) 225–30. Sees the poem as prompted by the poet's receiving from Cicero a gift of some of his poetry: "C. is flattered at receiving the literary gift, yet he cannot praise it; in his deft acknowledgment there is a touch of irony (between the lines), yet the poem is not as a whole ironical." (1997 commentary, 323)

Eric Laughton. "Disertissime Romuli nepotum." *Classical Philology* 65 (1970) 1–7. Summarizes earlier attempts to explain the situation behind the poem and proposes that it was Cicero's sending

Catullus "a specimen of his most recent poetry" (7).

Ernest A. Fredricksmeyer. "Catullus 49, Cicero, and Caesar." *Classical Philology* 68 (1973) 268–78.
Argues that the poem is a sincere note of thanks to Cicero for serving as intermediary in Catullus' reconciliation with Julius Caesar (see Suetonius, *Life of Caesar* 73).

W. P. Basson. "The Riddle of Catullus 49: Some Notes on Its Interpretation." *Acta Classica* 23 (1980) 45–52.

> At first blush . . . the poem appears to be purely eulogistic, particularly as a result of the use of high-sounding superlatives. On closer examination, however, one senses that the sustained exaggeration is suspect, and that the apparent eulogy is all but sincerely meant. In fact, the overall impression is one of consummate ambiguity, which is already implied by the very first word ('disertissime') and brought to a climax at the end. This ambiguity is intensified by the formal address of Cicero ('Marce Tulli'), the equally formal reference to Catullus himself ('Catullus'), sharp contrasts ('disertissime-pessimus'; 'pessimus-optimus'; 'poeta-patronus'), repetition ('pessimus-pessimus'; 'poeta-poeta'), and the use of words which may have an unfavourable connotation ('disertissime'; 'patronus'). (49)

Basson argues that poem 49 deals with poetic criticism and may, therefore, be intended as a defense of Catullus' poetry against the criticism of one who had no eye for the few poetry.

William C. McDermott. "Cicero and Catullus." *Wiener Studien* 14 (1980) 75–82. Views Catullus 49 as "ironic and hostile" (75).

W. Jeffrey Tatum. "Catullus' Criticism of Cicero in Poem 49." *Transactions of the American Philological Association* 118 (1988) 179–84.

> The obvious and emphatic irony of lines five and six transforms the last line of the poem into a subtle, urbane taunt which mocks Cicero's political and social pretensions. These seven hendecasyllables will have found a receptive and appreciative audience in Roman high Society—at any rate in Catullus' circle. (184)

Edward Frueh. "Sinistra Ut Ante Dextra: Reading Catullus 45." *Classical World* 84 (1990) 15–21.

> The verses addressed to Cicero (49) may be sincere and elegant praise of the great orator, or they may be a parodic subversion by means of overstatement, or perhaps a bit of amicable raillery. (21)

William Batstone. "Logic, Rhetoric, and Poesis." *Helios* 20 (1993) 143–72.

CATULLUS 50

1   Yesterday, Licinius, [while] at leisure,
2   we engaged in much play on my tablets,
3   having agreed to be frivolous:
4   both of us, writing scraps of verse,
5   played now in this meter, now in that,
6   answering each other's verses over laughs and drinks.
7   And I went away from there
8   inflamed by your charm, Licinius, and [your] wit,
9   so that as a result neither food relieved miserable/lovesick me,
10   nor did sleep cover my tender eyes with rest,
11   but wild with delirium/with uncontrollable delirium I was tossing
12   and turning over the whole bed, desiring to see the light [of dawn],
13   so that I might talk to you and be together with you.
14   But after my limbs, worn out with suffering,
15   lay half-dead on [my] little bed,
16   I wrote, [my] delightful [friend], this poem for you,

17   that you might be able to perceive my pain from it.
18   Now beware of being presumptuous and, I beg you,
19   of despising my prayers, dearest one,
20   that Nemesis may not exact a penalty from you.
21   She's a powerful goddess; beware of offending her.

By the testimony of the entire corpus, Catullus enjoyed no closer friendship and mutual understanding with anyone than with Calvus (see poems 53 and 96, which are in this book, and poem 14, which is not in this book). The two are cited together by later poets, including Ovid, for their close affinity in life and poetic practice. The present poem offers a glimpse of the two spending an afternoon together at leisure, drinking and laughing as they composed light verse. Catullus departed entranced or inflamed (**incēnsus**, 8) with Calvus' charm and wit (**lepōre**, 7, **facētiīs**, 8) and suffered through the night as if lovesick. He wrote the present poem pleading to be able to be with his friend and to talk with him again. The unusually powerful magnetism that draws Catullus back to the charm and wit of his friend is noteworthy and comparable in its power to the attraction that draws him to Lesbia in the love poems (see in particular, poem 51).

Initial Explorations

1.   When were Catullus and Calvus together? What were they doing? Where were they? Was anyone else there? (1–7)
     They were together the previous day. They were writing playful little verses in various meters on Catullus' writing tablets, matching or capping one another's verses, while joking and drinking. This presumably took place during normal working hours since the men are described as **ōtiōsī**, which implies a contrast with others who would be involved in business activities (**negōtia**) at the time. The location is not specified: not at Catullus' place (see line 7) nor at Calvus' since they do not use Calvus' tablets, but more likely at a drinking place somewhere in the city. There is no indication that anyone was present other than Catullus and Calvus.

2.   How are the two men and their activity characterized? (1–6)
     They were at leisure (**ōtiōsī**), i.e., not engaged in any of the usual business activities (**negōtia**) with which Romans would normally occupy themselves during the working hours of the day. They had a great deal of fun (**multum lūsimus**), writing on Catullus' tablets. They had agreed to enjoy themselves, to be frivolous or self-indulgent (**dēlicātōs**), presumably only for the duration of the time they were together this one day since this is something they specifically agreed upon; on other occasions they would doubtless be more serious. They were writing trifling little snatches of verse (**versiculōs**), playfully (**lūdēbat**), freely choosing their meters (**numerō modo hōc modo illōc**). The whole time the men were joking and drinking (**per iocum atque vīnum**).

3.   In what mental condition did Catullus depart from Calvus? (7–8) What result did this have for Catullus? (9–13)
     He was so inflamed with Calvus' charm and wit that he was miserable and food did not relieve his misery. He could not eat or sleep but tossed and turned over his whole bed, wanting only to see the light of day so that he could be with Calvus again and talk with him. He was in a state of intense mental excitement or derangement: *inflamed* (**incēnsus**, 8), *miserable/lovesick* (**miserum**, 9), and *unable to control himself* (**indomitus**, 11), because of *delirium* (**furōre**, 11).

4.   When and why did Catullus write the present poem? (14–17)
     He wrote the present poem when his limbs were exhausted from tossing and turning and lay half-dead on the bed, and he wrote it so that Calvus would learn of the mental or psychological pain (**dolōrem**) that he was suffering.

5.   Of what does Catullus warn Calvus? What are Catullus' **precēs**? (18–19)
     Catullus warns Calvus not to be presumptuous (**audāx**) and not to reject his prayers. His prayers, expressing what he now wants, have already been stated in line 13, namely, to

be with Calvus and talk with him.

6.   With what does Catullus threaten Calvus? (20–21)

He threatens him with punishment meted out by the goddess Nemesis, a powerful deity who punishes mortals for presumptuous acts that offend against the rightful respect owed to the gods. Thus Catullus appears to warn his dear friend not to despise his petition out of any thoughtless haughtiness ("hubris"), but to treat him as one would a suppliant.

Discussion

1.   Catullus describes Calvus and himself with the words ōtiōsī (1) and dēlicātōs (3). How is their life-style characterized in this poem? What would more traditionally-minded Romans such as the senēs sevēriōrēs referred to in Catullus 5.2 think about Catullus and Calvus' life-style here?

Segal (see Select Bibliography) provides a useful beginning for discussion of this topic:

Otiosi in the first line of poem 50 is, I suggest, a key word in the poem. It does not just fill out a vividly glimpsed scene in Catullus' life. Within its context it creates an antithesis to public life and suggests an elevation of the realm of the private, of personal mood and experience, to a new significance. In implicit opposition to the 'serious' work of law, politics, or business, it dwells upon the deliberately inconsequential activities, the frivolous— one might almost say, defiantly frivolous—pursuits of a privileged class of young men held together by common interests and tastes, and especially by common tastes in literature. The word, then, adumbrates both a mode of life and (indirectly) an aesthetic.

To appreciate the tone of defiance and the distinctive, 'non-conformist' attitude, one must realize that *otium* in this period has unfavourable, even 'disreputable' associations. Catullus, however, gives no hint of anything apologetic. Cicero, at the opposite pole, considers *otium* and *solitudo* to be *duae res quae languorem adferunt ceteris*, and sets it down to the credit of the elder Scipio Africanus that *et in otio de negotiis cogitare*.

Otiosi is followed by *lusimus, delicatos*, the diminutive *versiculos, ludebat, iocum atque vinum, lepore* (lines 2–7). Pucci, in his excellent study of 50, has noted the affinity of many of these words (and also *iucunde*, line 16) with Roman comedy. This connection, of course, increases the distance between the poem and the conventional morality of Catullus' respectable fellow citizens. (25–26)

2.   How does the poetic encounter with Calvus affect Catullus? What kind of language or what metaphor does Catullus use to describe the effect? Compare poem 35.

Catullus' poetic encounter with Calvus has a devastating effect on Catullus. He describes his condition metaphorically, using the language of love. Compare poem 35, in which a **puella** falls in love with Caecilius upon reading his newly begun poem on the Magna Mater (13–18). Reading Caecilius' poem has reduced the **puella** to a state of being **misella**, *lovesick* (35.14); in poem 50 Catullus departs from Calvus in a similar state of mind (**miserum**, 50.9). As Scott (see Select Bibliography) noted, the word **incēnsus** (8) "is borrowed from the standard erotic vocabulary of ancient love poetry"; Scott observed that it would usually be modified by **amōre**, but is here modified by **tuō lepōre / . . . facētiīsque** instead, "so that it connotes a strong intellectual, rather than erotic, friendship" (171). An erotic metaphor thus provides a basis for Catullus' description of his plight, but his plight is not that of a lover as is that of the **puella** of poem 35 but is intellectual, cerebral, and aesthetic, as Catullus is inflamed not by love or desire but by the *charm* and *wit* of Calvus and his versifications. "The emphasis is clearly on sociability and personality" (Finamore, 14, see Select Bibliography). The erotic parallel, however, is compelling. Compare, for example, the language used by Catullus in the lament of Ariadne, when she is deserted by her lover Theseus in poem 64. She is *inflamed* *in her mind* (**incēnsam . . . mente**, 64.97). Catullus describes himself as **miserum** (50.9), and Ariadne is repeatedly described with the same adjective (64.57, 71, 140, 196). Catullus describes himself as **indomitus furōre** (50.11), and Ariadne is described as **indomitōs in corde gerēns . . . furōrēs**, *bearing wild madness in her heart* (64.54). Later she is described as **inops, ārdēns, āmentī caeca furōre**, *helpless, blazing, blind with insane madness* (64.197). Those who are lovesick are described in ancient poetry as being unable to eat and sleep (Euripides, *Hippolytus* 131–40, 176–214; Theocritus, *Idyll* 2.81–92), and Catullus here remarks that food did not relieve his misery and that he was unable to sleep. The phrase **meum dolōrem** (50.17) will recall Catullus' reference to the **dolor** of his **puella** in poem 2.7, as she plays with her pet **passer** as a **sōlāciolum suī dolōris**. Catullus' desire to see the light of dawn so that he could be with Calvus and speak with him again (50.12–13) recalls the love-struck Medea's desire to see the light of dawn so that she could see Jason again (Apollonius, *Argonautica* 3.751–65). Note, however, that line 13 of Catullus' poem is in the rhetorical form of a hysteron proteron, with the chronological sequence of the items reversed, as Scott comments (171), in order "to emphasize the intellectual quality of this 'love affair'—'so that I might speak with you and be together with you.'" (Compare poem 9.)

After discussing the complex, metaphorical, and allusive language that Catullus uses to describe the effect that his poetic encounter with Calvus had on him, one should go back and reread the first six lines of the poem. Their vocabulary and grammar are fairly straightforward, and the situation described is fairly simple—Catullus and Calvus finding themselves at leisure decided to relax, play at responsive versification, joke, and drink. This is all very casual, and nothing in the description of the men's activities in lines 1–6 gives any hint of how this poetic encounter would devastate Catullus' poise, equanimity, and self-control and transform his state of mind into a kind of madness (**furor**), which he could describe only by calling on the language and situations of intense grief (there may be an allusion to Achilles' grieving over the dead Patroclus in *Iliad* 24.3–11 and 128–30) and overwhelming passionate love and heartache. A further index of the transformation of Catullus' attitude toward Calvus is seen in the series of vocatives, which progress from the fairly formal **Licinī** (1 and repeated in 8) to **iūcunde** (16) to the intimate expression of endearment, **ocelle** (19). The poet's recording of this transformation makes poem 50 one of the greatest and most unusual poems in the Catullan corpus. It has interesting parallels with poem 51, as we will see in discussion of that poem.

Select Bibliography

W. C. Scott. "Catullus and Calvus (c. 50)." *Classical Philology* 64 (1969) 169–73.
    The poet is speaking metaphorically: he has been moved as deeply and as completely as a lover is, not by some physical consideration, but by Calvus' wit and subtlety. (171)
Charles Segal. "Catullan *Otiosi*: The Lover and the Poet." *Greece & Rome* 17 (1970) 25–31. See above.
John Finamore. "Catullus 50 and 51: Friendship, Love, and *Otium*." *Classical World* 78 (1984) 11–19. Highly recommended.
Mark Williams. "Catullus 50 and the Language of Friendship." *Latomus* 47 (1988) 69–73. Builds on Scott's discussion of the poem.

CATULLUS 51

1 That man seems to me to be equal to a god,
2 that man, if it is possible, [seems to me] to surpass the gods,
3 who sitting opposite repeatedly
4   looks at you and listens to you

5 sweetly laughing, [a thing] that takes all sensation from me
6 [and makes me] miserable/lovesick: for as soon as [ever] I catch sight of you,
7 Lesbia, there is nothing left to me
8   [of voice on my lips,]

9 but my tongue is paralyzed, a thin flame
10 flows down through my limbs, my ears ring
11 with their own ringing, my eyes are covered
12   with a twofold night.

13 Leisure, Catullus, is troublesome for you;
14 in leisure you revel and exult too much;
15 Leisure in the past has destroyed both kings
16   and wealthy cities.

Poem 51 is the first of two poems that Catullus wrote in the Sapphic meter, and it may have been the first poem that he addressed to Lesbia. The other is poem 11, which expresses the poet's profound sense of loss at parting for good from his beloved Lesbia. Interpretation of poem 51 has been complicated by a number of unjustifiable assumptions scholars have made about it and in particular by controversy over its last stanza and the question whether it was originally a part of poem 51 or not. The interpretation of poem 51 offered here is based primarily on the words of the poem itself and tries to avoid the quagmires of 150 years of assumptions and hypotheses put forth by scholars,* and it is built on the assumption that the fourth stanza is and always was an integral part of the poem (contrary to the views of many scholars, including Fordyce, who comments, "Attempts to relate it to the rest of the poem are unplausible special pleading," 219). The first three stanzas are a close adaptation of a poem by Sappho, most of which is preserved for us in Pseudo-Longinus, *On the Sublime.* The best discussion of that poem of Sappho and of Catullus 51 is to be found in the article by Garry Wills (see bibliographical note).

N.B. Note that we give no indication in our presentation of the poem on pages 148–51 of the student's book that the first three stanzas are adapted from Sappho. We have done this so that teachers who wish to do so may have their students experience the poem first as simply a creation of Catullus and not as a "translation." For some students the initial impact of the poem will be greater when read this way. Study of the poem as containing an imitation of Sappho can then come later. Teachers may, of course, tell students immediately that part of the poem is adapted from Sappho, if they wish to do so.

The study material provided for poem 51 is more extensive than usual and includes comparison with poem 50, comparison with the original poem by Sappho (fragment 31 in modern editions of her poems), comparison with earlier poetry and with poetry contemporary with Catullus that incorporated elements from Sappho's poem and thus provided a tradition within which Catullus was working when he made his adaptation of her poem, and finally comparison with Catullus 11, the last poem in the Lesbia cycle. More material than usual is provided for Catullus 51, and the questions are fuller, as are also their answers, partly because this poem has been so widely misunderstood and partly because it is such an important poem, serving as it does as one of a pair of bookends within which the poems in the Lesbia cycle may be gathered and arranged. Note also that the Greek text of Sappho's poem is given on page 124 of the student's book with a facing translation on page 125. Under the heading **Another Comparison** below will be found notes on the vocabulary and dialect of Sappho's poem.

*[Especially to be avoided are attempts to reconstruct the situation that may have lain behind the composition of the poem, such as that of Jachmann, reported as follows by Fredricksmeyer (1965; see Select Bibliography):

> Catullus takes part in a social function of Caecilius Metellus Celer; there he comes to see Clodia, the wife of the host, and he feels himself *primo aspectu* swept away by her seductive charm. Unfortunately he has to see her, at the same time, flirting with another man, and so all hope disappears of winning her favors. . . . Thus he believes he must turn away from a way of life which brings with it the danger of involvement in unhappy passions. (156)

There is no basis for any of this in the poem itself, except for Catullus being "swept away by her seductive charm." In the poem there is no Caecilius Metellus Celer, Lesbia is not identified with Clodia (although that identification may be correct), there is no indication or even hint that Lesbia is married (although she may have been Clodia Metelli), there is no indication that she is flirting with *ille*, and, as Fredricksmeyer remarks, it is difficult to believe that Catullus would abandon all hope of winning Lesbia's favors just because he saw her flirting with another man. Better to examine the poem itself rather than to try to reconstruct some situation in real life that may have prompted its composition.]

Initial Explorations

1. Three people are involved in the first two stanzas of this poem. Who are they? What exactly are we told about the identity of each of them?

    First, there is a man referred to by the word **ille**. He is not named, and nothing is said about his identity; we have no way of knowing whether the pronoun **ille** was meant to refer to a real person or was a fiction adapted from Sappho. Speculation as to his identity is idle, and any assumptions as to his identity are likely to mislead and to interfere with interpretation of the poem itself. Second, there is the speaker or the poet, referred to by the pronoun **mī** in the first line and referred to in the second stanza with the words **miserō**, **mihi**, **aspexī**, and **mī**. Nothing is said about his identity, but he is assumed to be Catullus. Third, there is a woman referred to by the name **Lesbia**. Nothing is said about her identity, but she is assumed to be the Lesbia of the other love poems (usually identified, whether rightly or wrongly, as Clodia Metelli).

2. What rhetorical figure links the first two lines?

    Anaphora: **Ille . . . /ille**. The anaphora may be felt to continue with **quī** at the beginning of line 3.

3. What does the poet accomplish by adding the second line?

    He heightens the statement made in the first line.

4. Why does the poet add the parenthetical **sī fās est**?

    Fordyce (219) interprets this as a "characteristically Roman conventional formula of caution," inserted to avoid offending the gods. Thomson (327–28) rejects this interpretation and sees the clause as meaning nothing more than "if it is possible."

5. What is the man referred to by the word **ille** doing? (3–5)

    He is sitting opposite the woman and repeatedly looking at her and listening to her sweetly laughing.

6. What is the woman doing? (5)

    She is laughing sweetly.

7. To what does **quod** (5) refer?

    First, **quod** could refer to the whole scene of the man sitting opposite the woman, looking at her, and listening to her laughing sweetly. Second, **quod** could refer just to the ideas expressed in the **quī** clause of sitting opposite the woman, looking at her, and listening to her laughing sweetly. Third, **quod** could refer just to the woman's sweet laughter. Since in lines 6–8 the poet makes the generalization expressed in lines 5–6 specific by commenting on what happens when he looks just at the woman, with no mention of the man, either the second or the third interpretation above would appear to be preferable to the first.

Fredricksmeyer (1965, 158; see Select Bibliography) comments as follows: "It is not at once clear whether *quod* refers to the whole preceding picture . . . or only to the directly preceding image of the sweetly laughing Lesbia (*dulce ridentem*); but the following clause explains (*nam*): it is above all the sight of Lesbia herself that so unnerves the poet." So also Woodson (see Select Bibliography): "*quod* refers only to Lesbia's sweet laughter" (78). Wills (186) argues persuasively that **quod** refers to the two verbs of the **quī** clause, namely **spectat et audit**, and to their direct object, **tē / . . . / dulce rīdentem**; the relative pronoun **quod** could then be translated *which thing (namely, looking at you and listening to you sweetly laughing)*. The man referred to as **ille** is thus no longer of interest to the poet, and so jealousy is not the issue here; the issue is solely the effect that Lesbia has on the poet.

8. The pronoun **mihi** (6) is modified by **miserō** (5). Is it better to take **miserō** as an attributive adjective (*from miserable/lovesick me*) or to take it proleptically (*from me [and makes me] miserable/lovesick*)? Why is the adjective placed so early, even ahead of the relative pronoun that introduces the clause within which the adjective functions grammatically?

    It is probably better to take it proleptically: looking at the woman and listening to her sweet laughter takes all sensation away from the poet *and makes him miserable/lovesick*. The adjective is placed as early as possible, even before the relative pronoun, for emphasis; placed there and modifying, even alliterating with, **mihi** at the end of the clause, it also frames the clause, and, further, it sets this clause with its personal reference to the poet off in strong opposition to the first stanza, which describes **ille** and *his* relationship to the woman.

9. How does the word **miserō** (5) set the poet in opposition to the man referred to by the word **ille**?

    The man referred to by the word **ille** is equated with the gods or said to be superior to the gods. The adjective **miser**, *pitiable, poor, wretched, unfortunate, miserable, lovesick*, is particularly applicable to humans as opposed to gods and places Catullus firmly on the human level; **miserō** in its emphatic placement thus contrasts with **pār . . . deō** (1). With the divine or more than divine equanimity of the man referred to by the word **ille**, compare Lucretius' description of the gods (*De rerum natura* 3.18–24, trans., W. H. D. Rouse): "Before me appear the gods in their majesty, and their peaceful abodes, which no winds ever shake nor clouds besprinkle with rain, which no snow congealed by the bitter frost mars with its white fall, but the air ever cloudless encompasses them and laughs with its light spread wide abroad. There moreover nature supplies everything, *and nothing at any time impairs their peace of mind*" (italics ours).

10. What words in the first stanza are echoed by **simul tē / . . . aspexī** in the second?

    The words **identidem tē / spectat** (3–4) are echoed by **simul tē / . . . aspexī**. In both cases an adverb precedes the pronoun **tē**, and the parallel phrases sharpen the contrast between the man, who repeatedly looks at the woman, and Catullus, who as soon as he ever catches sight of the woman suffers debilitating physical symptoms.

11. What contrast is being drawn between Catullus in the second stanza and the man referred to by the word **ille** in the first?

    The contrast is between a man (the **ille**) who repeatedly looks at the woman and listens to her sweetly laughing and in so doing seems to be equal to a god or to surpass the gods on the one hand and Catullus on the other, who, far from being like the gods, loses his ability to speak as soon as he ever looks at the woman (6–8).

    An accurate understanding of this contrast is essential in interpreting the whole poem. Kinsey (see Select Bibliography) has it right: "For the contrast is not between an *ille* who is with Lesbia and a Catullus who is not, but between an *ille* who keeps on gazing at and listening to Lesbia and a Catullus who has not the power to do these things because of the immediate effect her presence has on him. . . . the contrast is between a man who *can* gaze upon, listen to and talk to Lesbia (*dulce ridentem* implies that *ille* has said something for Lesbia to laugh at) and Catullus who is immediately deprived of these powers by the sight of her" (375).

Wills (see Select Bibliography) argues persuasively that the words **miserō quod omnīs / ēripit sēnsūs mihi** (5–6) must ultimately be read as an implied apodosis of a contrary-to-fact condition. Wills paraphrases as follows: "Doing what he is doing—looking at her, and listening, close up, and long—takes away all my sensation (*i.e.* would do so *if* I were imitating him), since even a glance makes me aware of a series of physical disorders." Wills concludes that for Catullus to look at the woman repeatedly and listen to her sweetly laughing would be "unthinkably audacious, impossibly risky" (187).

12.   What four more debilitating effects does Catullus describe in lines 9–12?

  His tongue is paralyzed, a sensation as if of fire flows down his limbs, his ears ring (i.e., he becomes deaf), and darkness covers his eyes (i.e., he becomes blind). Note the asyndeton between the clauses, which emphasizes the non-stop effect on the senses.

13.   Examine the positions of the nouns and the verbs in the four clauses in lines 9–12 and identify the elements of a chiasmus.

  These are the elements of a chiasmus:

A	B	B	A
(NOUNS)	(VERBS)	(VERBS)	(NOUNS)
lingua	torpet	tintinant	aurēs
flamma	dēmānat	teguntur	lūmina

14.   What letters in lines 9–12 create a particularly effective alliteration?

  The letters *m* and *n* in the following words: **lingua, tenuis, flamma, dēmānat, sonitū, tintinant, geminā, teguntur, lūmina,** and **nocte.** Particularly effective is the repetition of **-min-** in <u>gemin</u>ā and <u>lūmina</u>.

15.   Find a transferred epithet in lines 9–12.

  The adjective **geminā** is a transferred epithet because grammatically it modifies **nocte** but in sense it goes with **lūmina**. The reader must make an effort to try to understand it both ways: the grammatically conveyed picture of the eyes (literally, *lights*) being covered with *a twin night* is daring, unconventional, and arresting, and it is with a sense of relief that the reader recognizes **geminā** as a transferred epithet and converts the picture into one of twin eyes being covered with darkness. As we read and reread the lines, both pictures persist and alternate in our understanding of them.

16.   What two words are most effectively juxtaposed in lines 9–12?

  The words **lūmina** and **nocte**, literally *lights* and *night*, metonymy for *eyes* and *darkness*. Compare the juxtaposition of **lūx** and **nox** in Catullus 5.5–6.

17.   How does the final clause, **geminā . . . / . . . nocte** (11–12), provide a fitting climax for the list of debilitating effects? How is the placement of the word **nocte** significant?

  The clause, describing blindness, is a fitting climax to the series of debilitating effects partly because it is the most catastrophic and partly because it concludes a series of effects produced by *sight*, i.e., by the poet's looking at Lesbia. The word **nocte**, *night*, is significantly placed as the last word in the list of debilitating effects because it expresses the darkness that covers the poet's eyes and renders him blind and unable any longer to look at the woman who has such a catastrophic effect on him.

18.   What rhetorical figure is most prominent in the final stanza? (13–16)

  Anaphora: **Ōtium . . . /ōtiō . . . /ōtium.**

19.   Point out several ways in which the placement of words and arrangement of clauses in the final stanza parallel the placement of words and arrangement of clauses in the first stanza of the poem.

  The anaphora in the last stanza (**Ōtium . . . /ōtiō . . . /ōtium**) echoes that in the first (**Ille . . . /ille . . . /quī**). The first two lines in each stanza each contain a complete clause (these are the only four lines in the poem where this is the case). The second line in each of the stanzas expands on the thought of the first line. The third and fourth lines of each stanza consist of potentially complete clauses (the clause in lines 3–4 does spill over into the next stanza, but it could have ended with line 4)—again these are the only stanzas in the poem where this occurs. The verbs of these clauses come in the fourth line of each stanza (once again this happens only in these stanzas).

The striking similarities between these two stanzas suggest that there are other, more profound relationships between them to be sought.

20. In the second and third stanzas Catullus has listed ways in which he is physically debilitated and devastated whenever he looks at Lesbia. On what does he place blame for this happening to him? (13)

He states in line 13 that it is **ōtium** that is troublesome (**molestum**) to him, and logically this must mean that he blames **ōtium** for what happens to him whenever he looks at Lesbia. Baker (see Select Bibliography) expresses it this way: "it is by . . . lack of enterprise in love, an inert surrender to the emotional and physical effects of love that reach their climax in stanza 3, that Catullus finds himself afflicted in stanza 4; and . . . it is by this sort of *otium* that he is held back from the god-like bliss of anonymous *ille* of stanza 1" (320).

21. How does Catullus rebuke himself for his employment of his leisure (**ōtium**)? (14)

He rebukes himself by declaring that he exults *too much* (**nimium**) in his leisure. He does not rebuke himself for cultivating leisure per se, but for indulging in it to excess. It was one of the commonplaces of ancient morality that doing or carrying anything to excess is dangerous and liable to lead to disaster. So here, the second line of the stanza makes it clear that Catullus does not blame **ōtium** per se for the devastating effects that looking at Lesbia has on him, but rather he blames his excessive indulgence in **ōtium**.

22. How is the effect that **ōtium** has had on kings and wealthy cities (15–16) a heightened parallel to the effect that looking at Lesbia has on Catullus?

Ōtium is said to have destroyed kings and rich cities, and presumably Catullus means that excessive indulgence in **ōtium** of the sort for which he rebukes himself has led to the destruction of kings and rich cities by putting kings, their guardians, and their armies off guard and thus exposing them to their enemies as easy prey. Something similar on a much smaller scale has happened to Catullus; his excessive indulgence in **ōtium** has put him off guard and made him so vulnerable to Lesbia's charms that merely glancing at her reduces him to speechlessness, deafness, and blindness.

Two of the clauses in the third stanza describing what happens to Catullus may prefigure the thought of cities being destroyed in the fourth stanza. First, the flame that devastates Catullus in lines 9–10 may prefigure cities being destroyed in the last stanza. Second, the final clause of the third stanza describing eyes covered with a twin night may remind the reader of Homeric warriors with darkness covering their eyes as they die on the battlefield (e.g., "and a mist of darkness clouded both eyes," Homer, *Iliad* 4.461, trans., Lattimore). The final image of Catullus in the third stanza is thus one of a vanquished and perishing lover and anticipates the image of destroyed cities in the final stanza.

23. How does Catullus' excessive indulgence in **ōtium** (14) account for his inability to look at Lesbia and listen to her sweetly laughing the way that the man referred to by the word **ille** is able to do?

The explanation lies in the concept of **ōtium** exposing and destroying kings and rich cities, and without the final two lines of the poem the answer to this question would not be clear. Catullus means that his excessive indulgence in **ōtium** puts him off guard and leaves him defenseless and vulnerable when exposed to Lesbia's captivating charms.

The man referred to by the word **ille** must be, Catullus claims, superhuman, possessing the equanimity and composure of the gods as described, for instance, by Lucretius, or even surpassing those gods, to be able repeatedly to look at Lesbia and listen to her sweetly laughing. This man, too, is enjoying **ōtium**, but he, Catullus says, must have superhuman resources and powers. He is not overwhelmed but remains in control of himself and the situation that he is in with Lesbia.

Catullus has a long way to go to become the equal of that man, if such is even possible. The final stanza with its self-rebuke and imagery of warfare points the way; Catullus must cease his excessive indulgence in **ōtium** and must develop himself, train himself, and steel himself until he has adequate defenses and resources to meet the challenge of Lesbia's captivating charm. As Wills (see Select Bibliography) concludes (197), "He must have a heroic ardor and energy, great enough to bear love's most excruciating bliss."

Baker (see Select Bibliography), after comparing Ovid's *Amores* 1.9 on the lover as soldier, comments: "Ovid found, just as Catullus had, that *otium* was *molestum* and inimical to the proper response to love. So he answered the call to arms. It is a similar call to action in love's warfare, issued in a manner more oblique than the characteristic clarion call of Ovid, which I believe we are meant to see Catullus addressing to himself at the beginning of stanza 4" (322). The oblique call to action here, then, anticipates Catullus' claim in poem 37 that he has loved Lesbia as much as no woman will ever be loved and that he has waged great wars on her account (**prō quā mihi sunt magna bella pugnāta**, 13); by the time of the composition of poem 37 Catullus has long since played the role of a valiant soldier of love, but unfortunately with no good result since Lesbia has now taken up with a motley crew of adulterers at a *whore-house tavern* (**salāx taberna**, 37.1).

Comparison

Compare this poem with Catullus 50:

1. In what ways are Catullus' encounters with Calvus and with Lesbia similar? In what ways are they dissimilar?

    They are similar in that both have devastating effects on Catullus. They are also similar in that both relationships are made possible by **ōtium**. They are dissimilar in that Catullus' encounter with Calvus is a poetic encounter with a man while his encounter with Lesbia is an erotic encounter with a woman.

2. Compare the effects suffered by Catullus from his poetic encounter with Calvus with the effects suffered by Catullus when he looks at Lesbia.

    The effects suffered by Catullus from his poetic encounter with Calvus are intellectual and cerebral; he is inflamed with Calvus' charm and wit, he is wild with delirium, and he desires to be with Calvus again so that he can speak with him. While Catullus' passion makes him miserable (**miserum**, 50.9) and disrupts the routine of his life, before the night is over he regains enough control to write poem 50 to Calvus. In poem 51 the devastation Catullus experiences at the sight of Lesbia also makes him miserable (**miserō**, 51.5) and precipitates a series of physical symptoms: speechlessness, flame-like sensations down his limbs, ringing in his ears, and blindness. At some point he recovers enough to compose poem 51 and to include a self-rebuke with the apparent purpose of putting himself on a path that will lead to a remedy of the problem that he records in the poem.

3. What role does **ōtium** play in the two poems?

    Leisure is essential in both poems. It provides the opportunity for Calvus and Catullus to indulge in their playful exchange of verses that ends up captivating Catullus, devastating him, and reducing him to delirium. In poem 51 the man referred to with the word **ille** and Lesbia are at leisure as the man looks at Lesbia and listens to her sweetly laughing. Catullus is also at leisure whenever he looks at Lesbia and suffers devastating physical reactions. **Ōtium** is thus essential to the "plots" of both poems. Without **ōtium** neither poem would have come into existence. The conception of **ōtium** is, however, more complex in poem 51, in that Catullus rebukes himself for indulging in it to excess and sees this excessive indulgence as the cause of the devastation that the sight of Lesbia produces throughout his body.

4. What resolution of his plight does Catullus envision in poem 50? What resolution of his plight in poem 51 does its final stanza hint at?

    In poem 50 Catullus seeks resolution in the form of another meeting with Calvus and an opportunity to speak with him again. He begs that Calvus comply with his wishes. In poem 51 Catullus extends no invitation to Lesbia but envisions resolution as being dependent on his adopting a new soldierly regimen of self-discipline in which he would abandon his excessive indulgence in **ōtium** and no longer allow himself to be overcome and vanquished by Lesbia's charms as kings and wealthy cities have been destroyed by excessive indulgence in **ōtium** in the past. If Catullus would only heed the positive advice implied in his self-rebuke in the final stanza, he could attain the position that the man referred to by the word **ille** occupies vis à vis Lesbia in the first stanza of the poem, i.e., he could repeatedly look at Lesbia and listen to her sweetly laughing without detrimental effect.

Another Comparison

Notes on the Greek of Sappho 31 (the Greek text is on page 124 of the student's book). Attic equivalents of Sappho's Aeolic forms are given below.

1 **Φαίνεται**: *(he) appears.*
   μοι: dat. sing., *to me.*
   κῆνος: = ἐκεῖνος, *that,* with ὤνηρ (2), *that man.*
   ἴσος: + dat., *equal* (to).
   θέοισιν: = θεοῖς, dat. pl., *to the gods.*
2 **ἔμμεν(αι)**: = εἶναι, *to be.*
   ὤνηρ: = ὁ ἀνήρ, *the man,* with κῆνος (1), *that man.*
   ὄττις: = ὅστις, *whoever, who.*
   ἐνάντιος: = ἐναντίος + dat., *opposite* (to).
   τοι: = σοι, dat. sing., *to you.*
3 **ἰσδάνει**: = ἱζάνει, *sits.*
   καί: conj., *and.*
   πλάσιον: = πλησίον, adv., *near, close at hand.*
   ἆδυ: = ἡδέως, adv., *sweetly.*
   φωνείσας: = φωνούσης, *speaking,* feminine genitive singular participle, modifying an implied *you,* object of ὑπακούει.
4 **ὑπακούει**: = ὑπακούει + gen., *listens to.*
5 **γελαίσας**: = γελώσης, *laughing,* feminine genitive singular participle, modifying the implied *you* (see note on line 3), object of ὑπακούει.
   ἰμέροεν: = ἱμερόεν, adv., *in a charming/lovely manner.*
   τό: = ὅ, relative pronoun, *which.*
   μ': = μοι, dat. of the possessor, *for me.*
   ἦ μάν: = ἦ μήν, *truly.*
6 **καρδίαν**: *heart.*
   ἐν: prep. + dat., *in.*
   στήθεσιν: dat. pl., *breast.*
   ἐπτόαισεν: = ἐπτόησεν, aorist of πτοέω, *to terrify, scare; to excite, set aflutter.* Translate the aorist as a present, *sets . . . aflutter.*
7 **ὡς . . . ὡς**: adv. = ὡς . . . ὡς, *when(ever) . . . then.*
   γάρ: conj., *for.*
   ἔς σ(ε): = εἴς σε, *at you.*
   ἴδω: *I (ever) look,* aorist subjunctive in an indefinite or general temporal clause (usually with κε or ἄν).
   βρόχε(α): = βραχέα, adv., *briefly, for a moment.*
   με φώναισ(αι): = με φωνῆσαι, aorist infinitive, *for me to speak.*
8 **οὐδ(ὲ) . . . ἔτ(ι)**: *no longer.*
   ἒν: = ἕν, *one thing.*
   εἴκει: *(it) is possible.*
9 **ἀλλά**: conj., *but.*
   κὰμ . . . ἔαγε: tmesis for κατέαγε, perfect of κατάγνυμι, *to shatter;* the perfect active form is here used in a passive sense, *has been/is shattered,* or as intransitive, *has snapped* (Campbell); our translation, *is tied.*
   μὲν . . . δ(έ) (10): particles, *on the one hand . . . on the other hand.*
   γλῶσσα: = γλῶττα, *tongue.*

μ(οι): dat. of the possessor, *my*, or ethical dative, *for me*.

λέπτον: = λεπτόν, *fine, delicate, thin*.

10 **αὔτικα**: = αὐτίκα, adv., *immediately, at once*.

χρῷ: = χρωτί, dat. sing., *skin*.

πῦρ: *fire, flame*.

ὑπαδεδρόμηκεν: = ὑποδεδρόμηκεν + dat., *has run beneath*.

11 **ὀππάτεσσι**: = ὄμμασι, dat. of means or instrument, *with [my] eyes*.

δ(έ): conj., *and*.

οὐδ(έ): adv., *not even*.

ἒν: = ἕν, *one thing*.

ὄρημμ(ι): = ὁρῶ, *I see*.

ἐπιρρόμβεισι: = ἐπιρρομβοῦσι, *(they) buzz*.

12 **ἄκουαι**: = ἀκοαί, *ears*.

13 **κὰδ . . . κακχέεται**: tmesis = καταχέεται, *pours down*.

μ(οι): = μοι = ἔμεθεν, *from me*.

ἴδρως: = ἰδρώς, *sweat*.

τρόμος: *trembling, quivering*.

14 **παῖσαν**: = πᾶσαν, *all, entire*; supply με and translate *all of me*.

ἄγρει = αἱρεῖ, *seizes, takes hold of*.

χλωροτέρα: *paler*.

ποίας: = πόης, gen. of comparison, *than grass*.

15 **ἔμμι**: = εἰμί, *I am*.

τεθνάκην: = τεθνάναι, *to be dead*.

ὀλίγω: = ὀλίγου, gen., *of little*.

(ἐ)πιδεύης: = ἐπιδευής + gen., *in want of, lacking*.

16 **φαίνομ(αι)**: *I seem*.

ἔμ(οι) αὔτᾳ: = ἐμοὶ αὔτᾳ, *to me myself*.

  τεθνάκην (15) . . . **αὔτᾳ** (16): *I seem to me myself lacking little to be dead = I seem to myself little short of being dead*.

17 **ἀλλὰ**: conj., *but*.

πὰν: = πᾶν, *all, everything*.

τόλματον: = τολμητόν, *has been/must be ventured/endured*.

ἐπεί: conj., *since*.

καί: adv., *even*.

πένητα: *a poor person*.

1. What are the major changes that Catullus has made in adapting the first three stanzas of Sappho's poem?

   a. Catullus' second line is new.
   b. Catullus adds **identidem** in line 3.
   c. Catullus adds **spectat** in line 4.
   d. Catullus adds **miserō** in line 5.
   e. Catullus changes "which truly sets / the heart in my breast aflutter" (Sappho 5–6) to **miserō quod omnīs / ēripit sēnsūs mihi** (5–6).
   f. Catullus reverses the order of the clauses in Sappho, lines 12–13, so as to put the reference to the ringing of his ears first (10–11) and the reference to blindness second (11–12).
   g. Catullus has heightened the rhetoric in his description of blindness (11–12) from Sappho's simple statement "I cannot see even one thing with my eyes" (12) to a statement containing striking alliteration, a transferred epithet, a metaphorical use of **lūmina** (*lights* = *eyes*) and **nocte** (*night* = *darkness*), effective clause framing by the two ablatives, effective antithesis of **lūmina** and **nocte**, climactic placement of **nocte**, and an allusion to Homeric warriors fallen on the battlefield.

2.   What reasons can you suggest for his having made each of these changes?

a.   Catullus' second line is new.
In the first place, Catullus likes hyperbole. He may also have added this line to suggest that he is attempting to "surpass" his Greek model. Structurally, he needed to add this line in order to reinforce the parallelism between his first and fourth stanzas; in each stanza the second line expands on the first. Much of the meaning of the poem depends on recognition of the relationship between the first and the fourth stanzas.

b.   Catullus adds **identidem** in line 3.
The purpose of this addition is to emphasize the essential, fundamental contrast between the man referred to by the word **ille** and Catullus. The former looks at and listens to Lesbia *repeatedly*, while Catullus immediately swoons and blacks out as soon as he ever looks at her.

c.   Catullus adds **spectat** in line 4.
Two things are achieved by this addition.
First, the word immediately combines with **audit** as representing the two primary senses (sight and hearing) by means of which we perceive the world outside of ourselves; these senses of sight and hearing then recur in stanzas two and three: sight (**aspexī**, 7, and **lūmina**, 12) and hearing (**aurēs**, 11).
Second, the addition of **spectat** before **audit** in line 4 establishes a powerful chiasmus with the third and fourth clauses in the third stanza, thus:

A	B	B	A
(SIGHT)	(HEARING)	(HEARING)	(SIGHT)
spectat	audit	sonitū suōpte / tintinant aurēs	geminā teguntur / lūmina nocte

Catullus has carefully engineered this chiasmus by deliberately making two changes: the addition of **spectat** in line 4 and the reversal from Sappho of the clauses describing the eyes and the ears in the third stanza. The result is a highlighting of the fundamental contrast between the man described by the word **ille** and Catullus: the former can look at and listen to Lesbia repeatedly, whereas Catullus loses hearing and vision as soon as he ever looks at her. The clauses in the third stanza negate the verbs in line 4 in reverse order in a brilliantly engineered rhetorical flourish and with uncompromising logic and irreversible finality.

d.   Catullus adds **miserō** in line 5.
This adjective sharpens the contrast between the divine status of the man referred to by the word **ille** and the mere mortal Catullus. It is also a favorite word for describing the misery of the lover suffering from unrequited love (cf. Catullus 8, 35.14, and 50.9).

e.   Catullus changes "which truly sets / the heart in my breast aflutter" (Sappho 5–6) to **miserō quod omnīs / ēripit sēnsūs mihi** (5–6).
Again, Catullus shows his preference for hyperbole. Also, Catullus with a strict sense of logic begins with a general statement referring to all of his senses and then lists the individual functions or senses beginning with line 7. This is more orderly than in Sappho, who begins with a very specific symptom ("which truly sets / the heart in my breast aflutter," 5–6) and then proceeds to other individual symptoms. Finally, Sappho at the end of her fourth stanza remarks that she is "little / short of being dead." Catullus did not overtly include the items in Sappho's fourth stanza, but his words **miserō quod omnīs / ēripit sēnsūs mihi** (5–6) imply a state of being near death or death itself. He thus puts right up front the concept of death, which Sappho leaves for her conclusion. It should also be noted that the idea of death implied in Catullus' lines 5–6 is picked up at the end of his third stanza in the allusion to dead Homeric warriors.

f.   Catullus reverses the order of the clauses in Sappho, lines 12–13, so as to put the reference to the ringing of his ears first (10–11) and the reference to blindness second (11–12).
See c above.

g. Catullus has heightened the rhetoric in his description of blindness (11–12) from Sappho's simple statement "I cannot see even one thing with my eyes" (12) to a statement containing striking alliteration, a transferred epithet, a metaphorical use of **lūmina** (*lights = eyes*) and **nocte** (*night = darkness*), effective clause framing by the two ablatives, effective antithesis of **lūmina** and **nocte**, climactic placement of **nocte**, and an allusion to Homeric warriors fallen on the battlefield.

    Again, Catullus is striving for hyperbole. He wants the antithesis of light/night as metaphors for life and death, and he wants the allusion to Homeric warriors. Wills (see Select Bibliography) catches the difference in style between Sappho and Catullus when he comments, "The poems shape the same thought, hers dancingly, his as a thing baroquely sculpted" (197).

3. What is Catullus doing in writing a completely different fourth stanza?

    He takes the thought expressed in the first words of Sappho's fifth stanza, "But all must be endured," which was most likely expanded in the remainder of the stanza now lost, and he transforms the thought from an exhortation to a self-rebuke, **ōtiō exsultās nimiumque gestīs** (14). He develops through the comment on kings and rich cities being destroyed by **ōtium** the idea that he must discipline himself and become more vigilant and aggressive, that he must become soldierly, if he is going to become strong enough to take his place in the presence of Lesbia and endure her captivating charms without losing his senses.

    It is possible that Sappho's fifth stanza expressed ideas similar to those in Catullus' fourth stanza and that he has adapted them just as he has adapted material from Sappho's first three stanzas. We will never know unless the remainder of Sappho's poem is retrieved.

More Comparisons

1. Find the words or phrases in the translation of Sappho's poem that one might recall when reading the underlined words and phrases in the passages above. Judging from the translations of Sappho and of these later poets provided above, do the descriptions of symptoms in the latter seem to have been written in such a way as to recall Sappho's poem to the reader's mind? If so, what purpose is served by such recall?

    Students should search Sappho's poem for words or phrases that are recalled by the underlined words and phrases in the passages from the later poets. They should be told something about how and why ancient poets imitated or alluded to their predecessors in order to establish traditional themes and traditional treatments of themes. This was done partly out of respect for earlier literary masters and partly out of a desire of the later poet to situate himself within a recognizable tradition. Imitation was not plagiarism, and the later poet always varied the expressions used by the earlier poet so that there was always **variātiō in imitātiōne**. The later poet would provide his own personal development of the imitated theme, while including enough reminiscences to remind his readers of his source. Allusion in the later poets to specific motifs that Sappho used to describe her physical and emotional symptoms adds credibility, authenticity, and a feeling of genuineness to the descriptions in the later poets. Students may also note ways in which the later poets have individualized their descriptions to fit the characters being described.

2. Sappho's is a female voice, and the descriptions of the catastrophic physical and emotional effects of love at first sight in Apollonius and Theocritus are descriptions of the effects suffered by women. Valerius Aedituus and Catullus adapted these descriptions that had by their time come to be traditionally associated with the physical and emotional suffering of women to describe their own suffering as men overcome by love. What is ironic or paradoxical about Catullus' appropriation to his own situation of Sappho and of her imagery that had become

traditional in descriptions of the physical and emotional suffering of *women* falling in love at first sight?

The very fact that Catullus appropriated Sappho and the imagery associated with women falling in love at first sight to a description of his own suffering whenever he looked at Lesbia speaking and laughing sweetly might well have seemed ironic or paradoxical to a Roman reader because of the reversals of role and gender. In the tradition it had been the woman who suffered extreme emotional effects and physical paralysis when falling in love at first sight, and in Apollonius and Theocritus it had become a situation of a woman falling in love with a man at first sight. One could also compare Phaedra's falling in love with Hippolytus at first sight, as described in Euripides' *Hippolytus* ("Phaedra saw him, and her heart was seized / with a terrible love," 27–28). All of this is ironically and paradoxically reversed in Catullus' poem, in which it is the man who suffers all of the emotional and physical symptoms traditionally associated with women.

3. How does an understanding of the tradition that lies behind Catullus' portrayal of himself in a female role as victimized by love contribute to an understanding of the unity of his poem 51, including the last stanza?

Vulnerability is a unifying theme in Catullus 51—Catullus' emotional and physical vulnerability whenever he looks at Lesbia and the vulnerability of kings and wealthy cities. Catullus is victimized by Love just as thoroughly as were the women in the traditional accounts of falling in love at first sight. An understanding of the tradition helps us understand how Catullus is portraying himself as the helpless victim of Lesbia's charms. In the last stanza Catullus blames the helpless victimization that he suffers on his excessive indulgence in **ōtium**, and he finds a parallel in the public sphere, in which kings and wealthy cities have been victimized and destroyed by their enemies due to excessive indulgence in **ōtium**. If the kings and cities are not to be destroyed, they must set aside their excessive indulgence in **ōtium** and mount their defenses in a more manly fashion. If Catullus is to become like the man referred to as **ille** and to be able repeatedly to look at Lesbia, to listen to her talking and sweetly laughing, and to interact with her as her lover, he must set aside his excessive indulgence in **ōtium**, and he must abandon the female role of helpless, vulnerable victim and become a manly soldier in the warfare of love. He must cease playing the role of a Sappho, a Phaedra, a Medea, or a Simaetha, and he must become a man.

A Final Comparison

1. Study the chiastic arrangement of themes in the two poems when set side by side:

Poem 11		Poem 51	
A	B	B	A
negōtium	Final parting of the ways	Love at first sight	**ōtium**
(travel and conquest) (lines 1–14)	(reminiscence of Sappho) (lines 21–24)	(adaptation of Sappho) (lines 1–12)	(destruction of kings and cities) (lines 13–16)

Each poem divides into two parts of unequal length. The longer section of poem 11, the travelogue, corresponds to the shorter section of poem 51, the stanza on **ōtium**; the longer section of poem 51, consisting of the adaptation of Sappho 31 and describing the symptoms the poet suffers whenever he looks at Lesbia (= love at first sight), corresponds to the shorter section of poem 11, which gives the poet's message of his final parting from Lesbia and the death of his love for her, using the image of the flower, which is derived from Sappho. The corresponding sections are chiastically arranged, with each corresponding section reversing its opposite in theme and in relative length (see Fredricksmeyer, 1983, 78–82, Select Bibliography).

2. How does the theme of travel developed in lines 1–14 of poem 11 answer the poet's self-rebuke for excessive indulgence in **ōtium** in poem 51.13–16?

The theme of travel to far-distant regions of the world represents the antithesis of the **ōtium** for which the poet rebukes himself at the end of poem 51. The projected travel is daring, bold, and far reaching; it will require vigorous physical activity and keen mental attentiveness. It is the opposite of **ōtium** in every way. While excessive **ōtium** leads to the destruction of kings and wealthy cities, Catullus' projected travels in poem 11 take him in the footsteps of the great generals, Alexander the Great, Crassus, and Caesar, who conquered cities and sought to establish or expand empires. Catullus' imagined stance toward life in his travels will be the opposite of what it was in poem 51. He will be active, not passive—an actor and a doer, not a victim (see Fredricksmeyer, 1993, 74–77, Select Bibliography). The irony, however, is that Catullus' imagined abandonment of **ōtium** and transformation of himself into the diametric opposite of what he was in poem 51 is expressed only in conjunction with his terminating his affair with Lesbia, only after his love has died, cut down by Lesbia's passing plow. The **magna bella** (37.13) that Catullus says he fought for Lesbia as a soldier of love were fought in vain. He is as much a victim of Lesbia in poem 11 as he was in poem 51.

3. How does the message of Catullus' final parting from Lesbia (11.21–24) echo and reverse his description of his original infatuation with her (51.1–12)?

The second and third paragraphs of the passage quoted from Duclos's essay provide partial answers to this question. Of particular note is repetition of the word **identidem** (51.3 and 11.19). The image of the flower in 11.22–24 recalls the poetry of Sappho, from which Catullus adapted the first twelve lines of poem 51. Basically, lines 1–12 of poem 51 record Catullus' initial attraction to the charms of Lesbia, while lines 21–24 of poem 11 record his ultimate turning away from her in revulsion.

Select Bibliography

D. L. Page. *Sappho and Alcaeus: An Introduction to the Study of Ancient Lesbian Poetry.* Oxford ENG: Oxford University Press, 1955. Best source for Sappho 31: text, translation, commentary, and interpretation.

C. M. Bowra. *Greek Lyric Poetry.* 2nd ed., 1961. See pages 185–89 for Sappho 31.

D. A. Kidd. "The Unity of Catullus 51." *Journal of the Australasian Universities Language and Literature Association* 20 (1963) 298–308. Contains some good observations on the structure of the poem.

E. A. Fredricksmeyer. "On the Unity of Catullus 51." *Transactions of the American Philological Association* 96 (1965) 153–63. An important study of the poem.

Garry Wills. "Sappho 31 and Catullus 51." *Greek, Roman, and Byzantine Studies* 8 (1967) 167–97. An extremely important study of the sequence of thought in these two poems. Highly recommended.

R. I. Frank. "Catullus 51: *Otium* versus *Virtus*." *Transactions of the American Philological Association* 99 (1968) 233–39. Contains a useful discussion of the negative attitudes toward love as a **perturbātiō animī** expressed by Roman writers.

Donald Norman Levin. "Propertius, Catullus, and Three Kinds of Ambiguous Expression." *Transactions of the American Philological Association* 100 (1969) 221–35. Ambiguity in lines 9–10: "Catullus has quite deliberately arranged his borrowed word-picture in such a way that the reader will be offered the opportunity to visualize not only a Sapphic 'slender flame,' but Catullan 'slender limbs' (Sappho supplies no limb at all, only 'skin' susceptible to inflammation) as well" (232).

T. E. Kinsey. "Catullus 51." *Latomus* 33 (1974) 372–87.
> The impression he produces in these first three stanzas (and let us pay him the compliment of supposing that it is the impression he is trying to produce) is not that of a man baring his soul, but of a *doctus poeta* writing an elegant set of complimentary verses to his lady which only the unsophisticated would assume had necessarily to be taken as meaning exactly what they said. (378)

A. J. Woodman. "Catullus 11 and 51." *Liverpool Classical Monthly* 3 (1978) 77–79.
> It follows from this interpretation that the difference between Catullus and the *ille* consists solely in their respective reactions to Lesbia's sweet laughter: those of *ille* are *spectat et audit*, whereas Catullus' *tintinnant aures, gemina teguntur / lumina nocte*, the contrast being emphasized by the chiasmus. In other words, the difference between the two men is one of ability: *ille* is thus *par deo* not in respect of his happiness or good fortune, but of his power or of his strength. . . . If this is so there is no good fortune of which Catullus may be supposed to be jealous. (79)

Robert J. Baker. "Propertius' Monobiblos and Catullus 51." *Rheinisches Museum* 124 (1981) 312–24.

E. A. Fredricksmeyer. "The Beginning and the End of Catullus' *Longus Amor*." *Symbolae Osloenses* 58 (1983) 63–88. A very important article on the relationship between poems 51 and 11.

John Finamore. "Catullus 50 and 51: Friendship, Love, and *Otium*." *Classical World* 78 (1984) 11–19. Highly recommended. "Catullus is every bit as serious about his desire for Calvus' friendship as for Lesbia's love" (14).

Dolores O'Higgins. "Sappho's Splintered Tongue: Silence in Sappho 31 and Catullus 51." *American Journal of Philology* 111 (1990) 156–67.
> For the Roman Neoteric poets *otium* was a symbol—the antithesis of *negotium*, a responsible citizen's official "activity," forensic, military, mercantile, or political. It was an attitude as much as the state of leisure, and could be considered the very soil which nourished elaborate, personal poetry. (165)

Paul Allen Miller. "Sappho 31 and Catullus 51: The Dialogism of Lyric." *Arethusa* 26 (1993) 183–99. On intertextuality in the Catullan corpus:
> If . . . we examine Catullus' translation of this . . . poem, the dialogical relation has changed. First, Catullus no longer thinks in terms of communal occasions [as had Sappho], but in terms of private readers or intimate friends. Second, the poem now not only gains its meaning from its relation to its audience, but also from its relation to other poems in the corpus. These poems provide the primary context in which the individual poem is to be understood. Our vision of Lesbia and Catullus is unalterably modified by our knowledge of these other poems, and thus the poem itself is in constant dialogue not only with its readers, but with the other poems of the collection. It is, in fact, this intertextual quality of Catullus' work that gives it that sense of intimacy which all readers perceive. We seem ever to be eavesdropping on the poet in dialogue with himself, but that dialogue is infinite because it is always being reshaped and remodelled by our own reading of the corpus. (189–90)

Karl Hayes. "Sappho 31 and Catullus 51." *Longman Latin Newsletter* (Spring 1997) 27–33. An important study that served as a basis for part of the interpretation of Catullus 51 and its relation to Sappho 31 that has been presented in the study questions in our student's book and in the answers to them in this teacher's guide.

CATULLUS 53

1   I laughed recently at someone from the crowd of bystanders,
2   who, when my dear Calvus had unfolded his charges
3   against Vatinius in marvelous fashion,
4   threw up his hands and in admiration said,
5   "Great gods, the little lecher is articulate!"

Poem 53 is difficult to interpret or appreciate adequately because the meaning of the final line, obviously intended to be humorous, is obscure. The problem is the Latin word **salapūtium**, the meaning of which is uncertain. The word occurs in the Catullan manuscripts as **salapantium**, but the elder Seneca (*Controversia* 7.4.7) refers to the passage in this way: **erat enim [Calvus] parvolus statūrā, propter quod etiam Catullus in hendecasyllabīs vocat illum "salapūtium disertum"**, *for Calvus was small in stature, on account of which Catullus also in his hendecasyllables calls him an "articulate **salapūtium**."* The word occurs nowhere else in Latin. Nevertheless, to judge by Seneca's comment, the word at least implies a diminutive stature, although many scholars have conjectured that it also carries some obscene connotations, perhaps being derived from **salāx**, *lascivious*, and **praepūtium**, *foreskin*, and being equivalent to **mentula salāx**.

Calvus was best known and admired in his own time as an orator in the courts. He was especially famous for the speeches that he delivered against Vatinius, one of Caesar's henchmen, who, like all things related to Caesar, was hated by Catullus (see poem 52, which is not in this book).

Initial Explorations

1.   How does the first word of the poem create suspense?
     It creates suspense by making the reader wonder what or whom it was that Catullus laughed at and why he laughed.
2.   Find an example of interlocking order or synchysis in lines 2–3.
     The words **Vatīniāna / meus crīmina Calvus** have interlocking order. The adjectives are placed first, and the nouns last, interlocking the adjective-noun phrases in parallel order: adjective A, adjective B, noun A, noun B. The words **meus . . . Calvus** are placed prominently in the middle line of the poem, right in its center.
3.   What word earlier in the poem does line 4 recall?
     It recalls the adverb **mīrificē**, prominently placed in the middle of the second line.
4.   How long is the reader held in suspense before learning what it was that Catullus laughed at?
     The reader is held in suspense until the very last word, **disertum**, since it is the paradox of the *little lecher* Calvus being so *articulate* that causes the spectator to utter the exclamation at which Catullus laughed. So, in translating, we should supply an **est** in the last line and treat **disertum** as a predicate adjective rather than translating the words **salapūtium disertum** as an exclamatory phrase, *what an articulate little lecher!*, which would make **salapūtium** and not **disertum** the key word. Catullus holds the key word until the very end. For discussion of the meaning of the adjective **disertus**, see Basson (Select Bibliography for poem 49), 47–48.

Discussion

1.   Compare this poem with Catullus 50. How do both poems express Catullus' admiration of Calvus? Is the expression of Catullus' admiration diminished in any way by quoting the word **salapūtium**, which may contain a gross obscenity?

     Poem 50 expresses Catullus' admiration of Calvus by recording the intense after-effects that Catullus experienced from a session of exchanging extemporaneous versification with Calvus. Catullus was so turned on by Calvus' charm and wit that he could not sleep and was reduced to a condition like that of a person experiencing love at first sight. In poem 50 Catullus thus expresses his intense admiration for Calvus' charm and wit, for his intellectual brilliance. In poem 53 he expresses admiration for Calvus' rhetorical brilliance, and he does it by quoting a paradoxical and probably obscene comment of a bystander. Whether one takes **salapūtium** to mean simply *little runt* or **mentula salāx** does not diminish the striking paradox and does not diminish the build-up from **mīrificē** through **admīrāns** and **manūs tollēns** and **"dī magnī"** to the climactic **disertum**. It is not that Catullus is calling his dear friend Calvus a **salapūtium**, but rather that he is taking the words that he overheard as an indication of the public admiration of his friend's high rhetorical skill.

2. What does the word **meus** tell us about the relation between Catullus and Calvus? Would it seem that this poem was written before or after Catullus 50?

    The word indicates that Catullus regards Calvus as a close mutual friend—close enough to allow Catullus to go public with stating their friendship prominently in this poem. It would seem therefore that this poem was written after poem 50, in which Catullus requests reciprocation and a continuing relation of friendship and intellectual camaraderie and which, as Thomson says, "may be supposed to date from an early stage in C's acquaintance with Calvus" (324).

3. Apart from its meter, what makes Catullus 53 poetic?

    This question might be approached by having students write a prose version of the event (Catullus' reaction to what he heard) and then comparing their prose versions with Catullus' poem. Obviously Catullus 53 is a poem because it is in meter, but other things about it are appropriate to poetry as opposed to prose, such as the compression of the narrative, the careful design and economy of the build-up to the climax, the mannered arrangement of words in lines 2 and 3 (**Vatīniāna / meus crīmina Calvus**), and the fact that the paradoxical phrase **salapūtium disertum** is left pointedly unexplained, although its meaning may not have been clear even to many contemporary Romans since the word **salapūtium** occurs only in this context in all extant Latin writings. A prose writer telling the story would most likely have given an explanation of the rare word or would have given a straightforward description.

Select Bibliography

E. S. Gruen. "Cicero and Licinius Calvus." *Harvard Studies in Classical Philology* 71 (1966) 215–33. Includes information on Calvus' prosecutions of Vatinius.

CATULLUS 62

Leader of the Chorus of Boys:

1 The evening star has come, young men, rise up: the evening star
2 only just now lifts its long-awaited light in the sky/Olympus. Now it is time to rise, now [it is
3 time] to leave the bountiful tables;
4 now the young maiden will come, now the marriage song will be sung.

Refrain:

5 Hymen O Hymenaeus, Hymen O Hymenaeus, come!

Leader of the Chorus of Girls:
6   Maidens, do you see the young men? Rise and face them;
7   without doubt the Nightbringer shows [his] Oetaean fires.
8   Here's why it's certain; do you see how nimbly they've leaped up?
9   Not for nothing have they leaped up; they will sing what is likely to win.

Refrain:
10   Hymen O Hymenaeus, Hymen O Hymenaeus, come!

Leader of the Chorus of Boys:
11   Not an easy palm [of victory], age-mates, awaits us;
12   look how the maidens search among themselves for what they've prepared.
13   Not in vain do they rehearse: they have something memorable;
14   and no wonder, since they work at it deep within with their whole mind.
15   We've divided our thoughts one way, our ears another;
16   rightly therefore we'll be outdone: victory loves/thrives on care.
17   Wherefore now give your full attention at least;
18   now they will begin to sing, now it will be proper to answer [them].

Refrain:
19   Hymen O Hymenaeus, Hymen O Hymenaeus, come!

The chorus of girls begins the singing match:
20   Hesperus, what more cruel fire is carried in the heavens?
21   Since you can bear to tear a daughter from the embrace of her mother,
22   tear a daughter, still clinging, from the embrace of her mother,
23   and deliver the chaste girl to a young man blazing [with lust].
24   What crueler thing does an enemy do upon the capture of a city?

Refrain:
25   Hymen O Hymenaeus, Hymen O Hymenaeus, come!

The chorus of boys responds:
26   Hesperus, what more pleasant fire shines in the heavens?
27   Since you confirm pledged marriages by your flame,
28   which men have arranged, which parents have arranged earlier,
29   but have not joined together before your fire has raised itself.
30   What more desired/welcome than [this] happy hour is given by the gods?

Refrain:
31   Hymen O Hymenaeus, Hymen O Hymenaeus, come!

The chorus of girls compares Hesperus to a thief; only the first line of the stanza has survived:
32   Hesperus, friends, has taken one of us away.
     [Five lines are missing here.]

Refrain:
32g   <Hymen O Hymenaeus, Hymen O Hymenaeus, come!>

The chorus of boys, in a stanza missing its first line, replies that when evening comes guards are wake-ful and that the Evening Star, when appearing as the Morning Star, catches thieves:
     [One line is missing here.]
33   For always a watchman is wakeful at your coming.
34   Thieves hide in the night, whom often when you return

35 you, Hesperus, catch [as the] Morning Star, the same [star] with a change of name,
36 but it pleases the unmarried [girls] to carp at you with feigned complaint.
37 What then, if they carp at [you], whom they seek with secret mind?

Refrain:
38 Hymen O Hymenaeus, Hymen O Hymenaeus, come!

The chorus of girls begins another theme:
39 As a flower grows set apart in an enclosed garden,
40 unknown to the flock, not torn up by any plow,
41 which the breezes stroke, the sun strengthens, the rains nurture;
41b <now all but   .   .   .   >
42 many boys, many girls desire it:
43 but when the same, plucked by a thin fingernail, has lost its flower,
44 no boys, no girls desire it:
45 so a maiden, as long as she remains untouched, is dear to her family;
46 but when she has lost her chaste blossom, her body sullied,
47 she does not remain pleasant/delightful to the boys, nor dear to the girls.

Refrain:
48 <Hymen O Hymenaeus, Hymen O Hymenaeus, come!>

The chorus of boys replies:
49 As an unwed vine, which grows in an open field,
50 never lifts itself up, never produces a sweet and juicy grape,
51 but bending down its tender body with downward leaning weight
52 now it all but touches its topmost shoot with its root;
53 this one no farmer, no oxen tend:
54 but if by chance the same [vine] has been joined together with an elm as its husband,
55 many farmers, many oxen tend it:
56 so a maiden, as long as she remains unmarried, grows old untended;
57 when at the proper time she has gained a well-matched marriage partner,
58 she is more dear to her husband and less hateful to her father.

Refrain:
58b <Hymen O Hymenaeus, Hymen O Hymenaeus, come!>

The leader of the chorus of girls addresses the bride:
   [One line is missing.]
59 And you, maiden, do not fight with such a husband.
60 It is not right to fight [with the one], to whom [your] father himself delivered you,
61 [your] father himself with [your] mother, whom you must obey.
62 Your virginity is not wholly yours, it's your parents in part,
63 a third is your father's, a third was given to your mother,
64 only a third is yours: do not fight against the two,
65 who have given to their son-in-law their rights [to your virginity] along with [your] dowry.

Refrain:
66 Hymen O Hymenaeus, Hymen O Hymenaeus, come!

Catullus 62 has the form of a singing match, in which a chorus of young men responds to the complaints made by a chorus of young women over the impending marriage of an unnamed maiden. (See the answer to Explorations question 19 for an outline of the structure of the poem.) The poet does not appear to be describing any particular wedding. Instead he imagines a generic wedding feast in an unidentified locale, at which the guests await the arrival of the bride and the marriage procession, which will take her to the groom's house. The arrival of Vesper, the evening star, signals the beginning of this last phase in the ancient wedding ceremony. The literary convention of the singing match belongs not to wedding ceremonies but to the tradition of pastoral poetry found in the early Hellenistic poet Theocritus and imitated by Vergil. In this convention one herdsman sings a short stanza of verse and is answered by another, who attempts to cap his predecessor's contribution by some clever piece of parody or ingenious counter statement. The incorporation of this amoebaean (i.e., responsive) form of verse into a wedding scene is unusual, but Catullus exploits the genre with pointed creativity to explore the conflicting psychologies of male and female at the rite of passage embodied in the rituals of marital union.

Our presentation of the text of the poem in the student's book and much of the interpretation in the answers to the Explorations questions are indebted to articles by Commager and Goud (see Select Bibliography) and to Thomson's commentary. There has been much debate as to whether the poem reflects Greek or Roman wedding ceremonies or a mixture of the two. Goud argues that it is consistent with what we know about Roman weddings (see answer to Explorations question 23), but he concludes: "If one pressed the details to the extreme, one would have to agree with Fraenkel that this wedding 'could not be celebrated anywhere in the ancient world,' but that its place is 'in a poetic sphere of its own.' And yet, that poetic sphere for this poem approaches far more closely the real world of Catullus' Rome than that of Sappho's Lesbos" (32).

Explorations

1.   What similarities can you detect between the words of the two chorus leaders? How does the leader of the chorus of girls model her words on those of the leader of the chorus of boys? (1–4 and 6–9)

They both address their respective choruses (**iuvenēs**, 1; **innūptae**, 6); they both speak of the rising of the evening star (1–2; 7). The leader of the chorus of girls borrows the verb **cōnsurgite** (6) from the leader of the chorus of boys (1). They both describe the rising or appearance of the evening star (1–2; 7).

2.   What different attitudes do the two chorus leaders take toward the evening star in their descriptions of it? (1–2 and 7)

The leader of the chorus of boys has been eagerly awaiting the rising of the star, as is shown by his words **exspectāta diū vix tandem** (2). In using the word **Olympō** (1) by metonymy for **caelō**, the chorus leader optimistically associates the evening star with the dwelling place of the gods. The leader of the chorus of girls coins the term **noctifer**, thus referring perhaps apprehensively to the evening star as the bringer of night as opposed to the more positive term **Vesper** used by the leader of the chorus of boys. The leader of the chorus of girls refers to the light of the star as fire, **ignēs** (7), picking up the word **lūmina** used by the leader of the chorus of boys but transforming that term for beautiful light or radiance into something potentially dangerous and destructive. The latter connotations are brought to the fore by use of the adjective **Oetaeōs**, which alludes ominously to the death of Hercules by fire as a result of his wife's attempt to revive his love for her after his affair with Iole. Note that the leader of the chorus of girls in line 7 deliberately varies the word order of line 2 by reversing the sequence of object and verb, creating a chiasmus: **lūmina** (2) A, **tollit** (2) B, **ostendit** (7) B, **ignēs** (7) A.

The leader of the chorus of girls thus describes the rising of the evening star in response to the description given by the leader of the chorus of boys, but in doing so she transforms it from a description of an eagerly awaited Olympian radiance to a description of an ominous fire that brings the darkness of night.

The different attitudes toward the evening star will be seen to prefigure diametrically opposed attitudes toward marriage on the part of the two chorus leaders and their respective choruses.

3.   How does the leader of the chorus of girls regard the boys' actions? (6–9)

While the leader of the chorus of boys simply directs the boys to rise (**cōnsurgite**, 1, and **Surgere iam tempus**, 3), the leader of the chorus of girls perceives their action as threatening—thus her command, **Cōnsurgite contrā** (6). (Note the strong alliteration in line 6: **Cernitis . . . ? Cōnsurgite contrā**.) Then, while the boys presumably simply rise in obedience to their leader, the leader of the chorus of girls with some apparent trepidation refers to their action as nimbly leaping up (**perniciter exsiluēre**, 8), and she repeats the verb in the next line (**exsiluēre**, 9), clearly perceiving the boys' action as threatening.

Considerable tension should already be evident between the two groups, with the girls on the defensive—a posture that is underscored by the prediction of their leader that the boys will win the competition (**canent quod vincere pār est**, *they will sing what is likely to win*, 9).

4.   How do the opening remarks of the leader of the chorus of boys (11–14) relate to what the leader of the chorus of girls has just said?

The leader of the chorus of girls, perhaps in an effort to spur the girls on, has said that it is likely that the boys will win (**canent quod vincere pār est**, 9). The leader of the chorus of boys, urging the boys not to be complaisant, tells them that no easy victory is at hand for them (**Nōn facilis nōbīs . . . palma parāta est**, 11). Indeed, the girls are busily rehearsing their words, and they will be memorable (12–14).

5.   How does the attitude of the girls toward the singing match differ from that of the boys? (12–17)

The perfect passive participle **meditāta** (12) suggests that what the girls will speak are thoughts that they have pondered, prepared, rehearsed, and practiced over a long period of time, not thoughts that just happen to come to them on the spur of the moment. They are busily consulting one another (**sēcum . . . requīrunt**, 12) in search of those thoughts. The leader of the chorus of boys is sure that what the girls will come up with will be **memorābile** (13) because they are laboring over (**labōrant**, 14) their thoughts deep within (**penitus**, 14) with total mental involvement (**tōtā mente**, 14). The boys, on the other hand, have not been concentrating their attention at all (15) or devoting any care (see **cūram**, 16) to the upcoming singing match, and so their leader is sure they will rightly lose (**iūre igitur vincēmur**, 16). Their leader has to tell them to pull their minds together and pay attention (17), something that the girls have already been busily doing.

The differences prefigure the attitudes toward marriage that the girls and boys will take in the singing match. The girls see marriage in strongly negative terms as, put bluntly, nothing more than legalized rape; the boys view marriage positively as a social contract that is part and parcel of mankind's civilized existence. The girls have apparently both individually and perhaps collectively long been pondering or brooding over what they see as the negative aspects of marriage, and now, as they are about to sing in opposition to the whole concept of marriage and in particular in opposition to the marriage that is about to take place, they busily consult among themselves in search of those thoughts that they have long pondered (**meditāta**, 12). The boys, thoroughly confident about the rightness and value of marriage, have not been obsessed over it in the past and come to the present wedding ceremonies with a cavalier confidence. Without having taken any great care (see **cūram**, 16) over preparation of their singing, they will extemporize in response to whatever the chorus of girls sings.

Note that while the first speech of the leader of the chorus of girls is spoken in response to the first speech of the leader of the chorus of boys and answers it point by point, this second speech of the leader of the chorus of boys is not answered by an immediately following speech by the leader of the chorus of girls. Instead, the singing match begins, with the chorus of girls going first in lines 20–24. There are, however, some minor verbal correspondences between 11–18 and 6–9: **nec mīrum** (14) picks up **nīmīrum** (7), and with **vincēmur** (16) the leader of the chorus of boys reverses the sense of **canent quod vincere pār est** (9) spoken by the leader of the chorus of girls. The eight-line stanza spoken by the leader of the chorus of boys (11–18) will ultimately be balanced by an eight-line stanza spoken by the leader of the chorus of girls at the end of the singing match (58c–65).

6. How do the girls' and the boys' conceptions of Hesperus differ, and how does this reflect their different attitudes toward the institution of marriage? (20–24 and 26–30)

The girls regard Hesperus as the most cruel star in the heavens (20), while the boys regard it as the most pleasant/delightful (26). The girls regard marriage, in which a daughter is torn away from the embrace of her mother and given to a young man blazing with lust (21–23), as being on a par with the rape of girls and women by the enemy when cities are captured (24). The boys regard marriage as the most welcome thing given by the gods to mankind (see **optātius**, 30) and as a joining together (see **iūnxēre**, 29) that is sanctioned by men and parents and is effected with proper ceremonies (see **dēspōnsa** and **conūbia**, 27) at the right time (29).

7. What words do the boys repeat from the girls' song in the same metrical positions? (20–24 and 26–30) What phrase of the girls do the boys reflect in their words **fēlīcī optātius hōrā** (30)?

Repeated words: **Hespere, quis caelō . . . ignis** (26 = 20); **Quī** (27 = 21); **Quid** (30 = 24). The words **fēlīcī optātius hōrā** (30) reflect the girls' words **captā crūdēlius urbe** (24).

8. How do the changes that the boys make in lines 26 and 30 reflect their different view of marriage from that of the girls?

The girls' description of Hesperus as a star being carried in the heavens (20) may subconsciously reflect their dire concern over marriage as a kind of rape, in which the bride is carried off. The boys, instead, focus happily on the light produced by Hesperus (**lūcet**, 26), and this is reminiscent of the male chorus leader's reference to the **lūmina**, *light/radiance*, of the evening star (2). The boys substitute **iūcundior** (26) for **crūdēlior** (20), reflecting their optimistic view of marriage. Finally, instead of the totally negative image of rape in captured cities (24), the boys, using the same grammatical construction as the girls had used, describe marriage as the most welcome thing given by the gods to mankind (30), and instead of focusing on the time when a city is captured (**captā . . . urbe**, 24), they mention the *auspicious/fortunate/happy hour* (**fēlīcī . . . hōrā**, 30) at which the bride is joined to her bridegroom. The various meanings of the adjective **fēlīcī** need to be kept in mind here, especially meanings such as *fruitful, productive, having a happy issue*, which point to positive future developments and in particular to the production of offspring; this adjective reverses the wholly negative image of the captured city cruelly destroyed by the enemy with girls and women raped and presumably doomed to bear bastard children.

9. Analyze the relationship between word-placement and meaning in lines 21–23.

The point that the girls are making is that it is cruel to tear a daughter away from the embrace of her mother and to give that girl to a young man blazing with lust.
Note in line 21: all spondees except the fifth foot; the word **nātam** separated from the word **mātris**, just as daughter will be torn away from mother; the word **complexū** occupying the middle of the line, between the critical players, the daughter and the mother; elision of **com-**

plexū and **āvellere**, uniting these two antithetical words that are at the heart of the dilemma into a single concept; **mātris** can be either objective or subjective genitive with **complexū**, i.e., either *from embracing her mother* or *from the embrace of her mother* (the girls probably want to take it both ways).

Note in line 22: four of the words are repeated from line 21; the nouns have been rearranged in chiastic order (**nātam**, 21, A; **mātris**, 21, B; **mātris**, 22, B; **nātam**, 22, A); the words **complexū** and **āvellere** are still in the same relative order in line 22, but while **āvellere** is in the same metrical position, **complexū** has been moved to emphatic position at the beginning of the line; the word **retinentem** has been added in the middle of the line as a pathetic touch focusing on the desperation of the daughter.

Note in line 23: chiasmus (**iuvenī** A, **ārdentī** B, **castam** B, **puellam** A); the sound of the endings of nouns and adjectives unites the words in each pair of words describing the young man and the girl (**iuvenī ārdentī** and **cast*am* . . . puell*am***); the infinitive **dōnāre** is placed as next-to-last word parallel to **āvellere** in the two lines above, emphasizing that the girl is torn away from her mother to be given over to the young man.

Everything here is engineered to reinforce the pathos and anguish of the girl being torn from her mother and being given to the lustful youth. The repetition of line 21 with variation in line 22 adds to the emotional effect. In line 23 **ārdentī** is juxtaposed to **castam**, emphasizing the unfairness of the chaste girl's being handed over to the lustful young man, almost as if to her enemy. This leads up to the indignant rhetorical question, **Quid faciunt hostēs captā crūdēlius urbe?** (24).

10. How does the chorus of boys in lines 27–29 respond to the apprehension and anxiety over marriage expressed by the girls in lines 21–24?

The point that the boys are making is that marriage is not at all like the rape of girls and women at the sack of cities when the will of the stronger prevails but is rather the result of a civilized contract entered into by the parents of both the bride and the groom that is best described as a uniting (see **iūnxēre**, 29) of the bridal couple, not as a tearing of a daughter from her mother and giving of her to a lustful young man, as if to an enemy.

The boys claim that marriage strengthens or confirms (see **firmēs**, 27) rather than tearing asunder. It is something that should be regarded as strengthening or confirming agreements entered into by men and parents (**dēspōnsa . . . conūbia . . . / quae pepigēre virī, pepigērunt ante parentēs**, 27–28) rather than as a sundering of natural ties such as those that unite daughter to mother and certainly something far different from the capricious violence perpetrated upon females at the sack of cities.

The boys attempt to reassure the girls with regard to the concept of fire as well. The girls saw the evening star as ominous Oetaean fire (9), and they persisted in using the word **ignis** of Hesperus in line 20. The boys pick this up (**ignis**, 26), but they reassuringly point out that it is the flame of Hesperus' fire (**flammā**, 27) that confirms the marriage that has been contracted by the parents (**dēspōnsa . . . conūbia**, 27). Further, while the girls complained of the bride being handed over **iuvenī ārdentī** (23) in no particular socially approved context, the boys remove the idea of burning or blazing from the groom and transfer it to Hesperus, addressed now as **ārdor** (29), at whose rising, and not before, the bridal couple is united in a socially approved marriage. Fire is no longer a threat but is here benign and provides the sanction for the legalized union of bride and groom.

Finally, note that just as the girls repeated their key verb **āvellere** (21, 22), so the boys repeat their key verb **pepigēre . . . pepigērunt** (28), countering the idea of forcible tearing away from the mother with the idea of civilized compacts entered into by the parents on both sides.

11. How does the girls' comparison of Hesperus to a thief (32) relate to their earlier description of Hesperus' actions (20–24)?

There they spoke of Hesperus as tearing daughter away from mother (21–22), and here they complain that Hesperus has taken a girl away from among themselves.

12.   How does the part of the boys' reply preserved in lines 33–35 counter the girls' complaint that Hesperus is a thief?

       The boys imply that instead of being a thief Hesperus helps catch thieves by indicating the time in the evening when guards should be wakeful and watchful (33) and that Hesperus returns as the Morning Star, Eos, and catches thieves (34–35). Hesperus is thus an upholder of law and order, rather than being a lawless thief. The boys' conception of Hesperus here harmonizes with their description of Hesperus in their previous stanza (26–30) as an upholder of the lawful marriage agreements made by parents. The negative, pejorative view of Hesperus held by the girls is being seriously undercut by the arguments of the boys.

13.   Of what do the boys accuse the girls in lines 36–37?

       They accuse them of carping at Hesperus with complaints that are made up and false (**fictō . . . carpere questū**, 36); the adjective **fictō** could even mean *knowingly false*. The boys accuse the girls of being insincere. In line 37 they go further and accuse the girls of hypocrisy in that they carp at Hesperus (= marriage), yet secretly, in the depths of their minds, they long for him (= marriage). The boys' charge of hypocrisy (**tacitā quem mente requīrunt**, 37) indicates a change in their attitude toward the girls and their motives, since earlier the leader of the chorus of boys had used the same verb of the girls' careful preparation for the match (**innūptae sēcum . . . meditāte requīrunt**, 12) and had praised them for laboring inwardly with their whole mind (**penitus . . . tōtā mente labōrant**, 14). The earlier phrase **tōtā mente** has been transformed into **tacitā mente** in the charge of hypocrisy.

14.   What is the final argument against marriage that the girls make? (39–47)

       They argue that it is far better to remain a virgin.

15.   The girls develop an elaborate simile comparing virginity or a virgin girl to a flower. How do details of the simile recall objections that the chorus of girls has already leveled against marriage? How do details of the simile counter what the boys have said in defense of the institution of marriage?

       The flower that grows (**nāscitur**, 39) in the enclosed garden is like the daughter (**nātam**, 21, 22) in the embrace of her mother; the chorus of girls thinks it is terrible for the daughter to be torn away from her mother (**āvellere**, 21, 22) and that it would be terrible for the flower to be damaged by sheep and cattle or torn up (**convulsus**, 40) by a plow (note that **āvellere** and **convulsus** are derived from the same root verb).

       The flower grows up set apart (**sēcrētus**, 39) and protected in an enclosed garden (**saeptīs . . . hortīs**, 39), and this reverses the image of the captured city with its inhabitants violated by the enemy (24).

       The chorus of girls describes the sun as strengthening the flower (**firmat sōl**, 41); this is the kind of strengthening or confirming that the girls wish for—a strengthening or confirming of their cherished maidenhood; this wish supplies an alternative to or answers the claim of the boys that Hesperus strengthens or confirms (see **firmēs**, 27) marriages that have been contracted (**dēspōnsa . . . conūbia**, 27).

       The chorus of girls comments that many boys and girls desire (**optāvēre**) the flower as long as it is unplucked (42); this counters the claim of the boys that nothing *more desired/welcome* (**optātius**, 30) has been given to mankind by the gods than marriage. The girls regard the unplucked flower of their virginity as the most desired/welcome thing in the world.

While the boys complained that the girls were carping at Hesperus/marriage unfairly and hypocritically (**carpere**, 36, **carpunt**, 37), the girls refute that complaint by using the same verb in the perfect passive participle and in its literal rather than its figurative sense (**carptus**, 43) to get at the crux of the matter: once the flower of a girl's virginity has been *plucked*, she is no longer desired by boys and girls (43–44).

Just as the chorus of girls spoke with revulsion earlier about the girl torn from her mother's embrace and given as a **castam . . . puellam** to the lustful young man (23), so here they contemplate the maiden's loss of her **castum . . . flōrem** (46) and the accompanying physical pollution (**pollūtō corpore**, 46) as rendering her no longer *pleasant/delightful* to boys and girls (47).

Finally, the girls argue that when a girl's maidenhood is lost, she is no longer **iūcunda**, *pleasant/delightful* to boys and girls (47), and this counters the boys' claim that there is no star **iūcundior** than Hesperus (26), which means that there is no condition more *pleasant/delightful* than marriage. The girls see the loss of maidenhood as the end of the **iūcunditās** that they associate with childhood. In expressing this idea, the girls conclude their stanza with a chiasmus (**puerīs** A, **iūcunda** B, **cāra** B, **puellīs** A) effectively grouped around the key word **manet** (see next paragraph).

In summary: "Where the boys look forward to the sexual satisfaction promised by Hesperus, the girls see the same occasion as marking a loss of innocence, the end to a happy past rather than the beginning of a desired future. Their repeated *manet . . . manet* (45, 47) reinforces their point. They wish things to remain as they have always been, the daughter still in her mother's embrace, the flower still untouched in its protected garden. What they find attractive is continuity (*iucunda manet*, 47), as opposed to the attractive change heralded, for the boys, by Hesperus' rising (*iucundior ignis*, 26)" (Commager, 29, see Select Bibliography).

This whole stanza can be read as a reaction on the part of the chorus of girls to the stinging charge of insincerity and hypocrisy leveled at them by the boys at the end of the previous stanza (36–37). Picking up on their verb **carpere**, which the boys used in the figurative sense, *to criticize, carp at*, the girls formulate the elaborate simile of the flower and place in its center the perfect passive participle of that very same verb, **carptus** (43), used in its literal sense to express their most sincere and heartfelt horror of being plucked and deflowered and losing their purity and innocent charm, which alone, in their view, make them *pleasant/delightful* (**iūcunda**, 47) to other boys and girls and *dear to their own* (**cāra suīs**, 45), i.e., presumably, to their own natural relatives. There is nothing insincere or hypocritical about the fear that the chorus of girls has deep in its heart over taking that critical and irreversible step across the great threshold that divides a girl's childhood from her life as an adult and separates her permanently from emotional bonding with her blood relatives and her childhood acquaintances. Stung by the boys' reproach, the girls formulate a brilliant defense of their virginal status quo, and in doing so they recapitulate much of what they have said before and refute much of what the boys have said against their views.

16. The boys reply by proposing a different simile. To what do they compare an unwed maiden?

    They compare an unwed maiden to a grapevine that has not been trained on a tree but has been left by itself, bends to the ground, and is neglected and unfruitful.

17. The boys in their reply repeat many of the words of the girls, usually in the same metrical positions. Locate all such repetitions. In a number of cases the boys echo words, phrases, and lines from the song of the girls but vary them by substituting different words. Locate all such echoes.

    In the following text, repetitions are underlined and echoes are in italic:
39 <u>Ut</u> *flōs in saeptīs sēcrētus* <u>nāscitur</u> *hortīs*,
40 ignōtus pecorī, nūllō convulsus arātrō,
41 quem mulcent aurae, firmat sōl, <u>ēducat</u> imber;

41b   <u><iam iam</u> .   .   .   >
42   *multī illum puerī, multae optāvēre puellae:*
43   īdem cum tenuī carptus dēflōruit unguī,
44   *nūllī illum puerī, nūllae optāvēre puellae:*
45   <u>sīc</u> virgō, <u>dum</u> *intācta* <u>manet, dum</u> cāra suīs est;
46   <u>cum</u> castum āmīsit *pollūtō corpore* flōrem,
47   nec puerīs *iūcunda* manet, nec <u>cāra</u> puellīs.

49   <u>Ut</u> *vidua in nūdō vītis* quae <u>nāscitur</u> *arvō,*
50   numquam sē extollit, numquam mītem <u>ēducat</u> ūvam,
51   sed tenerum prōnō dēflectēns pondere corpus
52   <u>iam iam</u> contingit summum radīce flagellum;
53   *hanc nūllī agricolae, nūllī coluēre iuvencī:*
54   at sī forte eadem est ulmō coniūncta marītō,
55   *multī illam agricolae, multī coluēre iuvencī:*
56   <u>sic</u> virgō, <u>dum</u> *innūpta* <u>manet, dum</u> inculta senēscit;
57   <u>cum</u> pār cōnubium *mātūrō tempore* adepta est,
58   <u>cāra</u> virō magis et minus est *invīsa* parentī.

18.   How does the simile of the vine reverse the implications of the simile of the flower to present a positive rather than a negative conception of marriage?

The flower flourishes as a thing of beauty only as long as it is sheltered and not plucked (**carptus**, 43) or torn up by a plow (**nūllō convulsus arātrō**, 40). The vine in order to flourish and bear fruit must be trained on a tree; otherwise it will bend to the ground (51–52) and not bear fruit (50). So the maiden must be joined with a man (**coniūncta**, 54); otherwise she *grows old untended* (**inculta senēscit**, 56) and *hateful to her father* (**invīsa parentī**, 58). The shift from flower to vine carries with it a major transformation of the image: while the image of the flower symbolizes marriage as a violent, physically rending, and destructive act of plucking (**carptus**, 43) or tearing up with a plow (**convulsus arātrō**, 40—the plow being, of course, a symbol of the male genitalia), the image of the vine joined to a tree for support (**ulmō coniūncta**, 54) contains no hint of any form of violence or of loss.

While the flower receives nourishment from the breezes, the sun, and the rain (41) in its isolated splendor, the vine lifts itself up and produces fruit when trained on a tree (50). The flower is here a passive recipient of natural nourishment (similar to a girl growing up in the nourishing embrace of her mother), whereas the vine *lifts itself up* (**sē extollit**, 50) and *produces a sweet and juicy grape* (**mītem ēducat ūvam**, 50). Note that in line 41 the verb **ēducat** is used of the rain *nourishing* the flower, while in line 50 the same verb is used of the vine *producing* grapes. Thus the vine even though trained onto a tree has a capability of its own (it *lifts itself up*), and it produces a highly desirable fruit. The grapes produced by the vine trained on the tree symbolize, of course, children produced by the marriage of bride and bridegroom, and this productivity and fruitfulness replace the simple but sterile beauty of the flower in the girls' simile. That flower of virginity at the moment of marriage necessarily loses its blossom (**dēflōruit**, 43), withers, and dies. The vine, however, when wed to the tree, lifts itself up and bears fruit. Marriage thus provides a supportive environment and a fruitfulness missing from the girls' image of the sheltered flower but symbolic of the maturity awaiting the maiden when she crosses the threshold into a new life of marriage.

While the flower when plucked loses its blossom and its desirability to boys and girls (43–44), the vine, unless it is married to a tree, sinks to the ground and is ignored by farmers and oxen, who otherwise would cultivate it (51–55). The girls see marriage as the plucking of a flower, which then loses its bloom (**carptus dēflōruit**, 43), whereas the boys see it as a joining of the vine to the elm tree as its husband (**ulmō coniūncta marītō**, 54).

The girls thought of livestock and farmers as dangerous to the flower, which had to be kept protected from them in its enclosed garden (39–40; note line 40 in particular, **ignōtus**

pecorī, nūllō convulsus arātrō). The boys reverse all of this and describe farmers and oxen as cultivators of the vine when married to the tree (**multī illam agricolae, multī coluēre iuvencī**, 55). Note the chiastic arrangement of **pecorī** (40) A, **arātrō** (40) B, **agricolae** (55) B, **iuvencī** (55) A.

While the world of the maiden is populated by boys and girls (**puerī . . . puellae**, 42 and 44, **puerīs . . . puellīs**, 47) and relatives (**suīs**, 45), the world that the boys describe is populated only by adults (**agricolae**, 53, 55, **virō**, 58, and **parentī**, 58).

The major reversal that Catullus has engineered in the movement from the song of the girls to that of the boys is a shift from a negative view of marriage to a positive one. This has been evident in the themes discussed above, but it is particularly evident in the lines in the second half of each song, where the verbal responsions and variations are the closest. There is an intricate pattern of reversals here. The girls' **multī . . . multae** (42) and **nūllī . . . nūllae** (44) are repeated by the boys but in the reverse order: **nūllī . . . nūllī** (53) and **multī . . . multī** (55). Thus, the girls begin with the unwed state as the positive (**multī illum puerī, multae optāvēre puellae**, 42) and then move to the wedded state as the negative (**nūllī illum puerī, nūllae optāvēre puellae**, 44), whereas the boys begin with the unwed state as the negative (**hanc nūllī agricolae, nūllī coluēre iuvencī**, 53), and then move to the wedded state as the positive (**multī illam agricolae, multī coluēre iuvencī**, 55). The alternation of positive-negative-negative-positive forms a chiastic sequence.

A similar chiastic sequence relates the last three lines of each of the songs. The girls' line 45, **sīc virgō, dum intācta manet, dum cāra suīs est**, is positive; the boys' corresponding line 56, **sīc virgō, dum innūpta manet, dum inculta senēscit**, is negative. The girls' last two lines are then negative (46–47), and the boys' last two lines are positive (57–58).

Thus, while the boys imitate the words and patterns of the girls' song as they transform the simile of the flower into the simile of the vine, they reverse the movements of the girls' thoughts that go from positive to negative and thereby emphasize marriage as a positive event, leaving a positive impression in the listener's mind. These two stanzas and the responsive relationship between them constitute a brilliant display of poetic pyrotechnics on the part of Catullus.

A few more reversals. The girls think, perhaps naively, that as long as their virginity is intact they will be dear to their own (45), i.e., to their relatives, especially their parents; this is countered by the boys' more realistic observation that unmarried females grow old **inculta**, *untended* (56), a highly undesirable situation. In line 46 the girls speak of the loss (**āmīsit**) of the flower of their purity; in the corresponding line the boys speak of the maiden not as losing anything but as getting (**adepta est**, 57) something, thus substituting the positive thought of the maiden getting an equally-matched partner (**pār cōnubium**, 57). And, instead of losing the flower of her virginity **pollūtō corpore**, *with sullied body* (46), she will gain her mate **mātūrō tempore**, *at the proper time* (57), emphasizing, as the boys have done before, the socially accepted proprieties and proper timing of the whole process of marriage (cf. 29, **nōn iūnxēre prius quam sē tuus extulit ārdor**). While the girls saw themselves as dear to their relatives and to boys and girls as long as they retained their virginity (45, 47), the boys counter this by placing the adjective **cāra** prominently at the head of their last line and following it with **virō magis**, implying that the married woman will be *more dear to her husband* than the unwed maiden was to her relatives and her playmates. And finally, while the girls thought of the maiden as **cāra suīs** (45), the boys point out far more realistically that when a daughter marries she is *less hateful to her father* (**minus . . . invīsa parentī**, 58). In saying that the daughter when married is *less hateful to her father*, the boys imply that prior to marriage she was hateful, thus touching on the traditional theme of girls as unwanted, useless, and burdensome members of a household. This shows the girls' description of the **virgō** as **cāra suīs** (45) to be naive if not outright false, and it suggests that even the relationship between the mother and the daughter (21–22) may be problematic. Surely there is bonding of the daughter with the mother, but the question is raised as to how much the mother shares the father's attitude toward the female child in the household. In marriage, the young woman will become unambiguously **cāra virō** (58). This should be a great consolation for her, as she escapes from the **invidia**, *ill will*, of her father.

In these many ways and in others that perceptive students will note for themselves, the simile of the vine reverses the implications of the simile of the flower to present a positive rather than a negative conception of marriage.

19. It is not certain to whom the last stanza should be assigned. In the past it was usually assigned to the chorus of boys, but Goud in a recent analysis of the structure of the poem as a whole concludes that it should be assigned to the leader of the chorus of girls, thus balancing the stanza comprised of lines 11–18, spoken by the leader of the chorus of boys. If this is so, then how should the structure of the entire poem be diagrammed?

The following is adapted from the discussion of the structure of poem 62 by Goud (see Select Bibliography):

Introduction

1–4	Leader of the chorus of boys instructs the boys to rise, since the bride will come soon.
6–9	The leader of the chorus of girls instructs the girls to rise in opposition to the boys.

Getting the Singing Match Going

11–18	The leader of the chorus of boys urges the boys to pay attention, since the girls, who have been consulting among themselves over what they have long rehearsed, are about to begin to sing and the boys will have to respond.

The Singing Match

20–24	Chorus of Girls
26–30	Reply by Chorus of Boys
32–32f	Chorus of Girls
32h–37	Reply by Chorus of Boys
39–47	Chorus of Girls
49–58	Reply by Chorus of Boys

Ending the Singing Match; Conclusion

58c–65	Leader of the Chorus of Girls

Responsions unify the structure of the poem. Lines 6–9 respond to 1–4; lines 58c–65 respond to 11–18; the singing match consists of three sets of stanzas, the second stanza in each set responding to the first. Both members of each set of corresponding stanzas have the same number of lines. Goud argues that in keeping with the overall symmetry of the structure, lines 58c–65 are to be spoken by the leader of the chorus of girls, and they correspond to lines 11–18.

20. How does the stanza above correspond to the stanza spoken by the leader of the chorus of boys in lines 11–18? Which side of the singing match does the leader of the chorus of girls appear to favor here? Is there a winner and a loser?

The leader of the chorus of boys in the earlier stanza was preparing the boys for the impending contest, marshaling his team for a verbal contest with the chorus of girls. The leader warns the boys that the chorus of girls is already preparing itself (12–14) and urges the boys to focus their attention (17) for the coming struggle (18). Language appropriate to athletic contests is used (**palma**, 11, **vincēmur**, 16, and **victōria**, 16).

The first line of the last stanza has been lost, and the speaker in the preserved lines does not address either of the two choruses but rather the bride. What she says to the bride, however, is applicable to the chorus of girls as well, since the chorus of girls was taking the side of the supposedly reluctant bride. The advice of the leader of the chorus of girls to the bride is not to fight (**nē pugnā**, 59, **nōn aequum est pugnāre**, 60, **nōlī pugnāre**, 64) but to obey her parents (**quibus parēre necesse est**, 61).

The leader of the chorus of girls thus seems to favor the boys' side in the singing match, but she does not openly proclaim victory for the boys. While lines 11–18 set up the expectation that the singing match will produce a winner and a loser, as would usually be the case in an athletic contest, no winner or loser is proclaimed by the speaker of lines 58c–65. Instead, the speaker turns away from the choruses and addresses the bride, who may already have entered the room and who may have heard the singing contest or who may just now be entering (see **iam veniet virgō**, 4), and tells her not to fight with her husband (**coniuge**, 59) or with her parents (**duōbus**, 64).

The final stanza spoken by the leader of the chorus of girls thus corresponds indirectly to the earlier stanza spoken by the leader of the chorus of boys. It terminates the singing match for which preparations were made in the earlier stanza; it is, however, addressed to the bride and not to either of the choruses, and it uses language appropriate to warfare (**nē pugnā**, 59, **nōn aequum est pugnāre**, 60, **nōlī pugnāre**, 64) rather than language appropriate to athletic contests (**palma**, 11, **vincēmur**, 16, and **victōria**, 16).

21. What explanation does the leader of the chorus of girls give for why the bride should not fight against marriage but should obey her parents?

The argument is one found only here in ancient literature: the maiden's virginity is not wholly hers, but one third of it belongs to her father, one third of it to her mother, and only one third of it is hers; her parents have given their rights to her virginity to the groom along with the dowry.

22. What relationship does the explanation that the leader of the chorus of girls gives to the bride have to concerns expressed by the choruses in the singing match?

The chorus of boys had described marriage as a legal contract arranged by the groom-to-be and the bridal couple's parents (**dēspōnsa . . . conūbia . . . / quae pepigēre virī, pepigērunt . . . parentēs**, 27–28), and the leader of the chorus of girls at the end also emphasizes the parents' legal rights over their daughter. In this focus on legal principles the leader of the chorus of girls appears to be siding with the arguments of the boys.

The chorus of girls had fearfully described marriage as a tearing of the maiden away from her embrace of her mother (or her mother's embrace of her) (21–22), and the leader of the chorus of girls appears to be allaying these fears by emphasizing that both mother and father have handed the maiden over to the groom (**pater cui <u>trādidit</u> ipse, / ipse pater <u>cum mātre</u>**, 60–61) and that both parents have given their rights to the girl's virginity to the groom along with the dowry (**quī generō sua iūra simul cum dōte <u>dedērunt</u>**, 65).

Marriage is not really forcible rape, in which the girl is torn away from a mother who tries to hold her back, but is a handing over (the verb **trādere** used in line 60 is a technical term for handing over the bride to the groom in marriage) or a giving (**dedērunt**, 65). And, far from any similarity to rapes taking place in captured cities, with which the chorus of girls seems obsessed (24), marriage is not only a voluntary handing over of the girl by her parents to the groom, but the girl is even accompanied by the gift of a dowry, equally freely given; the metaphor of rape in a captured city is thus exposed as totally erroneous, and any fears the girl may harbor on this score should be eliminated.

Goud (see Select Bibliography) remarks: "The arguments of the final lines continue the boys' legal tone, but with the girls' emphasis on the family, especially the mother. The girls complained that Hesperus tears the maiden away from her mother's embrace (21–22), while the boys drew attention to the fact that the men had made an agreement (28). As Commager notes: 'The girls' appeal to the family, and the boys' appeal to law, are at last one.' In the final lines the bride is urged to accept this husband because both her father and her mother have given their rights in her virginity to the groom. . . . the two viewpoints [are blended]" (28).

23. Situate the action of the poem in the sequence of events in a wedding as described in the

paragraph preceding this poem.

Goud (see Select Bibliography) does this for us as follows: "The moment of Catullus 62 is that of the ritual tearing away of the bride from her mother's embrace in order to begin the *domum deductio*. The introductory material sets the time: Hesperus has just risen; the banquet is over; it is time to prepare for the procession. The first strophe and antistrophe of the singing contest are concerned entirely with the seizure of the bride. The second pair of stanzas clearly continue on this line. The feigned violence of this 'rape' easily accounts for the remorse of the girls and for their emphasis on the physical 'pollution' of the bride's body, which we find in the third strophe. The resolution comes when the leader of the chorus of girls, assuming, as it were, the rôle of the *pronuba*, turns to the bride and urges her not to fight but to yield. It is right to do so. The procession may now begin!" (31–32).

Select Bibliography

Eduard Fraenkel. "Vesper adest (Catullus LXII). *Journal of Roman Studies* 45 (1955) 1–8.
The poem *Vesper adest* presents to us a wedding such as could not be celebrated anywhere in the ancient world. The place of this epithalamium is neither in Greece nor in Rome but in a poetic sphere of its own. It owes some basic elements of its setting, above all the type of the feast, either to Greek life or to Greek poetry or to both, but it also employs freely some non-Greek elements. (7)

A. Davison. "A Marriage Song of Sappho's." *Archilochus to Pindar*, New York, 1968: 242–46. Examines the possible relationship of Sappho 105c to Catullus 72.39–47 and of Sappho 105a to Catullus 72.49–58.

W. R. Nethercut. "The Art of Catullus 62." *Studies in Latin Literature and Roman History*, Vol. 1. Bruxelles: Collection Latomus, 1979, 229–38. Analyzes the poem as "offering a psychological study of male and female as they await the approaching ceremony" (229).

Steele Commager. "The Structure of Catullus 62." *Eranos* 81 (1983) 21–33. A close, perceptive reading of the poem.

E. Courtney. "Three Poems of Catullus." *Bulletin of the Institute of Classical Studies of the University of London* 32 (1985) 85–100. Agrees with Tränkle that "the dramatic setting of the poem is wholly consistent with the customs of a Greek wedding" (85). Examines the possible relationship of Sappho 105c to Catullus 72.39–47 and of Sappho 105a to Catullus 72.49–58.

T. Goud. "Who Speaks the Final Lines? Catullus 62: Structure and Ritual." *Phoenix* 49 (1995) 23–32. A masterful analysis of the structure of the poem, closely followed in our presentation of it.

CATULLUS 70

1 My woman says that she prefers to marry no one more
2   than me, not if Jupiter himself were to woo her.
3 [So] she says; but what a woman says to a desirous lover
4   ought to be written on the wind and the swiftly flowing water.

Catullus imitates an epigram of Callimachus that treats the untrustworthiness of lovers' vows. His imitation is carefully crafted and subtly adjusted to his own purposes, and the Explorations questions focus on Catullus' supreme artistry in his transformation of the Greek poem into Latin. Poem 70 is, of course, far more than a literary exercise, since this is the first poem in a series of deeply probing, epigrammatic examinations of Catullus' tortured love affair with Lesbia. (We can assume that the **mulier mea** of poem 70 is Lesbia, as the companion poem 72 makes evident.) The general theme of this series of poems is that of the lover's dilemma. He repeatedly confesses his own deep love for Lesbia, but at the same time he admits that he cannot trust her faithfulness to him. In this poem the series begins with Lesbia's declaration that she prefers to marry no one other than Catullus, but the poet greets her protestation with cynical disbelief. Careful study of the changes Catullus has made in adapting Callimachus' epigram to his own purposes is the best way to approach poem 70 and the best preparation for understanding some of the epigrams that follow.

Comparison

Catullus adapted this epigram from an epigram of the Greek poet Callimachus (ca. 305–ca. 240 B.C.). Here is a translation of Callimachus' epigram:

1   Callignotus swore to Ionis that he would hold
2   neither man nor woman dearer than her.
3   He swore: the truth is that lovers' oaths
4   do not enter the ears of the immortals.
5   Now he burns for a man, while of the poor girl,
6   as of the Megarians, there is no word or record.

Explorations

1.   Which lines of Callimachus' poem has Catullus used?

    He has used only the first four.

2.   What are the similarities between Catullus' epigram and the first two couplets of Callimachus'?

    In both poems one member of a pair of lovers swears or declares that he/she loves the other more than anyone else in the world. In the second couplet in each poem the poet declares that lovers' oaths and words are not to be trusted.

3.   Of what significance are the following differences between Catullus' epigram and the first two couplets of Callimachus'?
    a.   Callimachus is writing about fictional characters, while Catullus is writing about himself and his **mulier**.

    Callimachus' poem is not about himself or a love affair of his own, but is rather an amusing story about fictional characters illustrating the theme of the untrustworthiness of lovers' oaths. The characters and their actions are contrived by the poet to serve as illustrations of the proverbial saying that "love's oaths do not enter the ears of the immortals." The poet is a distanced observer of the fictional characters that he has invented, and he shows no deep emotional involvement with any of them. For example, he expresses no indignation over Callignotus' breaking of his oath, he expresses no congratulations or pity for the new object of Callignotus' passion, and he expresses only the most conventional sympathy for the betrayed girl, calling her "poor girl," before losing track of her completely in the last line of the poem. The name Callignotus is significant, since it means "Known as Handsome," thus perhaps implying that the man bearing the name has seemed attractive to many people and has had many lovers. Further, his oath "that he would hold neither man nor woman dearer than her" may imply that he has had love affairs with many people of both sexes, all of whom he is forswearing now in favor of Ionis. Ionis should have known better than to trust such a gadabout and should have realized that she would be only one in a series of people victimized by Callignotus and would soon drop into oblivion. Having sworn "that he would hold / neither <u>man</u> nor woman dearer than her" (1–2), Callignotus has now dumped her and "burns for a <u>man</u>" (5). Callimachus observes his fictional characters from a distance, as it were, enjoying with ironic detachment the proof that he is providing of the truth of the proverbial statement that is at the center of the poem. The poem begins in the past ("Callignotus swore," 1, and "He swore," 3), moves into timelessness with the proverbial truth (3–4), and then into the present ("Now he burns. . . . ," 5). The reader will project the drama on into the future, realizing that the man for whom Callignotus now burns will not be the last in the series of those deceived by Callignotus' oaths.

Catullus, on the other hand, participates in his own poem, and his characters are not fictional but consist of his woman and himself (**mulier mea**, 1, **mihi**, 2). It is his own beloved who declares that she prefers no one to Catullus, and personal references can be felt even in line 3, which could be translated *[So] she says; but what [my woman] says to [me] [her] desirous lover*. It is not until reading the last line that one realizes that the third line is part of the proverb, which should be translated *What a woman says to a desirous lover / ought to be written on the wind and the swiftly flowing water*. Catullus assesses the truthfulness of his woman's statement in the light of the proverb and realizes how hollow her words ring, but he comes to this realization only through being himself the victim of his woman's deceitful words. He is the eager lover (**cupidō . . . amantī**), and it is his woman who brings home the truth of the proverb. Catullus in writing about himself and his **mulier** thus produces a poem far more personal, searing, and disturbing than was Callimachus' distanced, objective, ironic, and humorous view of Callignotus' series of loves.

Note also that Catullus' poem is even more intensely personal in that it concentrates on one moment in the present (**dīcit**, 1, **Dīcit**, 3, **dīcit**, 3), during which the poet comes to the realization of the truth of the proverb at the very moment when he vividly perceives himself as the *desirous lover* (**cupidō . . . amantī**). Catullus' poem takes us into the recesses of his mind at one moment in present time as he himself repeats the words of his **mulier**, feels his own desire and love for her, and realizes the emptiness of her words.

b.   In Callimachus' epigram it is a man who swears the oath, while in Catullus it is a woman who makes the statement.

This is a fundamental change of roles that Catullus has engineered in adapting the epigram of Callimachus. In Callimachus it is the male who is in the position of control, manipulating Ionis with his oath just as he has presumably manipulated many men and women in the past and will continue to do so in the future. Catullus has reversed all of this and made himself the recipient of the woman's false words; Catullus plays Ionis opposite the role of Callignotus played by Catullus' **mulier**.

Through this exchange of gender roles, Catullus has opened up a world of self-awareness totally absent from Callimachus' poem. In Callimachus' poem it is only the poet who is aware of the proverb, and it is he who states its truth. Neither Callignotus nor Ionis has any awareness of the proverb or of how it is applicable to their love affair. In Catullus' poem, however, it is the poet himself in his role as Ionis, the recipient of deceitful words, who becomes aware of the emptiness of those words and perceives the truth of the proverb. While in Callimachus Callignotus and Ionis both blithely go their own ways ignorant of the wisdom of the proverb that their lives illustrate, in Catullus the full weight of the realization of the truth of the proverb falls crushingly on the poet, who has received the empty words of his **mulier** but sees through them.

c.   Catullus has introduced the idea of marriage and the possibility of marriage with Jupiter.

In Callimachus' poem there is no mention of marriage because the heterosexual affairs of lovers in Hellenistic Greek epigrams are those of free-born Greek men for women of lower social status or courtesans. Marriage is not even a possibility in these affairs. Catullus, however, in having his **mulier** speak of marriage, has brought the relationship between himself and his **mulier** (whatever her status may be; the poem tells us nothing about it except that she is able to conceive of marriage with Catullus) within the realm of established social customs and has raised the discourse between himself and his **mulier** to a level far more serious than that of the Greek epigram.

The reference to Jupiter is playful hyperbole on the part of the **mulier**, but it has ironic overtones that betray the insincerity of her words. Jupiter is already married and is never thought of as seeking a new marriage partner. Rather, he is constantly involved in extramarital affairs with mortal women, so if Catullus' **mulier** fantasizes about any relationship between Jupiter and herself it is going to be a casual affair, a seduction or a rape. While she speaks of marriage, she can be thinking only of herself as being one in the endless series of Jupiter's loves. While she claims to reject such "marriage" with Jupiter in favor of marriage with Catullus, her whole conception of marriage is put in doubt. Perhaps it is exactly this hyperbolic reference to Jupiter that shows the insincerity of her words and leads Catullus to his realization of the truth of the proverb.

4. Why do you suppose Catullus did not use Callimachus' third couplet?

Callimachus' third couplet implies the complete breakup of the affair between Callignotus and Ionis, with the former (whose role is played by the **mulier** in Catullus' poem) off with a new lover and with the latter (whose role is played by Catullus in his poem) totally out of the picture. Catullus' affair with his woman has not yet reached that point. His **mulier** is still **mulier mea**, *my woman*. It will not be until much later, at the stage recorded in poem 11, that the situation described in the third couplet of Callimachus' epigram will be realized in Catullus' affair, with Lesbia fornicating with three hundred other lovers just as Callignotus "burns for a man," and with Catullus' love cut down like the flower at the edge of the meadow and disappearing forever just as the "poor girl" Ionis disappears from sight and mind in Callimachus' epigram.

Select Bibliography

Brooks Otis, *Virgil: A Study in Civilized Poetry*. Oxford ENG: Clarendon Press, 1963, 1st ed., 102–5.
On poems 70, 72, and 76:
The Lesbia poems as a whole—both the elegies and lyric polymetra—describe an amour extending through several stages, from initial passion to both preliminary and final disillusionment. This is certainly a Roman phenomenon in that we can find no such continuity in Greek lyric or elegy: Sappho's emotions, for example, are intense but not, so far as we can tell, related in anything like a dramatic sequence of lyrics. (105)
Paul Miller, "Catullus, C. 70. A Poem and Its Hypothesis." *Helios* 15 (1988) 127–32.
The inversion of the original Callimachean sex roles makes it possible for Catullus to occupy the role of the passive recipient of Lesbia's speech. And though Catullus has judiciously omitted the final distich of Callimachus's poem, the reader knows only too well that Catullus, in the end, will play Ionis to Lesbia's Callignotus, just as in C. 11, he plays the flower to her plough. (129)

CATULLUS 72

1   You used to say that you knew only Catullus/that only Catullus knew you,
2   Lesbia, and that you didn't wish to hold Jove more than me.
3   I cherished you then not only as anyone from the common herd [loves] a friend/prostitute,
4   but as a father cherishes his sons and his sons-in-law.
5   But now I know you: so, although I burn at greater expense/more heavily,
6   you are much cheaper and lighter in my eyes.
7   How can this be, you ask? Because the wrong you've done
8   forces a lover to love more, but to wish well less/have less affection.

Poem 72, a more complex restatement of the point of poem 70, is perhaps the best example of what Catullus achieved in his short elegiacs: a forthright, unsparing expression of his profoundly debilitating emotional conflict, though in a poetic form that evinces in every way a disciplined mastery of self-control and elegant restraint. This would be a substantial accomplishment in itself, but Catullus also manages to find very original and striking language to conceptualize his love for Lesbia. In the Explorations questions for poem 72, students are invited to build their interpretation of this poem on a careful comparison of it with poem 70 and the epigram of Callimachus on which that poem is based.

Explorations

1.   Compare this poem with Catullus 70. What are the similarities and differences?

Similarities:
a.   the verb **dīcēbās** (72.1) recalls the triple use of **dīcit** in poem 70; the woman's words are reported in indirect speech in both poems.
b.   In both poems the woman is recorded as stating her preference for Catullus even to Jupiter.
c.   In both poems the poet recognizes the emptiness of the woman's words.
Differences:
a.   In poem 72 the poet addresses Lesbia directly (note the vocative, **Lesbia**, 2, the second person verbs **dīcēbās**, 1, **es**, 6, and **inquis** 7, and the repeated **tē**, 1, 3, 5) and carries on a kind of dialogue with her, while poem 70 is an internal monologue in which the poet speaks only to himself, thus the third person form **dīcit**.
b.   In poem 72, Lesbia's statements are put into the past, introduced by **dīcēbās**, and the poet now contrasts the past (1–4) with the present (5–8).
c.   While in 70 the poet refers obliquely to his love for the **mulier** in the words **cupidō . . . amantī**, here he describes the love he felt for Lesbia in an entire couplet (3–4).
d.   While in poem 70 the poet simply records the one moment of time in which he comes to realize the emptiness of the words of his **mulier**, in poem 72 he describes in lines 5–8 how that realization has now changed how he loves Lesbia in the present.

2.   What has Catullus borrowed in this poem from Callimachus' epigram (see Catullus 70) that he did not borrow in poem 70?

He has here borrowed the contrast between past and present:
Callimachus, lines 1 and 3, "Callignotus swore" and "He swore" = past.
Callimachus, line 5, "Now he burns for a man" = present.
Catullus 72.1, 3, **Dīcēbās** and **dīlēxī** = past.
Catullus 72.5, **Nunc tē cognōvī** = present.
The contrast between past and present is even sharper if one compares the original Greek, in that Callimachus places the word that means "he swore" at the beginning of lines 1

and 3, so that Catullus deliberately echoes Callimachus as follows:

	Callimachus	Catullus
Line 1	"He swore. . . ."	**dīcēbās. . . .**
Line 3	"He swore. . . ."	**dīlēxī. . . .**
Line 5	"Now. . . ."	**Nunc. . . .**

Note that Catullus has not borrowed the motif of the breakup of the affair as it is presented in Callimachus, where Callignotus takes a new love and Ionis is totally forgotten. In Catullus the affair between the poet and Lesbia continues even after the poet's recognition in present time of Lesbia's unfaithfulness. It is this continuation of the affair under these circumstances and the emotional condition that it produces in Catullus that moves poem 72 well beyond the situation of poem 70 (which limits itself to the realization of the emptiness of the words of the **mulier**) and sets 72 off as a very different poem from that of Callimachus where there is only a touch of sympathy for the betrayed Ionis ("the poor girl," line 6) before she drops completely from sight. The betrayed Catullus takes center stage in the second half of poem 72.

3. How is what Lesbia is reported to have said in lines 1 and 2 of poem 72 different from what the **mulier** is reported to say in the first two lines of poem 70?

Rather than just saying that she would prefer to marry no one other than Catullus, Lesbia in poem 72 is reported to have repeatedly (note the imperfect tense) declared her total faithfulness to Catullus alone in a clause that can be read two ways: **sōlum tē nōsse Catullum**, *that you knew only Catullus* (with **tē** as subject of the infinitive) or *that only Catullus knew you* (with **tē** as object of the infinitive). No matter which way one reads the clause, it expresses Lesbia's total faithfulness to Catullus alone. (It should be noted that within the context of line 1 itself, the second translation is the more natural, since **sōlum** comes first, but in conjunction with line 2 the first translation must be adopted since **tē** must serve as the subject of the infinitive **velle** in line 2; in any case the words **sōlum . . . Catullum** protectively surround the word that refers to Lesbia, **tē**, thus emphasizing by word picture the inviolable togetherness of the two lovers.) The ambiguity within line 1 thus emphasizes Lesbia's declared status of being **ūnivira**, with her having known no one other than Catullus and with no one having known her except Catullus.

Catullus is here building on the Roman concept of the **matrōna ūnivira**, for which, see Gordon Williams (Select Bibliography), "The ideal of marriage to one husband finds frequent expression on Roman epitaphs, often with the word *solus*: for instance, *Carm. Epigr.* 455 *solo contenta marito*; 548, 5 *dedita coniugi soli suo*; 597, 3 *quae mihi solus coniunx Aelius . . .* ; 652, 7 *soli servasse marito*; 1872, 5 *maritum quem solum norat. . . .*" (23).

4. How does Catullus define his love for Lesbia in lines 3–4?

First, he uses the milder, more nuanced verb **dīligere**, *to esteem, cherish, love*, rather than the more physical **amāre**. Then there are the similes through which Catullus tries to define his own unique feelings, his own unique experience of his love for Lesbia, describing it as a combination (**nōn tantum . . . / sed. . . .**, *not only . . . but [also]. . . .*) of forthright sexuality (**ut vulgus amīcam**, *as anyone from the common herd [loves] a friend/prostitute*) and of the familial affection and loyalty (what the Romans would call **pietās**) that bind fathers to sons and even to sons-in-law (**pater ut gnātōs dīligit et generōs**). Compare poem 87 where Catullus asserts that his relationship to Lesbia is characterized by both love (1–2) and faithfulness (**fidēs**, 3–4). Loyalty and faithfulness would be major components of a father's relationship to his sons and to his sons-in-law in social and political alliances formed by marriage between families in the Roman world.

From the first two couplets one could assume that Catullus and Lesbia would make the perfect couple—she dedicated only to Catullus as Acme is to Septimius in poem 45 and Catullus loving Lesbia with all his sexual prowess and affection. The echoes of poem 70, however, a poem in which Catullus calls the declarations of his **mulier** into question, and the tenses of the verbs here (**dīcēbās**, 1, and **dīlēxī**, 3) with their insistence on all of this having been in the past forebode trouble and subvert the similarity to Acme and Septimius. The first words of the third couplet then descend like a sledgehammer.

5.   What has Catullus come to know (5) and what effect has that knowledge had on him (5–6)?

He has come to know Lesbia for what she really is, i.e., the opposite of what she claimed in line 1. Note the bitterly ironic use of **cognōvī** (5) picking up **nōsse** (1): "You claimed that you 'knew' only Catullus, but now I have come to know you = I know you for what you really are." (The shift of tenses from past in **Dīcēbās**, 1, and **dīlēxī**, 3, in the first half of the poem to **Nunc tē cognōvī**, 5, where the perfect tense has a present meaning, helps articulate the structure of the poem.) This recognition of Lesbia's unfaithfulness or promiscuity has not, however, brought Catullus' love for her to an end, but, paradoxically, he now *burns* (**ūror**, 5) even more than before, but Lesbia, on the other hand, is now much cheaper and lighter in his eyes (**multō mī . . . vīlior et levior**, 6). Catullus' balanced love for Lesbia in the past that combined forthright sexuality with familial affection and loyalty (3–4) has now shifted toward sexual passion (**ūror**, 5), such as anyone from the common herd indulges with prostitutes (cf. Flavius and his **scortum febrīculōsum** in poem 6), and Lesbia has become cheap and inconsequential in his eyes (6), instead of being an object of the kind of affection and concern that a father would show toward his sons and sons-in-law. Lines 5 and 6 thus record the upsetting of the delicate balance of sexual passion and familial affection/loyalty that Catullus felt toward Lesbia in the past and reduce her in his eyes to the status of an **amīca**, here, of course, a euphemism for a prostitute.

It should be noted how the two meanings of **impēnsius**, *at greater expense* and *more heavily* (5) are picked up by the two adjectives **vīlior et levior**, *cheaper and lighter* (6). The increase of Catullus' sexual desire for Lesbia is thus in exact proportion and correspondence to the decrease of his respect for her (see Commager, Select Bibliography, 94–95).

6.   What is accomplished by the addition of the final couplet, introduced by Lesbia's reported question?

The poem could have ended with lines 5 and 6, which state unambiguously the effect that Catullus' recognition of Lesbia's unfaithfulness has had on him, and would have done so with a brilliant verbal flourish in the sequence of the words **impēnsius**, **vīlior**, and **levior**, which would have brought the epigram to an artistically satisfying conclusion.

But Catullus does not stop there.

The final couplet gives Lesbia a speaking part at least in the form of a quoted question (**Quī potis est, inquis?** 7), and this turns the epigram into a kind of dialogue (cf. poem 7). That in turn allows the poet in his response to Lesbia's question to restate his awareness of his present feelings in abstract, impersonal, proverbial terms, **Quod amantem iniūria tālis / cōgit amāre magis, sed bene velle minus** (7–8), and to end the poem with a pentameter that weighs increased sexual desire against diminished benevolence (**cōgit amāre magis, sed bene velle minus**). But none of this advances us beyond what we have learned in the first three couplets. Why the final couplet?

The most important thing accomplished in the final couplet is the revelation of Catullus' awareness of Lesbia's complete lack of understanding of what is happening to him. Her baffled question, **Quī potis est?** *How can this be?* needs to be read with reference to the entire third couplet. It shows on the one hand that Lesbia *cannot* understand, or perhaps, better, does *not want* to understand *why* Catullus has changed; she cannot or does not want to understand *why* recognition of her promiscuousness should have any great effect on Catullus. Her statements reported indirectly in lines 1 and 2 must now be re-evaluated and seen not as serious, sincere declarations but as the playful phrases of a coquette, cajoling her lover into an illusory sense of security in order to take advantage of his gullibility. Lesbia's words were part of her role-playing of the part that Callignotus plays in Callimachus' epigram. They were meant to deceive and were all part of a game and never intended to be taken seriously.

Lesbia's reported question also shows that she does not understand the *effect* that her promiscuity has had on Catullus, even after he has explained it quite clearly in lines 5 and 6. Again, it may be that Lesbia does not *want* to understand what Catullus has said, since his words in lines 5 and 6 move her down toward the level of a common prostitute and equate her with the **amīca** of line 3. All Catullus can do in answer to Lesbia's reported question is to restate what her infidelity has done to him and to restate it in abstract, proverbial terms in case that language might get across to her better than his personal statement of the same thing in lines 5 and 6. The poem ends with Catullus leaving the ringing and unforgettable words in Lesbia's ears, **cōgit amāre magis, sed bene velle minus.**

The dialogue has resolved nothing; it has highlighted the disparity between Lesbia's and the poet's conceptions of love. Its conclusion points ominously forward toward more poems in the cycle that will explore how all of this plays itself out.

7. Examine the relationship between the sentences and clauses in this epigram and the metrical structures of the hexameter and the pentameter lines. How do the grammatical and metrical structures enhance the meaning expressed in each of the couplets?

Each of the first three couplets consists of a single sentence. The first two couplets are similar in that each consists of sentences with two main clauses, the first contained in the hexameter and the second in the pentameter; the second clause is introduced by **nec** (2) in the first couplet and by **sed** (4) in the second. The two couplets referring to past time are thus parallel in grammatical structure, each consisting of compound sentences, the clauses of which flow easily through the hexameter and pentameter lines.

The third couplet also consists of a single sentence, but it is far more complex in grammar. The first three words form a complete main clause; the second main clause begins in the middle of the hexameter with the word **quāre** and is interrupted by a subordinate clause, **etsī impēnsius ūror**, before being completed in the pentameter. The grammatical complexity of the couplet reflects a complexity of thought and slows the reader down to ponder the meaning.

In each of the first three couplets the end of the hexameter coincides with the end of a clause, the thought of which is expanded in the pentameter.

The final couplet begins with two short main clauses, **Quī potis est** and **inquis**, and then the remainder of the couplet consists of one sentence that flows without a break from the hexameter into the pentameter (the only place where this happens in the epigram), emphasizing the singular importance of the thought that it expresses.

8. Locate significant placement of words and repetition of words, rhythms, and sounds in the epigram. How do they enhance the meaning?

Placement and repetition of words:
Dīcēbās (1), **dīlēxī** (3), and **Nunc** (5) are emphatically placed at the head of their couplets. The adverb-pronoun phrase **Nunc tē** (5) echoes the adverb-pronoun phrase **tum tē** (3), emphasizing the contrast between past and present and hammering on the pronoun **tē**. The conjunction **quāre** (5) is echoed in **Quod** (7), both of which introduce descriptions of the present state of Catullus' feelings.

Repetition of rhythms:
Lines 1, 3, and 5 have the same metrical pattern of spondees everywhere except in the fifth foot. These lines are all heavy and ponderous, and their metrics suggest the weighty seriousness with which Catullus treats the whole subject of this epigram. Contrast these lines with the beginning of the final hexameter where Lesbia's voice is heard in her reported question: **Quī potis est?**—the only hexameter that opens with a light dactylic rhythm, suggesting, perhaps, Lesbia's frivolous attitude toward her whole involvement in the affair.

Lines 2 and 4, the pentameters in the couplets that refer to past time, both have the same metrical pattern.

Note also that line 6 opens with three long syllables, ominously highlighting the words **multō** and **mī**.

Finally, note the rapid dactylic rhythms in the final line, which sear the words on the memory: **cōgit amāre magis, sed bene velle minus**.

Repetition of sounds:
>   Line 1: sō**lum** . . . Catul**lum**
>   Line 3: **tum tē** . . . **tan**tum
>   Line 4: gnā**tōs** . . . gene**rōs**
>   Line 6: vīl**ior** . . . lev**ior**
>   Line 7: po**tis est,** inqu**is**

Select Bibliography

Gordon Williams. "Some Aspects of Roman Marriage Ceremonies and Ideals." *Journal of Roman Studies* 48 (1958) 16–29. On the ideal of the **matrōna ūnivira**.

Steele Commager. "Notes on Some Poems of Catullus." *Harvard Studies in Classical Philology* 70 (1965) 83–110. Excellent observations on the following epigrams, in this order: 85, 72, 76.

H. Akbar Khan. "A Note on the Expression *solum . . . nosse* in Catullus." *Classical Philology* 62 (1967) 34–37. On the ideal of the **matrōna ūnivira**.

J. T. Davis. "Poetic Counterpoint: Catullus 72." *American Journal of Philology* 92 (1971) 196–201.
>   In this single brief poem Catullus has interwoven three sets of structural patterns all based on contrasts: a reverie on the past with the agonized reality of the present; carnal desire with romantic love; and his feelings with those of his mistress. Catullus uses all these means in order to define completely his feelings for Lesbia. (200)

G. S. Duclos. "Catullus 11: Atque in perpetuum, Lesbia, ave atque vale." *Arethusa* 9 (1976) 76–89. Comparison of poem 72 with poem 11:
>   c.72 hinges on the contrast between the "past" Lesbia and the "present" Lesbia, between the woman who once professed that Catullus was her only lover and the woman who now wantonly abandons herself to indiscriminate lust. In the halcyon days of their relationship, Lesbia had claimed that she would rather hold Catullus in her arms than Jove (*nec prae me uelle tenere Iouem*, 72.2). Whom, now, in c.11 does the "present" Lesbia hold? Not Catullus, not even Jove—but hundreds of adulterers. (80)

Ellen Greene. "The Catullan Ego: Fragmentation and the Erotic Self." *American Journal of Philology* 116 (1995) 77–93.
>   The way in which "Catullus" and Lesbia know one another according to her version of their love (*nosse*) conflicts with "Catullus'" description of their love as primarily spiritual. Her statement to "Catullus" at the beginning shows that her standard for judging their erotic union and for knowing "Catullus" is primarily in terms of physical passion. But by telling Lesbia that the basis of his love is radically different from hers, "Catullus" reveals to her that he is, indeed, unlike the "Catullus" she knows. . . . We can now see that the speaker's hatred of Lesbia comes not only from her rejection of him, but from what he perceives to be her violation of his moral ideal of a *sancta amicitia*. (86)

CATULLUS 73

1   Stop wishing to have a claim in any way on anyone's gratitude
2   or thinking that anyone is able to be faithful to social obligations.
3   The whole world is ungrateful/all the things one does are unappreciated, to have acted
         kindly/generously
4   is not beneficial at all, rather it even wearies [one] and is harmful instead;

or
3   The whole world is ungrateful/all the things one does are unappreciated, to have acted
         kindly is nothing;
4   rather it even wearies [one], it wearies [one] and is harmful instead;

5   as in my case, whom no one oppresses more heavily or cruelly
6   than he who recently had me as his one and only friend.

Poem 73 is a particularly compressed expression of Catullus' reaction to being betrayed, a not uncommon theme in his poetry. In particular one may compare poem 30, which is not included in this book, and poem 77. Here Catullus does not speak of being betrayed by Lesbia, but by some unidentified man. In poem 30 he identifies Alfenus as the culprit, in 77 Rufus. Because of the similarity of poems 73 and 77 many scholars have conjectured that Rufus might also be the offending one here and furthermore that Rufus may be Caelius Rufus, the young protégé of Cicero, who became the lover of Clodia Metelli in a tumultuous affair that eventually led to Clodia's orchestration of a prosecution against Caelius in a Roman law court. We have Cicero's speech, *Pro Caelio*, defending Caelius and attacking Clodia in the matter. The identification of the unidentified man in poem 73 with the Rufus of 77, the identification of that Rufus with Caelius Rufus, the identification of the betrayal in poems 73 and 77 as involving Clodia, and the identification of Clodia Metelli with the Lesbia of Catullus' poems are all speculative. Our only clue to the identity of the betrayer in poem 73 is the single masculine pronoun **quī** in the last line, which is in fact no clue at all, and nothing is said or hinted as to the matter that caused Catullus to feel betrayed. Focusing on the poem itself will be more productive than speculating about its relationship to Catullus' life.

Explorations

1.   How does the large number of infinitives (five of them) in lines 1–2 affect your ability to comprehend what is being expressed in these lines? Does the similarity of sound of the words **quōquam**, **quicquam**, and **aliquem** help or hinder your understanding of the meaning of the lines? How does alliteration bind the words together? What is the tone of the lines?

     The large number of infinitives will slow down most readers and force them to sift through the various infinitives in order to sort out the grammatical function of each. The similarity of sounds of the words **quōquam**, **quicquam**, and **aliquem**, all pronouns, will initially add to the grammatical complexity or almost confusion of the lines. The three pronouns are linked by alliteration, as are the final three words of the couplet. The tone is admonitory, highlighted by the initial imperative, and one of high seriousness, as evident in the tightly worded grammatical structures, the alliterations, and the high-sounding diction, in particular the phrase **bene . . . merērī** and the word **pium**. The lines are also abstract and generalizing, addressed to no particular person and citing no particular example as a reason for the admonition. It is unusual for Catullus to start with a generalization rather than a specific event or addressee (poems 76, 96, and 107 are parallel).
     Also interesting is the word play with **bene velle** (1). The words appear in the last line of poem 72 and the first line of 73, but in poem 72 **bene** modifies **velle**, while in 73 it modifies **merērī**.

2.   Which version of lines 3–4 is more effective?

   Most readers will probably feel that Thomson's version of the text is more effective. The clause **nihil fēcisse benignē / prōdest**, *to have acted kindly/generously is not beneficial at all*, expresses the same basic meaning as Thomson's **nihil fēcisse benignē est**, *to have acted kindly/generously is nothing/is no good*, but the conciseness of expression in the latter phrasing adds weight. Beginning the pentameter with **immō** is more effective than having this word come in second position, and the emphatic repetition of **taedet** in the middle of the pentameter with the second **taedet** expanded with the following **obestque** is very striking. Finally, **magis** at line-end repeats and reinforces **immō** at line-beginning to highlight the contrast with **nihil fēcisse benignē est** in the preceding line. The only thing that is lost in Thomson's version is the play on the words **prōdest** and **obest** in line 4.

3.   What is the logical relationship of the second couplet to the first?

   The second couplet in stating that the whole world is ungrateful or that all the things one does are unappreciated and that acting generously does no good and is in fact detrimental explains why one should stop wishing to have a claim on anyone's gratitude or to think that anyone is able to be faithful to social obligations. The second couplet thus explains the reason for the admonition expressed in the first.

4.   The words **merērī** (1), **pium** (2), **ingrāta** (3), **benignē** (3), and **prōdest** (4) refer to traditional values in Roman society. These values put great store in a network of mutual loyalties, favors, and gratitude between individuals, between individuals and the state, and between individuals and the gods. What view does Catullus urge that the reader take of these mutual interrelationships in the first two couplets of this poem?

   He urges that the reader take a completely cynical attitude toward them by urging that one should never premise one's behavior on trust that others will be grateful or will reciprocate kindness or generosity. No one, he declares, is able to be **pius**, *faithful to moral, religious, or social obligations*, and acting kindly or generously reaps no reward from those treated with kindness or generosity but instead makes one regret one's actions and is positively harmful to the one who does the good deeds. The two couplets express a complete disillusionment with the moral foundation of Roman culture.
   For the moral/political concept of **pietās** in interpersonal relationships in Roman society, see Ross's chapter titled "Lesbia and the Vocabulary of Political Alliance" (see Select Bibliography). The following passage may be useful in discussing poem 73:
   [Ross quotes R. Syme, *The Roman Revolution*, Oxford, 1956, 157] "Roman political factions were welded together, less by unity of principle than by mutual interest and by mutual services (*officia*), either between social equals as an alliance, or from superior to inferior, in a traditional and almost feudal form of clientship: on a favorable estimate the bond was called *amicitia*, otherwise *factio*." "Idcirco amicitiae comparantur ut commune commodum mutuis officiis gubernetur," as Cicero himself so very clearly stated (*Sex. Rosc.* 111). Mutual services were the result or expression of unanimity: *benevolentia* (with the verb *bene velle*) has an important place in the dialogue between political *amici*, a prop to *amicitia* almost as tangible and practical as the actual *officia* or *beneficia* conferred. The result of mutual favors and *benevolentia* is specifically *gratia.* . . . (86)

5.   What is the effect of the elisions in the last line of the poem?

   They give the impression that it is very difficult for the poet to articulate the horrible truth that he feels he must express in this poem. The words do not come easily; they do not flow smoothly. Instead they get caught and tangled in one another by repetition of sound (**ūnum . . . ūnicum amīcum**) and by the five elisions, which make the line very awkward and difficult to read. It is as if the poet is so emotional in his disillusionment with his friend's betrayal of the special relationship between them that he can scarcely utter the words that describe how close their friendship was in the past.

6.   What imagery (use of descriptive language to represent people or objects, often appealing to our senses) does Catullus use in this poem, if any? How many nouns can you find? Of what significance are your findings? From what does this poem draw its power?

There is no descriptive imagery, and there is only one noun in the whole poem, the word **amīcum** in the last line. This is so because the poem is not about specifics but transcends whatever the situation was in which Catullus felt betrayed and raises the level of discourse to a highly abstract level with a black-and-white contrast between his friend's past and present behavior and a cynical admonition to the reader to abandon all faith in one's fellow human beings. It is from this high level of abstraction and compression that the poem draws its power in describing the poet's alienation from the moral corruption that surrounds him.

7.   Some scholars believe that Catullus arranged his poems in essentially the order in which they are preserved in the manuscripts; others believe that the arrangement is due to an editor who collected Catullus' poems after his death. Why would either Catullus or an editor put poem 73 after poem 72?

Both poems deal with betrayal, with the contrast between what was or appeared to be close reciprocal relationships in the past between Catullus and Lesbia (poem 72) and between Catullus and his close friend (poem 73) on the one hand and the disillusioning recognition that the poet's kindness and generosity toward Lesbia (poem 72) and toward his unnamed friend (poem 73) have not been reciprocated but that his trust and loyalty have been betrayed in both cases. There is also the word play on **bene velle** between the two poems (see the answer to Explorations question 1 above).

Select Bibliography

W. A. Oldfather, "'The Most Extreme Case of Elision in the Latin Language'?" *Classical Journal* 38 (1943) 478–79. Clyde Murley had observed that in poem 73 "the last six words of the last line . . . run together by elision into a single word," and had noted this as "probably the most extreme case of elision in the Latin language." Oldfather quoted lines from Caecilius Statius (**Sentīre eā aetāte eumpse esse odiōsum alterī**) and Lucilius (**frīgore inluviē inbalnitiē inperfunditiē incūriā**) with more words elided, and he commented: "I . . . feel inclined to doubt whether such lines as these could be readily understood if actually nineteen and twenty-two syllables respectively were 'run together into a single word'" (479). Indeed, it seems that "elided" syllables must have been sounded in some way in order for meaning to be conveyed to a listener and not "run together into a single word."

David O. Ross, Jr. "Lesbia and the Vocabulary of Political Alliance." *Style & Tradition in Catullus.* Cambridge MA: Harvard University Press, 1969, 80–95. See above.

CATULLUS 75

1   To this point my mind has been reduced, Lesbia, thanks to your unfaithfulness,
2   and it itself has so destroyed itself by [performing] its own function/by its own devotion
3   that now it couldn't wish well for you/hold you in affection, if you were to become
          the best [woman of all],
4   nor could it cease to love [you], if you were to do [anything and] everything.

The thought of poem 75 in part repeats the point of poem 72, that Catullus, at this stage in his relationship with Lesbia, has reached the point that he can no longer hold her in affection (**bene velle**), although he continues to love her (**amāre**). He gives this point a new twist in poem 75 by the claim that he has been brought to this state of conflicting emotions by his own devotion (**officium**). Through the words **culpā** and **officium**, Catullus imparts a moral dimension to his understanding of his relationship with Lesbia. He expresses his awareness of his situation in the traditional Roman language of moral responsibilities, with respect to which this poem is to be compared with poem 73.

Explorations

1.   Catullus has put strong emphasis on the opening word, **Hūc**. To what state of mind does **Hūc** refer? How does the compound verb **est . . . dēducta** color the assertion?

      The opening word **hūc**, *to this point*, refers to the strained and ambivalent state of mind that Catullus describes in the second couplet, the first word of which, **ut**, *so that*, picks up the initial **hūc**. The state of mind that Catullus describes here is revealed in his inability to wish Lesbia well/feel affection for her on the one hand and his inability to stop loving her on the other (cf. 72.8). The compound verb **est . . . dēducta** implies that Catullus feels that in having come into this state of mind he has been *dragged down*, *reduced*, perhaps *degraded* to a level of despair and despondency.

2.   In lines 1–2, what is Catullus claiming he did and that Lesbia did not do? Consider the words **culpā** (1) and **officiō** (2) in your answer. What is the consequence of Catullus' actions according to line 2?

      Essentially, Catullus claims that he has been devoted to Lesbia but that she has not been faithful in her obligations to him. The simple words **tuā . . . culpā** point to her unfaithfulness. Catullus' devotion to Lesbia is expressed in far more complex language. Catullus says that his very mind has destroyed itself **officiō . . . suō**, i.e., *by [performing] its own function/by its own devotion*—one level of the meaning of the phrase **officiō . . . suō**. The proper, essential *function/job* of the mind, however, would be to keep track of one's duties and obligations to one's fellow human beings, so that the phrase **officiō . . . suō** can also mean *by its own devotion*. What Catullus is saying here is that his mind has destroyed itself in his attempt to fulfill his commitment or maintain his devotion to Lesbia. This is the consequence to himself of what he has done in the course of his love affair with Lesbia.

3.   In your own words state what the last two lines say. The phrase **bene velle** (3) clearly relates this poem to Catullus 72, where the same phrase is used in the final line. What are the similarities and the differences between the two poems?

      Quite literally Catullus is saying here that his mind would not be able to wish Lesbia well, i.e., have benevolent/generous thoughts toward her, not even if she should change completely and become the best of all women and that at the same time his mind would not be able to stop loving Lesbia no matter what she were to do, i.e., if she became the worst of all women.

Poem 72 is longer and contrasts the past when Lesbia professed complete faithfulness to Catullus and Catullus loved her both physically and familially with the present when Catullus has come to recognize Lesbia's faithlessness. Poem 75 differs in that it begins in the present, but it is similar in the way that Lesbia's unfaithfulness has affected the poet. In poem 72 the poet states that the injury Lesbia has done to their relationship causes him to love her more but to wish her well less. This idea is repeated in poem 75, but it is heightened; the poet is now reduced to a greater depth of despair by an awareness that his affair with Lesbia has reached an irremediable impasse, so that he would not be able to have benevolent/generous thoughts toward her if she were to become the best of women and he would not be able to stop loving her if she were to become the worst of women.

4. Specific words in Catullus 73 highlight traditional Roman values based on mutual loyalties, favors, and gratitude between individuals. What words in Catullus 75 highlight these values? Are any words of this sort found in Catullus 72?

The key words here in poem 75 are **culpa** and **officium**. The word **culpa** here refers to wrongdoing that is blameworthy in the context of relationships between people, here in the amatory relationship between Catullus and Lesbia. The word **officium** refers to the dutiful adherence to obligations that should bind people together in mutual good will and reciprocal, beneficent actions. These words are part of the vocabulary of traditional Roman values that was explored in question 4 on poem 73. The phrase **bene velle** found in 72.8 is part of this vocabulary. The loyalty of fathers to sons and sons-in-law (72.4) also reflects the language of political obligations.

5. Read the poem in meter. Where do you feel that the first comma should go in line 1? Find a chiastic arrangement of words in lines 1 and 2. Analyze the parallel structure of lines 3 and 4. How many elisions do you find? Why are the ones in line 4 so effective?

However one places the comma, the effective antithesis of **tuā** and **mea** should be noted. With the comma after **mea**, there is an interlocking chiasmus of **mēns** A, **tuā** B, **mea** B, **culpā** A, effectively juxtaposing and interlocking the words describing the poet's mind and Lesbia's unfaithfulness. With the comma after **tuā**, there is a parallel arrangement of adjectives and nouns, **tuā, mea Lesbia, culpā**, a neat framing of **mea Lesbia** by **tuā ... culpā**, and a strikingly paradoxical implication that Lesbia is still the poet's Lesbia, just as she was, for example, in poem 5 (**Vīvāmus, mea Lesbia, atque amēmus**) in spite of her unfaithfulness—the very idea that is spelled out in lines 3–4 of poem 75. If we remember that Catullus may not have punctuated his own text, it is possible that he intended deliberate ambiguity here.

The words **tuā ... culpā / ... officiō ... suō** form a chiasmus, effectively juxtaposing Lesbia's unfaithfulness with Catullus' devotion.

The words **nec bene velle queat tibi** (3) find their antithesis in **nec dēsistere amāre** [queat] (4); **sī optima fīas** (3) is echoed by **omnia sī faciās** (4), with <u>optima</u> picked up by <u>om</u>-ni<u>a</u> and with **fīas** (3) echoed and reversed by its active counterpart **faciās** in line 4. There are three elisions; the ones in line 4 are particularly effective because the first links the two infinitives into a single utterance and the second links the two halves of the pentameter and ironically juxtaposes and unites **amāre** and **omnia**.

Select Bibliography

G. S. Duclos. "Catullus 11: Atque in perpetuum, Lesbia, ave atque vale." *Arethusa* 9 (1976) 76–89. Comparison of poem 11 with poem 75:

Catullus' love for Lesbia ... was ruthlessly destroyed by a human agency, as a flower is cut down by the passing plough. Lesbia herself was this agent of destruction: *illius culpa* (11.22). [Catullus] had expressed this before, in the earlier c.75: *huc est mens deducta tua mea, Lesbia, culpa* (1), but he had qualified the concept by admitting his own culpability: *atque ita se officio perdidit ipsa suo* (2). Now, however, the responsibility is totally hers. . . . Lesbia's *culpa* has been so blatant, so disgusting that it has destroyed forever Catullus' love. No longer is he poised on the horns of the dilemma of 75.3–4. . . . He can now flatly declare that his love has died because of her conduct and underline this by the finality of the image of the flower which has perished after being crushed by a passing plough. (81)

CATULLUS 76

1   If a man has any pleasure remembering previous good deeds,
2   when he thinks that he [has been and] is dutiful,
3   and that he has not violated any sacred trust, and not abused in any formal agreement
4   the divinity of the gods in order to deceive people,
5   many joys remain for you over a long life,
6   Catullus, acquired out of this love that has been received with no gratitude.
7   For whatever people can say or do well to anyone
8   has been said and done by you,
9   all which things have perished/been lost upon having been entrusted to an
            ungrateful/thankless mind.
10   Why now should you torment yourself further?
11 Why don't you become strong in [your] heart and withdraw yourself from there
12   and since the gods are unwilling [that she love you in return] cease being miserable?
13 It is difficult to put aside a long love affair in a moment.
14   It is difficult, but you must somehow bring it about;
15 this is your one salvation, you must win this victory,
16   you should do this, whether it is possible or not possible.
17 O gods, if it is within you to feel compassion, or if ever you have
18   brought any last-minute help to those on the verge of death,
19 look upon me in my wretchedness, and, if I have led a pure life,
20   take away from me this destructive disease/ruinous plague,
21 which creeping into my innermost joints like a paralysis
22   has driven joy out of my whole heart.
23 No longer do I seek that she love me in return,
24   or, what is not possible, that she wish to be chaste;
25 I wish myself to be well and to put aside this foul disease.
26   O gods, repay me this in return for my dutifulness.

In the short elegiac poems Catullus works with sharp contrasts in vocabulary, metaphors, moods, and thinking. Structural balance and antithesis are essential characteristics of his composition. Poem 76 stretches the limits of the epigrammatic form by its length and complexity. Catullus first recalls his faithful devotion to his beloved, which, he tells us, is beyond reproach or criticism: *for whatever people can say or do well to anyone / has been said and done by you* (7–8). But his love has been received with no gratitude (**ingrātō . . . amōre**, 6), and he asks, *Why now should you torment yourself further?* (10).

The poet then conducts an internal dialogue with himself and exhorts himself to put away his love in a series of questions, jussive subjunctives, and a very emphatic passive periphrastic **tibi pervincendum** (15). Here at the center of the poem we find the poet's realization of his overwhelming need to be freed from a love affair that is destroying him and his simultaneous awareness of how difficult or impossible it is suddenly to lay aside a long love.

The poet then prays to the gods for deliverance from his love, which he now describes as a foul disease. The first and last sections of the poem contrast directly with each other in comparing the poet's selfless devotion in love with his present wretched plight as he tries to free himself from the hold that love still exerts over him. The first section is the poet's confession of having lived dutifully, which logically undergirds the prayer for deliverance in the last section, as line 19 makes clear: **sī vītam pūriter ēgī**.

Comparison is invited in the student's book between poem 76 and poem 8, and poem 76 seems to take its place shortly before Catullus' final parting of the ways with Lesbia recorded in poem 11.

Explorations

1. When doing what might a person experience pleasure (**voluptās**)? (1–4)

   A person might experience pleasure when remembering his/her previous good deeds, recognizing that one has been and still is dutiful, that one has not violated any sacred trust, and that one has not abused the divinity of the gods in order to deceive anyone in any formal agreement

2. What lies in store for Catullus? (5–6) Why is this so? (7–8)

   Many joys (**multa . . . gaudia**, 5–6) lie in store for Catullus, because he has said and done well all the things that anyone could say or do well for anyone (7–8), thus accumulating many *benefacta*, the memory of which, as postulated in lines 1–4, produces pleasure (**voluptās**, 1).

3. A syllogism consists of a major and a minor premise and a conclusion. Identify the elements of a syllogism in the thoughts contained in lines 1–8 (the elements of the syllogism are there, but not in the usual order).

   Major premise: People experience pleasure in remembering their prior good deeds (1–4).
   Minor premise: I have said and done well all the things that anyone could ever do for anyone (7–8).
   Conclusion: Therefore many joys lie in store for me (5).

4. It was a philosophical commonplace in antiquity "that the recollection of past good deeds is a source of pleasure," as Powell (see Select Bibliography) remarks (199). He continues: "One of the chief problems in ancient moral philosophy was the need to show that virtue is profitable to those who practise it. One of the arguments employed to this end was that virtuous deeds are a source of pleasurable memories and that the enjoyment of a good conscience has a greater value than more mundane pleasures" (199). Powell quotes the following example of this thinking from Cicero's *De senectute* (9): **cōnscientia bene āctae vītae multōrumque benefactōrum recordātiō iūcundissima est**, *knowledge of a life well lived and memory of many good deeds is most pleasant.* Compare Cicero's statement with lines 1–5 of Catullus 76.

   The passages are very similar.

Cicero	Catullus
cōnscientia	**recordantī** (1)
bene	**benefacta** (1), **bene** (7)
benefactōrum	**benefacta** (1)
recordātiō	**recordantī** (1)
iūcundissima	**voluptās** (1), **multa . . . gaudia** (5–6)

   Both passages deal with the pleasure one may derive from a good conscience and a memory of one's good deeds.

5. Is there anything in lines 1–5 that would lead you to expect that this poem will deal with a love affair?

   The language is very general, dealing with abstract moral, ethical, and religious concepts (good deeds, being dutiful, not violating sacred trusts, and not abusing the divinity of the gods in order to deceive anyone in any formal agreement). These are the abstract moral, ethical, and religious concepts that the Romans traditionally held as ideals that should govern the relationships among people and between people and the gods (see Ross, quoted below in answer to Explorations question 6). Nothing in these lines prepares us to expect that these concepts and ideals will be applied to a love affair.

6.   Are lines 5–6 straightforward? That is, is Catullus flooded with **voluptās** and **gaudia** at the thought of his good deeds and clean conscience? If not, why not? What words in line 6 undercut the optimism of lines 1–5?

Lines 5–6 are bitterly ironic. The words **hōc ingrātō . . . amōre**, *this love that has been received with no gratitude* (6) surround and negate the word **gaudia**. With these words in line 6 the reader suddenly and unexpectedly realizes that something is wrong. The moral, ethical, and religious language of lines 1–4 implies a reciprocity of dutiful conduct between people: good deeds should be met with gratitude, dutifulness should be reciprocated, sacred trusts should be kept by both parties, and neither party to a formal agreement should deceive the other by abusing the divinity of the gods.* In line 6 we are suddenly informed that in the particular episode of Catullus' life in which he has displayed all the virtues and from which his conduct should entitle him to many joyful memories of his goodness something was and is terribly wrong. His **benefacta** have not been received with gratitude or reciprocated. He has been betrayed in his dutiful conduct toward his beloved.

*[Ross's comments are useful here (see Select Bibliography): "Catullus . . . has portrayed his affair with Lesbia in the terminology of a political alliance: it is to be an *amicitia*, a *foedus*, based on *fides*, the concrete expressions of which are the mutual *benevolentia* and *benefacta* of the two parties, resulting in *gratia* arising from the performance of *officia*; the relationship is to be protected by divinity, as it must be religiously observed with *pietas* by both parties. . . ." (90).]

7.   The truth or falsity of the conclusion of a syllogism depends on the truth or falsity of each of its premises. Which premise (1–4, 7–8) when applied to Catullus' situation may be false here?

The first premise appears to be false. While usually one feels pleasure and joy in remembering one's good deeds, Catullus may be so overwhelmed by the negative reception of those good deeds and by the betrayal with which his good words and deeds have been met that he is not able to feel the pleasure and joy to which he should be entitled. Powell remarks: "Catullus is saying that it does not work: he *has* acted virtuously, he *has* kept faith with Lesbia, but the recollection of this does nothing to alleviate the pain caused by her ingratitude" (200).

8.   Explain the commercial connotations of the words **periērunt** and **crēdita** (9).

crēdita: = *entrusted*, as if a loan or a deposit of money, which one would expect to be returned, perhaps with interest.

periērunt: = *have perished/been lost*, i.e., have not been returned by the person to whom they were entrusted, and certainly not with interest. (For a similar use of the verb **pereō**, cf. Catullus 8.2, **et quod vidēs perīsse perditum dūcās**.)

The concept behind both of the words as used here is often expressed by the phrase **dō ut dēs**, *I give in order that you may give [something back to me]*. The phrase expresses the balanced giving and receiving that should be at the heart of all commercial exchanges between those doing business with one another and by extension in all civil relationships between individuals and in all relationships between men and gods.

9.   Compare the idea expressed in lines 8–9 with line 3 of Catullus 73. What specific example of ingratitude does the poet give in poem 76?

The first 9 lines of poem 76 have many similarities to poem 73. Both poems begin with a generalization to be demonstrated in Catullus' case. In poem 73 Catullus in a totally disillusioned and pessimistic state of mind enjoins the reader (there is no addressee) to stop wishing to have a claim on anyone's gratitude (1) and to stop thinking that anyone is able to become dutiful (**pium**, 2). He says this because through personal experience he has come to realize the truth of what he says in lines 3–4, **Omnia sunt ingrāta. . . . ,** *The whole world is ungrateful/None of the things one does is received with gratitude.* The personal experience in question is some kind of betrayal by a man whom he previously held as his best friend (5–6). So in poem 76, all the things that Catullus has said and done well in his affair with his beloved *have perished/been lost upon having been entrusted to an ungrateful/thankless mind.* While Catullus has been dutiful (**pium**, 76.2) in his relations to his beloved, she has not reciprocated; so, in poem 73 Catullus warns against thinking that any other person can be **pius**.

In poem 76 Catullus is viewing his beloved with the same disillusioned pessimism that he expressed in poem 73; the unnamed man of poem 73 and the unnamed beloved (undoubtedly Lesbia) of poem 76 have shown themselves equally ungrateful and have equally betrayed the dutiful trust that Catullus has put in them.

10.   What is the relationship between the question in line 10 and what has preceded it in the poem?

The initial adverb, **Quārē**, must refer to both of the main ideas that have been expressed so far in the poem and must mean something like: (1) *since many joys should lie in store for you as you remember the good deeds you have done and your faithful dutifulness* and (2) *since everything you have done for your beloved has fallen with no return upon an ungrateful mind.* This simultaneous awareness of the *pleasure* (**voluptās**, 1) and the *joys* (**gaudia**, 6) that Catullus deserves to feel on the one hand and the total futility of everything that he has done (**omnia quae ingrātae periērunt crēdita mentī**, 9) on the other lead him to ask the anguished question, **cūr tētē iam amplius excruciēs?** (10). While Catullus deserves to feel pleasure and joy over his good deeds and his dutifulness, in reality he despairs over the unresponsiveness of his beloved and her betrayal of his dutiful trust. Since he is in no way to blame for what has happened, having said and done everything he could possibly say and do and since the problem lies totally with the unresponsiveness of his beloved, he asks, **cūr tētē iam amplius excruciēs?** *why now should you torment yourself further?* He recognizes that he is tormenting himself and asks why he continues to do so, now that he recognizes the total futility of his generous and dutiful conduct.

11.   What answer does Catullus give in lines 11–12 to the question he asks of himself in line 10?

Catullus answers the question he asks in line 10 with an ascending tricolon of questions through which he urges himself to become strong in mind, withdraw himself from the affair with his beloved, and cease being miserable. The phrase **dīs invītīs**, if it means *since the gods are unwilling [that she love you in return]*, points to the unresponsiveness of his beloved but views that unresponsiveness not as a personal choice on the part of his beloved but as the fated will of the gods, making it an obstacle that would be not only impossible to surmount but also impious even to attempt to surmount. For Catullus to continue his so far futile wooing of his beloved would thus not merely continue his self-torture but would also render him **impius** and deprive him of the sense of dutifulness in which he took great pride at the beginning of the poem (**cum sē cōgitat esse pium**, 2).

The phrase **dīs invītīs** is, of course, open to many interpretations. Freis (see Select Bibliography) paraphrases: "*since* the gods are unwilling that Lesbia love him, it would be prudent and pious for him to withdraw from the affair; *although* Catullus has lost what he formerly considered his one hope of happiness, he must *now* try to give over his misery through the prudent and pious course of withdrawing from the affair" (47). Dyson (see Select Bibliography): "since the gods do not wish you to continue loving her" or "since the gods do not wish you to be unhappy" (141). Thomson: "when Heaven itself opposes <the love that makes you *miser*>" (501).

12.   Lines 13–14 stand in the exact middle of the poem. Explain them as an internal dialogue.

Poem 76 is similar to poem 8 in many ways, and the two are set side by side in the Comparison section. Poem 8 is an internal monologue or dialogue. Here at the very heart of poem 76 when Catullus has just told himself that the only way for him to stop torturing himself is to withdraw from the affair with his beloved, the internal dialogue form is employed. In the first nine lines of the poem it might seem as if the poet is talking about an affair that is over, perhaps terminated long ago (see **priōra**, 1, and the perfect tense infinitives and finite verbs throughout). It is only with line 10 that the reader realizes that Catullus is still involved, still "in love" with the ungrateful and unresponsive woman. In lines 10–12 the second person pronouns become prominent, as if, as in poem 8, a rational Catullus were addressing an emotional Catullus: *Why don't you become strong in [your] heart and withdraw yourself from there / and since the gods are unwilling [that she love you in return] cease being miserable?* In line 13 the internal dialogue continues as Catullus' emotional self gives an answer: **Difficile est longum subitō dēpōnere amōrem**. (Note the effective juxtaposition of **longum** and **subitō**, emphasizing the difficulty of the task.) Catullus' rational self then counters: **Difficile est, vērum hoc quā lubet efficiās** (14). As Powell (see Select Bibliography) remarks, "The repetition of *difficile est* exemplifies the familiar technique of countering an objection by echoing the words of the opponent" (202). Note that line 13 reads as a formal **sententia** or emblematic statement.

13.   What devices of rhetoric, grammar, and meter does Catullus use in lines 15–16 to emphasize the necessity of accomplishing the task? Does he think he can accomplish it?

The anaphora of **haec . . . hōc . . . / hoc** (15–16), picking up **hoc** in line 14, hammers on the task to be accomplished. The polysyllabic gerundive expressing necessity, **pervincendum**, creates an unusual heavy spondaic rhythm at the end of line 15. The phrases **sīve id nōn pote sīve pote**, with the negative phrase coming first, suggest that the task is certainly beyond the capabilities of the "emotional Catullus," who objected, **Difficile est longum subitō dēpōnere amōrem** (13), probably beyond the capabilities of the "rational Catullus," and even beyond the capabilities of the "whole Catullus." It is a task that has already been shown in poem 8 to be humanly impossible.

14.   To whom does Catullus turn in his helplessness?

He turns to the gods.

15.   Catullus incorporates standard elements of ancient prayers to the gods, such as the if-clauses in lines 17–18, but how are these two clauses particularly relevant to Catullus' condition?

He is in need of the gods' pity (**miserēri**, 17), and it seems to be implied that he feels that the self-torment that he is inflicting on himself (10) has brought him to the verge of death (**ipsā in morte**, 18). (Note how the adjective and noun that frame the line, **extrēmam . . . opem**, embrace the implied figure of the dying man (**iam ipsā in morte**).
    Some readers perceive a play on the words **Ō dī** (17, 26) and the opening word of poem 85, **Ōdī**.

16.   What lines at the beginning of the poem do the words **sī vītam pūriter ēgī** (19) recall?

Lines 2–4, in which Catullus describes the goodness of his life.

17.   For what does Catullus pray? (20–22)

He prays that the gods may snatch away from him the *destructive disease/ruinous plague* (**pestem perniciemque**, 20), i.e., his irrational love, which has paralyzed him and driven joy out of his heart.

18. With what kind of imagery does the poet now describe his love? (20) What words in the remaining lines of the poem develop this imagery?

He uses imagery of disease (**pestem**, 20), which is developed in **subrēpēns īmōs . . . torpor in artūs** (21), **valēre** (25), and **taetrum . . . morbum** (25).

19. What words in lines 19–21 recall words in Catullus 51, which may have been the first poem that Catullus addressed to Lesbia?

Compare the underlined words in these stanzas of Catullus 51 with the underlined words in lines 19–22 of Catullus 76 below:

5   dulce rīdentem, <u>miserō</u> quod omnīs
6   <u>ēripit</u> sēnsūs mihi: nam simul tē,
7   Lesbia, <u>aspexī</u>, nihil est super mī
8   <vōcis in ōre,>

9   lingua sed <u>torpet</u>, tenuis sub <u>artūs</u>
10   flamma dēmānat, sonitū suōpte
11   tintinant aurēs, geminā teguntur
12   lūmina nocte.

19   mē <u>miserum</u> <u>aspicite</u> et, sī vītam pūriter ēgī,
20   <u>ēripite</u> hanc pestem perniciemque mihi,
21   quae mihi subrēpēns īmōs ut <u>torpor</u> in <u>artūs</u>
22   expulit ex omnī pectore laetitiās.

The indicatives **ēripit** (51.6) and **aspexī** (51.7) become imperatives in poem 76: **aspicite** (19) and **ēripite** (20). In both poems, Catullus describes himself as *miserable/lovesick* (**miserō**, 51.5) and **miserum**, 76.19). In both poems Catullus describes physical symptoms of paralysis; compare **lingua sed <u>torpet</u>, tenuis sub <u>artūs</u> / flamma dēmānat** (51.9–10) with **quae mihi subrēpēns īmōs ut <u>torpor</u> in <u>artūs</u>** (76.21). McGushin (see Select Bibliography) remarks: "The physical effects of the emotions aroused in him by Lesbia's beauty, as he attempted to describe them in 51.9–11, have changed their character in 76.21–22 and their end product is not the ecstasy of love but the *morbus* (76.25) of a blighting and unworthy affection" (91).

20. What two words in the first part of the poem are recalled by the word **laetitiās** (22)?

The words **voluptās** (1) and **gaudia** (6) are recalled by **laetitiās**. While Catullus deserved to enjoy **voluptās** and **gaudia** when remembering his good deeds, it is now clear with line 22 that the emotional paralysis caused by his unrequited love and his betrayal by his beloved has driven any experience of joy over those memories or over anything else out of his heart.

21. What does Catullus no longer seek, and why? (23–24)

He no longer seeks that the unnamed woman (Lesbia?) love him in return, and he no longer seeks that she be *chaste* (**pudīca**). He no longer seeks the latter because, as he explicitly states, **nōn potis est**, *it is not possible* for her to wish to be **pudīca**. Catullus does not state why he does not seek that she love him in return (**contrā ut mē dīligat illa**, 23; note that he uses the same verb here as in 72:3–4), but several explanations are possible. He may not want a woman who is **impudīca** to love him because what he longs for and the only thing that will not torment him is a reciprocal relationship between man and woman who are equally **pius**, *dutiful*, and **fidēlis**, *faithful*, to one another. Furthermore, he has already come to realize that *the gods are unwilling* that she love him in return (**dīs invītīs**, 12), and to pray for something contrary to the will of the gods would be impious. He also knows that for her to cherish him in return is simply not going to happen.

22.   What line earlier in the poem is echoed by line 25 and to what effect?

Line 25, **ipse valēre optō et taetrum hunc dēpōnere morbum**, in the final couplet of the poem, recalls line 13 in the central couplet of the poem, **Difficile est longum subitō dēpōnere amōrem**, and bitterly equates his long love with a foul disease. The recall also emphasizes the fact that Catullus himself is incapable of laying aside his love; he must pray to the higher powers of the gods to rid him of the foul disease and return him to health (**valēre**).

23.   How does the last line of the poem round out the prayer to the gods and the poem as a whole?

It rounds out the prayer to the gods by echoing the first line of the prayer (Ō dī, 26 = Ō dī, 17), and it rounds out the poem as a whole by echoing the theme of Catullus' dutifulness at the beginning (pium, 2) in the phrase prō pietāte meā (26) at the end. At the beginning of the poem the poet describes the pleasure and joys that should attend memories of good deeds and dutiful behavior such as Catullus has shown toward his beloved. Ironically, at the end of the poem Catullus prays that in exchange for his dutiful behavior (prō pietāte meā) the gods free him from the foul disease that his love has become, something that he himself is unable to do.

Comparisons

How does Catullus 76 compare with Catullus 8 in theme and in tone?

Readers have often felt the similarity in these two poems, since in both Catullus seeks deliverance from an overpowering passion with which he helplessly struggles; in both he contrasts an idyllic past with a present torment; in both he exhorts himself to do what he acknowledges may not be possible to do. The crisis of a divided will is marked also by similar vocabulary. Lines 11–12 of poem 76, **quīn tū animō offirmās atque instinc tē ipse reducis, / et dīs invītīs dēsinis esse miser** allude unmistakably to the earlier poem: **animō offirmās** recalls **obstinātā mente perfer, obdūrā** (8.11), and **dēsinis esse miser** echoes **miser Catulle, dēsinās ineptīre** (8.1). Nevertheless, there are important differences in the way the poet works with the same basic theme. In poem 8 Catullus muses on the happiness shared by the two lovers in better days, whereas there is in poem 76 a more emphatic moral tone. The past is not to be marked so much for the happiness Catullus experienced—that hardly counts now as a consideration—as for the singular faithfulness and religiously faultless devotion with which the poet behaved toward his beloved. Hence, there is a more perplexing philosophical conundrum in the present poem. One can naturally understand how emotional happiness might turn to despair (such an experience is part of the natural ups and downs of life), but it is a far more perplexing problem to explain why morally virtuous conduct should not be reciprocated and rewarded. What is at doubt in Catullus 8 is whether the poet will be able to carry out his resolve to be quit of a love that has turned sour; what is at doubt in Catullus 76 is whether the gods are in any sense just. If it is within them to feel compassion on those who suffer and yet have led a pure life as has the poet, then it follows that they must deliver him, but the issue is left in doubt. Just as we suspect at the end of poem 8 that the poet's resolve to be quit of his beloved is not all together intact, so here we may question, as philosophers as early as the writer of *Job* have questioned, whether happiness must necessarily attend the lives of good people. The traditional religious formulation, at Rome as elsewhere, has it that it must be so, but the poet's cast of the problem invites doubt. We are left with a stronger impression of the pitiable debilitation that he suffers, described in the figurative language of plague and disease, than of the certainty of his deliverance.

Project

Carl Rubino (see Select Bibliography) comments: "Though Poem 76 is obviously quite interesting and effective in itself, it can also be read as a sort of summary and model of the entire elegiac and erotic segment of the Catullan *oeuvre*. . . . Catullus 76 is full of references to many of the other poems which together establish the erotic world that is created within the *oeuvre*" (289). After students have read at least the love poems in this book, have them locate all of the echoes of other poems that they can find in poem 76. They may begin with the comparisons suggested by Rubino: 76.1–2 and 6–8, cf. poem 73; 76.3–4, cf. poems 87 and 109; 76.10, cf. poem 85; 76.11–12, cf. poem 8; 76.20, cf. poem 77; 76.21–22, cf. poem 51; 76.23, cf. poem 72. Then have students write essays in which they show how an awareness of these echoes of other poems enhance their understanding of poem 76.

Select Bibliography

P. McGushin. "Catullus' *Sanctae Foedus Amicitiae*." *Classical Philology* 62 (1967) 85–93.

Richard Freis. "Form and Thought in Catullus 76." *Agon* 1 (1968) 39–58. Highly recommended.
Catullus acknowledges the unresponsiveness of his mistress . . . (1–9); tries to assimilate that fact and choose a new course out of his misery (10–16); and . . . discovers the ineluctability of his love-*furor* (17–26). (40)

L. A. Moritz. "*Difficile est longum subito deponere amorem*." *Greece and Rome* 15 (1968) 53–58.
The struggle that must be won is not with her but with himself and with the sinister force that has hold of him and threatens to destroy him; and it is a struggle that he cannot win without the help of the gods, which he implores but which he also feels entitled to claim as the due return for his 'devotion.' (57)

David O. Ross, Jr. "Lesbia and the Vocabulary of Political Alliance." *Style & Tradition in Catullus*. Cambridge MA: Harvard University Press, 1969, 80–95. See above.

M. Dyson. "Catullus 8 and 76." *Classical Quarterly* 23 (1973) 127–43. A penetrating study of poems 8 and 76.
The general conclusion to be drawn from consideration of poems 8 and 76 and recent critical discussion on them is that an autobiographical approach is unsatisfactory and that they are best understood as poetic ideas made vivid by an appearance of autobiography. (142)

Carl A. Rubino. "The Erotic World of Catullus." *Classical World* 68 (1975) 289–98. Provocative.
The poetic lover is always uncertain of his beloved's fidelity to him, for he knows that *she has already been unfaithful to her husband*: without that unfaithfulness there could be no relationship between the lover and beloved at all. . . . Thus the elegiac world is always teetering on the brink of destruction, and the elegiac hero is always on the verge of going mad, *if he takes his situation seriously*. (291)

G. S. Duclos. "Catullus 11: Atque in perpetuum, Lesbia, ave atque vale." *Arethusa* 9 (1976) 76–89. Comparison of poem 76 with poem 11:
[Catullus] is reduced to speaking of his love as a *pestis*, a *pernicies*, a *morbus* (c.76) which he prays he may shake off so that he can grow strong and whole again: *ipse valere opto et taetrum hunc deponere morbum* (76.25). Catullus can be healthy and strong only if he rids himself of his love for Lesbia. . . . By declaring that his love is dead (11.22), Catullus has attained his wish for health. (80)

Marilyn B. Skinner. "Disease Imagery in Catullus 76.17–26." *Classical Philology* 82 (1987) 230–33.

J. G. F. Powell. "Two Notes on Catullus." *Classical Quarterly* 40 (1990) 199–206.

Ellen Greene. "The Catullan Ego: Fragmentation and the Erotic Self." *American Journal of Philology* 116 (1995) 77–93.
The problem is that in order to maintain his personal erotic ideal, Catullus has to preserve the illusion that the elegiac world is the real world. Poem 76 dramatizes the extent to which the two worlds are indeed in conflict by showing the impossibility of incorporating Roman cultural values into the private world of the lover. (88) At the end of poem 76, the multi-voiced Catullan poetic *ego* seems hopelessly tangled up in the oppositional discourses of the

private and public worlds. . . . Catullus' complex multilayered consciousness, which culminates in poem 76, reveals a lyric subjectivity new to Western literature. (91)

Joan Booth. "All in the Mind: Sickness in Catullus 76." *The Passions in Roman Thought and Literature,* ed. Susanna Morton Braund and Christopher Gill. New York NY: Cambridge University Press, 1997, 150–68.

The sickness is to be identified with an externally generated emotion: love of a complex kind, both spiritual and sexual, unsatisfied and unsatisfying, yet irresistible. But it also embraces the wider effects of this love, which are mental, not physical. It is a condition of the psyche which is serious and has gradually been getting worse: it is, in short, a progressive mental *crippling*. It has taken over Catullus completely, and makes him feel that life is not worth living. He considers it to be utterly beyond his ability to control or remedy. Moreover, to be cured is not to be granted the positive happiness which would come if his beloved suddenly reformed, but is to return to a normal and tranquil state of mind, and nothing short of a hardly-to-be-expected miracle can bring that about. By the end of the poem we can see, then . . . that the 'foul sickness' of which Catullus is desperate to be healed is *both* the emotion of love *and* the mental crippling which has in his case resulted from it. (167)

CATULLUS 77

1   Rufus, whom I in vain and without good cause believed to be a friend
2   (in vain? rather at great cost and suffering),
3   is this how you wormed your way into my confidence, and burning me deeply
4   stole all my happiness from me, wretch that I am?
5   You stole it, alas, alas, cruel poison
6   of our life, alas, alas, plague of our friendship.

This poem shares the theme of betrayed friendship and similar vocabulary with poem 73. For the possible identification of the Rufus of this poem with M. Caelius Rufus, see Explorations question 8. Here as in poem 73 the specific circumstances of the poet's betrayal at his friend's hands are not explained, only the terrible emotional cost the poet has suffered, which has blighted his life and his confidence in being able to share intimate friendship with others. This is the particular pattern of Catullus' epigrams, which do not prosaically tell a story but express and define the essential suffering of the spirit borne by the disillusioned poet.

Explorations

1.   Compare the theme of this poem with that of Catullus 73. What are the similarities? What are the differences?

     Both poems deal with the theme of friendship betrayed. In poem 73 the emphasis is on the futility of behaving toward anyone with the kindness and generosity that would engender friendship; in poem 77 the emphasis is on the villainy of a friend who has destroyed a mutual friendship by some insidious actions. Neither poem specifies what the friend is doing or has done to undermine the friendship.

2.   Poems 73 and 77 both find echoes in poem 76. What lines in poems 73 and 76 express the futility of behaving toward anyone with the kindness and generosity that would engender friendship? What lines in poem 76 are recalled by words, phrases, and clauses in poem 77?

Discussion may center on the following underlined words, phrases, and clauses:

a.   Poem 73.3–4:

> <u>Omnia sunt ingrāta</u>, nihil <u>fēcisse benignē</u>
>   prōdest, <u>immō etiam taedet obestque magis</u>;

Poem 76.7–9:

> Nam quaecumque hominēs <u>bene</u> cuiquam aut dīcere possunt
>   aut <u>facere</u>, haec ā tē dictaque factaque sunt,
> <u>omnia quae ingrātae periērunt crēdita mentī</u>.

b.   Poem 76.20–25:

> ēripite hanc <u>pestem</u> perniciemque mihi,
> quae mihi <u>subrēpēns īmōs ut torpor in artūs</u>
>   expulit ex omnī pectore <u>laetitiās</u>.
> Nōn iam illud quaerō, contrā ut mē dīligat illa,
>   aut, quod nōn potis est, esse pudīca velit:
> ipse valēre optō et taetrum hunc dēpōnere <u>morbum</u>.

Poem 77.3–6:

> sīcine <u>subrēpstī</u> mī atque <u>intestīna perūrēns</u>
>   ei miserō <u>ēripuistī omnia nostra bona</u>?
> Ēripuistī, heu heu nostrae crūdēle <u>venēnum</u>
>   vītae, heu heu nostrae <u>pestis</u> amīcitiae.

Also note the change in meaning from **ēripite** (76.20) to **ēripuistī** (76.4).

3.   Locate four nouns in the vocative case.

> **Rūfe** (1), **amīce** (1), **venēnum** (5), **pestis** (6).

4.   In lines 1–2 locate an ascending triad of two adverbs and a prepositional phrase.

> **frūstrā** (1), **nēquīquam** (1), **magnō cum pretiō atque malō** (2)

5.   In lines 3–6 locate the members of an ascending tricolon.

> **subrēpstī mī** (3), **intestīna perūrēns** (3), **ei miserō ēripuistī omnia nostra bona** (4)

6.   Study the pattern of *m-*, *s-*, and *ō*-sounds in the poem. How do they enhance its effectiveness?

> The *m*s draw attention to the speaker (**mihi**, 1; **mī**, 3), the theme of friendship (**amīce**, 1; **amīcitiae**, 6); the agent that destroys the friendship (**venēnum**, 5), and the misery (**miserō**, 4) of the speaker, betrayed in his friendship. The *s*s emphasize the slithering insidiousness of the treacherous friend (**sīcine subrēpstī mī atque intestīna perūrēns**, 3). The *o*s highlight the great loss suffered by the speaker when his friendship is betrayed (**immō magnō cum pretiō atque malō**, 2).

7.   Locate all repeated words. How does repetition emphasize the forward movement of the rhetorical structures in the poem?

> The repetition of **frūstrā** (1) in the rhetorical **frūstrā?** (2) introduces the third element of the ascending tricolon that emphasizes the devastating effect on the speaker of the betrayal of his friendship for Rufus.

The repetition of **ēripuistī** (4) in the speaker's answering of his own question in line 5 prevents the poem from becoming a dialogue and moves it to its conclusion with the speaker's own evaluation of Rufus as a **crūdēle venēnum** (5) and a **pestis** (6).

The repetition of **heu heu** (5) in **heu heu** (6) allows the poet to formulate a doublet (**nostrae crūdēle venēnum / vītae**, 5–6 = **nostrae pestis amīcitiae**, 6), the second member of which while shorter than the first is climactic in the poem as a whole in that its final word echoes **amīce** at the end of the first line of the poem, thus emphasizing the theme of friendship betrayed.

8. The Rufus of this poem is sometimes identified with M. Caelius Rufus, a lover of Clodia Metelli, the woman who is often identified as Catullus' Lesbia. If these two identifications were to be made, how would this affect your interpretation of this poem? How would your interpretation of the poem be different if these two identifications were not made?

Readers who make the two identifications often then conclude that the betrayal of the friendship between Catullus and Rufus consisted of the latter's stealing the former's beloved Lesbia/Clodia from him. They see allusions to Lesbia in the words **omnia nostra bona** (4, with **nostra** equaling **mea**), in the words **nostrae . . . vītae** (5–6, seen as a reference to Catullus' love affair with Lesbia/Clodia), and in the words **nostrae . . . amīcitiae** (6, seen also as a reference to Catullus' love for Lesbia, which Catullus describes as a form of **amīcitia** in poem 109.6). Arkins (see Select Bibliography): "Given the traditional identification of Lesbia with Clodia Metelli and the traditional chronology of Catullus' affair with her, then Poem 77 could very probably refer to the fact that Marcus Caelius Rufus became Clodia Metelli's lover and so supplanted Catullus in her affections" (308).

Compare the statements on this matter by Fordyce, Quinn, and Thomson. Fordyce states, "This Rufus, it is suggested, is M. Caelius Rufus, and it was he who supplanted Catullus in Clodia's favours" (xvi); in his introduction to poem 77, Fordyce states: "The theme of the false friend has already appeared in 30 and 73. Here the charge is explicit; Rufus has stolen Catullus' love from him" (369). Quinn is less certain: "Whether the Rufus of Poems 69 (and presumably 71) and 77 is Clodia's lover we cannot tell" (xix); Quinn entertains the possibility of seeing references to Lesbia in the words **ēripuistī omnia nostra bona** (4) ("Usually taken to mean 'you have stolen Lesbia from me'. . . . ," Quinn, 412) and **nostrae crūdēle venēnum / vītae** (5–6)— "we should perhaps remember that for C. *uita* becomes synonymous with Lesbia. . . . ," Quinn, 412. Thomson (504) advises caution by referring to "the difficulty of choosing among the many men of senatorial rank who bore the name Rufus," citing Wiseman (see Select Bibliography), but he comments as follows on the phrase **omnia nostra bona** (4): "almost certainly = <life with> Lesbia. . . . *omnia bona* alludes to her at 68.158." For Quinn, the whole question of the identity of Rufus arouses "exasperation" (xix), and students should be aware of the limits of our knowledge of some of the very important facts of Catullus' life.

If the identifications are not made and if no hidden allusions to Lesbia are seen in the poem, then it takes its place alongside poem 73 as a record of a falling out with a friend for some reason that is not reported in the poem.

Select Bibliography

T. P. Wiseman. *Cinna the Poet and Other Roman Elegists.* Leicester: Leicester University Press, 1974. On the identity of Rufus, 107–8.

B. Arkins. "Caelius and Rufus in C." *Philologus* 127 (1983) 306–11. See above.

CATULLUS 83

1   Lesbia in the presence of her husband heaps a great deal of abuse on me:
2   this is the greatest joy to that fool.
3   Mule, don't you discern anything at all? If she ignored me and was silent,
4   she would be emotionally sound: but now inasmuch as she snarls and reviles,
5   not only does she think of me, but what is much more serious,
6   she is mad. That is, she burns and so she speaks.

Catullus elegantly makes the point that disparaging words in the case of lovers are a sign of their strong attachment. The idea is a stimulating one that was taken up by later elegists. Here he draws his epigrammatic point from a brief sketch of a scene between Lesbia and her husband. Whether Catullus is actually present or not does not really affect the basic sense of the poem. When she badmouths Catullus, the husband is happy, thinking that she has no significant attachment with the young friend. But the poet understands the matter in a reverse sense. The fact that she is angry proves her love, for her angry speaking proceeds from her deep attachment to her lover. The crucial, figurative word **ūritur** is cleverly appropriate, since its metaphorical meanings can embrace both anger and love at the same time.

Holoka (see Select Bibliography and Explorations question 7) makes the attractive suggestion that Catullus is deluding himself, perhaps deliberately.

Explorations

1.   What is the situation described in this poem? Some commentators identify Lesbia with Clodia Metelli and believe that the reader is to imagine Catullus as being with Lesbia/Clodia and her husband, Q. Metellus Celer. Others, noting the words **nostrī oblīta** (3) and **meminit** (5), maintain that Catullus cannot be imagined as being present. Others deny the identification of Lesbia with Clodia Metelli. Which interpretation makes greater sense for the poem as a whole?

Holoka's observations provide useful background for this question:

If Lesbia is Clodia, but her *uir* is not Metellus, we may entertain the possibility of a second marriage, subsequent to 59 (the year of Metellus' death), and, concomitantly, a later date of composition for this poem. If the *uir* is no husband at all, but rather a "recognized lover," we may indulge in supposition about his identity. Is he, perhaps, the Rufus of poem 77, the M. Caelius Rufus defended by Cicero in 56? And what if Lesbia is not Clodia Metelli? (119)

Quinn and the Loeb translator have Catullus present with Lesbia and her husband (identified as Metellus by Quinn). Quinn comments, "all three actors are present in this little drama—Lesbia isn't just abusing C. behind his back" (417), but Thomson remarks, "In the scene depicted in this poem, C. is not present (otherwise there would be no point in either *oblita* or *meminit)"* (510). Readers will have to make up their own minds on this issue. Use of the pronoun **mī** does not imply that Catullus receives the abuse in person. If Catullus is thought of as being present, then the scene could be imagined as limited to the three people, or it could include others as well. If on the other hand Catullus is not imagined as being present, then a scene could be imagined with any number of other people being present, including Lesbia's husband (**praesente virō**, 1). If Catullus is present, then Lesbia is abusing him (perhaps to his face, perhaps not) in the presence of her husband. If Catullus is not present but others (including her husband) are, then Lesbia is abusing Catullus in conversation with some unidentified interlocutor(s) with her husband overhearing her words.

2. Why does Catullus call the husband a mule in the second couplet?

    For the comparison to a mule, see poem 17.25–26 (a poem not included in this edition). Thomson comments: "The mule is cited, not because it is sterile or because it is proverbial for stupidity or obstinacy . . . but because of its excessive patience and complaisance . . . making it a suitable figure for the indifference of the husband" (510). The husband in poem 83 is just as imperceptive as the husband who is compared to an alder tree and then to a mule in poem 17: compare **Mūle, nihil sentīs** (83.3) with **tantundem omnia sentiēns quam sī nūlla sit usquam**, *perceiving everything just as much as if it* (i.e., itself, the alder tree) *did not exist at all* (17.20).

3. How will your translation of **obloquitur** (4) depend on your answer to question 1 above?

    If the scene consists of Lesbia, her husband, and Catullus, **obloquitur** could mean *interrupts*, and **loquitur** in line 6 could have the same meaning. If Catullus is not present and the scene is imagined as including a number of people, then **obloquitur** probably means *reproaches/abuses/reviles*, and simply extends the meaning of **gannit**.

4. What word in line 6 corresponds to **sāna** in line 4?

    The word **īrāta** in line 6 corresponds to **sāna** by reversing its meaning.

5. If the reading **loquitur** is kept in line 6, how should the word be translated here? Thomson prints **coquitur**. Can that reading be defended? What words in line 3 might suggest that **loquitur** should be retained in line 6?

    If **obloquitur** (4) is translated *interrupts*, then **loquitur** (6) could be translated the same way. Fordyce regards **coquitur** as "over-ingenious," and Quinn rejects it as simply repeating **ūritur**. The reading **ūritur et loquitur** may seem flat because the vivid, metaphorical word comes first and the simple **loquitur** comes as the final word in the poem, but Catullus' point is that her speaking is the result of her burning, i.e., she burns and therefore she speaks, so that the word **loquitur** delivers a special punch at the end of this poem.

6. Propertius, a love poet of the Augustan age, had Catullus 83 in mind when he wrote a poem on "the theme that an angry tongue is a proof of love" (Quinn, 418). The following lines are extracts from Propertius' poem (3.8.3–4, 9–12, 27–28). Does Propertius' imitation help you interpret Catullus' poem?
    When, crazed with wine, you knock over the table and fling full cups at me with frenzied hand, you are without question giving me tokens of true ardor: for no woman smarts unless hers is a serious passion. She whose raging tongue spits out insults is grovelling at the feet of mighty Venus. . . . I should always wish to be the wan lover of an angry mistress (**semper in īrātā pallidus esse velim**). (trans., G. P. Goold)

    Propertius' poem should help readers understand the argument that Catullus is making that Lesbia's abuse of him and her anger are signs that she is passionately in love with him.

7. Some see in lines 3–6 "a deliberate evasion of the unpleasant conclusions that might be drawn from the situation described in lines 1–2" (Holoka, 119). Is this view defensible?

    Holoka's view of the poem is attractive (see Select Bibliography). Catullus may be deluding himself, perhaps deliberately, in insisting that Lesbia's behavior is not to be taken at its face value but is, paradoxically, evidence that she is passionately in love with him. Perhaps the truth of the matter is not that the husband does not perceive the truth (**Mūle, nihil sentīs?** 3) but that Catullus is unable or refuses to admit the truth that Lesbia's abuse of him and anger are at least to some extent genuine. Holoka comments as follows:

> In 83 and later in 92 we are witnessing a mental event: an act of therapeutic self-deception. . . . The bravado of the apostrophe to the insensitive and asinine *uir* is a ruse to conceal from the poet's addressee—himself—a more typical lack of self-assurance (cf. poems 70, 72, 75, 109); the over-elaborated rationalization of the last four lines bespeaks a mind in need of confirmation. Finally, the *hoc est* of line 6 has a ring of nervous assertion and acceptance of a willful misrepresentation: "that's it" = "that *must* be it" ("I will not allow myself to believe it is otherwise"). (119–20)

Select Bibliography

J. P. Holoka. "Self-Delusion in Catullus 83 and 92." *Classical World* 69 (1975) 119–20.

CATULLUS 84

1   "Hadvantages" Arrius used to say, when he meant
2   "advantages," and "hambush" when he meant "ambush."
3   And he used to flatter himself that he had spoken remarkably well,
4   whenever he said "hambush" with as much force as possible.
5   I believe his mother had spoken this way, and so his "free" uncle,

or
5   I believe his mother had spoken this way, and so always his uncle,

6   and so his maternal grandfather and grandmother.
7   When he had been sent to Syria, everyone's ears got a rest:
8   they heard these same [words pronounced] smoothly and softly,
9   and after that they weren't afraid of such words,
10   when suddenly a horrible message is brought,
11   that the Ionian waves, after Arrius had gone there,
12   were no longer "Ionian" but "Hionian."

On the surface Catullus 84 is a mildly amusing satire directed against a certain Arrius, a social climber who had a proclivity to use the *h* sound improperly at the beginning of certain words to show that he was *au courant* with current fads among the educated elite. Students should be invited to relish the humor and the biting satire of the poem and to enjoy a break from the increasingly agonizing poems of the Lesbia cycle that surround it. Students should also be invited to compare poem 84 with poems 12 and 22, in which someone is described as doing something that he thinks is witty or sophisticated but that is just the opposite.

Explorations

1.   How does Catullus use word placement and chiasmus to highlight Arrius' humorous mispronunciations? (1–2)

The two aspirated words (**chommoda** and **hīnsidiās**) are emphasized by being placed at the beginning and end of the couplet; the chiasmus is formed by the pattern: aspirated (**chommoda**) A, unaspirated (**commoda**) B, unaspirated (**īnsidiās**) B, aspirated (**hīnsidiās**) A. It calls attention to the pairs of words and further emphasizes the aspirated words which are at the extremities of both the couplet and the chiasmus.

In English we do not distinguish in spelling between initial aspirated and unaspirated *k*-sounds, but we pronounce the word *cat* with an aspirated *k*-sound (note the puff of breath) and the word *kitten* with an unaspirated *k*-sound (no puff of breath). So, **chommoda** should be pronounced with a puff of breath, **commoda** without.

2. What do we learn about Arrius in lines 3–4? Compare this behavior to that of Suffenus described in lines 15–17 of Catullus 22. What is the similarity? What is the poet's attitude toward this behavior?

We learn that Arrius' mistaken aspiration of words was not inadvertent or a mere slip of the tongue but was deliberate and something that he took pride in. Just as Suffenus in poem 22 was never so happy and never rejoiced and admired himself so much as when he was composing his atrocious verses, so Arrius flatters himself on his mispronunciations. Catullus makes fun of the misguided pretensions and posturing of both Suffenus and Arrius.

3. Arrius' mispronunciations are often explained as misguided attempts on the part of someone of lower class to imitate the speech of the upper classes. Explain this in the light of the information on aspiration supplied in the notes on lines 1 and 2 and in the light of what Cicero says about Quintus Arrius (see note on line 2), assuming that he is the Arrius of this poem.

This background information is often put together to lead to the conclusion that Arrius, uneducated and of low birth but an ambitious social climber, aspirated initial consonants and vowels that should not have been aspirated in an attempt to imitate the educated speech of the upper classes and to latch onto the current vogue even among the educated of excessive aspiration. So Arrius shows that he can keep up with the most reckless of the educated imitators of Greek pronunciation by aspirating initial consonants, and he shows how far he has moved away from the popular, lower-class speech that had dropped aspiration of initial vowels by aspirating initial vowels that were never aspirated before. He does all of this deliberately and with great gusto, and he prides himself on his hypersophisticated pronunciation. His verbal posturing is all part of his social climbing.

4. Why does Catullus mention Arrius' family in lines 5–6? Is **līber** to be taken literally or sarcastically? What is implied about the social status of Arrius' maternal relatives?

On one level lines 5–6 simply offer a partial explanation of why Arrius pronounces words the way he does; it is because his relatives on his mother's side of his family pronounced them that way. Arrius' mispronunciations are no invention or affectation of his own. The word **līber** is generally agreed to be sarcastic, as if it were in quotation marks as a reference to the uncle's pretensions to free-born status, with his being in fact a slave or a freedman. Just as the uncle had pretensions to free-born status, so all the members of the family are characterized as social climbers by their misuse of aspiration, an affectation by which they hope to emulate the status of the upper classes. On a deeper level, then, Catullus adds lines 5–6 to extend the sting of his satire and ridicule back from Arrius himself to his mother, his mother's family, and his grandfather and grandmother. Readers may feel that Catullus is here being bitter, harsh, and not a little nasty in satirizing the affectations and pretensions of a whole clan. There may be something here that a contemporary audience would have picked up on but to which we are not privy.

5. What do the words **Hōc missō in Syriam** (7) and **requiērant** <u>omnibus</u> **aurēs** (7) imply about the social status of Arrius at this time?

The words **Hōc missō in Syriam** imply that Arrius was important enough to be sent on a diplomatic mission, possibly by the great Crassus himself. This would fit with Cicero's descriptions of Arrius as having gained the attention of certain patrons and as being a hench-man of Crassus. His social climbing has gotten himself somewhere.

If everyone's ears found relief in Arrius' absence (**requiērant omnibus aurēs**), then he must have been well known to all for his mispronunciations, thus possibly indicating his status as an orator or an advocate in the law courts.

6. How do the words **lēniter** and **leviter** (8) correspond to descriptions of Arrius' speech in lines 1–4?

The word **lēniter** means that these words are now pronounced without aspiration, as they should be, rather than with aspiration as Arrius had done. The word **leviter** implies that these words are now pronounced in a normal, quiet tone of voice and not *with as much force as possible*, as Arrius had pronounced them (**quantum poterat**, 4).

7. Explain the point of the final couplet.

The point is that everyone thought they were rid of Arrius and his affected aspirations, but no, he hurls one more at them even in his absence!

Select Bibliography

E. S. Ramage. "Note on Catullus' Arrius." *Classical Philology* 54 (1959) 44–45.
Correct employment of the aspirate was an important constituent of *urbanitas*, which repre-sented the sum of those elements that set the speech of the city dweller off from that of the people outside Rome. . . . Catullus would appear to be describing here one of a group at Rome composed of 'climbers and also born aristocrats of defective education' whose 'zeal outstripped their knowledge.' Arrius, then, would be a member of the pseudosophisticated and pseudointellectual set in the city. . . . Just as this C. Arrius of Cicero is 'hyperurbanized,' so it is a hyperurbanism . . . that Catullus is criticizing in his poem. (45)

Donald Norman Levin. "Arrius and His Uncle." *Latomus* 32 (1973) 587–94. Surveys the major scholarly debates on this poem.

Bruce A. Marshall and Robert J. Baker. "The Aspirations of Q. Arrius." *Historia* 24 (1975) 220–31. These scholars argue for identifying Arrius with Quintus Arrius and describe his association with Crassus.

Elizabeth Vandiver. "Sound Patterns in Catullus 84." *Classical Journal* 85 (1990) 337–40.
Catullus carefully manipulates the letter *h* (used both correctly and incorrectly), the letter *s*, the metrical positions of certain aspirated words, and elision to enhance his points about pronunciation and mispronunciation. . . . The reiterated hissing of *s* throughout poem 84 is noticeable in its absence in one line, and one line only, that contains not a single *s*. This is line 8, "audibant eadem haec leniter et leuiter." This line describes the relief occasioned to Roman ears by Arrius' absence; thus the line's sound, in which the repeated hissing of *s* ceases for the only time in the poem, supports the meaning conveyed by the line's content. (337, 339)

Francis Xavier Ryan. "Two Persons in Catullus." *Giornale Italiano di Filologia: Rivista Trimestrale di Cultura* 48 (1996) 85–91. Rejects the identification of Arrius with the C. Arrius of Cicero's *Brutus* 242 and prefers identifying him with the C. Arrius of Cicero's *Letters to Atticus* 2.14 or with the son of the Arrius mentioned in the *Brutus*.

CATULLUS 85

1   I hate and I love. Why do I do that, perhaps you ask?
2   I don't know, but I feel that [it] is being done [to me] and I'm crucified/tormented.

Structural balance and antithesis play a crucial role in Catullus' short elegiac verse. Perhaps nowhere better is this illustrated than in poem 85. There is a chiastic ring compositional pattern to this couplet (ABCCBA), which conveys well the poet's feeling of being dominated by a superior force against which he is helpless. The basic antithesis of the poem is revealed in the way the active voice used by the poet in the first line is undermined, even nullified, by the passive voice in the second line. Compelling love and helpless dissolution could not be more forcefully stated. Hence, Catullus has managed within the compass of this single couplet to express not only the ambivalence of his love/hate relationship with Lesbia, but also his own inner demoralization and psychological paralysis resulting from that relationship.

In expressing this psychological paralysis, Catullus not only employs an elaborate chiastic ring compositional pattern of words, phrases, and clauses (analyzed in the Explorations questions), but he also cleverly plays on sounds; note the chiastic pattern of *qu, f, f, qu* in **Quārē id faciam, fortasse requīris** (1; see Ferguson, Select Bibliography, 138), and note the reversal of the order of the first three letters in the two words that stand at the beginning of the two halves of the pentameter: *nes- > sen-* in **Nescio . . . sentiō** (2).

Explorations

1. How many verbs are there in this couplet? How many nouns and adjectives can you find? On what does the poet focus in poem 85?

    There are eight verbs (counting the infinitive as a verb) out of fourteen words in the poem. There are no nouns and no adjectives. Compare poem 73, which contains only one noun. In poem 85 the poet focuses almost entirely on active and passive verb forms that express conflicting emotions.

2. Read the poem aloud and in meter. How many elisions can you find and what is the effect of the first and of the last elision?

    The following words are elided: **Ōdī et; Quārē id;** and **sentiō et**. The first elision helps unite the first three words into a distinct group with a metrical pattern of long-short-short-long and with initial and final long *o*. The last elision helps unite the last three words into a group that doubles the metrical pattern of the first three words, giving long-short-short-long-short-short-long. Thus the final elision helps establish a relationship between the words **senti(ō) et excrucior** and the first words **Ōd(ī) et amō**.

3. Identify the members of an ascending tricolon in the poem. What word does the ascending tricolon highlight?

    (1) Ōdī et amō.
    (2) Quārē id faciam, fortasse requīris?
    (3) Nescio, sed fierī sentiō et excrucior.

    The ascending tricolon highlights the final word of the third colon, namely, **excrucior**.

4. Locate two caesuras in the first line and two diaereses in the second line.

    The caesuras in the first line occur after **amō** and **faciam**. The diaereses in the second line occur after **Nescio** and **fierī**.

5. Divide the poem into segments based on the pauses (caesuras, diaereses, and sentence-ends).

> **Ōdī et amō**
> **Quārē id faciam**
> **fortasse requīris**
> **Nesciō**
> **sed fierī**
> **sentiō et excrucior**

6. Using these divisions of the poem into segments, label each of the segments as members of a ring composition or chiasmus consisting of ABCCBA.

> A **Ōdī et amō**
> B **Quārē id faciam**
> C **fortasse requīris**
> C **Nesciō**
> B **sed fierī**
> A **sentiō et excrucior**

7. Label the members of the ring composition or chiasmus as (A) feelings felt by an active agent, (B) action performed by an active agent, (C) inquiry by an active agent, (C) response by an active agent, (B) suffering experienced by a passive victim, and (A) feelings felt by a passive victim. What pattern do you detect?

> A **Ōdī et amō**: feelings felt by an active agent
> B **Quārē id faciam**: action performed by an active agent
> C **fortasse requīris**: inquiry by an active agent
> C **Nesciō**: response by an active agent
> B **sed fierī**: suffering experienced by a passive victim
> A **sentiō et excrucior**: feelings felt by a passive victim

The second line reverses the first line as the active agent becomes a passive victim. The elements labeled C serve as a pivot, with the inquiry of the active agent at the end of line 1 being answered by Catullus as an active agent at the beginning of line 2 but with a negative answer that indicates his lack of understanding and control and that leads merely to descriptions of his suffering and his feelings as a passive victim, with no deeper understanding of what afflicts him.

8. How does the final word of the poem relate to the first three words?

The final word has the same metrical pattern as the first three words taken together: long-short-short-long. The image of crucifixion suggests being drawn in two opposite directions, both vertically and horizontally; this expresses the opposite pulls of hate and love expressed in the first two words. On the other hand, the final verb reverses the sense of the first two verbs in that the final verb is passive while the first two verbs are active, suggesting that at the beginning of the poem the speaker is an active agent expressing his feelings while at the end of the poem the speaker is a passive victim of forces beyond his control (he is crucified as if by an executioner).

9. How do the words that immediately precede the second pause in each line (labeled B in the ring composition or chiasmus) relate to one another?

These two words, **faciam**, and **fierī**, relate to one another as active and passive forms of the same verb (recognizing that **faciō** and **fīō** are really one and the same verb, the one its active form, the other its passive form). As active and passive, however, they are opposites. In the clause **Quārē id faciam**, the poet takes responsibility as an active agent for his actions of hating and loving, but in the clause **sed fierī sentiō** the poet takes responsibility only for perceiving what is happening to him as a passive victim of forces beyond his control. The poet takes issue with the notion that falling in love is something one does. It happens to one as a passive rather than an active event.

10.   What are the main oppositions or antitheses in the poem?

The main oppositions or antitheses are hating versus loving and active versus passive, the first of which is expressed most vividly in the opening words **Ōdī et amō**, and the latter of which is expressed most vividly in the antithesis of **faciam** (1) and **fierī** (2). There is also the antithesis of knowing versus feeling.

11.   Who is the *you* of **requīris**?

A number of answers are possible here. It could be Catullus' rational self as opposed to his emotional self (compare the implied dialogue in poem 8). It could be Lesbia (compare poem 72.7, **Quī potis est, inquis?**). It could be an anonymous "friend" of Catullus, to whom he is confiding his torment (**Ōdī et amō**). Most likely, it could be simply any and every reader of this epigram. Some have suggested that Catullus is here imitating funerary inscriptions in which a conversation is carried on with any passer-by who happens to read the inscription: the deceased makes a statement; the imaginary passer-by asks a question; and the deceased answers the question.

12.   Compare this poem with Catullus 72 and 75. How does it carry to its logical conclusion and crystallize the basic antithesis expressed in those poems?

The antithesis between loving (**amāre**, 72.8, 75.4) and not wishing well (**bene velle**, 72.8, 75.3) is here carried to its logical conclusion in the antithesis between loving (**amō**, 85.1) and hating (**ōdī**, 85.1). In the three words that open poem 85, Catullus crystallizes the dilemma expressed in milder terms in poems 72 and 75.

13.   Catullus 72 contains elements of a dialogue. How does the implied dialogue in Catullus 85 lead the poet to a different conclusion and to a different state of mind?

In poem 72 the dialogue results in the poet simply restating in the penultimate half line and the final line what he had already stated in the second half of line 5 and in line 6, giving the statement a proverbial twist in reply to Lesbia's question but with the poet still functioning as a positive agent as a lover. In poem 85 the dialogue leads to a division between the speaker (**sentiō**, *I feel*) and the contradictory emotions that he experiences as a passive sufferer (**fierī**, *[it] being done [to me], [myself] experiencing [it]*) and climaxes with an image of the speaker paralyzed as a helpless victim of forces beyond his control (**excrucior**).

14.   In poem 72 the clause **Nunc tē cognōvī** (5) shows the poet fully in command of his rational faculties, and with these rational faculties he clearly describes his emotional situation twice over, first in the second half of line 5 and line 6 and then in answer to Lesbia's reported question, in the second half of line 7 and line 8. What word in Catullus 85 reverses this sense of intellectual knowledge expressed in Catullus 72?

The word **nesciō** in 85.2 reverses the intellectual assurance of poem 72. While in poem 72 the poet clearly describes his emotional situation twice over, the second time in ringing proverbial language, in poem 85 he describes his emotional situation even more clearly in the first three words, **Ōdī et amō**, but the rhetorical question posed in the poem, namely,

Quārē id faciam, demands not a description of his emotional situation but something far more difficult to deal with, namely an explanation of *why* he finds himself subjected to these contradictory emotions. This he cannot give, and with the pivotal word **Nesciō** at the beginning of the second line he admits his loss of clarity, his ignorance, and his inability to explain his feelings. All he can do in the remainder of the poem is to express his awareness that what the first three words of the poem state is indeed what he feels and that he is being torn apart by it. The sense of intellectual knowledge expressed in Catullus 72 is replaced by ignorance and an inability to give a rational account of his situation.

Project

Have students diagram the structure of the poem in a drawing, painting, or collage.

Select Bibliography

Steele Commager. "Notes on Some Poems of Catullus." *Harvard Studies in Classical Philology* 70 (1965) 83–110 (92–94 for poem 85). "The eighty-fifth poem seems an example . . . of the kind of poetry Robert Graves describes:

> Poems should not be written, like novels, to entertain or instruct the public; or the less poems they. The pathology of poetic composition is no secret. A poet finds himself caught in some baffling emotional problem. . . . The poem is either a practical answer to his problem, or else it is a clear statement of it; and a problem clearly stated is half-way to solution. Some poets are more plagued than others with emotional problems, and more conscientious in working out the poems which arise from them—that is to say more attentive to their service to the Muse, and unless he despises his fellow-men, he will not deny them the pleasure of reading what he has written while inspired by the Muse, once it has served his purpose of self-information. (93–94; the quotation is from R. Graves, *The Crowning Privilege*, New York, 1956, 191).

John Ferguson. "Catullus 85." *Liverpool Classical Monthly* 12 (1987) 138.

CATULLUS 86

1   Quintia is beautiful in the eyes of many. To me she is of good complexion, tall,
2   straight: these points I admit severally.
3   But I deny that the whole effect is "beautiful": for there is no charm,
4   no grain of spice in all that large body.
5   Lesbia is beautiful, who is not only all together pretty
6   but also has alone stolen from all women all the charms of Venus.

In many of his poems Catullus reveals a discriminating taste that sets him apart from traditional Roman standards. In other poems he uses words such as **lepidus, venustus, facētus, salsus**, and their opposites to define his own refined taste and preferences. Here he distinguishes his taste from that of the many by insisting on his own definition of the adjective **fōrmōsa**, and in the process he flatters Lesbia as the quintessential embodiment of this quality. Compare poems 22 and 43 for the contrast between public opinion and Catullus' aesthetic. Papanghelis (see Select Bibliography) suggests that the beauty contest is a metaphor for Catullus' neoteric poetic preferences.

Explorations

1. Where in the first line does Catullus deliberately place words next to each other in order to set himself and his values against society and its values?

   He does this with **multīs** and **Mihi**, setting his view off against that of the many.

2. Examine the placement of the word **fōrmōsa** in each of the three couplets. What do you discover?

   The word, which is used only here by Catullus, is used in exactly the same metrical position in lines 1 and 5 and in an only slightly delayed position in line 3. Its repetition in a similar position helps to establish the theme and the structure of the poem.

3. What qualities does Catullus admit that Quintia has? (1–2)

   He admits that she has a pleasing complexion (**candida**, 1), stature (**longa**, 1), and good posture (**rēcta**, 2), all qualities that were admired in women in antiquity. See the passages from Ovid, Propertius, Varro, and Horace quoted by Fordyce (378–79); the ideal courtesan is described by Horace (*Satires* 1.2.123) as **candida rēctaque**; Ovid has **longa** as an ideal of womanly beauty at *Amores* 2.4.33 and 3.3.8.

4. Why does Catullus refuse to admit that Quintia measures up to the full definition of the word **fōrmōsa**? (3–4)

   He refuses to admit this because she lacks **venustās** (3) and **sal** (4), which Catullus insists are essential to the full meaning of **fōrmōsa**.

5. What does Lesbia have that Quintia does not? (5–6)

   She has **venustās** and **sal**.

6. What does Catullus mean by the phrase **omnīs . . . Venerēs** (6)?

   The words call to mind the qualities of charm and attraction that the goddess Venus has, apparently transcending in Catullus' conception mere physical beauty. Catullus does not go on to define or illustrate the phrase, but we might think it would include such things as the particular way a woman laughs, talks, smirks, coyly demurs, cracks a joke, angrily rebuts an insult, turns her head, throws back her hair, rolls her eyes, or cocks an elbow. In short, one can imagine a thousand personal gestures, expressions, and mannerisms—physical, intellectual, and emotional—that may make up an indelible impression of charm and attraction. These are all qualities that work more on the personal sensibilities and aesthetic capacities of the human imagination. We all know they exist, and we all know the influence they wield; to define them may be impossible, and when we try to define them they are somehow diminished.

Select Bibliography

T. D. Papanghelis. "Catullus and Callimachus on Large Women (A Reconsideration of *c.* 86)." *Mnemosyne* 44 (1991) 372–86. "
   The comparison between Quintia and Lesbia and the notions which underlie it may be seen as a translation into beauty-contest terms of Callimachus' poetic theory and as a witty allusion to the relevant Callimachean passages" (374). "charm resides in modest-sized and fine-spun compositions, not in long ones" (375). "Quintia lacks *uenustas* and *sal* not despite but *because* of her physical *megethos* [size]. . . . Lesbia [has] the qualities of the ideal Neoteric

work in contrast to the un-Neoteric Quintia. . . . A Neoteric Lesbia and an un-Neoteric Quintia are a Callimachean Lesbia and an un-Callimachean Quintia by axiomatic extension. (379)

CATULLUS 87

1   No woman can truly say that she has been loved
2   as much as my Lesbia has been loved by me.

or
2   as much as you, my Lesbia, have been loved by me.

3   No faithfulness so great was ever in any contract,
4   as has been found in love for you on my part.

The two couplets of this epigram appear to parallel one another. In the first, Catullus states the great love he has shown for Lesbia. This recalls the earlier avowal of his love in poem 8.5: **amāta nōbīs quantum amābitur nūlla**. In the second couplet we expect his unparalleled love to be matched by Lesbia's unparalleled faithfulness. The poem turns out, however, to be completely about Catullus, and it says nothing about Lesbia at all. By way of contrast, compare the reciprocity of love and faithfulness expressed in the dialogue between Septimius and Acme in Catullus 45.

Explorations

1.   What words establish a parallelism between the two couplets of this poem?

     Three sets of words establish a parallelism of vocabulary and grammar between the two couplets: first, **Nūlla** (1), **Nūlla** (3); second, **tantum . . . / . . . quantum** (1–2), **tanta . . . quanta** (3–4); and third, **mea est** (2), **meā est** (4). The first and last of these echoes stand in the same metrical positions in their respective lines, thus enhancing the parallelism; **tanta** and **quanta** stand next to each other at the end of the third line and the beginning of the fourth, emphasizing the correlatives and thus highlighting the parallelism with the first couplet.

2.   What is gained and what is lost by reading **es** instead of **est** in line 2?

     If **es** is read, the poem gains the immediacy of a named addressee, **Lesbia . . . mea**, in the first couplet. The poem also gains coherence with the second person addressee in the first couplet and the second person reference in the words **in amōre tuō** in the second couplet. With this reading, some of the parallelism of the final two words of the couplets is sacrificed, as we get **mea es** (2) and **meā est** (4).

3.   How does alliteration enhance the diction in line 3?

     The alliteration of *f*s in **fidēs, fuit**, and **foedere** enhance the key words **fidēs** and **foedere**.

4.   Thomson remarks, "The sting of this epigram lies, of course, in *ex parte mea*." Explain how this could be true. What is the flaw in this unparalleled love?

     The words **ex parte . . . meā** reverse the expectation that has been built up that the poem will end with the words **ex parte . . . tuā**. This is a poem of correlations, as expressed in the words **tantum . . . / . . . quantum** (1–2) and **tanta . . . quanta** (3–4). The first couplet expresses Catullus' unparalleled love for Lesbia; one expects the second couplet, beginning as it does with **Nūlla fidēs**, to express Lesbia's unparalleled faithfulness to Catullus. As one reads the second couplet for the first time, one finds a confirmation of this expectation in the words **in amōre tuō** (4), which can most naturally be interpreted to mean *in your love [for me]*. Up to this point the second couplet will then be translated *No faithfulness so great was ever in any contract, / as in your love [for me]. . . .* With this meaning of the lines in mind, one reads on expecting the words **ex parte reperta** to be completed with the words **tuā est**, *has been found on your part*. This would make the two couplets exactly correlative with one another, with Catullus' unparalleled love in the first couplet matched by Lesbia's unparalleled faithfulness in the second couplet. This reading of the poem is shattered, however, by the single word **meā**, which requires the reader to revise the interpretation of **in amōre tuō** to mean *in [my] love for you* and results in the following translation of the second couplet: *No faithfulness so great was ever in any contract, / as has been found in love for you on my part.* The poem now is completely about Catullus (his love and his faithfulness), and it says nothing about Lesbia at all. Thus, the sting of the epigram lies in the words **ex parte . . . meā**, which shatter the illusion of love answered by faithfulness that has been built up to just before the penultimate word of the epigram. Not only does the sting of the epigram lie in those last words, but much of the power of the piece lies in the antithesis between the expected theme of love reciprocated by faithfulness and the actual theme of one-sided love and faithfulness with nothing said about either being reciprocated by Lesbia. Therein lies the flaw in this unparalleled love. The effect of all of this is greater if **mea es** is read in the first couplet so that the entire epigram is addressed to Lesbia, who at no point enters into a dialogue (as she does in poem 72.7 and may be thought to do in 85.1). Her silence is deafening.

With the theme of **fidēs** here, which is claimed solely on Catullus' part, compare Williams's remarks on Roman marriage (see Select Bibliography):

> Very exceptionally the husband claims credit for faithfulness to one wife: cf. e.g. *CIL* 1, 2, 1221. But clearly the normal view was that such faithfulness was a becoming and necessary virtue in woman, not in men. So too the eternal nature of the marriage-bond applies normally only to the wife. The essential one-sidedness of the whole conception is neatly illustrated in Prop. IV, 11, where Cornelia boasts of being *uniuira* but envisages Paullus' marrying again. (23, n. 27)

5. Compare the reciprocity of love and faithfulness expressed in the dialogue between Septimius and Acme in Catullus 45 with the one-sided declaration of love and faithfulness in Catullus 87.

Septimius swears both desperate and eternal love for Acme (2–5), and Acme swears both continual and intense love for Septimius (13–16). The mutuality of their love is expressed in line 20, and their faithfulness to each other is expressed in lines 21–24, in which the adjective **fidēlis** is used of Acme. Poem 45 thus portrays a completely reciprocal relationship of love and faithfulness in contrast to the one-sided declaration of love and faithfulness in poem 87, which contains no hint of reciprocity of either love or faithfulness from the side of the woman.

The use of hyperbole to express intensity of emotion is similar in both poems.

Select Bibliography

Gordon Williams. "Some Aspects of Roman Marriage Ceremonies and Ideals." *Journal of Roman Studies* 48 (1958) 16–29.

CATULLUS 92

1   Lesbia is always heaping abuse upon me and she is never silent
2   about me: may I perish if Lesbia doesn't love me.
3   By what sign [do I make this judgment]? Because it's the same for me [lit., my (things) are the
            same]: I pray to be rid of her
4   constantly, but may I perish if I don't love [her].

   This poem offers a variation on the theme of poem 83, and comparison with poem 104 may increase the probability that Catullus is indulging in self-deception in both 83 and 92.

Explorations

1.   What examples of parallel wording do you find in this poem?

      Lesbia mī (1) is echoed by **Lesbia mē** (2), and **dispeream nisi amat** (2) is echoed by **dis-
      peream nisi amō** (4).

2.   What is unusual about the word order of the two clauses contained in the words **Lesbia mē
      dispeream nisi amat** (2)?

      It is unusual to have a main clause (here **dispeream**) sandwiched in the middle of a sub-
      ordinate clause (here the words **Lesbia mē . . . nisi amat** = **nisi Lesbia mē amat** in normal
      word order).

3.   What is the structural and logical point of the phrase **quō signō** (3)?

      The phrase introduces the second couplet as the logical proof of the first. Lesbia must love
      him because she's always heaping abuse upon him, but how does the latter prove the former?
      Because the poet himself behaves the same way toward her, and he knows that he loves her.

4.   How would you best translate **dēprecor** in line 3?

      Based on the literal meaning, *entreat relief from*, Quinn suggests that the word would
      mean that Catullus "keeps wishing (aloud) that he could be rid of Lesbia" (429). Students
      should consider the meanings of the other words that Gellius adduces to explain what Catul-
      lus means by **dēprecor** here. Gellius concludes his discussion of this poem as follows (7.16.13):
      **Sīc igitur Catullus eadem sē facere dīcit quae Lesbiam, quod et maledīceret eī palam
      respueretque et recūsāret dētestārēturque assiduē et tamen eam penitus dēperīret**, *So
      therefore Catullus says that he is doing the same as Lesbia, because he publicly speaks ill of her, scorns
      and rejects her, and constantly prays to be rid of her, and yet loves her to madness.*

5.   Compare the theme of this poem with that of Catullus 83.

      In both poems Catullus interprets Lesbia's heaping of abuse upon him as a sign that she
      loves him. In poem 92 he carries this further by saying that he is sure this is true because it is
      true of himself, i.e., he continually curses Lesbia, but he knows that he loves her. The husband
      plays no role in poem 92, and it has no addressee, while poem 83 was addressed to Lesbia's
      husband. Holoka suggests that Catullus in poem 92 is again indulging in self-deception in
      his interpretation of the abusive language that Lesbia directs against the poet (see Select Bib-
      liography).

6.   Compare poem 104, given below in Latin and a very literal English translation. Does Catul

lus' denial there that he was ever able to heap abuse upon Lesbia suggest a flaw in the argument of poem 92?

If he was never capable of heaping abuse upon her and never did so, then the argument of poem 92 is weakened because it depends on his knowing from his own experience that abusive language and love can go hand in hand. Comparison with poem 104 may strengthen the probability that Holoka is correct in seeing self-deception in poems 83 and 92.

Select Bibliography

J. P. Holoka. "Self-Delusion in Catullus 83 and 92." *Classical World* 69 (1975) 119–20.

CATULLUS 95

1   The *Zmyrna* of my friend Cinna finally published after the ninth harvest
2   and the ninth winter after it was begun,
3   while for his part the [man] of Hatriensis in one
4   \<year has vomited forth five hundred thousand verses,\>
5   the *Zmyrna* will be sent far off to the deep-channeled waves of the Satrachus,
6   the *Zmyrna* gray-haired generations will go on unrolling for a long time.
7   But the *Annals* of Volusius will die by the Padua itself
8   and will often provide loose tunics for mackerel.
9   May the small works of my \<"Philetas"\> [i.e., Cinna] be dear to me,
10   but let the people be happy with [their] swollen "Antimachus" [i.e., Volusius].

This poem has several textual problems, including the reading **Hatriēnsis in** in line 3, the reading of the lost line 4, the question of whether the final couplet belongs to this poem or should be printed as a separate poem (95b), and filling in the word missing from the manuscripts at the end of line 9. We have made certain choices and decisions in printing the version in the student's book, and we believe that that version gives a coherent poem that contrasts Cinna's *Zmyrna* with the *Annals* of Volusius and ends with the poet's staking out his own poetic stance with reference to the Greek poets Philetas and Antimachus and the Latin poets Cinna and Volusius.

Hortensius, who appears in line 3 of the poem as presented in the Oxford Classical Text and in the editions of Fordyce, Quinn, and Thomson, has no place in this poem, as Solodow has persuasively argued (1987, see Select Bibliography). The reading **Hatriēnsis** in line 3 refers to Volusius, and his poetry is then the topic of both the second and the fourth couplets. He is introduced as **Hatriēnsis** in order to locate his home in northern Italy in the Po River delta and thus prepare for mention of the Padua in line 7, which will then be recognized as in the area of Volusius' home town.

Solodow (1989, see Select Bibliography) summarizes the poem as follows:

The qualities of the *Smyrna* and of the *Annals* are established for each by their absence from the other. The three linked points of comparison, which justify Cinna's success and coming renown, are: care in composition (small vs. swollen); subject and, by implication, narrative form (epyllion vs. annals); and intended audience (coterie of friends vs. the common people). And in carrying out the comparison, though his sentiments are manifest, Catullus is strictly even-handed in the allotment of space: a couplet to one, a couplet to the other, the same again, then the final couplet divided evenly. (317)

Explorations

1. What contrast is being made between Cinna's production of poetry as described in the first couplet and Volusius' production of poetry as described in the second couplet?

    It took Cinna nine full years to produce one poem, his *Zmyrna*, while Volusius produces 500,000 verses per year. The contrast involves the length of time it takes each poet to produce his poetry.

2. What words in the first couplet mirror the time frame of a human pregnancy?

    The repeated **nōnam** (1, 2) suggests the normal term of a woman's pregnancy; the noun **messem** (1) puns on the noun **mēnsem** (which was actually written here by the scribe of manuscript O); and the participle **ēdita** can suggest the idea of *being born* as well as of *being given forth* in the sense of *being published*. The suggestion of childbearing is further facilitated by the fact that the title of the poem that has been produced is that of a human being, Zmyrna.

3. What word in the second couplet suggests that Volusius' production of poetry can best be described with vocabulary describing a bodily function? How does it contrast with the vocabulary of the first couplet?

    The verb **ēvomuit** describes Volusius' production of poetry in terms of a disgusting bodily function that contrasts sharply with the gestation and childbearing suggested in the first couplet. It should be remembered, however, that line 4 has been supplied by a modern editor and is not necessarily what Catullus wrote. In support of the conjectured verb **ēvomuit**, however, one may adduce the even more disgusting description of Volusius' *Annals* in poem 36 as **cacāta carta**, *papyrus expelled as excrement* (36.1, 20).

4. What words are highlighted by their placement in line 3?

    Two of the numerical words, **mīlia** and **ūnō**, are highlighted by their placement at line-beginning and line-end.

5. In what other poem does Catullus castigate a poet for writing too many verses?

    In poem 22 he castigates Suffenus for writing **mīlia aut decem aut plūra [versuum]** (4).

6. What rhetorical device is used in lines 5 and 6?

    Anaphora of **Zmyrna**, repeating the initial word of the poem.

7. How do lines 5 and 7 contrast the fate of Cinna's poem with the fate of Volusius' verses?

    Cinna's poem will travel far; it will be sent far off to the Satrachus River in Cyprus, which would have been the setting for at least part of the section of the poem dealing with Adonis. By saying that it will be sent there, Catullus means that it will be read there, i.e., that its readership will extend very far from Italy, clear off into the Greek world of the eastern Mediterranean. Volusius' *Annals*, however, will travel nowhere, but will perish at Padua, i.e., in the vicinity of the poet's birthplace (assuming that he was born at Hatria). The contrast is sharpened by the two different meanings of the word **ad**; in line 5 it means *to* and expresses the distance that Cinna's poetry will travel, while in line 7 it means *at* and emphasizes the fact that Volusius' *Annals* will not go beyond his native region.

8. How do lines 6 and 8 contrast the fate of Cinna's poetry with the fate of Volusius' verses in a different way from that seen in lines 5 and 7?

Line 6 describes the longevity of Cinna's poetry, which will be read by *gray-haired generations* (a striking phrase that invites readers to puzzle over its exact meaning). Readers *will go on unrolling* (**pervoluent**) the papyrus roll containing the *Zmyrna*. And, they will unroll it, i.e., read the poem written on it, *for a long time* (**diū**). On the other hand, instead of being unrolled for reading, the expendable *Annals* of Volusius will be wrapped loosely around mackerel and, if Thomson is right, consigned to the flames as the fish wrapped in it are cooked. The papyrus rolls of Volusius' poetry are so many in number that people will not need to economize in their use of them for wrapping fish, but will be able to afford to wrap the fish *loosely*, in spite of the fact that papyrus was so expensive that it was rarely wasted. While people will read the *Zmyrna* **diū**, *for a long time* (6), people will *often* (**saepe**, 8) wrap fish in Volusius' *Annals*. Lines 6 and 8 thus highlight the longevity of Cinna's poem and the length of time people will devote to reading it as opposed to the short life of Volusius' *Annals* and the fact that people will either not read it at all or having read it will consign it to the flames. The respect that will be shown to Cinna's poem is contrasted with the lack of respect that will be shown to Volusius' *Annals*.

Note that while this analysis sets line 7 against line 5 and line 8 against line 6, there is a certain parallelism between lines 5 and 8 that further relates these two couplets to one another, namely, the parallelism of **cavās . . . undās** (5) and **laxās . . . tunicās** (8). Further, the word **morientur**, *will die* (7), contrasts with the theme of the longevity of the *Zmyrna* in line 6.

9. The production and publication of Cinna's *Zmyrna* were described in the first couplet in language suggesting child-birthing. How do lines 6 and 7 continue the metaphor of poetry as a living creature?

The metaphor is continued most explicitly in line 7 where it is said that Volusius' *Annals* will die (**morientur**); in line 6 it is implied that Cinna's *Zmyrna*, whose birth is described in the first couplet, will live for a long time.

10. What is the poet's wish for himself in line 9? What does he order the vulgar crowd to do in line 10? What contrasts are established?

Catullus wishes/prays that the writings of Cinna (here referred to by metonymy as Philetas) may be pleasing/dear to himself, while he orders the vulgar crowd to be happy with the bloated poetry of Volusius (here referred to by metonymy as Antimachus). There is a contrast between the small-scale poems of Cinna (**parva . . . monimenta**, 9) and the bloated, pretentious (**tumidō**, 10) poetry of Volusius. There is also a contrast between the implied good taste and discrimination of Catullus in his preference for Cinna/Philetas and the complete lack of taste of those who enjoy the bloated poetry of Volusius/Antimachus. The lack of taste on the part of the latter is indicated partly by the pejorative adjective **tumidō** and partly by use of the word **populus**, here in the disparaging sense of the vulgar crowd, hoi polloi, as the Greeks would put it.

11. What is accomplished by Catullus' referring to Cinna with the phrase **meī . . . Philītae** and by his referring to Volusius as Antimachus?

In referring to Cinna as *my Philetas*, Catullus would appear to be acknowledging the position and the importance of Cinna as a kind of Roman Philetas, i.e., as the founder of a school of scholar-poets in Italy just as Philetas had founded such a school in Greece in the third century B.C. (For Cinna's crucial role in bringing Alexandrian poetics to Italy in the person of Parthenius, see Clausen's article in the Select Bibliography and Thomson, 14–15.) By referring to Cinna as a Philetas and Volusius as an Antimachus, Catullus is suggesting a parallel between the controversy over poetry that raged in third-century Alexandria and pitted Philetas and Callimachus against the likes of Antimachus and the controversy in his own day and age that was pitting the new poets (Cinna, Catullus, Calvus, Cornificius, Ticidas, Furius Bibaculus, etc.) against the well-established, traditional school of epic poetry deriving in Italy from Ennius. By using the names Philetas and Antimachus Catullus is defining the poetics of his own day and age in terms of the past and clearly staking out his own and Cinna's position as followers in the footsteps of Philetas and his great pupil Callimachus.

12.   How is this poem structured?

    Solodow (1989; see Select Bibliography) describes the overall structure as follows: "In the first pair of couplets Catullus expresses through numbers the pains taken by Cinna and Volusius over their work. Then in the next pair he uses rivers to mark the extent of the fame they will win as a consequence. Finally, he summarizes what has been said and affirms his own stance" (318). Further, the first couplet deals with Cinna's poem, the second, with Volusius' poetry; the third deals again with Cinna's poem, the fourth, introduced by **At**, deals again with Volusius' poetry. Then the final couplet repeats this pattern, dealing in its first line with Cinna's poetry and in its second line, introduced again by **at**, with Volusius' poetry. While the first four couplets deal first with the production of Cinna's and Volusius' poetry and then with the life of the one and the death of the other, in the final couplet the poet abandons his third-person narrative description and states his own personal point of view—his own preference for Cinna/Philetas and his own rejection of Volusius/Antimachus.

13.   What is Catullus saying in this poem about good poetry and bad poetry, and how does what he says compare with what Callimachus says about poetry in the passage for comparison?

Good Poetry:	Bad Poetry:
is composed over long periods of time.	is composed quickly.
will be read far and wide over a long period of time.	is voluminous.
	will not be read widely and will perish soon.
is small in scale.	is bloated.
need not, should not, appeal to the vulgar tastes of hoi polloi.	appeals to the vulgar tastes of hoi polloi.

    Clausen (see Select Bibliography, 189) suggests that Catullus wants to include mention of the two rivers, "the broad familiar Po with its mud and flotsam, the exotic Satrachus, deep-channeled, swift and clear," as an allusion to the final lines of Callimachus' *Hymn to Apollo*. The Assyrian river, which carries much filth and refuse, would correspond to the voluminous and bloated poetry of Volusius, and the trickling spring would correspond to the small-scale, meticulously composed poetry of Cinna. The water of the trickling spring is "the choicest, the flower of its kind," and so is Cinna's poetry, which does not seek to appeal to the tastes of hoi polloi. Catullus' poetic preferences correspond to those expressed by Callimachus.

Select Bibliography

Wendell Clausen. "Callimachus and Latin Poetry." *Greek, Roman and Byzantine Studies* 5 (1964) 181–96 (188–91 for poem 95). See above.

D. F. S. Thomson. "Interpretations of Catullus—II: Catullus 95.8: 'et laxas scombris saepe dabunt tunicas'." *Phoenix* 18 (1964) 188–91. See above.

Joseph Solodow. "On Catullus 95." *Classical Philology* 82 (1987) 141–45. Defends keeping lines 9–10 (i.e., 95b) along with lines 1–8 as a unified poem; defends Housman's **Hatriēnsis** in line 3.

Joseph Solodow. "Forms of Literary Criticism in Catullus: Polymetric vs., Epigram." *Classical Philology* 84 (1989) 312–318. Proposes **Philītae** in line 9.

J. D. Morgan. "The Waters of the Satrachus (Catullus 95.5)." *Classical Quarterly* 41 (1991) 252–53. Proposes **sacrās** for **cavās** in line 5 and accepts **Hatriēnsis** in line 3.

CATULLUS 96

1   If anything pleasing or welcome to silent graves [i.e., to the silent dead in their graves]
2   can happen, Calvus, from our grief,
3   by means of which desire/longing we renew old loves
4   and [because of which desire/longing] we weep for long-departed friendships,
5   surely untimely death is not of such great grief
6   to Quintilia, as she rejoices in your love.

Poem 96 is a tightly-argued consolation addressed to Catullus' friend Calvus upon the death of Quintilia, who was possibly his wife but probably his mistress. In seeking to define Calvus' grief, Catullus succeeds in defining Calvus' love, which consists of both **amor** and **amīcitia**, both intensely experienced. Catullus can then easily assure Calvus that the grief that Quintilia feels over her premature death is no match for the joy she feels over Calvus' great love for her.

The last two lines of poem 96 appear to contain an allusion to a line in an elegy that Calvus himself wrote on his dead wife, **forsan hōc etiam gaudeat ipsa cinis**, *perhaps her ash itself may even rejoice in this*. Another fragment of Calvus' elegy is also preserved: **cum iam fulva cinis fuerō**, *when I will be brown ash*. Ovid (*Tristia* 2.431–32) comments that Calvus revealed his secret love affairs (**fūrta**) in his verse. Fraenkel pieced this evidence together into an interpretation of Catullus 96, which is summarized as follows by Fordyce (386):

> Fraenkel concludes that in his elegy Calvus had made the dead Quintilia herself reproach him for his infidelities . . . ; *cum iam fulua cinis fuero*, she had said, you will be sorry for your *furta*, and he had hoped that his repentance would comfort her shade (*gaudeat ipsa cinis*). Using his own words, Catullus gently reassures him; *ueteres amores* and *missae amicitiae* are the love that Calvus had lightly abandoned and the generalizing plural tenderly spares his feelings.

Much of this reconstruction of the background of the poem was swept aside by Davis (see Select Bibliography), who regards Quintilia as Calvus' mistress and not his wife and who sees no allusion in Catullus 96 to Calvus' alleged **fūrta**. Davis (299) offers the following explanation of Catullus 96 and its background:

> Quintilia is Calvus' mistress and Catullus imagines that Calvus' affection for her was of the same nature as Catullus' own love for Lesbia. At her death Calvus wrote an elegy in which he conversed with her ghost who was imagined as saying "I will remember you even in death and may you also remember me." Calvus' reply was that he would remember her and that he hoped this would please her shade. Catullus' poem is the poet's assurance that Quintilia is pleased with and accepts Calvus' expression of affection.

With only meager fragments of Calvus' poem preserved it is better to concentrate on close analysis of Catullus 96 in its own right. It is one of Catullus' finest poems, and its coupling of **amor** and **amīcitia** is important for understanding poem 109.

The answers to some of the Explorations questions are based closely on Davis's excellent analysis of the poem.

Explorations

1.   What is the grammatical structure of the single sentence of which this poem is composed?

>   It is a conditional sentence. The first couplet is the protasis or if-clause, the second couplet expands the protasis with a relative clause, and the third couplet is the apodosis or conclusion.

2. What proposition does the poet put forth in the first and the third couplets?

The poet proposes that if anything pleasing or welcome (**grātum acceptumve**, 1) for the dead can come from the grief (**ā . . . dolōre**, 2) of the living, then death is not a source of grief (**dolōrī**, 5) to Quintilia; rather, she rejoices (**gaudet**, 6) in Calvus' love. (Davis, 300)

3. What words in the third couplet recall a specific word and a specific phrase in the first couplet? What central thematic contrast in the poem do these words and this phrase define?

The word **dolōrī** (5) recalls **dolōre** (2), and the word **gaudet** (6) recalls and corresponds to the phrase **grātum acceptumve** (1). These words and this phrase define a central thematic contrast between joy (expressed in the phrase **grātum acceptumve**, 1, and the word **gaudet**, 6) and grief (expressed in the words **dolōre**, 2, and **dolōrī**, 5). The grief of the living (**nostrō . . . dolōre**, 2) and the happiness of the dead (**gaudet**, 6) are the poles of the poem. The poem explores the relationship between these two emotions. (Davis, 300)

4. How does the relative clause that makes up the second couplet define its antecedent, **dolōre** (2)?

First, it defines **dolōre** by substituting for it a new word, **dēsīderium**, and incorporating that word into the relative clause as a repeated antecedent. The relative clause thus moves from the very general concept of painful grief, **dolōre** (2) to the more specific concept of painful longing for a lost beloved, **dēsīderiō** (3). Second, it defines the new term, **dēsīderium**, through the two clauses that make up the compound relative clause, first through the clause in line 3, in which the ablative phrase **quō dēsīderiō** is used instrumentally, and second through the clause in line 4, in which the ablative phrase is to be taken to express cause rather than instrument.

5. What are the similarities and what are the differences between the two clauses in lines 3 and 4?

The second clause, **ōlim missās flēmus amīcitiās** has wording parallel to that in the first clause, **veterēs renovāmus amōrēs**, but it expands and does not merely repeat the first clause. (Davis, 300) In the first clause **dēsīderium**, *desire/longing,* is the <u>instrument or means</u> *by which we renew old loves.* In the second clause the operation of **dēsīderium** is different as it becomes the <u>cause</u> *on account of which we weep for long-departed friendships*; the instrumental ablative would make no sense here, giving *by means of which desire/longing we weep for long-departed friendships,* which is nonsense. The different operations of **dēsīderium**, first as instrument and then as cause correspond to the different objects of longing expressed in the two clauses, **amōrēs**, *loves,* and **amīcitiae**, *friendships*. The former, Catullus is saying, are renewed by **dēsīderium**; the latter can only be wept over (and by implication can never be renewed), and **dēsīderium** is what causes the weeping. So, men renew old loves <u>by means of</u> their longing/desire, and they weep over departed friendships <u>because of</u> that same longing/desire.

6. What words suggest that Catullus is generalizing about the human condition in lines 1–5?

First, the word **quicquam**, *anything,* is general. Second, the phrase **ā nostrō . . . dolōre** means not *from your grief and mine* but more generally *from the grief of us human beings*. Catullus is generalizing here and not talking specifically about Calvus' grief for his lost Quintilia. Third, the first person plural verbs **renovāmus** (3) and **flēmus** (4) generalize to include all human beings. Fourth, the phrases **veterēs . . . amōrēs** (3) and **ōlim missās . . . amīcitiās** (4) generalize by being in the plural and generalize also through the modifiers **veterēs** and **ōlim missās**, which do not refer specifically to Calvus' recent loss of his Quintilia but to people's longing in general for things of the past. In these lines, then, Catullus is defining certain important aspects of the human condition in general without specific reference to the example of Calvus and Quintilia.

7. How do lines 3 and 4 lead to the conclusion expressed in the final couplet?

In the first couplet Catullus talks simply of grief (**dolōre**, 2), but in lines 3 and 4 he describes the content or the operation of that grief by redefining it with the term **dēsīderium** and then showing how **dēsīderium** operates with respect to lost loves and friendships. While lines 3 and 4 continue to generalize as did the first couplet, they also surely apply to Calvus' specific **dolor** and his specific **dēsīderium** and describe how he renews his lost love for Quintilia and weeps over his departed friendship with her. His love for/friendship with Quintilia would be one instance of the **amōrēs** and **amīcitiae** of lines 3–4. Lines 3–4 have thus redefined the **dolor** of line 2 as an expression not simply of grief but as an expression of on-going longing/desire relating to love/friendship. This leads to the conclusion in the final couplet:

So when Catullus describes Quintilia's joy he says that she is happy because of Calvus' love (*gaudet amore tuo*, v. 6), not his grief. If the feelings of the living can touch the dead, then the real meaning of grief is that it expresses a love in which even the dead can rejoice. (Davis, 300)

Select Bibliography

John T. Davis. "Quo desiderio: The Structure of Catullus 96." *Hermes* 99 (1971) 297–302. See above; highly recommended.

CATULLUS 101

1 Having traveled through many peoples and through many seas
2   I arrive, brother, for the purpose of these pitiful offerings for the dead,
3 to bestow upon you the final duty/offering associated with death,
4   and to speak to your silent ashes, useless as that is,
5 since fortune has robbed me of you yourself,
6   alas, pitiful brother, undeservedly taken away from me.
7 Now at any rate receive these things, which in the ancient manner of our parents/ancestors
8   have been handed over [by me] for the purpose of offerings for the dead as a sad
          duty/offering,
9 dripping heavily with a brother's tears,
10   and forever, brother, hail and farewell.

This is one of Catullus' most famous poems. In it he speaks upon arrival at the grave of his brother in the Troad. Catullus also speaks of his grief for his dead brother in poems 65 (5–14) and 68 (19–26, 89–100). Some think that the occasion of Catullus' visit to his brother's grave was on his way to his service on the governor's staff in Bithynia (57 B.C.) or on his way home (56 B.C.), but inclusion of a description of the journey in the first line of poem 101 makes it more likely that a separate journey was undertaken to visit the grave; the impression conveyed is one of a separate pilgrimage to the site. Poem 101 should be compared with poem 96 on the death of Quintilia. The assumption in that poem that the dead can perceive the feelings of the living, thus opening the possibility of communication between the living and the dead, lurks in the background in line 4 of poem 101 but is found to be mistaken in this profoundly sad poem.

This is an excellent poem to have students memorize and recite. In the process of doing so, students will come to appreciate the subtlety and finesse of elisions, word placement, and sound effects such as alliteration, assonance, and homoioteleuton. There are superb opportunities for modulation of tone of voice and expression in this brief epigram.

Explorations

1. What letters and sounds predominate in lines 1–4?

    The heavy alliteration of *m*s, which is noticeable throughout the poem, is signaled by the initial *m* in **multās** and **multa** in the first line. Notice, moreover, how the *m*s intensify as the sentence progresses. There is only one instance of *m* in the second line but four each in lines 3 and 4, the heaviest concentration in all of the poem. Since lines 3–4 announce the poet's intentions of bestowing on his brother the final duty/offering associated with death and of speaking to his silent ashes, the heavy alliteration enhances the emotional weight of the statement.

    Also notable is the anaphora of **Multās . . . multa** at the beginning of the successive phrases in line 1 and the triple repetition of -**ās** in **hās miserās . . . īnferiās** in line 2, with **miserās** positioned at the end of the first half of the line and **īnferiās** at the end of the second half of the line. The long *a* of **frāter** is echoed in the surrounding words **hās miserās . . . īnferiās**.

2. Read lines 1–4 aloud. How does Catullus use dactyls and spondees effectively here?

    Students should be asked to describe the effects produced by the heavy pattern of three spondees followed by the lighter pattern of two dactyls in the first line, the second line containing no spondees, and the third and fourth lines containing as many spondees as possible for normal hexameter and pentameter verses.

    Students should also notice the elision across the normal diaeresis in the middle of the fourth line, which joins the adverb **nēquīquam** with the verb that it modifies, **alloquerer**, into one unit of sound and sense that emphasizes the emptiness of the poet's proposed speaking to the ashes of his brother.

3. How does Catullus effectively position words in lines 3 and 4 to highlight the verbs?

    In line 3 an adjective and its noun (**postrēmō . . . mūnere**) surround the verb (**dōnārem**), which occupies the middle of the line; in line 4 an adjective and its noun (**mūtam . . . cinerem**) surround the elided adverb and verb (**nēquīquam alloquerer**), which together occupy the middle of the line. In both cases the verbs, which express the poet's intention of performing the ritual actions (namely, giving offerings and addressing the dead), are highlighted.

4. How does the poet evoke sympathy for his task in the first four lines?

    To bring funeral offerings and to perform funerary rituals for a brother who has died prematurely are sad tasks by any measure, but Catullus has enhanced the emotional piquancy of the gesture by the particular way in which he has described it here. Since his brother was buried in the vicinity of Troy, as we learn from poems 65.7 and 68.89–92, going to visit his grave required a long journey across many lands and seas. Hence, the initial line of poem 101, which recalls that journey, has reminded some readers of the epic journey of Odysseus. Lines 3–4 of Homer's *Odyssey* read: "He saw the cities and learned the thought of many *men*, / and he suffered many pains in his heart on the *sea*." Homer's summary shows the same order of **gentēs** and **aequora** as in Catullus' poem. Catullus, however, has given the motif an unusual twist. An epic hero's quest, undertaken with arduous exertion and suffering, will meet with some suitable recompense, and Catullus, as he made the long pilgrimage to his brother's grave, may have been building up unrealistic expectations of what awaited him, what Quinn refers to as "some possibility of communication transcending normal experience" (*Latin Explorations*, London: Routledge and Kegan Paul, 1963, 81). But the journey Catullus makes brings him only to speak to the silent ashes of his brother, which he recognizes as a useless exercise (**nēquīquam**, 4), and to address three final words to him, **Avē atque valē** (10). Hence, the emotional piquancy of the Catullan poem lies in the fact that there is no suitable resolution to the poet's longing and to the great exertion he has made to visit his brother's grave. Instead he must confront the reality of his loss (see the next question and its answer), which is a bitter and permanent one. All he can do, to borrow language from poem 96, is to weep over **ōlim missās . . . amīcitiās** (4).

It is also interesting to compare this poem to poem 11. In that poem Catullus contrasts the grand public mission Furius and Aurelius are ready to undertake with him to the private, intimate favor he actually requests of them. So here, Catullus begins his poem with epic language and theme—a trip to Troy—, but shows in the body of the poem that his focus is on a private and very personal episode in his life. He speaks not of heroic accomplishment but of private loss.

5.   Observe the placement of the words in line 4: **et mūtam nēquīquam alloquerer cinerem**. What would be expressed by taking **nēquīquam** as modifying **mūtam**?

Reading the sentence as it unfolds, the reader will first associate **nēquīquam** with **mūtam**. The idea of *mute in vain* would suggest that something could be communicated, just as the bed in poem 6, which is described as **nēquīquam tacitum** (7), actually shouts (**clāmat**, 7) the truth about Flavius. As one continues with the second half of the line, however, one more naturally takes **nēquīquam** with **alloquerer**, so that the poet's stated intention is to speak to the mute ash, although realizing that to be an empty gesture, rather than to speak to the ash that is mute in vain. The initial temptation, however, to take **mūtam** and **nēquīquam** together may continue to haunt the meaning of the line and suggest that Catullus may have journeyed to the Troad in anticipation of some communication with his deceased brother "transcending human experience," as Quinn puts it. Lines 5 and 6 dash any such expectations and clearly indicate that no communication will be possible with the deceased since fortune/death has taken Catullus' brother away from him.

6   What feelings are expressed in lines 5–6? Look closely at the individual words in this couplet. What is the point of using **tētē** and **ipsum** in combination? What is the force of the words **abstulit** and **adēmpte**? How do the three words **heu miser indignē** build on each other? Why is **mihi** repeated?

Feelings of anger and indignation over the cruelty of fortune that has taken his brother from him are expressed in line 5, and sympathy for his brother's pitiable demise is expressed in line 6. The placement of **mihi** next to the emphatic **tētē** effectively emphasizes the poet's loss, and this is emphasized further by the adjective **ipsum** at the end of the line, with **tētē . . . ipsum** here in stark contrast to **mūtam . . . cinerem**, the *mute ashes* in line 4, which do not represent the brother's real self. The words **abstulit** and **adēmpte** further highlight the loss that the poet has suffered; the ascending syllable counts in **heu miser indignē** emphasize the pathos of the brother's death and of the poet's loss; and the repetition of **mihi** focuses on the poet and his emotional trauma caused by his brother's death.

7.   What is the structure of the poem?

As in Catullus' other short elegiac verse, the present poem has a logical, symmetrically balanced structure to it. The first four lines, describing the poet's journey and stating its purpose, are balanced against the last four lines, in which Catullus describes himself completing the funerary rituals at his brother's grave. These two sections are mediated in the center of the poem by the highly emotional invocation to his dead brother (5–6). That direct invocation is contained in a subordinate clause that begins with **quandoquidem**. Syntactically this subordinate clause could be attached either to the first or to the last four lines of the poem, and indeed editors punctuate the poem differently to attach it to the one or the other group of lines. The Oxford Classical Text edition joins it to the last four lines, putting a full stop after the word **cinerem** at the end of line 4. Conversely, the text given here follows Thomson, who puts a comma after **cinerem** and the full stop after **mihi** (6). However we punctuate, the central lines 5 and 6 appropriately qualify what is said in both the first and the last four lines of the poem. The poet's journey (the first four lines) and his performance of the rituals (the last four lines) are carried out with an ultimate awareness of the sad fact of the impossibility of communication with the dead that is realized most fully in the central lines 5 and 6.

8.   What is the effect of the threefold repetition of **frāter** in the poem?

Thomson comments as follows on the ritual background: "The poem can be seen, in view of the triple repetition of *frater* . . . as enshrining a literary version of the ritual known as *conclamatio*, by which the relatives of the deceased called his name loudly, three times (originally no doubt as a precaution, in the belief that this might evoke a spark of recognition if any life remained)" (537).

In each of the three structural sections of the poem, the poet directly addresses his brother (2, 6, 10). Moreover, the word **frāter** is in the same metrical position in each of these lines and is bracketed by emotionally charged terms in every case: **miserās, frāter, ad īnferiās** (2: the pitiful task); **indignē frāter adēmpte** (6: the tragedy, which the poet finds so difficult to accept); **in perpetuum, frāter, avē atque valē** (10: the final plaintive farewell). The effect of this highly crafted artistry is a stirring cri-du-cœur that is quite overpowering.

9.   Comment on alliteration and assonance in the last four lines.

The pattern of alliteration of *m*s continues in the last four lines, although it is not as pronounced as in lines 1–4. Nevertheless, the emotive phrase **multum mānantia** hits a particularly plaintive note. What is distinctive, however, about this last section in comparison with the first four lines is the other forceful patterns of alliteration, which build up to a crescendo here in the poem. Notice the concentration of *s*s and *p*s, for example, but even more pronounced are the heavy *t*s, three in line 7 and four in each of the last three lines. The most elegant and emotive blend of these alliterative patterns is found in the exquisite phrase **frāternō multum mānantia flētū** (9). Notice also the beautiful assonance of the final cri-de-coeur, which repeats the pattern of vowel sounds, *a* and *e*, although we have to allow for elision: <u>av</u><u>ē</u> atque <u>val</u><u>ē</u>.

10.   This poem speaks of last rites performed by the poet for his brother. How does the poem itself enact and become part of the ritual?

The relatives of the dead would ritually call upon the name of the deceased loudly three times; the poem itself does this through the threefold repetition of **frāter**.

The poet speaks of arriving for the purpose of making pitiful offerings for the dead (**hās miserās . . . ad īnferiās**, 2); these offerings would normally be milk, honey, wine, or flowers. In lines 7–9 Catullus asks his brother to receive **haec**, *these things,* which are not identified but are described in the relative clause in lines 7–8: **prīscō quae mōre parentum / trādita sunt trīstī mūnere ad īnferiās**, *which in the ancient manner of our parents/ancestors / have been handed over [by me] for the purpose of offerings for the dead as a sad duty/offering.* Note that **trādita** is to be translated "'given' (as I have now done), rather than 'handed down' by tradition" (Thomson, 538). The word **haec** thus need not necessarily refer to things handed down by tradition (such as the usual milk, honey, wine, or flowers), although those things need not be ruled out. Eleanor Cederstrom (see Select Bibliography) has suggested that **haec** may include the poem itself in which the word occurs: "the unspecified **haec** of line 7, referring ostensibly to the traditional gifts of milk and honey, wine and flowers, may also be interpreted as the poem itself. The poem is Catullus's last gift to his brother" (117). In describing the things being offered as *dripping heavily with a brother's tears* (**multum mānantia flētū,** 9), the poet could be referring to his own poem, the composition of which must surely have been accompanied by much suffering and tears (metaphorical or real).

In this poem Catullus not only describes the customary rituals performed for the dead but also enacts the ceremony through his ritual cry, through the gift of the poem itself—the greatest possible tribute of one brother to another—, and finally through the farewell he utters, **avē atque valē**, which is a formula found on tombstone inscriptions.

Postscript

Invite students to compare poem 101 with poem 96, especially on themes of the relationship of the living to the dead and the function of grief. The passage from the letter of Sulpicius to Cicero should be included in the discussion.

Select Bibliography

C. E. Robinson. "Multas per Gentes." *Greece & Rome* 12 (1965) 62–63. Supports punctuating with a comma after line 4 and a period after line 6, as does Thomson and as we do.
Eleanor Cederstrom. "Catullus' Last Gift to His Brother (c. 101)." *Classical World* 75 (1981) 117–18. See above.

CATULLUS 107

1   If anything [ever] happens to someone desiring and wishing [for it to happen],
2   [while] not expecting [that it would ever happen], it is [always] welcome in the true sense
            of the word to [his/her] heart.
3   Therefore this is welcome to us [i.e., to me], and more precious than gold,
4   that you bring yourself back into favor, Lesbia, with me desiring [that you would do so],
5   you bring yourself back into favor [with me] desiring [that you would do so] and not
            expecting [that it would ever happen], you yourself bring yourself back
6   to us [i.e., to me]. O day of a whiter mark!
7   Who lives more happily than I alone/who is happier than I myself, or who will ever
8   be able to lead a life more to be desired?

Catullus has created in this poem a mosaic of words, of which the most important are: **cupidō** (1, 4, 5), **optantī** and **optandam** (1, 8), **īnspērantī** (2, 5), **grātum** (2, 3), and **restituis** (4, 5). These five words encompass the basic point of the poem, that Lesbia's restoring herself to Catullus is a special blessing because it has not only been desired and wished for but was also unexpected. The unusual rhetorical strategy in this poem is that Catullus does not make a simple statement of this matter but that he repeats it with rhetorical emphasis and ingenuity. Is he simply celebrating the return of his beloved, or is he trying to convince himself that his newfound happiness must be true? Thomson has said that the repetitions "have an almost incantatory effect" (543).

See the standard commentaries for discussion of the textual problems in lines 3 and 7–8. We print the emendations of Heyworth and Lyne. Dettmer supports Lyne's reconstruction of lines 7–8 and diagrams the verbal repetitions in the poem. See Select Bibliography.

Explorations

1. What is the logical structure of thought in this poem?

    The first couplet expresses a generalized observation that it is especially welcome if something happens to someone that that person desires and wishes to happen but does not expect to happen. The second and third couplets at the center of the poem apply this general statement to a specific case and draw the conclusion (introduced by **Quārē**, *Therefore*, 3) that it is welcome to Catullus that Lesbia is reinstating herself in his favor, something that he desired but did not expect to happen. In the rhetorical questions that make up the final couplet, Catullus expresses just how welcome this event is to him.

2. Catullus has created an extraordinarily elaborate verbal mosaic in this poem. What words are repeated from the first couplet in the last couplet?

    The words **optantī** (1) and **umquam** (1) are repeated in **umquam** (7; same position in the line) and **optandam** (8). Pattern: ABBA = chiasmus; caution: remember that **umquam** in line 7 is a modern conjecture without manuscript authority.

3. What words are repeated from the first couplet in the central second and third couplets?

    The words **cupidō** (1), **īnspērantī** (2), and **grātum** (2) are repeated in **grātum** (3), **cupidō** (4), **cupidō** (5), and **īnspēranti** (5). Pattern: ABCCAB.

4. What words are repeated within the central two couplets?

    The words **nōbīs** (3), **tē** (4), **restituis** (4), and **cupidō** (4) are repeated in **restituis** (5), **cupidō** (5), **tē** (5), and **nōbīs** (6). Pattern: ABCDCDBA; AB . . . BA= chiasmus; CDCD = parallel.

5. Are any words repeated in the final couplet from the central second and third couplets?

    No. The echoes felt in the final couplet are of words in the first couplet, thus rounding out the structure of the poem.

6. Analyze the example of conduplicatio that is at the exact center of the poem.

    The words **tē restituis, Lesbia, mī cupidō** (4) are repeated with variation in **restituis cupidō atque īnspēranti** (5), and the lines in which these words occur lie at the exact center of the poem.

7. Identify the members of a tricolon in the central second and third couplets.

    The members of the tricolon are: (1) **tē restituis, Lesbia, mī cupidō** (4), (2) **restituis cupidō atque īnspēranti** (5), and (3) **ipsa refers tē / nōbīs** (5–6).

8. Comment on the placement of the name Lesbia in line 4.

    The single occurrence of the name of Catullus' beloved is artfully bracketed between **tē restituis** and **mī cupidō**. The poet's desire and his beloved's return enfold the name Lesbia (word picture).

9. What words in lines 3 and 6 highlight how welcome what has happened is?

    The word **grātum** (3) expresses the idea explicitly; then two images highlight it: **cārius**

aurō, *more precious than gold* (3), and **Ō lūcem candidiōre notā!** *O day of a whiter mark!* (6). These two images surround the central statements about Lesbia and express through the idea of great value and through the gleaming of the precious metal and the brilliant whiteness of the happy day just how welcome Lesbia's return is to Catullus.

10.   What is unusual about this poem when you compare it with the rest of the short elegiac poems you have read?

All the other Lesbia poems among Catullus' short elegiac poems treat of his betrayal at the hands of his beloved. It is odd that against this strong, unanimous testimony there would be one poem alone that speaks of a reconciliation. It is impossible to locate such an event precisely in the course of the real or fictional love affair. Is Catullus speaking of something that happened early in the affair or in its later stages? Some scholars who have attempted to reconstruct an outline of the affair have given a great deal of weight to this poem, claiming a late reconciliation between the lovers. But the singular testimony of the poem strikes a note of doubt, and the poem itself seems to hint at the fact that Lesbia's restoration is too good to be true. Maybe we should leave it at that.

Postscript

Have students compare the question at the end of this poem with that at the end of poem 45. Are these questions ironic in any way?

Select Bibliography

Stephen Heyworth. "Catullus 107.3—A Response." *Liverpool Classical Monthly* 9.9 (Nov. 1984) 137. Responds to Thomson and proposes the reading that we print in line 3.

D. F. S. Thomson. "Catullus 107.3–4 and 109.1–2." *Liverpool Classical Monthly* 9.9 (Oct. 1984) 119. Proposes **quāre hoc est grātum nōbīs, quod cārius aurō est, / quod tē restituis. . . .** (3–4), with **quod** meaning *which* in line 3 and *the fact that* in line 4.

R. O. A. M. Lyne. "The Text of Catullus CVII." *Hermes* 113 (1985) 498–500. Proposes the reconstruction that we print for lines 7–8.

Helena Dettmer. "Catullus 107.7–8." *Classical World* 80 (1987) 371–373. See above.

CATULLUS 109

1   You propose a pleasant thing, my life: that this love
2   of ours will be everlasting to the end between us.

or

1   You propose, my life, that this our love between us
2   will be pleasant and everlasting.

or

1   You propose, my life, a pleasant love—this one of ours
2   between us—[and] that it will last forever.

3   Great gods, cause her to be able to promise truly
4   and to say this sincerely and from [her] heart,

5   so that it may be permitted to us to extend through all our life
6   this eternal compact of sacred friendship.

This poem may be compared with poems 70 and 72 in the skepticism it expresses towards Lesbia's protestations of love (assuming that **mea vīta**, 1, here refers to Lesbia). In the first couplet of all three epigrams the poet quotes a statement made by Lesbia and then reacts against it. In poem 109 Catullus prays to the gods, implying that superhuman intervention is needed to bring it about that Lesbia may be able to promise truly, sincerely, and from the heart. Lesbia uses the conventional word **amōrem** to describe their love. The adjective **perpetuum** is also unexceptional and the kind of thing one would expect a lover to say. Catullus, however, conceptualizes his view in the last line of the poem in language drawn from the world of political alliances (**amīcitia**) and describes a solemn commitment based on mutually binding obligations of an eternal nature. Lesbia professes everlasting mutual love (**amōrem / hunc nostrum inter nōs perpetuum usque fore**, 1–2), and Catullus dreams of an eternal bond (**aeternum . . . foedus**, 6). Catullus' ideal goes beyond Lesbia's profession of everlasting mutual love by introducing the language of political alliances (see Ross, Select Bibliography). For the ideal that combines **amor** and **amīcitia**, compare poem 96.

Explorations

1.   Compare Thomson's version of the first couplet printed in the text above with the traditional version printed below the notes on the opposite page. Do you find any problems with the traditional version? Is Thomson's version an improvement?

Quinn comments as follows on the traditional version: "The words *iucundum . . . amorem hunc nostrum inter nos perpetuumque fore* are usually regarded as accusative + infinitive dependent on *proponis*. But *iucundum*, though a word C. is fond of, sounds odd on Lesbia's lips in this context, and rather an inadequate partner for *perpetuum*. Perhaps we should take *iucundum . . . amorem* as the direct object of *proponis* (*iucundum* then expressing C.'s—ironic—appraisal, not hers) and *hunc nostrum inter nos* as an appositional expansion . . . and *perpetuumque fore* as a further expansion ('and it will last for ever, you say')" (448). W. A. Camps (see Select Bibliography) commented: "The opening word *iucundum* does not seem to be in place here. The prospect desired is not that the *amor* should be *iucundus*, which it obviously is already, but that it should be permanent" (442). Camps proposed reading **continuum** in place of **iūcundum**. Thomson rejects Camps' emendation on paleographical grounds. The reading Thomson offers eliminates the need to take the words **amōrem / hunc nostrum inter nōs** together as a single phrase (which is an awkward pleonasm), and it puts the emphasis of the first couplet squarely where it should be—on the life-long continuance of the love between Catullus and Lesbia (assuming that the latter is intended here in the vocative **mea vīta**, 1).

2.   What is the relationship between the first couplet and the remainder of the poem? Compare the structures of Catullus 70 and 72.

In the first couplet Catullus indirectly quotes a statement made by Lesbia, just as he does in the first couplets of poems 70 and 72. (Note that in poem 70 Catullus refers to the *woman* [= Lesbia?] in the third person, while in 72 he addresses Lesbia by name.) In the second and third couplets of poem 109, Catullus responds to Lesbia's statement with a prayer to the gods, not with an address to Lesbia. In poem 70 he responds with a proverbial statement; in poem 72 he continues with a direct address to Lesbia in the second person and even enters into a kind of dialogue with her in lines 7–8. In poem 109, Catullus does not reply directly to Lesbia but formulates his prayer to the gods with references to Lesbia in the third person (*cause her to be able to promise truly / and to say this sincerely*, 3–4); he does not say *Great gods, bring it about that you, my life, may be able to promise truly. . . .* That is, he does not develop this poem into a genuine dialogue but uses it as an opportunity to express his own anxiety and his own deepest wishes.

3.   In poem 70 Catullus is skeptical of Lesbia's protestations, and in poem 72 he has caught her lying. Through his prayer to the gods in lines 3–4 of poem 109, what attitude does Catullus reveal toward Lesbia's proposal in lines 1–2?

The ascending triad of adverbs (**vērē** 3, **sincērē**, 4) and the adverbial phrase **ex animō** (4) in his prayer to the gods reveals his anxiety and his skepticism as to Lesbia's truthfulness and sincerity. He does not simply pray or wish that Lesbia may be promising *truly*, *sincerely*, and *from the heart*, but he calls upon the *great gods* to bring it about that she be capable of doing so. In praying to the gods, Catullus implies that superhuman intervention is needed to bring it about that Lesbia may be able to promise *truly*, *sincerely*, and *from the heart*.

With the prayer to the gods here, compare poem 76.17–26.

4.   What result does Catullus envision in the third couplet as coming from the gods' enabling Lesbia to promise *truly*, *sincerely*, and *from the heart*?

The result would be that Catullus and Lesbia would be permitted to carry out the terms of an eternal compact of sacred friendship throughout their whole lives. It is implied here that Catullus is ready to carry out his role in the compact; it is Lesbia's readiness that is in question, and that depends on whether the gods can bring it about that she may be able to keep her promises.

5.   The two major themes of this poem are (1) life-long continuance of love/friendship and (2) sincerity. How are the themes allocated to couplets?

The theme of life-long continuance of love/friendship appears in the first and the third couplets, while the theme of sincerity occurs in the middle couplet. The poem thus has a balanced thematic structure with the theme of sincerity highlighted in the center and with the theme of life-long continuance of love/friendship occupying the initial couplet that sets the main theme of the whole piece and the final couplet that gives that theme its most distinctive expression in all of Catullus' poetry in the words **aeternum hoc sānctae foedus amīcitiae**.

6.   Consider the final line of the poem. Locate its interlocked word order. Are there examples of transferred epithets here? If so, what are their implications? What kind of relationship is described in these words?

The two phrases, **aeternum hoc . . . foedus** and **sānctae . . . amīcitiae** are interlocked. Note that the phrase **hoc . . . foedus** will mean *the pact you are proposing*, as Quinn, 449, suggests; but note also that it is Catullus who introduces the term **foedus**, while Lesbia had said simply that their love would be *everlasting to the end between us*, **inter nōs perpetuum usque fore**, 2.

It could be argued that both **aeternum** and **sānctae** are examples of transferred epithets. It is surely the **amīcitia** that Catullus wishes to be eternal, and it is surely the **foedus** that should be sanctified by the gods. The adjective **sānctae** is thus positioned neatly next to **foedus**, and the two words **aeternum** and **amīcitiae** neatly occupy first and last position in the line, thus framing the words in between. The upshot of this is that all of these words relate to one another and that Catullus is envisioning an eternal and sanctified compact of eternal and sanctified friendship.

As Ross (see Select Bibliography) has demonstrated so clearly, the concept of the relationship that is described in the last line of this poem in language reminiscent of other Catullan elegiacs is one that would have been immediately recognizable to any Roman reader. As Ross explains:

Catullus . . . has portrayed his affair with Lesbia in the terminology of a political alliance: it is to be an *amicitia*, a *foedus*, based on *fides*, the concrete expressions of which are the mutual *benevolentia* and *benefacta* of the two parties, resulting in *gratia* arising from the performance of *officia*; the relationship is to be protected by divinity, as it must be religiously observed with *pietas* by both parties. (90)

This may all sound rather abstract and formulaic, but it should be remembered that the social, political, and religious life of the Romans was guided and ruled by formulaic language handed down from their ancestors. Catullus was no exception. The concept, however, of **amīcitia**, conceived of as "the central, controlling concept of political connections" (Ross, 84) and here transferred to the relationship between Catullus and Lesbia, does not express the whole of Catullus' ideal conception of his relationship with Lesbia. There was **amor**, too; see below.

7. What is the relationship between **amōrem** (end of line 1) and **amīcitiae** (end of line 6)? With the concepts and words here, compare Catullus 72.3–4 and Catullus 96.3–4.

The two words are prominently positioned in the poem, and both clearly refer to what it is that joins Catullus and Lesbia together (note the words **nostrum**, 2, **inter nōs**, 2, and **foedus**, 6). In line 6 the term **amīcitia** is substituted for or takes the place of the term **amor** used in line 1. The two terms could possibly even be interchanged in this poem, but they are not synonyms. Comparison with poems 72.3–4 and 96.3–4 will help clarify why Catullus needs to use both terms in this poem. Here are lines 3–4 of poem 72: **Dīlēxī tum tē nōn tantum ut vulgus amīcam / sed pater ut gnātōs dīligit et generōs**. Catullus here defines his own unique feelings, his own unique experience of his relationship with Lesbia, by describing it as a combination (**nōn tantum . . . / sed. . . .**, *not only . . . but [also]. . . .*) of forthright sexuality (**ut vulgus amīcam**, *as anyone from the common herd [loves] a friend/prostitute*) and the familial affection and loyalty that bind fathers to sons and even to sons-in-law (**pater ut gnātōs dīligit et generōs**). The former would go under the heading of **amor**, the latter under the heading of **amīcitia**; both are part of Catullus' relationship to Lesbia. Then there are lines 3–4 of poem 96: **quō dēsīderiō veterēs renovāmus amōrēs / atque ōlim missās flēmus amīcitiās**. Here Calvus' grief (the **dolor** of line 2) for Quintilia, his lost wife or mistress, is defined as **dēsīderium**, *longing/desire*, by which he renews his past love (his **amor**) for the woman and because of which he weeps over his past friendship (his **amīcitia**) with the departed. Calvus' **dolor** thus reveals both his love and his friendship with Quintilia, and both of these terms are reunited in the word *love* when in the last line of the poem Quintilia is said to rejoice in Calvus' love (**gaudet amōre tuō**). In this poem Catullus sees the relationship between Calvus and Quintilia as involving both **amor** and **amīcitia**, just as he separated his own emotional attachment to Lesbia under two headings in poem 72. So here, in poem 109, Catullus' devoutly-sought relationship with Lesbia involves both **amor** (1) and **amīcitia** (6). While in poem 72 he united the two terms under the heading of the verb **dīligere** and while in poem 96 he united them under the term **amor**, here he ends the poem with the word **amīcitia**, but he clearly has the **amor** of Lesbia's proposition in mind as well. Love in Catullus' understanding is not merely a passion but a moral commitment under binding obligations of an eternal nature, **aeternum . . . foedus** (109.6). In addition, love is not merely a sexual relationship at a physical level but must involve genuinely reciprocal affection and goodwill such as the gods themselves sanction, **sānctae . . . amīcitiae** (109.6). This is his dream: **tōtā perdūcere vītā / aeternum hoc sānctae foedus amīcitiae**, *to extend through all our life / this eternal compact of sacred friendship* (109.5–6). A pity that it appears never to have been realized!

Postscript

Many facets of the political alliance that the Romans called **amīcitia** are clearly set forth in a letter written by Cicero to Crassus in 54 B.C (*Epistulae ad familiares* 5.8). It is too long to reproduce here, but it is an excellent document to set side by side with Catullus 109 and to analyze in depth, comparing Cicero's relationship with Crassus to Catullus' relationship with Lesbia.

Select Bibliography

David O. Ross, Jr. "Lesbia and the Vocabulary of Political Alliance." *Style & Tradition in Catullus.*
Cambridge MA: Harvard University Press, 1969, 80–95.

> Catullus, in what must be an early poem to Lesbia, answers her proposition of a pleasant little affair (*iucundum . . . amorem*, 109.1) with an emphatic expression of something very different, *aeternum hoc sanctae foedus amicitiae* (the last line, 6). That the metaphor is definitely that of a political alliance is made clear repeatedly. (88–89)

M. Vinson. "Party Politics and the Language of Love in the Lesbia Poems of Catullus." *Studies in Latin Literature and Roman History* VI (Collection Latomus 217) 1992, 163–80. See pages 163–64 for discussion of alternatives to Ross's views quoted above.

BIBLIOGRAPHY

All items are listed under their headings in chronological, not alphabetical, order. Articles cited in the Select Bibliographies are usually not included in this bibliography.

Translations:

Frank O. Copley. *Catullus: The Complete Poetry*. Ann Arbor: University of Michigan Press, 1957.
Roy Arthur Swanson. *Odi et Amo*. New York: Liberals Arts Press, 1959.
Peter Whigham. *The Poems of Catullus*. Harmondsworth ENG: Penguin Books, 1966.
Charles H. Sisson. *The Poems of Catullus*. New York: Viking, 1969.
Celia and Louis Zukofsky. *Catullus (Gai Valeri Catulli Veronensis Liber)*. London: Cape Golliard Press, 1969. [accompanying Latin text]
Charles Martin. *The Poems of Catullus*. Omaha: University of Nebraska Press, 1979.
G. P. Goold. *Catullus*. London: Duckworth, 1989 (2nd ed.). [accompanying Latin text]

See also:

Eleanor Shipley Duckett. *Catullus in English Poetry*. Smith College Classical Studies, Number 6, 1926. Northampton, MASS: Departments of Greek and Latin. This is the source of the following translations/adaptations by English poets contained in the student's book: Andrew Lang, p. 22; Thomas Campion, p. 46; Ben Jonson, p. 46; Robert Herrick, p. 47; Richard Crashaw, p. 47; Ben Jonson, p. 58; John Oldham, p. 59; Thomas Campion, p. 64; Christopher Smart, p. 142; William Walsh, p. 192; and Walter Savage Landor, p. 207.

Commentaries:

Elmer T. Merrill. *Catullus*. Boston: Ginn, 1893.
C. J. Fordyce. *Catullus: A Commentary*. Oxford ENG: Clarendon Press, 1961.
Kenneth Quinn. *Catullus: The Poems*. London ENG: Macmillan, 1973 (2nd ed.).
Phyllis Young Forsyth. *The Poems of Catullus: A Teaching Text*. Lanham: University Press of America, 1986.
Daniel H. Garrison. *The Student's Catullus*. Norman: University of Oklahoma Press, 1989.
D. F. S. Thomson. *Catullus*. Toronto: University of Toronto Press, 1997.

Bibliographies:

H. J. Leon. "A Quarter Century of Catullan Scholarship (1934–1959)." *Classical World* 53 (1960) 104–13; 141–48; 173–80; 281–83.
D. F. S. Thomson. "Recent Scholarship on Catullus (1960–1969)." *Classical World* 65 (1971) 116–26.
J. Granarolo. "Catulle 1948–1973." *Lustrum* 17 (1973–74) 27–70.
Kenneth Quinn. "Trends in Catullan Criticism." *Aufstieg und Niedergang der Römischen Welt* 1.3 (1973) 369–89.
H. Harrauer. *A Bibliography to Catullus*. Hildesheim GERMANY: Gerstenberg, 1979.
J. P. Holoka. *Gaius Valerius Catullus: A Systematic Bibliography*. New York: Garland, 1985.

General Books:

Roger A. Hornsby. *Reading Latin Poetry*. Norman: University of Oklahoma Press, 1967.
E. J. Kenney and W. V. Clausen, eds. *The Cambridge History of Classical Literature: II: Latin Literature*. Cambridge ENG and New York: Cambridge University Press, 1982. [W. V. Clausen, "The New Directions in Poetry," 178–206]

T. James Luce, ed. *Ancient Writers: Greece and Rome: Volume II: Lucretius to Ammianus Marcellinus.* New York: Charles Scribner's Sons, 1982. [James E. G. Zetzel, "Catullus," 643–67]

H. H. Scullard. *From the Gracchi to Nero: A History of Rome 133 BC to AD 68.* London ENG and New York: Rutledge, 1982 (5th ed.).

Gian Biagio Conte. *Latin Literature: A History*, trans. by J. B. Solodow. Baltimore: The Johns Hopkins University Press, 1994.

Books on Catullus:

E. A. Havelock. *The Lyric Genius of Catullus.* Oxford ENG: Blackwell, 1939.

A. L. Wheeler. *Catullus and the Traditions of Ancient Poetry.* Berkeley: University of California Press, 1964.

C. L. Neudling. *A Prosopography to Catullus.* "Iowa Studies in Classical Philology," 12. Oxford ENG: Oxford University Press, 1955.

Kenneth Quinn. *The Catullan Revolution.* Cambridge ENG: W. Heffer and Sons, Ltd., 1969.

David O. Ross. *Style and Tradition in Catullus.* Cambridge: Harvard University Press, 1969.

T. P. Wiseman. *Catullan Questions.* Leicester: Leicester ENG University Press, 1969.

Kenneth Quinn (ed.). *Approaches to Catullus.* New York: Barnes and Noble, 1972.

Kenneth Quinn. *Catullus: An Interpretation.* New York: Barnes and Noble, 1973.

T. P. Wiseman. *Cinna the Poet and Other Roman Essays.* Leicester ENG: Leicester University Press, 1974.

R. O. A. M. Lyne. *The Latin Love Poets: From Catullus to Horace.* Oxford ENG: Clarendon Press, 1980.

Eve Adler. *Catullan Self-Revelation.* New York: Arno Press, 1981.

Marilyn B. Skinner. *Catullus' Passer: The Arrangement of the Book of Polymetric Poems.* New York: Arno, 1981.

Richard Jenkyns. *Three Classical Poets: Sappho, Catullus, and Juvenal.* London: Duckworth, 1982.

Stuart P. Small. *Catullus: A Reader's Guide to the Poems.* Lanham: University Press of America, 1983.

T. P. Wiseman. *Catullus and His World: A Reappraisal.* Cambridge ENG: Cambridge University Press, 1985.

John Ferguson. *Catullus.* Oxford ENG: Clarendon Press, 1988.

Charles Martin. *Catullus.* New Haven: Yale University Press, 1992.

Julia Gaisser. *Catullus and His Renaissance Readers.* Oxford: Clarendon Press, 1993.

General Articles on Catullus:

Frank O. Copley. "Emotional Conflict and Its Significance in the Lesbia-poems of Catullus." *American Journal of Philology* 70 (1949) 22–40.

Luigi Alfonsi. "Lesbia." *American Journal of Philology* 71 (1950) 59–66.

J. P. Elder. "Notes on Some Conscious and Unconscious Elements in Catullus' Poetry." *Harvard Studies in Classical Philology* 60 (1951) 101–36.

R. Syme. "Piso and Veranius in Catullus." *Classica et Mediaevalia* 17 (1956) 129–34.

M. Owen Lee. "Illustrative Elisions in Catullus." *Transactions of the American Philological Association* 93 (1962) 144–53.

Wendell Clausen. "Callimachus and Latin Poetry." *Greek, Roman and Byzantine Studies* 5 (1964) 181–96.

Steele Commager. "Notes on Some Poems of Catullus." *Harvard Studies in Classical Philology* 70 (1965) 83–110.

W. M. A. Grimaldi. "The Lesbia Love Lyrics." *Classical Philology* 60 (1965) 87–95.

Erich S. Gruen. "Cicero and Licinius Calvus." *Harvard Studies in Classical Philology* 71 (1966) 215–33.

Charles Segal. "The Order of Catullus, Poems 2–11." *Latomus* 27 (1968) 305–21.

H. D. Rankin. "Clodia II." *L'Antiquité Classique* 38 (1969) 501–06.

O. Skutsch. "Metrical Variation and Some Textual Problems in Catullus." *Bulletin of the Institute of Classical Studies of the University of London* 16 (1969) 38–43.

Wendell Clausen. "Catullus and Callimachus." *Harvard Studies in Classical Philology* 74 (1970) 85–94.

N. B. Crowther. "οἱ νεώτεροι," *poetae novi*, and *cantores Euphorionis*." *Classical Quarterly* 20 (1970) 322–27.

N. B. Crowther. "Catullus and the Traditions of Latin Poetry." *Classical Philology* 66 (1971) 246–49.

H. D. Rankin. "The Progress of Pessimism in Catullus, Poems 2–11." *Latomus* 32 (1972) 744–51.

R. Seager. "*Venustus, Lepidus, Bellus, Salsus*. Notes on the Language of Catullus." *Latomus* 33 (1974) 891–94.

H. D. Rankin. "Catullus and the Privacy of Love." *Wiener Studien* 9 (1975) 67–74.

Carl Rubino. "The Erotic World of Catullus." *Classical World* 68 (1975) 289–97.

T. P. Wiseman. "Clodia, Some Imaginary Lives." *Arion* 2 (1975) 96–115.

Wendell Clausen. "Catulli Veronensis Liber." *Classical Philology* 71 (1976) 37–43.

N. B. Crowther. "Parthenius and Roman Poetry." *Mnemosyne* 29 (1976) 65–71.

Phyllis Y. Forsyth. "Catullus: The Mythic Persona." *Latomus* 35 (1976) 555–66.

H. D. Rankin. "Catullus and the Beauty of Lesbia." *Latomus* 35 (1976) 3–11.

S. F. Wiltshire. "Catullus Venustus." *Classical World* 70 (1977) 319–26.

R. O. A. M. Lyne. "The Neoteric Poets." *Classical Quarterly* 28 (1978) 167–87.

R. G. M. Nisbet. "Notes on the Text of Catullus." *Proceedings of the Cambridge Philological Society* 24 (1978) 91–115.

A. J. Woodman. "Catullus 11 and 51." *Liverpool Classical Monthly* 3 (1978) 77–79.

M. B. Skinner. "Parasites and Strange Bedfellows. A Study in Catullus' Political Imagery." *Ramus* 8 (1980) 137–52.

M. B. Skinner. "Pretty Lesbius." *TAPA* 112 (1982) 197–208.

Brian Arkins. "Caelius and Rufus in Catullus." *Philologus* 127 (1983) 306–11.

Ernest A. Fredricksmeyer. "The Beginning and the End of Catullus' *Longus Amor*." *Symbolae Osloenses* 58 (1983) 63–88.

Michael C. J. Putnam. "The Future of Catullus." *Transactions of the American Philological Association* 113 (1983) 243–62.

M. B. Skinner. "Clodia Metelli." *Transactions of the American Philological Association* 113 (1983) 273–82.

T. K. Hubbard. "The Catullan Libellus." *Philologus* 127 (1983) 218–37.

John F. Finamore. "Catullus 50 and 51: Friendship, Love, and *Otium*." *Classical World* (78 (1984) 11–19.

Wendell Clausen. "Cicero and the New Poetry." *Harvard Studies in Classical Philology* 90 (1986) 159–70.

J. D. Minyard. "The Source of the *Catulli Veronensis Liber*." *Classical World* 81 (1988) 343–53.

Marilyn B. Skinner. "Aesthetic Patterning in Catullus: Textual Structures, Systems of Imagery and Book Arrangements: Introduction." *Classical World* 81 (1988) 337–40. This is an introduction to six articles by Minyard, Richlin, Traill, Dettmer, King, and Hallett.

J. B. Solodow. "Forms of Literary Criticism in Catullus: Polymetric vs. Epigram." *Classical Philology* 84 (1989) 314–19.

T. Fear. "Catullus: A Poet in Transition." *Liverpool Classical Monthly* 15.2 (Feb. 1990) 18–24.

Martha Vinson. "Party Politics and the Language of Love in the Lesbia Poems of Catullus." *Studies in Latin Literature and Roman History* VI, 163–80.

G. Edward Gaffney. "*Severitati Respondere*: Character Drawing in *Pro Caelio* and Catullus' *Carmina*." *Classical Journal* 90 (1995) 4233–31.

Ellen Greene. "The Catullan Ego: Fragmentation and the Erotic Self." *American Journal of Philology* 116 (1995) 77–93.

W. Jeffrey Tatum. "Friendship, Politics, and Literature in Catullus: Poems 1, 65 and 66, 116." *Classical Quarterly* 47 (1997) 482–500.

TEXT ENLARGEMENTS

CATULLUS 1

1 Cui dōnō lepidum novum libellum
2 āridā modo pūmice expolītum?
3 Cornēlī, tibi: namque tū solēbās
4 meās esse aliquid putāre nūgās
5 iam tum, cum ausus es ūnus Ītalōrum
6 omne aevum tribus explicāre cartīs
7 doctīs, Iuppiter, et labōriōsīs.
8 Quārē habē tibi quidquid hoc libellī
9 quālecumque; quod, <ō> patrōna virgō,
10 plūs ūnō maneat perenne saeclō.

CATULLUS 2

1 Passer, dēliciae meae puellae,
2 quīcum lūdere, quem in sinū tenēre,
3 cui prīmum digitum dare appetentī
4 et ācrīs solet incitāre morsūs,
5 cum dēsīderiō meō nitentī
6 cārum nescio quid lubet iocārī,
7 et sōlāciolum suī dolōris,
8 crēdō, ut tum gravis acquiēscat ārdor;
9 tēcum lūdere sīcut ipsa possem
10 et trīstīs animī levāre cūrās!

CATULLUS 2b

1 Tam grātum est mihi quam ferunt puellae
2 pernīcī aureolum fuisse mālum,
3 quod zōnam soluit diū ligātam.

CATULLUS 3

1 Lūgēte, ō Venerēs Cupīdinēsque
2 et quantum est hominum venustiōrum:
3 passer mortuus est meae puellae,
4 passer, dēliciae meae puellae,
5 quem plūs illa oculīs suīs amābat.
6 Nam mellītus erat suamque nōrat
7 ipsam tam bene quam puella mātrem,
8 nec sēsē ā gremiō illius movēbat,
9 sed circumsiliēns modo hūc modo illūc
10 ad sōlam dominam usque pīpiābat;
11 quī nunc it per iter tenebricōsum
12 illūc, unde negant redīre quemquam.
13 At vōbīs male sit, malae tenebrae
14 Orcī, quae omnia bella dēvorātis:
15 tam bellum mihi passerem abstulistis.
16 Ō factum male! Ō miselle passer!
17 Tuā nunc operā meae puellae
18 flendō turgidulī rubent ocellī.

CATULLUS 4

1   Phasēlus ille, quem vidētis, hospitēs,
2   ait fuisse nāvium celerrimus,
3   neque ūllius natantis impetum trabis
4   nequīsse praeterīre, sīve palmulīs
5   opus foret volāre sīve linteō.
6   Et hoc negat mināsis Hadriāticī
7   negāre lītus īnsulāsve Cȳcladās
8   Rhodumque nōbilem horridamque Thrāciam
9   Propontida trucemve Ponticum sinum,
10 ubi iste post phasēlus anteā fuit
11 comāta silva; nam Cytōriō in iugō
12 loquente saepe sībilum ēdidit comā.
13 Amastri Pontica et Cytōre buxifer,
14 tibi haec fuisse et esse cognitissima
15 ait phasēlus: ultimā ex orīgine
16 tuō stetisse dīcit in cacūmine,
17 tuō imbuisse palmulās in aequore,
18 et inde tot per impotentia freta
19 erum tulisse, laeva sīve dextera
20 vocāret aura, sīve utrumque Iuppiter
21 simul secundus incidisset in pedem;
22 neque ūlla vōta lītorālibus deīs
23 sibi esse facta, cum venīret ā marī
24 novissimō hunc ad usque limpidum lacum.
25 Sed haec prius fuēre: nunc recondita
26 senet quiēte sēque dēdicat tibi,
27 gemelle Castor et gemelle Castoris.

CATULLUS 5

1   Vīvāmus, mea Lesbia, atque amēmus,
2   rūmōrēsque senum sevēriōrum
3   omnēs ūnius aestimēmus assis!
4   Sōlēs occidere et redīre possunt;
5   nōbīs cum semel occidit brevis lūx,
6   nox est perpetua ūna dormienda.
7   Dā mī bāsia mīlle, deinde centum,
8   dein mīlle altera, dein secunda centum,
9   deinde usque altera mīlle, deinde centum;
10   dein, cum mīlia multa fēcerīmus,
11   conturbābimus illa, nē sciāmus,
12   aut nē quis malus invidēre possit,
13   cum tantum sciat esse bāsiōrum.

CATULLUS 6

1   Flāvī, dēliciās tuās Catullō,
2   nī sint illepidae atque inēlegantēs,
3   vellēs dīcere nec tacēre possēs.
4   Vērum nescio quid febrīculōsī
5   scortī dīligis: hoc pudet fatērī.
6   Nam tē nōn viduās iacēre noctēs
7   nēquīquam tacitum cubīle clāmat
8   sertīs ac Syriō fragrāns olīvō,
9   pulvīnusque peraequē et hīc et ille
10   attrītus, tremulīque quassa lectī
11   argūtātiō inambulātiōque.
12   Nam nīl stupra valet, nihil, tacēre.
13   Cūr? Nōn tam latera ecfutūta pandās,
14   nī tū quid faciās ineptiārum.
15   Quārē, quidquid habēs bonī malīque,
16   dīc nōbīs. Volo tē ac tuōs amōrēs
17   ad caelum lepidō vocāre versū.

CATULLUS 7

1   Quaeris quot mihi bāsiātiōnēs
2   tuae, Lesbia, sint satis superque.
3   Quam magnus numerus Libyssae harēnae
4   lāsarpīciferīs iacet Cyrēnīs
5   ōrāclum Iovis inter aestuōsī
6   et Battī veteris sacrum sepulcrum,
7   aut quam sīdera multa, cum tacet nox,
8   fūrtīvōs hominum vident amōrēs;
9   tam tē bāsia multa bāsiāre
10 vēsānō satis et super Catullō est,
11 quae nec pernumerāre cūriōsī
12 possint nec mala fascināre lingua.

CATULLUS 8

1   Miser Catulle, dēsinās ineptīre,
2   et quod vidēs perīsse perditum dūcās.
3   Fulsēre quondam candidī tibī sōlēs,
4   cum ventitābās quō puella dūcēbat
5   amāta nōbīs quantum amābitur nūlla.
6   Ibi illa multa cum iocōsa fīēbant,
7   quae tū volēbās nec puella nōlēbat,
8   fulsēre vērē candidī tibī sōlēs.
9   Nunc iam illa nōn volt; tū quoque, inpotē<ns, nōlī>,
10 nec quae fugit sectāre, nec miser vīve,
11 sed obstinātā mente perfer, obdūrā.
12 Valē, puella. Iam Catullus obdūrat,
13 nec tē requīret nec rogābit invītam.
14 At tū dolēbis, cum rogāberis nūlla.
15 Scelesta, vae tē! Quae tibī manet vīta?
16 Quis nunc tē adībit? Cui vidēberis bella?
17 Quem nunc amābis? Cuius esse dīcēris?
18 Quem bāsiābis? Cui labella mordēbis?
19 At tū, Catulle, dēstinātus obdūrā.

CATULLUS 9

1 Vērānī, omnibus ē meīs amīcīs

2 antistāns mihi mīlibus trecentīs,

3 vēnistīne domum ad tuōs penātēs

4 frātrēsque ūnanimōs anumque mātrem?

5 Vēnistī. Ō mihi nūntiī beātī!

6 Vīsam tē incolumem audiamque Hibērum

7 nārrantem loca, facta, nātiōnēs,

8 ut mōs est tuus, applicānsque collum

9 iūcundum ōs oculōsque suāviābor.

10 Ō quantum est hominum beātiōrum,

11 quid mē laetius est beātiusve?

CATULLUS 10

1   Vārus mē meus ad suōs amōrēs
2   vīsum dūxerat ē forō ōtiōsum,
3   scortillum, ut mihi tum repente vīsum est,
4   nōn sānē illepidum neque invenustum.
5   Hūc ut vēnimus, incidēre nōbīs
6   sermōnēs variī: in quibus, quid esset
7   iam Bīthȳnia; quō modō sē habēret;
8   et quōnam mihi prōfuisset aere.
9   Respondī, id quod erat, nihil neque ipsīs
10 nec praetōribus esse nec cohortī,
11 cūr quisquam caput ūnctius referret,
12 praesertim quibus esset irrumātor
13 praetor, nec faceret pilī cohortem.
14 "At certē tamen," inquiunt, "quod illīc
15 nātum dīcitur esse, comparāstī
16 ad lectīcam hominēs." Ego, ut puellae
17 ūnum mē facerem beātiōrem,
18 "Nōn," inquam, "mihi tam fuit malignē,
19 ut, prōvincia quod mala incidisset,
20 nōn possem octō hominēs parāre rēctōs."
21 At mī nūllus erat nec hīc neque illīc,
22 frāctum quī veteris pedem grabātī
23 in collō sibi collocāre posset.
24 Hīc illa, ut decuit cinaediōrem,
25 "Quaesō," inquit, "mihi, mī Catulle, paulum
26 istōs commoda; nam volō ad Serāpim
27 dēferrī." "Mane," inquiī puellae,
28 "istud quod modo dīxeram mē habēre,
29 fūgit mē ratiō: meus sodālis—
30 Cinna est Gāius—is sibī parāvit.
31 Vērum, utrum illius an meī, quid ad mē?
32 Ūtor tam bene quam mihī parārim.
33 Sed tū īnsulsa male et molesta vīvis,
34 per quam nōn licet esse neglegentem."

CATULLUS 11

1   Fūrī et Aurēlī, comitēs Catullī,
2   sīve in extrēmōs penetrābit Indōs,
3   lītus ut longē resonante Eōā
4   tunditur undā,

5   sīve in Hyrcānōs Arabasve mollēs,
6   seu Sagās sagittiferōsve Parthōs,
7   sīve quae septemgeminus colōrat
8   aequora Nīlus,

9   sīve trāns altās gradiētur Alpēs,
10 Caesaris vīsēns monimenta magnī,
11 Gallicum Rhēnum horribile aequor ulti-
12   mōsque Britannōs,

13 omnia haec, quaecumque feret voluntās
14 caelitum, temptāre simul parātī,
15 pauca nūntiāte meae puellae
16   nōn bona dicta.

17 Cum suīs vīvat valeatque moechīs,
18 quōs simul complexa tenet trecentōs,
19 nūllum amāns vērē, sed identidem omnium
20   īlia rumpēns;

21 nec meum respectet, ut ante, amōrem,
22 quī illius culpā cecidit velut prātī
23 ultimī flōs, praetereunte postquam
24   tāctus arātrō est.

CATULLUS 12

1   Marrūcīne Asinī, manū sinistrā
2   nōn bellē ūteris: in iocō atque vīnō
3   tollis lintea neglegentiōrum.
4   Hoc salsum esse putās? Fugit tē, inepte;
5   quamvīs sordida rēs et invenusta est.
6   Nōn crēdis mihi? Crēde Polliōnī
7   frātrī, quī tua fūrta vel talentō
8   mūtārī velit: est enim lepōrum
9   differtus puer ac facētiārum.
10 Quārē aut hendecasyllabōs trecentōs
11 exspectā, aut mihi linteum remitte,
12 quod mē nōn movet aestimātiōne,
13 vērum est mnēmosynum meī sodālis.
14 Nam sūdāria Saetaba ex Hibērīs
15 mīsērunt mihi mūnerī Fabullus
16 et Vērānius; haec amem necesse est
17 ut Vērāniolum meum et Fabullum.

CATULLUS 13

1   Cēnābis bene, mī Fabulle, apud mē
2   paucīs, sī tibi dī favent, diēbus,
3   sī tēcum attuleris bonam atque magnam
4   cēnam, nōn sine candidā puellā
5   et vīnō et sale et omnibus cachinnīs.
6   Haec sī, inquam, attuleris, venuste noster,
7   cēnābis bene—nam tuī Catullī
8   plēnus sacculus est arāneārum.
9   Sed contrā accipiēs merōs amōrēs
10 seu quid suāvius ēlegantiusve est:
11 nam unguentum dabo, quod meae puellae
12 dōnārunt Venerēs Cupīdinēsque,
13 quod tū cum olfaciēs, deōs rogābis
14 tōtum ut tē faciant, Fabulle, nāsum.

CATULLUS 22

1 Suffēnus iste, Vāre, quem probē nōstī,
2 homō est venustus et dicāx et urbānus,
3 īdemque longē plūrimōs facit versūs.
4 Putō esse ego illī mīlia aut decem aut plūra
5 perscrīpta, nec sīc ut fit in palimpsestō
6 relāta: cartae rēgiae, novī librī,
7 novī umbilīcī, lōra rubra membrānae,
8 dērēcta plumbō et pūmice omnia aequāta.
9 Haec cum legās tū, bellus ille et urbānus
10 Suffēnus ūnus caprimulgus aut fōssor
11 rūrsus vidētur: tantum abhorret ac mūtat.
12 Hoc quid putēmus esse? Quī modo scurra
13 aut sī quid hāc rē scītius vidēbātur,
14 īdem īnficētō est īnficētior rūre,
15 simul poēmata attigit, neque īdem umquam
16 aequē est beātus ac poēma cum scrībit:
17 tam gaudet in sē tamque sē ipse mīrātur.
18 Nīmīrum idem omnēs fallimur, neque est quisquam
19 quem nōn in aliquā rē vidēre Suffēnum
20 possīs. Suus cuique attribūtus est error;
21 sed nōn vidēmus manticae quod in tergō est.

CATULLUS 27

1 Minister vetulī puer Falernī,
2 inger mī calicēs amāriōrēs,
3 ut lēx Postumiae iubet magistrae
4 ēbriōsō acinō ēbriōsiōris.
5 At vōs quō lubet hinc abīte, lymphae,
6 vīnī perniciēs, et ad sevērōs
7 migrāte. Hīc merus est Thyōniānus.

CATULLUS 31

1 Paene īnsulārum, Sirmiō, īnsulārumque
2 ocelle, quāscumque in liquentibus stagnīs
3 marīque vastō fert uterque Neptūnus,
4 quam tē libenter quamque laetus invīsō,
5 vix mī ipse crēdēns Thȳniam atque Bīthȳnōs
6 līquisse campōs et vidēre tē in tūtō.
7 Ō quid solūtīs est beātius cūrīs,
8 cum mēns onus repōnit, ac peregrīnō
9 labōre fessī vēnimus larem ad nostrum,
10 dēsīderātōque acquiēscimus lectō?
11 Hoc est quod ūnum est prō labōribus tantīs.
12 Salvē, ō venusta Sirmiō, atque erō gaudē
13 gaudente, vōsque, ō Lȳdiae lacūs undae,
14 rīdēte quidquid est domī cachinnōrum.

CATULLUS 34

1   Diānae sumus in fidē
2   puellae et puerī integrī:
3   <Diānam puerī integrī>
4   puellaeque canāmus.

5   Ō Lātōnia, maximī
6   magna prōgeniēs Iovis,
7   quam māter prope Dēliam
8   dēposīvit olīvam,

9   montium domina ut forēs
10   silvārumque virentium
11   saltuumque reconditōrum
12   amniumque sonantum:

13   tū Lūcīna dolentibus
14   Iūnō dicta puerperīs,
15   tū potēns Trivia et nothō es
16   dicta lūmine Lūna;

17   tū cursū, dea, mēnstruō
18   mētiēns iter annuum,
19   rūstica agricolae bonīs
20   tēcta frūgibus explēs.

21   Sīs quōcumque tibi placet
22   sāncta nōmine, Rōmulīque,
23   antīquē ut solita es, bonā
24   sōspitēs ope gentem.

CATULLUS 35

1   Poētae tenerō, meō sodālī,
2   velim Caeciliō, papȳre, dīcās
3   Vērōnam veniat, Novī relinquēns
4   Cōmī moenia Lāriumque lītus:
5   nam quāsdam volo cōgitātiōnēs
6   amīcī accipiat suī meīque.
7   Quārē, sī sapiet, viam vorābit,
8   quamvīs candida mīliēs puella
9   euntem revocet, manūsque collō
10 ambās iniciēns roget morārī.
11 Quae nunc, sī mihi vēra nūntiantur,
12 illum dēperit impotente amōre:
13 nam quō tempore lēgit incohātam
14 Dindymī dominam, ex eō misellae
15 ignēs interiōrem edunt medullam.
16 Ignōscō tibi, Sapphicā puella
17 mūsā doctior: est enim venustē
18 Magna Caeciliō incohāta Māter.

CATULLUS 36

1 Annālēs Volusī, cacāta carta,
2 vōtum solvite prō meā puellā.
3 Nam sānctae Venerī Cupīdinīque
4 vōvit, sī sibi restitūtus essem
5 dēsīssemque trucēs vibrāre iambōs,
6 ēlēctissima pessimī poētae
7 scrīpta tardipedī deō datūram
8 īnfēlīcibus ūstulanda lignīs,
9 et hoc pessima sē puella vīdit
10 iocōsē lepidē vovēre dīvīs.
11 Nunc, ō caeruleō creāta pontō,
12 quae sānctum Īdalium Ūriōsque apertōs
13 quaeque Ancōna Cnidumque harundinōsam
14 colis quaeque Amathunta quaeque Golgōs
15 quaeque Dyrrachium Hadriae tabernam,
16 acceptum face redditumque vōtum,
17 sī nōn illepidum neque invenustum est.
18 At vōs intereā venīte in ignem,
19 plēnī rūris et īnficētiārum
20 annālēs Volusī, cacāta carta.

CATULLUS 43

1 Salvē, nec minimō puella nāsō
2 nec bellō pede nec nigrīs ocellīs
3 nec longīs digitīs nec ōre siccō
4 nec sānē nimis ēlegante linguā.
5 Dēcoctōris amīca Fōrmiānī,
6 tēn prōvincia nārrat esse bellam?
7 Tēcum Lesbia nostra comparātur?
8 Ō saeclum īnsipiēns et īnficētum!

CATULLUS 44

1 Ō funde noster seu Sabīne seu Tīburs
2 (nam tē esse Tīburtem autumant, quibus nōn est
3 cordī Catullum laedere; at quibus cordī est,
4 quōvīs Sabīnum pignore esse contendunt),
5 sed seu Sabīne sīve vērius Tīburs,
6 fuī libenter in tuā suburbānā
7 vīllā, malamque pectore expulī tussim,
8 nōn inmerentī quam mihī meus venter,
9 dum sūmptuōsās appetō, dedit, cēnās:
10 nam, Sestiānus dum volō esse convīva,
11 ōrātiōnem in Antium petītōrem
12 plēnam venēnī et pestilentiae lēgī.
13 Hīc mē gravēdō frīgida et frequēns tussis
14 quassāvit usque, dum in tuum sinum fūgī,
15 et mē recūrāvī ōtiōque et urtīcā.
16 Quārē refectus maximās tibī grātēs
17 agō, meum quod nōn es ulta peccātum.
18 Nec dēprecor iam, sī nefāria scrīpta
19 Sestī recepsō, quīn gravēdinem et tussim
20 nōn mī, sed ipsī Sestiō ferat frīgus,
21 quī tunc vocat mē, cum malum librum lēgī.

CATULLUS 45

1 Acmēn Septimius suōs amōrēs
2 tenēns in gremiō, "Mea," inquit, "Acmē,
3 nī tē perditē amō atque amāre porrō
4 omnēs sum assiduē parātus annōs,
5 quantum quī pote plūrimum perīre,
6 sōlus in Libyā Indiāque tostā
7 caesiō veniam obvius leōnī."
8 Hoc ut dīxit, Amor sinistrā ut ante
9 dextrā sternuit approbātiōnem.
10 At Acmē leviter caput reflectēns
11 et dulcis puerī ēbriōs ocellōs
12 illō purpureō ōre suāviāta,
13 "Sīc," inquit, "mea vīta Septimille,
14 huic ūnī dominō usque serviāmus,
15 ut multō mihi maior ācriorque
16 ignis mollibus ārdet in medullīs."
17 Hoc ut dīxit, Amor sinistrā ut ante
18 dextrā sternuit approbātiōnem.
19 Nunc ab auspiciō bonō profectī
20 mūtuīs animīs amant amantur.
21 Ūnam Septimius misellus Acmēn
22 māvult quam Syriās Britanniāsque:
23 ūnō in Septimiō fidēlis Acmē
24 facit dēliciās libīdinēsque.
25 Quis ūllōs hominēs beātiōrēs
26 vīdit, quis Venerem auspicātiōrem?

CATULLUS 46

1 Iam vēr ēgelidōs refert tepōrēs,
2 iam caelī furor aequinoctiālis
3 iūcundīs Zephyrī silēscit aureīs.
4 Linquantur Phrygiī, Catulle, campī
5 Nicaeaeque ager ūber aestuōsae:
6 ad clārās Asiae volēmus urbēs.
7 Iam mēns praetrepidāns avet vagārī,
8 iam laetī studiō pedēs vigēscunt.
9 Ō dulcēs comitum, valēte, coetūs,
10 longē quōs simul ā domō profectōs
11 dīversae variē viae reportant.

CATULLUS 49

1 Disertissime Rōmulī nepōtum,
2 quot sunt quotque fuēre, Mārce Tullī,
3 quotque post aliīs erunt in annīs,
4 grātiās tibi maximās Catullus
5 agit pessimus omnium poēta,
6 tantō pessimus omnium poēta
7 quantō tū optimus omnium patrōnus.

CATULLUS 50

1   Hesternō, Licinī, diē ōtiōsī

2   multum lūsimus in meīs tabellīs,

3   ut convēnerat esse dēlicātōs:

4   scrībēns versiculōs uterque nostrum

5   lūdēbat numerō modo hōc modo illōc,

6   reddēns mūtua per iocum atque vīnum.

7   Atque illinc abiī tuō lepōre

8   incēnsus, Licinī, facētiīsque,

9   ut nec mē miserum cibus iuvāret

10   nec somnus tegeret quiēte ocellōs,

11   sed tōtō indomitus furōre lectō

12   versārer, cupiēns vidēre lūcem,

13   ut tēcum loquerer simulque ut essem.

14   At dēfessa labōre membra postquam

15   sēmimortua lectulō iacēbant,

16   hoc, iūcunde, tibī poēma fēcī,

17   ex quō perspicerēs meum dolōrem.

18   Nunc audāx cave sīs, precēsque nostrās,

19   ōrāmus, cave dēspuās, ocelle,

20   nē poenās Nemesis reposcat ā tē.

21   Est vēmēns dea; laedere hanc cavētō.

CATULLUS 51

1 Ille mī pār esse deō vidētur,
2 ille, sī fās est, superāre dīvōs,
3 quī sedēns adversus identidem tē
4   spectat et audit

5 dulce rīdentem, miserō quod omnīs
6 ēripit sēnsūs mihi: nam simul tē,
7 Lesbia, aspexī, nihil est super mī
8   <vōcis in ōre,>

9 lingua sed torpet, tenuis sub artūs
10 flamma dēmānat, sonitū suōpte
11 tintinant aurēs, geminā teguntur
12   lūmina nocte.

13 Ōtium, Catulle, tibī molestum est;
14 ōtiō exsultās nimiumque gestīs;
15 ōtium et rēgēs prius et beātās
16   perdidit urbēs.

CATULLUS 53

1 Rīsī nescio quem modo ē corōnā,
2 quī, cum mīrificē Vatīniāna
3 meus crīmina Calvus explicāsset,
4 admīrāns ait haec manūsque tollēns:
5 "Dī magnī, salapūtium disertum!"

CATULLUS 62

Leader of the Chorus of Boys:

1 Vesper adest; iuvenēs, cōnsurgite; Vesper Olympō
2 exspectāta diū vix tandem lūmina tollit.
3 Surgere iam tempus, iam pinguīs linquere mēnsās;
4 iam veniet virgō, iam dīcētur hymenaeus.

Refrain:

5 Hȳmēn ō Hymenaee, Hymēn ades ō Hymenaee!

Leader of the Chorus of Girls:

6 Cernitis, innūptae, iuvenēs? Cōnsurgite contrā;
7 nīmīrum Oetaeōs ostendit Noctifer ignēs.
8 Sīc certēst; viden ut pernīciter exsiluēre?
9 Nōn temere exsiluēre; canent quod vincere pār est.

Refrain:

10 Hȳmēn ō Hymenaee, Hymēn ades ō Hymenaee!

Leader of the Chorus of Boys:

11 Nōn facilis nōbīs, aequālēs, palma parāta est;
12 aspicite, innūptae sēcum ut meditāta requīrunt.
13 Nōn frūstrā meditantur: habent memorābile quod sit;
14 nec mīrum, penitus quae tōtā mente labōrant.
15 Nōs aliō mentēs, aliō dīvīsimus aurēs;
16 iūre igitur vincēmur: amat victōria cūram.
17 Quārē nunc animōs saltem convertite vestrōs;
18 dīcere iam incipient, iam respondēre decēbit.

Refrain:

19 Hȳmēn ō Hymenaee, Hymēn ades ō Hymenaee!

The chorus of girls begins the singing match:

20   Hespere, quis caelō fertur crūdēlior ignis?
21   Quī nātam possīs complexū āvellere mātris,
22   complexū mātris retinentem āvellere nātam,
23   et iuvenī ārdentī castam dōnāre puellam.
24   Quid faciunt hostēs captā crūdēlius urbe?

Refrain:

25   Hȳmēn ō Hymenaee, Hymēn ades ō Hymenaee!

The chorus of boys responds:

26   Hespere, quis caelō lūcet iūcundior ignis?
27   Quī dēspōnsa tuā firmēs conūbia flammā,
28   quae pepigēre virī, pepigērunt ante parentēs,
29   nec iūnxēre prius quam sē tuus extulit ārdor.
30   Quid datur ā dīvīs fēlīcī optātius hōrā?

Refrain:

31   Hȳmēn ō Hymenaee, Hymēn ades ō Hymenaee!

*The chorus of girls compares Hesperus to a thief; only the first line of
the stanza has survived:*

32   Hesperus ē nōbīs, aequālēs, abstulit ūnam.
32b   .   .   .
32c   .   .   .
32d   .   .   .
32e   .   .   .
32f   .   .   .

Refrain:

32g   <Hȳmēn ō Hymenaee, Hymēn ades ō Hymenaee!>

The chorus of boys, in a stanza missing its first line, replies that when evening comes guards are wakeful and that the Evening Star, when appearing as the Morning Star, catches thieves:

32h   .   .   .

33   namque tuō adventū vigilat custōdia semper.

34   Nocte latent fūrēs, quōs īdem saepe revertēns,

35   Hespere, mūtātō comprendis nōmine Eōus

36   at lubet innūptīs fictō tē carpere questū.

37   Quid tum, sī carpunt, tacitā quem mente requīrunt?

Refrain:

38   Hȳmēn ō Hymenaee, Hymēn ades ō Hymenaee!

The chorus of girls begins another theme:

39   Ut flōs in saeptīs sēcrētus nāscitur hortīs,

40   ignōtus pecorī, nūllō convulsus arātrō,

41   quem mulcent aurae, firmat sōl, ēducat imber;

41b   <iam iam   .   .   .   >

42   multī illum puerī, multae optāvēre puellae:

43   īdem cum tenuī carptus dēflōruit unguī,

44   nūllī illum puerī, nūllae optāvēre puellae:

45   sīc virgō, dum intācta manet, dum cāra suīs est;

46   cum castum āmīsit pollūtō corpore flōrem,

47   nec puerīs iūcunda manet, nec cāra puellīs.

Refrain:

48   Hȳmēn ō Hymenaee, Hymēn ades ō Hymenaee!

The chorus of boys replies:

49 Ut vidua in nūdō vītis quae nāscitur arvō,

50 numquam sē extollit, numquam mītem ēducat ūvam,

51 sed tenerum prōnō dēflectēns pondere corpus

52 iam iam contingit summum rādīce flagellum;

53 hanc nūllī agricolae, nūllī coluēre iuvencī:

54 at sī forte eadem est ulmō coniūncta marītō,

55 multī illam agricolae, multī coluēre iuvencī:

56 sic virgō, dum innūpta manet, dum inculta senēscit;

57 cum pār cōnubium mātūrō tempore adepta est,

58 cāra virō magis et minus est invīsa parentī.

Refrain:

58b <Hӯmēn ō Hymenaee, Hymēn ades ō Hymenaee!>

The leader of the girls' chorus addresses the bride:

58c   .   .   .

59 Et tū nē pugnā cum tālī coniuge, virgō.

60 Nōn aequum est pugnāre, pater cui trādidit ipse,

61 ipse pater cum mātre, quibus parēre necesse est.

62 Virginitās nōn tōta tua est, ex parte parentum est,

63 tertia pars patrīst, pars est data tertia mātrī,

64 tertia sōla tua est: nōlī pugnāre duōbus,

65 quī generō sua iūra simul cum dōte dedērunt.

Refrain:

66 Hӯmēn ō Hymenaee, Hymēn ades ō Hymenaee!

CATULLUS 70

1   Nūllī sē dīcit mulier mea nūbere mālle
2   quam mihi, nōn sī sē Iuppiter ipse petat.
3   Dīcit; sed mulier cupidō quod dīcit amantī,
4   in ventō et rapidā scrībere oportet aquā.

CATULLUS 72

1   Dīcēbās quondam sōlum tē nōsse Catullum,
2   Lesbia, nec prae mē velle tenēre Iovem.
3   Dīlēxī tum tē nōn tantum ut vulgus amīcam,
4   sed pater ut gnātōs dīligit et generōs.
5   Nunc tē cognōvī; quārē, etsī impēnsius ūror,
6   multō mī tamen es vīlior et levior.
7   Quī potis est, inquis? Quod amantem iniūria tālis
8   cōgit amāre magis, sed bene velle minus.

CATULLUS 73

1   Dēsine dē quōquam quicquam bene velle merērī
2   aut aliquem fierī posse putāre pium.
3   Omnia sunt ingrāta, nihil fēcisse benignē
4   <prōdest,> immō etiam taedet obestque magis;
5   ut mihi, quem nēmō gravius nec acerbius urget
6   quam modo quī mē ūnum atque ūnicum amīcum habuit.

CATULLUS 75

1   Hūc est mēns dēducta tuā mea, Lesbia, culpā
2   atque ita sē officiō perdidit ipsa suō,
3   ut iam nec bene velle queat tibi, sī optima fīās,
4   nec dēsistere amāre, omnia sī faciās.

CATULLUS 76

1   Sī qua recordantī benefacta priōra voluptās
2   est hominī, cum sē cōgitat esse pium,
3   nec sānctam violāsse fidem, nec foedere nūllō
4   dīvum ad fallendōs nūmine abūsum hominēs,
5   multa parāta manent in longā aetāte, Catulle,
6   ex hōc ingrātō gaudia amōre tibi.
7   Nam quaecumque hominēs bene cuiquam aut dīcere possunt
8   aut facere, haec ā tē dictaque factaque sunt,
9   omnia quae ingrātae periērunt crēdita mentī.
10   Quārē cūr tētē iam amplius excruciēs?
11   Quīn tū animō offirmās atque istinc tē ipse redūcis
12   et dīs invītīs dēsinis esse miser?
13   Difficile est longum subitō dēpōnere amōrem.
14   Difficile est, vērum hoc quā lubet efficiās;
15   ūna salūs haec est, hōc est tibi pervincendum,
16   hoc faciās, sīve id nōn pote sīve pote.
17   Ō dī, sī vestrum est miserērī, aut sī quibus umquam
18   extrēmam iam ipsā in morte tulistis opem,
19   mē miserum aspicite et, sī vītam pūriter ēgī,
20   ēripite hanc pestem perniciemque mihi,
21   quae mihi subrēpēns īmōs ut torpor in artūs
22   expulit ex omnī pectore laetitiās.
23   Nōn iam illud quaerō, contrā ut mē dīligat illa,
24   aut, quod nōn potis est, esse pudīca velit;
25   ipse valēre optō et taetrum hunc dēpōnere morbum.
26   Ō dī, reddite mī hoc prō pietāte meā.

CATULLUS 77

1 Rūfe mihi frūstrā ac nēquīquam crēdite amīce
2   (frūstrā? immō magnō cum pretiō atque malō),
3 sīcine subrēpstī mī atque intestīna perūrēns
4   ei miserō ēripuistī omnia nostra bona?
5 Ēripuistī, heu heu nostrae crūdēle venēnum
6   vītae, heu heu nostrae pestis amīcitiae.

CATULLUS 83

1 Lesbia mī praesente virō mala plūrima dīcit;
2   haec illī fatuō maxima laetitia est.
3 Mūle, nihil sentīs? Sī nostrī oblīta tacēret,
4   sāna esset; nunc quod gannit et obloquitur,
5 nōn sōlum meminit, sed, quae multō ācrior est rēs,
6   īrāta est. Hōc est, ūritur et loquitur.

CATULLUS 84

1 Chommoda dīcēbat, sī quandō commoda vellet
2   dīcere, et īnsidiās Arrius hīnsidiās,
3 et tum mīrificē spērābat sē esse locūtum,
4   cum quantum poterat dīxerat hīnsidiās.
5 Crēdō, sīc māter, sīc līber avunculus eius,
6   sīc māternus avus dīxerat atque avia.
7 Hōc missō in Syriam requiērant omnibus aurēs:
8   audībant eadem haec lēniter et leviter,
9 nec sibi postillā metuēbant tālia verba,
10   cum subitō affertur nūntius horribilis,
11 Īoniōs flūctūs, postquam illūc Arrius īsset,
12   iam nōn Īoniōs esse sed Hīoniōs.

CATULLUS 85

1 Ōdī et amō. Quārē id faciam, fortasse requīris?
2   Nescio, sed fierī sentiō et excrucior.

CATULLUS 86

1 Quīntia fōrmōsa est multīs. Mihi candida, longa,
2   rēcta est: haec ego sīc singula cōnfiteor.
3 Tōtum illud "fōrmōsa" negō: nam nūlla venustās,
4   nūlla in tam magnō est corpore mīca salis.
5 Lesbia fōrmōsa est, quae cum pulcerrima tōta est,
6   tum omnibus ūna omnīs surripuit Venerēs.

CATULLUS 87

1 Nūlla potest mulier tantum sē dīcere amātam
2   vērē, quantum ā mē Lesbia amāta mea est.
3 Nūlla fidēs ūllō fuit umquam foedere tanta,
4   quanta in amōre tuō ex parte reperta meā est.

CATULLUS 92

1 Lesbia mī dīcit semper male nec tacet umquam
2   dē mē: Lesbia mē dispeream nisi amat.
3 Quō signō? Quia sunt totidem mea: dēprecor illam
4   assiduē, vērum dispeream nisi amō.

CATULLUS 95

1   Zmyrna meī Cinnae nōnam post dēnique messem
2   quam coepta est nōnamque ēdita post hiemem,
3   mīlia cum intereā quīngenta Hatriēnsis in ūnō
4   <versiculōrum annō putidus ēvomuit,>
5   Zmyrna cavās Satrachī penitus mittētur ad undās,
6   Zmyrnam cāna diū saecula pervoluent.
7   At Volusī annālēs Paduam morientur ad ipsam
8   et laxās scombrīs saepe dabunt tunicās.
9   Parva meī mihi sint cordī monimenta <Philētae>,
10   at populus tumidō gaudeat Antimachō.

CATULLUS 96

1   Sī quicquam mūtīs grātum acceptumve sepulcrīs
2   accidere ā nostrō, Calve, dolōre potest,
3   quō dēsīderiō veterēs renovāmus amōrēs
4   atque ōlim missās flēmus amīcitiās,
5   certē nōn tantō mors immātūra dolōrī est
6   Quīntiliae, quantum gaudet amōre tuō.

CATULLUS 101

1   Multās per gentēs et multa per aequora vectus
2   adveniō hās miserās, frāter, ad īnferiās,
3   ut tē postrēmō dōnārem mūnere mortis
4   et mūtam nēquīquam alloquerer cinerem,
5   quandoquidem fortūna mihī tētē abstulit ipsum,
6   heu miser indignē frāter adēmpte mihi.
7   Nunc tamen intereā haec, prīscō quae mōre parentum
8   trādita sunt trīstī mūnere ad īnferiās,
9   accipe frāternō multum mānantia flētū,
10   atque in perpetuum, frāter, avē atque valē.

CATULLUS 107

1 Sī quicquam cupidō optantīque optigit umquam
2   īnspērantī, hōc est grātum animō propriē.
3 Quārē hōc est grātum nōbis, et cārius aurō,
4   quod tē restituis, Lesbia, mī cupidō,
5 restituis cupidō atque īnspērantī, ipsa refers tē
6   nōbīs. Ō lūcem candidiōre notā!
7 Quis mē ūnō vīvit fēlīcior, aut magis umquam
8   optandam vītam dūcere quis poterit?

CATULLUS 109

1 Iūcundum, mea vīta, mihi prōpōnis: amōrem
2   hunc nostrum inter nōs perpetuum usque fore.
3 Dī magnī, facite ut vērē prōmittere possit,
4   atque id sincērē dīcat et ex animō,
5 ut liceat nōbīs tōtā perdūcere vītā
6   aeternum hoc sānctae foedus amīcitiae.